TAG

MAJOR
BUS and COACH
FLEETS

AREA 3
SOUTH WEST
ENGLAND

PRINTED IN ENGLAND BY BOOKCRAFT (BATH) LTD.
FOR TAG PUBLICATIONS   WEST EWELL   SURREY   KT19 9SH
JULY 2002

ISBN 1-871115 55 8   COPYRIGHT TAG PUBLICATIONS 2002

INTRODUCTION

Welcome to the latest TAG,an update of our 1999 South West volume(56:Ron)

Included in the Independents section are all fleets in the area with 4 or more vehicles,those with 3 and under appear in the Other PSV Vehicles section.

We've once again received a wealth of information from "The Brains Trust" and would especially like to thank Alan Walker,Tim & Simon Jennings,Graham Radcliffe,Dave Godley, Ken Lansdowne,Roger Storr,Ron Mesure,Steve Jenner & Dave Nicol & the Swindon Vintage Omnibus Society for checking our original draft and either rewriting much of it,or pointings us in the right direction to do it ourselves.

On the Major's front,we have received no fleetlist from First Badgerline or Stagecoach Devon,but have obviously received unofficial information from other sources.

Thanks must go to the PSV Circle,"The Brains Trust" and the many operators who responded to our requests.

A.N. & Andrew N. Goddard
36 Poole Road,
West Ewell,
Surrey,
KT19 9SH.

July 2002

E-Mail: tagpubs.transport@virgin.net

4

CONTENTS

FIRST GROUP PLC

1 FIRST BRISTOL BUSES LTD   FIRST CITY LINE LTD

Garages:
BH BATH(Lower Bristol Road)
*   DEVIZES(Station Road)(5 ex BH)*
*   FROME(Station Yard)(6 ex BH)*
HE BRISTOL(Hengrove Park,Hengrove)
LH BRISTOL(Easton Rd,Lawrence Hill)
MH BRISTOL(Marlborough Street)
MR BRISTOL(Muller Road,Horfield)

*   RADSTOCK(Haydon IE)(5 ex BH)*
*   TROWBRIDGE(Canal Road)(10 ex BH)*
*   WELLS(Priory Road)(joint WM)(18)*
WM WESTON-SUPER-MARE(Searle Crescent)
*   WOTTON-UNDER-EDGE(School)(4 ex MH)*
*   YATE(?)(6 ex MH)*

100-13 Volvo B10M-56 Alexander DP53F Badgerline 100etc 96
  D100-9/11-3 GHY.

100 WM	102 MH	104 WM	106 BH	108 BH	111 WM	112 WM	113 MH
101 WM	103 WM	105 BH	107 BH	109 BH			

* * * * * * *

121-36 Dennis Lance Plaxton B49F Badgerline 121etc 96
  L121-30/2-6 TFB.

121 WM	123 WM	125 MH	127 MH	129 MH	132 MH	134 BH	136 BH
122 WM	124 MH	126 MH	128 MH	130 MH	133 MH	135 BH	

* * * * * * *

137 BH	M137 FAE	Dennis Lance SLF	Wright B37F	Badgerline 137 96
138 BH	M138 FAE	Dennis Lance SLF	Wright B37F	Badgerline 138 96
140 BH	M140 FAE	Dennis Lance SLF	Wright B37F	Badgerline 140 96
141 BH	M141 FAE	Dennis Lance SLF	Wright B37F	Badgerline 141 96
142 BH	M142 FAE	Dennis Lance SLF	Wright B37F	Badgerline 142 96

* * * * * * *

203-42 *Dennis Dart Plaxton B40F Badgerline 203etc 96
          *206 ex Southern National 206 00
       L203-9 SHW,L211-21/3-5 VHU,N228-42 KAE.

203 BH	208 MH	214 BH	219 BH	225 MH	231 MH	235 BH	239 WM
204 WM	209 BH	215 BH	220 BH	228 WM	232 BH	236 BH	240 BH
205 MH	211 BH	216 BH	221 BH	229 WM	233 BH	237 BH	241 BH
206 WM	212 BH	217 BH	223 BH	230 WM	234 BH	238 BH	242 MH
207 MH	213 BH	218 BH	224 BH				

* * * * * * *

243-57 Dennis Dart Plaxton B40F New 96
  N243-50 LHT,P251-7 PAE.

243 MH	245 MH	247 MH	249 MH	251 MH	253 MH	255 MH	257 WM
244 MH	246 MH	248 MH	250 MH	252 MH	254 MH	256 WM	

* * * * * * *

258 WM	P258 PAE	Dennis Dart SLF	Plaxton B39F	New 96
259 WM	P259 PAE	Dennis Dart SLF	Plaxton B39F	New 96
260 WM	P260 PAE	Dennis Dart SLF	Plaxton B39F	New 96
261 WM	P261 PAE	Dennis Dart SLF	Plaxton B39F	New 96
262 WM	P262 PAE	Dennis Dart SLF	Plaxton B39F	New 96
263 WM	P263 PAE	Dennis Dart SLF	Plaxton B39F	New 96
264 WM	P264 PAE	Dennis Dart SLF	Plaxton B39F	New 96

* * * * * * *

265-72 *Dennis Dart SLF Plaxton B35F Yorkshire Rider 3302/3/14/21/0,
              *265/6/72/3 are B39F   3313/04/5 02
         P302/3 AUM,P827/34/3/26 YUM,P304/5 AUM.

265 MH	266 MH	267 MH	268 MH	269 MH	270 MH	271 MH	272 MH

* * * * * * *

273 MH	W809 VMA	Dennis Dart SLF	SCC B37F	Mainline 100 02
297 BH	R297 AYB	Dennis Javelin	Plaxton C49FT	New 98
299 BH	R299 AYB	Dennis Javelin	Plaxton C49FT	New 98
328 MR	K328 KYC	Dennis Dart	Wright DP37F	Southern Nat. 806 01
329 MR	K329 KYC	Dennis Dart	Wright DP37F	Southern Nat. 807 01
330 MR	K330 KYC	Dennis Dart	Wright DP37F	Southern Nat. 808 01

* * * * * * *

803-11 Dennis Dart Plaxton B32F First London DP3-11 02
  N803-11 FLW.

803 -	805 -	806 LH	807 -	808 -	809 -	810 -	811 LH
804 -						

1222-30 Dennis Lance Plaxton B49F Midland Red West 222-30 98
          L322,223-30 AAB.
1222 BH 1224 MH 1225 MH 1226 MH 1227 MH 1228 BH 1229 BH 1230 BH
1223 BH
                    * * * * * * *
1503-59 Dennis Dart Plaxton B35F New 94-6
          L503-8 VHU,M509-19 DHU,M520-38 FFB,N539-47 HAE,N549-54/6-9 LHU.
1503 LH 1510 LH 1517 LH 1524 LH 1531 LH 1538 HE 1545 MR 1553 MR
1504 LH 1511 LH 1518 MR 1525 LH 1532 LH 1539 MR 1546 MR 1554 HE
1505 MH 1512 LH 1519 LH 1526 LH 1533 LH 1540 MR 1547 HE 1556 HE
1506 LH 1513 LH 1520 LH 1527 LH 1534 LH 1541 MR 1549 HE 1557 MR
1507 LH 1514 LH 1521 LH 1528 LH 1535 LH 1542 MR 1550 HE 1558 HE
1508 LH 1515 LH 1522 LH 1529 LH 1536 LH 1543 HE 1551 HE 1559 LH
1509 LH 1516 LH 1523 LH 1530 LH 1537 HE 1544 MR 1552 HE
                    * * * * * * *
1600-62 Leyland LX2R B49F New 89/90
          F600/9-25/30-2 RTC,H633/4/6-62 YHT.
1600 MR 1615 HE 1622 HE 1632 HE 1639 HE 1645 WM 1651 LH 1657 LH
1609 BH 1616 HE 1623 MR 1633 HE 1640 BH 1646 LH 1652 LH 1658 LH
1610 WM 1617 HE 1624 MR 1634 HE 1641 BH 1647 LH 1653 LH 1659 LH
1611 WM 1618 HE 1625 HE 1636 HE 1642 BH 1648 LH 1654 LH 1660 LH
1612 MH 1619 MR 1630 BH 1637 HE 1643 WM 1649 LH 1655 LH 1661 LH
1613 WM 1620 MR 1631 WM 1638 HE 1644 WM 1650 LH 1656 LH 1662 LH
1614 HE 1621 MR
                    * * * * * * *
1701-29 Dennis Dart SLF Plaxton B29F or B35F(1720-9) New 97-9
          R701-12/4-8 BAE,R719 RAD,S720-5 AFB,T726-9 REU
1701 HE 1705 HE 1709 HE 1714 BH 1718 HE 1721 HE 1724 HE 1727 BH
1702 HE 1706 HE 1710 HE 1715 BH 1719 LH 1722 HE 1725 HE 1728 BH
1703 HE 1707 HE 1711 HE 1716 BH 1720 HE 1723 HE 1726 BH 1729 WM
1704 HE 1708 HE 1712 HE 1717 BH
                    * * * * * * *
1730-8 Dennis Dart SLF Alexander B35F or B37F(1730/1) New 99/00
          T730/1 REU,V732-8 FAE.
1730 WM 1732 HE 1733 HE 1734 HE 1735 HE 1736 HE 1737 HE 1738 HE
1731 WM
                    * * * * * * *
1740 MR R130 FUP Dennis Dart SLF Plaxton B33F Yorkshire Rider 3379 02
1741 WM R221 MSA Dennis Dart SLF Plaxton B37F First Aberdeen 221 02
1742 WM R222 MSA Dennis Dart SLF Plaxton B37F First Aberdeen 222 02
                    * * * * * * *
1801-34 Volvo B6BLE Wright B35F or B36F(1801/10) New 99/00
          T801 FHW,V810 EFB,W811-9/21-9/31-4 PFB.
1801 HE 1812 HE 1815 HE 1818 HE 1822 HE 1825 HE 1828 MR 1832 MR
1810 HE 1813 HE 1816 HE 1819 HE 1823 HE 1826 MR 1829 MR 1833 MR
1811 HE 1814 HE 1817 HE 1821 HE 1824 HE 1827 MR 1831 MR 1834 MR
                    * * * * * * *
1901-10 Volvo B10BLE Wright B47F New 98
          R901-10 BOU..
1901 BH 1903 WM 1905 WM 1906 WM 1907 WM 1908 WM 1909 WM 1910 BH
1902 WM 1904 WM
                    * * * * * * *
1911 BH R460 VOP Volvo B10BLE   Wright B44F   Volvo(Demonstrator) 99
                    * * * * * * *
1912-20 Volvo B10BLE Wright B47F New 98
          R912-9 BOU,R920 COU.
1912 BH 1914 BH 1915 WM 1916 BH 1917 BH 1918 BH 1919 BH 1920 BH
1913 BH
                    * * * * * * *
1921 BH S806 RWG Volvo B10BLE   Wright B41F   Mainline 806 02
1922 BH S807 RWG Volvo B10BLE   Wright B41F   Mainline 807 02
1923 BH S808 RWG Volvo B10BLE   Wright B41F   Mainline 808 02
1924 BH S809 RWG Volvo B10BLE   Wright B41F   Mainline 809 02
2000 BH V610 GGB Volvo B10LA   Wright AB55D   First London AV10 02
2001 BH V606 GGB Volvo B10LA   Wright AB55D   First London AV6 02
2002 BH V607 GGB Volvo B10LA   Wright AB55D   First London AV7 02
2003 BH V608 GGB Volvo B10LA   Wright AB55D   First London AV8 02
2326 MR JDZ 2326 Dennis Dart   Wright B30F   Centrewest DW26 01

```
2327 MR  JDZ 2327   Dennis Dart        Wright B30F   Centrewest DW27 01
2328 MR  JDZ 2328   Dennis Dart        Wright B30F   Centrewest DW28 01
2329 MR  JDZ 2329   Dennis Dart        Wright B30F   Centrewest DW29 01
2330 MR  JDZ 2330   Dennis Dart        Wright B30F   Centrewest DW30 01
2331 MR  JDZ 2331   Dennis Dart        Wright B30F   Centrewest DW31 01
2332 MR  JDZ 2332   Dennis Dart        Wright B30F   Centrewest DW32 01
2500 MH  D500 GHY   Volvo B10M-61      Van Hool C48FT Badgerline 2500 96
2501 BH  D501 GHY   Volvo B10M-61      Van Hool C53F  Badgerline 2501 96
2503 BH  D503 GHY   Volvo B10M-61      Van Hool C48FT Badgerline 2503 96
2564 BH  TDZ 3265   Volvo B10M-60      Plaxton C49FT First Wessex 6166 01
2567 BH  865  GAT   Volvo B10M-60      Plaxton C49FT First Wessex 6167 01
2570 BH  WV02 EUP   Volvo B12M         Plaxton C46FTL New 02
2571 BH  WV02 EUR   Volvo B12M         Plaxton C46FTL New 02
2572 BH  WV02 EUT   Volvo B12M         Plaxton C46FTL New 02
2573 BH  WV02 EUU   Volvo B12M         Plaxton C46FTL New 02
2600 MH  WYY  752   Volvo B10M-61      Van Hool C57F  Badgerline 2600 96
3169 MR  NDZ 3169   Dennis Dart        Wright B26F   Centrewest DW169 02
3610 WM  H610 YTC   Leyland LX2R       B49F          Badgerline 3610 96
3611 WM  H611 YTC   Leyland LX2R       B49F          Badgerline 3611 96
3612 WM  H612 YTC   Leyland LX2R       B49F          Badgerline 3612 96
3613 WM  H613 YTC   Leyland LX2R       B49F          Badgerline 3613 96
3614 WM  H614 YTC   Leyland LX2R       B49F          Badgerline 3614 96
3615 WM  H615 YTC   Leyland LX2R       B49F          Badgerline 3615 96
3616 WM  H616 YTC   Leyland LX2R       B49F          Badgerline 3616 96
                         * * * * * * *
```

3850-9 Mercedes-Benz 709D Reeve Burgess B23F Badgerline 3850etc 96
     J850-5/7-9 FTC.
```
3850 WM  3852 WM  3853 WM  3854 WM  3855 WM  3857 WM  3858 WM  3859 WM
3851 WM
```
                         * * * * * * *

3860-76 Mercedes-Benz 709D Plaxton B23F Badgerline 3860etc 96
     J860-6 HWS,K867-76 NEU.
```
3860 WM  3863 WM  3865 WM  3867 BH  3869 WM  3871 BH  3873 BH  3875 BH
3861 WM  3864 WM  3866 WM  3868 BH  3870 BH  3872 BH  3874 BH  3876 BH
3862 WM
```
                         * * * * * * *
```
3877 BH  L877 TFB   MB 711D            Plaxton B23F   Badgerline 3877 96
```
                         * * * * * * *

3878-908 Mercedes-Benz 709D Plaxton B23F Badgerline 3878etc 96
     L878-81 VHT,M882 BEU,L883-7/9-93/5-9,901-8 VHT.
```
3878 BH  3882 BH  3886 BH  3891 BH  3896 WM  3899 WM  3903 WM  3906 WM
3879 BH  3883 BH  3887 BH  3892 BH  3897 MH  3901 WM  3904 WM  3907 WM
3880 BH  3884 BH  3889 BH  3893 BH  3898 HE  3902 WM  3905 WM  3908 WM
3881 BH  3885 BH  3890 BH  3895 BH
```
                         * * * * * * *
```
3912 BH  E694 UND   MB 609D            MM B21F        Durbin Coaches 96
3914 BH  J850 OBV   MB 709D            Plaxton B23F   Badgerline 3914 96
3915 BH  L390 UHU   MB 709D            Plaxton B23F   Badgerline 3915 96
3916 BH  K 29 OEU   MB 709D            Wright B29F    Badgerline 3916 96
3917 BH  K922 VDV   Iveco 59-12        Mellor B28F    First Hampshire 254 00
3934 BH  K434 XRF   MB 709D            Plaxton B24F   PMT 434 01
3936 MH  Y 36 HBT   Optare Solo M850   B29F           New 01
3937 MH  Y 37 HBT   Optare Solo M850   B29F           New 01
3938 MH  Y 38 HBT   Optare Solo M850   B29F           New 01
3939 MH  Y 39 HBT   Optare Solo M850   B29F           New 01
3941 MH  K441 XRF   MB 709D            Plaxton B24F   PMT 441 01
3942 WM  K442 XRF   MB 709D            Plaxton B24F   PMT 442 01
3954 BH  L554 HVT   MB 709D            Marshall B23F  PMT 554 01
3955 MH  L455 HVT   MB 709D            Marshall B23F  PMT 555 01
3956 MH  L556 HVT   MB 709D            Marshall B23F  PMT 556 01
3994 MH  L494 HRE   MB 709D            Dormobile B24F PMT 494 01
3995 MH  L495 HRE   MB 709D            Dormobile B24F PMT 495 01
5107 MR  KDZ 5107   Dennis Dart        Wright B30F    First Beeline 107 02
```
                         * * * * * * *

5700-14 Volvo B10M-50 Alexander CH47/35F Badgerline 5700etc 96
     D700-11 GHY,E217 BTA.
```
5700 WM  5702 WM  5704 WM  5706 WM  5708 WM  5710 WM  5711 WM  5714 WM
5701 WM  5703 WM  5705 WM  5707 WM  5709 WM
```

7801-79 Mercedes-Benz 709D Plaxton B22F New 93-5
         L801-4/6-9/20/2/4-6 SAE,L827/9/30 WHY,M833-8/43-68/70-4 ATC,
         N875-9 HWS.

7801 MH	7820 MR	7833 HE	7844 LH	7851 LH	7858 HE	7865 HE	7873 LH
7802 MH	7822 MR	7834 LH	7845 LH	7852 HE	7859 HE	7866 HE	7874 MH
7803 MR	7824 MR	7835 BH	7846 LH	7853 HE	7860 HE	7867 HE	7875 MH
7804 MR	7825 MR	7836 WM	7847 LH	7854 LH	7861 HE	7868 HE	7876 LH
7806 MR	7826 MR	7837 -	7848 LH	7855 LH	7862 HE	7870 MR	7877 MH
7807 MR	7827 LH	7838 MR	7849 LH	7856 LH	7863 HE	7871 LH	7878 MH
7808 MR	7829 MR	7843 WM	7850 LH	7857 LH	7864 HE	7872 MH	7879 MH
7809 MR	7830 MR					

* * * * * * *

8201 BH	X201 HAE	Dennis Dart SLF	Plaxton B29F	New 00
8202 BH	X202 HAE	Dennis Dart SLF	Plaxton B29F	New 00
8203 BH	X203 HAE	Dennis Dart SLF	Plaxton B29F	New 00
8300 BH	P828 KTP	Iveco 59-12	UVG B27F	Streamline,Bath 97
8301 BH	P829 KTP	Iveco 59-12	UVG B27F	Streamline,Bath 97
8302 BH	N 34 FWU	DAF DE02LTSB220	Ikarus B49F	Streamline,Bath 97
8303 BH	N 28 FWU	DAF DE02LTSB220	Ikarus B49F	Streamline,Bath 97
8304 BH	N 29 FWU	DAF DE02LTSB220	Ikarus B49F	Streamline,Bath 97
8305 BH	M606 RCP	DAF SB220LT550	Ikarus B49F	Streamline,Bath 97
8306 BH	M968 USC	MB 814D	Plaxton C33F	Streamline,Bath 97
8307 WM	M 45 BEG	MB 811D	Marshall B31F	Streamline,Bath 97
8308 BH	M 46 BEG	MB 811D	Marshall B31F	Streamline,Bath 97
8309 BH	M857 XHY	MB 811D	Marshall B31F	Streamline,Bath 97
8310 BH	M 48 BEG	MB 811D	Marshall B31F	Streamline,Bath 97
8311 HE	K690 UFV	MB 709D	Plaxton B23F	Streamline,Bath 97
8312 BH	K691 UFV	MB 709D	Plaxton B23F	Streamline,Bath 97
8313 MH	K692 UFV	MB 709D	Plaxton B23F	Streamline,Bath 97
8314 BH	K693 UFV	MB 709D	Plaxton B23F	Streamline,Bath 97
8315 BH	K694 UFV	MB 709D	Plaxton B23F	Streamline,Bath 97
8600 BH	RTH 931S	BL VRT/SL3/501	ECW CO43/31F	Badgerline 8600 96
8605 BH	VDV 143S	BL VRT/SL3/6LXB	ECW CO43/31F	Badgerline 8605 96
8606 BH	VDV 137S	BL VRT/SL3/6LXB	ECW CO43/31F	Badgerline 8606 96
8608 BH	UFX 860S	BL VRT/SL3/6LXB	ECW CO43/31F	Badgerline 8608 96
8609 MH	A809 THW	Leyland ONLXB/1R	Roe CO47/29F	Badgerline 8609 96
8610 WM	A810 THW	Leyland ONLXB/1R	Roe CO47/29F	Badgerline 8610 96
8611 WM	A811 THW	Leyland ONLXB/1R	Roe CO47/29F	Badgerline 8611 96
8612 WM	A812 THW	Leyland ONLXB/1R	Roe CO47/29F	Badgerline 8612 96
8613 WM	A813 THW	Leyland ONLXB/1R	Roe CO47/29F	Badgerline 8613 96
8614 WM	A814 THW	Leyland ONLXB/1R	Roe CO47/29F	Badgerline 8614 96
8615 BH	JHW 107P	BL VRT/SL3/6LXB	ECW O43/29F	Badgerline 8615 96
8616 BH	JHW 108P	BL VRT/SL3/6LXB	ECW O43/29F	Badgerline 8616 96
8617 WM	JHW 109P	BL VRT/SL3/6LXB	ECW O43/29F	Badgerline 8617 96
8620 BH	LEU 256P	BL VRT/SL3/6LX	ECW O43/27D	Badgerline 8620 96
8621 BH	LEU 269P	BL VRT/SL3/6LXB	ECW O43/27D	Badgerline 8621 96
8656 BH	A756 VAF	Leyland ONLXB/1R ECW CH45/32F		Western Nat. 1809 97
8657 BH	A757 VAF	Leyland ONLXB/1R ECW CH45/32F		Western Nat. 1810 97

* * * * * * *

8916-24 Dennis Lance Wright B34D Centrewest LLW16-24 01
         ODZ 8916/8-24.

8916 -	8918 LH	8919 LH	8920 LH	8921 LH	8922 LH	8923 LH	8924 -

* * * * * * *

8980 BH	V980 XUB	Optare Solo M850	B30F	New 00
9005 BH	G905 TWS	LD ONCL10/1RZ	LD H47/31F	Badgerline 9005 96
9006 BH	G906 TWS	LD ONCL10/1RZ	LD H47/31F	Badgerline 9006 96
9007 BH	G907 TWS	LD ONCL10/1RZ	LD H47/31F	Badgerline 9007 96
9008 BH	G908 TWS	LD ONCL10/1RZ	LD H47/31F	Badgerline 9008 96
9009 BH	G909 TWS	LD ONCL10/1RZ	LD CH43/29F	Badgerline 9009 96
9010 BH	G910 TWS	LD ONCL10/1RZ	LD CH43/29F	Badgerline 9010 96
9425 MR	CUB 25Y	Leyland ONLXB/1R	Roe H47/29F	Yorkshire Rider 5025 00
9431 MR	CUB 31Y	Leyland ONLXB/1R	Roe H47/29F	Yorkshire Rider 5031 00
9440 MR	CUB 40Y	Leyland ONLXB/1R	Roe H47/29F	Yorkshire Rider 5040 00
9445 MR	CUB 45Y	Leyland ONLXB/1R	Roe H47/29F	Yorkshire Rider 5045 00
9477 MR	EWY 77Y	Leyland ONLXB/1R	Roe H47/29F	Yorkshire Rider 5077 00

* * * * * * *

9506-68 *Leyland ONLXB/1R Roe H47/29F New 82-4
          *9506/7/10-2/4/6/31/2 ex Badgerline 9506etc 96 & are CH43/29F
     JHU 905/6/9-11/3/4X,LWS 32/44/5Y,NTC 129-31/3-6/8/42Y,
     A945/6/8-50/2-4 SAE,A955-9/61-8 THW.

9506 BH	9514 MH	9530 MH	9536 BH	9546 MR	9553 LH	9558 LH	9564 MR
9507 BH	9515 BH	9531 MH	9538 BH	9548 MR	9554 LH	9559 LH	9565 LH
9510 MH	9516 MH	9532 MH	9539 MR	9549 LH	9555 LH	9561 -	9566 MH
9511 MH	9528 MR	9534 MH	9543 MR	9550 MR	9556 LH	9562 LH	9567 LH
9512 MH	9529 MR	9535 BH	9545 MR	9552 LH	9557 LH	9563 LH	9568 MR

* * * * * * *

9606-30 Leyland ON2R Northern Counties H47/29F New 93
          K606-30 LAE.

9606 MR	9610 MR	9613 MR	9616 MR	9619 MR	9622 MR	9625 MR	9628 MR
9607 MR	9611 MR	9614 MR	9617 MR	9620 MR	9623 MR	9626 MR	9629 MR
9608 MR	9612 MR	9615 MR	9618 MR	9621 MR	9624 MR	9627 MR	9630 MR
9609 MR							

* * * * * * *

9631-54 Volvo YN2RC Northern Counties H47/29F New 93/4
          L631-54 SEU.

9631 HE	9634 HE	9637 HE	9640 HE	9643 HE	9646 HE	9649 BH	9652 BH
9632 HE	9635 HE	9638 HE	9641 HE	9644 HE	9647 HE	9650 BH	9653 BH
9633 HE	9636 HE	9639 HE	9642 HE	9645 HE	9648 HE	9651 BH	9654 BH

* * * * * * *

9655-91 *Volvo Olympian Northern Counties H43/29F New 97/8
            *9655-60 are H47/29F & 9688-91 are CH43/29F
     P655-60 UFB,R661-4 NHY,S665/7-91 AAE

9655 MH	9660 MH	9665 HE	9671 HE	9676 HE	9680 LH	9684 LH	9688 WM
9656 MH	9661 LH	9667 HE	9672 HE	9677 LH	9681 LH	9685 LH	9689 WM
9657 MH	9662 LH	9668 HE	9673 HE	9678 LH	9682 LH	9686 LH	9690 WM
9658 MH	9663 LH	9669 HE	9674 HE	9679 LH	9683 LH	9687 WM	9691 WM
9659 MH	9664 LH	9670 HE	9675 HE				

* * * * * * *

9701-17 Dennis Trident East Lancs H49/30F New 99/00
          V701 FFB,W702-8 PHT,W709/11-7 RHT.

9701 HE	9703 HE	9705 HE	9707 HE	9709 BH	9712 BH	9714 BH	9716 BH
9702 HE	9704 HE	9706 HE	9708 HE	9711 BH	9713 BH	9715 BH	9717 BH

* * * * * * *

9801-39 Volvo B7TL Alexander H49/29F New 00-2
          W801-9/11-9/21-4 PAE,WU02 KVE-H/J-M/O/P/R-T/V/W.

9801 LH	9806 LH	9812 LH	9817 LH	9823 LH	9828 HE	9832 HE	9836 HE
9802 LH	9807 LH	9813 LH	9818 LH	9824 LH	9829 HE	9833 HE	9837 HE
9803 LH	9808 LH	9814 LH	9819 LH	9825 HE	9830 HE	9834 HE	9838 HE
9804 LH	9809 LH	9815 LH	9821 LH	9826 HE	9831 HE	9835 HE	9839 HE
9805 LH	9811 LH	9816 LH	9822 LH	9827 HE			

~~~~~~

OTHER VEHICLES OWNED BY THE COMPANY
* * * * * * *

3809 BH	E809 MOU	MB 811D	Optare B31F	Trainer
3817 LH	E817 MOU	MB 811D	Optare B31F	Trainer
3823 BH	E823 MOU	MB 811D	Optare DP27F	Trainer
4944 WM	E944 LAE	Fiat 49-10	RH B13F	Trainer
7473 LH	C473 BHY	Ford Transit	Dormobile B16F	Staff Bus
8152 BH	E202 BDV	Ford Transit	Mellor B7F	Staff Bus
8154 BH	E204 BDV	Ford Transit	Mellor B7F	Staff Bus
8158 LH	C158 TLF	Volvo B10M-46	Plaxton C43F	Trainer
8159 LH	C159 TLF	Volvo B10M-46	Plaxton C43F	Trainer
8256 LH	C256 CFG	Volvo B10M-46	Plaxton C43F	Trainer
8317 BH	G229 EOA	Fiat 49-10	Carlyle B25F	Trainer
8752 LH	E752 YGY	Volvo B10M-46	Plaxton C43F	Trainer
-	AAX 466A	LD TRCTL11/3R	Plaxton C51F	Trainer

~~~~~~

TDZ 3265*L64 UOU(3/01), WYY 752*D600 GHY(3/98), 865 GAT*L67 UOU(3/01),
AAX 466A*SDW 917Y(4/87), C256 CFG*   ? (?/??), M857 XHY*M47 BEG(3/99) &
W809 VMA*REL 905(3/01)
~~~~~~

2   FIRST SOUTHERN NATIONAL LTD

Garages:
```
BL BRISTOL(Croydon Street)              MK MARTOCK(Gt Western Rd/Coat Rd)
BR BRIDGWATER(East Quay)                   STURMINSTER NEWTON( ? )(ex YL)
BT BRIDPORT(Tannery Road)               TN TAUNTON(Hamilton Road)
   BURNHAM-ON-SEA( ? )(ex TN)           WH WEYMOUTH(Edward Street)
   CHARD(Millfield IE)(ex TN/YL)           WILLAND( ? )(ex TN)
   DORCHESTER(Grove TE)(ex WH)             WINCANTON(c/o South West)(2 ex YL)
   HONITON( ? )(ex TN)                     WIVELISCOMBE( ? )(ex TN)
   MINEHEAD(Mart Road IE)(10 BR/TN) YL YEOVIL(Reckleford)
```

```
  5 BT  B895 YYD  LD TRCTL11/3RH   Plaxton C51F   New 85
 12 -    620 HOD  LD TRCTL11/3R    Plaxton C53F   Ambassador Travel 85
201 TN  L201 SHW  Dennis Dart      Plaxton B40F   First Bristol 201 00
202 YL  L202 SHW  Dennis Dart      Plaxton B40F   First Bristol 202 00
210 BT  L210 VHU  Dennis Dart      Plaxton B40F   First Bristol 210 00
226 YL  N226 KAE  Dennis Dart      Plaxton B40F   First Bristol 226 00
227 YL  N227 KAE  Dennis Dart      Plaxton B40F   First Bristol 227 00
                     * * * * * * *
228-37  Dennis Dart  Plaxton B37F  First London D627-31,33-7 01
        P627-31 CGM,N633-7 ACF.
228 BR   230 YL   232 YL   233 WH   234 WH   235 WH   236 WH   237 WH
229 TN   231 YL
                     * * * * * * *
238 TN  NDZ 3163  Dennis Dart   Wright B29F   First London DW163 02
239 TN  NDZ 3165  Dennis Dart   Wright B29F   First London DW165 02
240 TN  NDZ 3162  Dennis Dart   Wright B29F   First London DW162 02
241 TN  NDZ 3164  Dennis Dart   Wright B29F   First London DW164 02
555 WH  ATA 555L  Bristol VRT/SL6G   ECW O43/32F  Western National 555 83
559 -   ATA 559L  Bristol VRT/SL6G   ECW O43/32F  Western National 559 83
560 WH  MBZ 7140  BL VRT/SL3/6LXB    ECW O43/31F  Stephenson,Rochford 98
574 -   VOD 594S  BL VRT/SL3/6LXB    ECW H43/31F  Western National 574 83
                     * * * * * * *
650-7  MB 609D  Frank Guy B20F  Eastern Counties 942/3/5/9/51/3/62/3 00
       M372/3 XEX,N605/9/11/3/22/3 GAH.
650 TN   651 TN   652 BR   653 BR   654 YL   655 YL   656 YL   657 YL
                     * * * * * * *
701-10  Mercedes-Benz 709D  Carlyle B29F  New 91
        H906/8-10/2-6 WYB.
701 -    704 WH   705 WH   706 -    707 WH   708 WH   709 -    710 -
703 -
                     * * * * * * *
719 WH  J969 EYD  MB 709D   Carlyle DP29F   New 92
720 WH  J241 FYA  MB 709D   Carlyle DP29F   New 92
721 WH  J580 FYA  MB 709D   Carlyle DP29F   New 92
722 WH  J601 FYA  MB 709D   Carlyle DP29F   New 92
725 YL  M305 TSF  MB 709D   ARB B29F        New 94
                     * * * * * * *
726-35  Mercedes-Benz 709D  Alexander B29F  New(SN) 94/5
        M804/3/5/2 UYA,M278/9/81/2 UYD,M239/40 VYA.
726 YL   728 TN   730 YL   731 YL   732 WH   733 BR   734 TN   735 TN
727 BR   729 YL
                     * * * * * * *
736 YL  M220 PMS  MB 709D   Alexander B29F  Alexander(Demonstr.) 95
737 WH  N 46 OAE  MB 709D   ARB B29F        Enza(Demonstrator) 95
738 YL  N556 EYB  MB 709D   ARB B29F        New 96
739 YL  N557 EYB  MB 709D   ARB B29F        New 96
740 TN  N558 EYB  MB 709D   ARB B29F        New 96
741 YL  N559 EYB  MB 709D   ARB B29F        New 96
742 TN  N561 EYB  MB 709D   ARB B29F        New 96
743 TN  L 26 LSG  MB 709D   ARB B25F        Bryans,Denny 96
744 BR  E814 XHS  MB 709D   AR DP25F        Williams,Crosskeys 96
745 YL  L 23 LSG  MB 709D   ARB B25F        Henderson,Hamilton 97
746 YL  L 24 LSG  MB 709D   ARB B25F        Henderson,Hamilton 97
747 YL  M 14 ABC  MB 709D   Alexander B25F  Collison,Stonehouse 97
748 BR  M 19 ABC  MB 709D   Alexander B29F  Collison,Stonehouse 97
749 YL  L 92 NSF  MB 709D   ARB B25F        Henderson,Hamilton 97
```

751-62 Mercedes-Benz 811D Wright B33F New 92-4
     K751 VFJ,L650-2 CJT,L329/30 MYC,L67/8 EPR.

751 YL	756 BT	757 TN	758 YL	759 YL	760 TN	761 TN	762 TN

* * * * * * *

766 BT	M766 FTT	MB 811D		Marshall B33F	New 94
770 YL	M241 VYA	MB 811D		Wright B33F	New 95
771 YL	M242 VYA	MB 811D		Wright B33F	New 95
772 TN	M508 VYA	MB 811D		Wright B33F	New 95
773 BT	M509 VYA	MB 811D		Wright B33F	New 95
774 WH	F154 RHK	MB 811D		RB B33F	Jackson,Bicknacre 95
775 BT	J185 LGE	MB 811D		Alexander B31F	Harte,Greenock 97
776 WH	K776 AFS	MB 811D		Alexander B31F	Rowe,Muirkirk 97
780 BR	P442 KYC	MB 711D		ARB B29F	New 96
781 YL	P443 KYC	MB 711D		ARB B29F	New 96
782 TN	P445 KYC	MB 711D		ARB B29F	New 96
783 TN	P446 KYC	MB 711D		ARB B29F	New 96
784 TN	P447 KYC	MB 711D		ARB B29F	New 96
785 YL	P448 KYC	MB 711D		ARB B29F	New 96
786 TN	P179 LYB	MB 711D		Plaxton B25F	New 97
787 YL	P180 LYB	MB 711D		Plaxton B25F	New 97
788 TN	P181 LYB	MB 711D		Plaxton B25F	New 97
789 TN	P182 LYB	MB 711D		Plaxton B25F	New 97
790 TN	P183 LYB	MB 711D		Plaxton B25F	New 97
802 TN	H802 GDV	Dennis Dart		Carlyle B40F	New 91
817 BT	S817 KPR	Dennis Dart SLF		Plaxton B39F	New 98
818 BT	S818 KPR	Dennis Dart SLF		Plaxton B39F	New 98
819 BT	S819 KPR	Dennis Dart SLF		Plaxton B39F	New 98
820 WH	S820 KPR	Dennis Dart SLF		Plaxton B39F	New 98
821 WH	S821 KPR	Dennis Dart SLF		Plaxton B39F	New 98
822 WH	S822 KPR	Dennis Dart SLF		Plaxton B39F	New 98
823 WH	S823 KPR	Dennis Dart SLF		Plaxton B39F	New 98
824 TN	S824 WYD	Dennis Dart SLF		EL B35F	New 99
825 TN	S825 WYD	Dennis Dart SLF		EL B35F	New 99
826 WH	T826 AFX	Dennis Dart SLF		Plaxton B39F	New 99
827 WH	T827 AFX	Dennis Dart SLF		Plaxton B39F	New 99
828 WH	T828 AFX	Dennis Dart SLF		Plaxton B39F	New 99
829 WH	T829 AFX	Dennis Dart SLF		Plaxton B39F	New 99
830 BR	T830 RYC	Dennis Dart SLF		EL B37F	New 99
831 BR	T831 RYC	Dennis Dart SLF		EL B37F	New 99
832 TN	V832 DYD	Dennis Dart SLF		EL B37F	New 99
833 TN	V833 DYD	Dennis Dart SLF		EL B37F	New 99
834 TN	V834 DYD	Dennis Dart SLF		EL B37F	New 99
835 TN	V835 DYD	Dennis Dart SLF		EL B37F	New 99
836 TN	ODZ 8911	Dennis Lance		Wright B38F	First Bristol 8911 01
837 TN	ODZ 8912	Dennis Lance		Wright B38F	First Bristol 8912 01
838 TN	ODZ 8913	Dennis Lance		Wright B38F	First Bristol 8913 01
839 TN	ODZ 8914	Dennis Lance		Wright B38F	First Bristol 8914 01
840 TN	ODZ 8915	Dennis Lance		Wright B38F	First Bristol 8915 01
841 TN	T366 NUA	Dennis Dart SLF		Alexander B37F	Yorkshire Rider 3366 01
842 TN	T367 NUA	Dennis Dart SLF		Alexander B37F	Yorkshire Rider 3367 01
843 TN	T368 NUA	Dennis Dart SLF		Alexander B37F	Yorkshire Rider 3368 01
844 TN	T369 NUA	Dennis Dart SLF		Alexander B37F	Yorkshire Rider 3369 01
845 TN	T370 NUA	Dennis Dart SLF		Alexander B37F	Yorkshire Rider 3370 01
846 WH	P836 YUM	Dennis Dart SLF		Plaxton B35F	First Cymru 02
847 WH	P407 MLA	Dennis Dart SLF		Plaxton B34F	First London L7 02

* * * * * * *

854-64 Mercedes-Benz O810D or O814D(857/60-4) Plaxton B27F New 98
     R501-8 NPR,S340 WYB,S863/4 LRU.

854 WH	856 WH	858 WH	860 WH	861 WH	862 YL	863 TN	864 TN
855 WH	857 WH	859 WH					

* * * * * * *

934 WH	VDV 134S	BL VRT/SL3/6LXB	ECW CO43/31F	Western National 934 83
942 WH	VDV 142S	BL VRT/SL3/6LXB	ECW CO43/31F	Devon General 942 83
950 TN	M392 KVR	MB 709D	ARB B27F	North Western 172 97
951 BL	M393 KVR	MB 709D	ARB B27F	North Western 173 97
952 TN	M386 KVR	MB 709D	ARB B27F	North Western 174 97
953 YL	M674 RAJ	MB 709D	ARB B25F	Go Ahead(OK) 474 98
954 YL	M675 RAJ	MB 709D	ARB B25F	Go Ahead(OK) 475 98
958 TN	M381 KVR	MB 709D	ARB B27F	Eastern Counties 98

```
 959 TN  M382 KVR  MB 709D         ARB B27F     Essex Buses 98
 968 BR  N585 WND  MB 709D         ARB B27F     Western Buses 062 98
 969 TN  N584 WND  MB 709D         ARB B27F     Williamson,Knockin H 98
 970 TN  N586 WND  MB 709D         ARB B27F     Thompson,South Bank 98
 971 BR  N583 WND  MB 709D         ARB B27F     Richmond,Epsom 99
1111 BR  VDV 111S  BL VRT/SL3/6LXB ECW H43/31F  Western Nat. 1111 83
                       * * * * * * *
```

1122-93 Bristol VRT/SL3/6LXB ECW H43/31F Western National 1122etc 83
     VDV 122S,AFJ 764/6-8/70/3T,FDV 779-81,837V.

```
1122 YL  1159 BT  1161 BT  1166 TN  1167 YL  1168 BR  1169 BR  1193 BR
1157 BR  1160 BR  1163 BT
                       * * * * * * *
1626 TN  F626 RTC  Leyland LX2R    B49F         First Bristol 1626 00
1627 WH  F627 RTC  Leyland LX2R    B49F         First Bristol 1627 00
1628 WH  F628 RTC  Leyland LX2R    B49F         First Bristol 1628 00
1629 TN  F629 RTC  Leyland LX2R    B49F         First Bristol 1629 00
  -      D875 ELL  Leyland LX112   DP49F        PMT 843 02
  -      D501 LNA  Leyland LX563   B48F         PMT 02
  -      D502 LNA  Leyland LX563   B48F         PMT 02
  -      D503 LNA  Leyland LX563   B48F         PMT 02
  -      F361 YTJ  Leyland LX112   B51F         PMT 845 02
  -      F362 YTJ  Leyland LX112   B51F         PMT 846 02
  -      F363 YTJ  Leyland LX112   B51F         PMT 847 02
  -      G936 YRY  Leyland LX112   B51F         PMT 850 02
                       * * * * * * *
```

1802-9 Volvo B6BLE Wright B36F New 99
     V802-9 EFB.

```
1802 WH  1803 WH  1804 WH  1805 WH  1806 WH  1807 WH  1808 WH  1809 WH
                       * * * * * * *
1813 YL  A685 KDV  Leyland ONLXB/1R ECW H45/32F Devon General 1813 90
1814 TN  G901 TWS  LD ONCL10/1RZ   LD H47/31F   First Bristol 9001 00
1815 TN  G902 TWS  LD ONCL10/1RZ   LD H47/31F   First Bristol 9002 00
1816 TN  G903 TWS  LD ONCL10/1RZ   LD H47/31F   First Bristol 9003 00
1817 TN  G904 TWS  LD ONCL10/1RZ   LD H47/31F   First Bristol 9004 00
                       * * * * * * *
```

1819-26 LD ONLXB/1R Roe H47/29F First Bristol 9527/40-2/51/03-5 00
     LWS 43Y,NTC 139-41Y,A951 SAE,JHU 902-4X.

```
1819 WH  1820 WH  1821 WH  1822 WH  1823 WH  1824 WH  1825 WH  1826 WH
                       * * * * * * *
2213 BR  A690 AHB  LD TRCTL11/3R   Marshall B57F   MOD 96
2214 BR  A696 YOX  LD TRCTL11/3R   Marshall B57F   MOD 95
2215 BR  UOB 366Y  LD TRCTL11/3R   Marshall B57F   MOD 95
2216 TN  B591 FOG  LD TRCTL11/3R   Marshall B57F   MOD 96
2217 BR  A649 YOX  LD TRCTL11/3R   Marshall B57F   MOD 95
2218 BR  A624 YOX  LD TRCTL11/3R   Marshall B57F   MOD 95
2219 TN  A622 YOX  LD TRCTL11/3R   Marshall B57F   MOD 95
2220 BR  LIL 5851  LD TRCTL11/3R   Plaxton C53F    Lancaster 620 93
2221 MK  HHJ 372Y  LD TRCTL11/2R   Alexander C53F  Essex Buses 1111 98
2223 TN  A695 OHJ  LD TRCTL11/2R   Alexander C53F  South Wales 186 99
2224 TN  A691 OHJ  LD TRCTL11/2R   Alexander C53F  South Wales 184 99
2225 TN  HHJ 381Y  LD TRCTL11/2R   AR DP53F        Eastern Counties 3 99
2226 TN  HHJ 382Y  LD TRCTL11/2R   Alexander C53F  Eastern Counties 4 99
2227 MK  UFX 940   LD TRCTL11/2R   Alexander C53F  Eastern Counties 1 98
2228 BT  595 JPU   Volvo B10M-60   Plaxton C46FT   New 91
2229 TN  UFX 330   Volvo B10M-60   Plaxton C46FT   New 91
2230 MK  HHJ 375Y  LD TRCTL11/2R   Alexander C53F  Essex Buses 1114 98
2231 MK  HHJ 376Y  LD TRCTL11/2R   Alexander C53F  Essex Buses 1115 98
2920 YL  VBG 114V  LN NL116L11/1R  B49F         Merseyside 6114 98
2921 YL  VBG 127V  LN NL116L11/1R  B53F         Merseyside 6127 98
2923 YL  XLV 143W  LN NL116AL11/1R B53F         Merseyside 6143 98
2924 -   VBG 120V  LN NL116L11/1R  B53F         Merseyside 6120 98
2925 YL  VBG 118V  LN NL116L11/1R  B53F         HMB,Gateshead 98
2931 YL  DMS 22V   LN NL116L11/1R  B53F         Red & White 515 98
2932 -   RSG 815V  LN NL116L11/1R  B52F         Red & White 505 98
6104 BL  T104 JBC  Volvo B7R-63    Plaxton C49F    New 99
6105 BL  T105 JBC  Volvo B7R-63    Plaxton C49F    New 99
6106 BL  T106 JBC  Volvo B7R-63    Plaxton C49F    New 99
6161 WH  K792 OTC  Volvo B10M-60   Plaxton C46FT   New 93
                       * * * * * * *
```

6169-94 *Volvo B10M-62 Plaxton C49FT or C46FT(6169) New 94-00
    *6189/91-4 are C44FT
   M92 BOU,M765 CWS,M413 DEU,M439/40 FHW,M41 FTC,P944-6 RWS,
   R813/4 HWS,R943 LHT,T310 AHY,X191-4 HFB.

```
6169 BL   6178 WH   6180 BL   6182 BL   6184 BL   6186 BL   6191 BL   6193 BL
6176 BL   6179 BL   6181 BL   6183 BL   6185 BL   6189 BL   6192 BL   6194 BL
6177 BL
```

* * * * * * *

6201-12 Dennis Javelin Plaxton C49FT New 95/6
   N471-4 KHU,N913/4 KHW,N821/2 KWS,N319-22 NHY.

```
6201 BL   6203 BL   6205 BL   6207 BL   6209 BL   6210 BL   6211 BL   6212 BL
6202 BL   6204 BL   6206 BL   6208 BL
```

* * * * * * *

```
6301 BL   WX51 AJV   Volvo B12M        Plaxton C44FT   New 01
6302 BL   WX51 AJU   Volvo B12M        Plaxton C44FT   New 01
6303 BL   WX51 AJY   Volvo B12M        Plaxton C44FT   New 01
6304 BL   WX51 AKY   Volvo B12M        Plaxton C49FT   New 01
7003 BT   KDU  648   Volvo B10M-61     Van Hool C49FT  Taylors,Tintinhull 93
7004 MK   RIL 1056   Volvo B10M-61     Plaxton C53F    Taylors,Tintinhull 93
7009 YL   TPR  354   LD TRCTL11/3R     Plaxton C53F    Taylors,Tintinhull 93
7022 -    RIL 1053   Dennis Javelin    Plaxton C53F    Hayball,Warminster 96
7026 MK   A694 OHJ   LD TRCTL11/2R     Alexander C53F  Eastern Counties 5 98
7616 TN   M248 NNF   Iveco 59-10       Marshall B25F   First Bristol 7616 00
7617 TN   M249 NNF   Iveco 59-10       Marshall B25F   First Bristol 7617 00
7618 TN   K929 VDV   Iveco 59-12       Mellor B28F     First Hampshire 257 00
7619 TN   M413 RND   Iveco 59-10       Marshall B20F   First Bristol 7619 00
```

* * * * * * *

7831-907 Mercedes-Benz 709D Plaxton B22F First Bristol 7831etc 00
   M831/2 ATC,N880-7/9-99,901-7 HWS.

```
7831 YL   7882 WH   7886 YL   7891 TN   7895 BR   7898 BR   7902 YL   7905 YL
7832 YL   7883 WH   7887 YL   7892 TN   7896 BR   7899 BR   7903 YL   7906 YL
7880 WH   7884 BT   7889 TN   7893 BR   7897 BR   7901 YL   7904 YL   7907 YL
7881 BT   7885 -    7890 TN   7894 BR
```

* * * * * * *

```
8013 -    KFX  791   LD TRCTL11/3R     Plaxton C53F    Arlington(Demonstr.) 83
8015 TN   RIL 1069   LD TRCL10/3ARZM   Plaxton C45FT   Hill,Tredegar 91
8016 BT   USV  821   LD TRCTL11/3RH    Plaxton C46FT   New(SN) 84
8021 TN   IIL 2490   LD TRCTL11/2RH    Plaxton C53F    Lancaster C90 93
8025 TN   8683 LJ    Dennis Javelin    Duple C53F      Brighton & Hove 501 97
8026 TN   OJI 8786   Dennis Javelin    Duple C53F      Brighton & Hove 502 97
9001 WH   GIL 1684   Volvo B10M-61     Van Hool C53F   Philp,Dunfermline 94
9002 WH   TJI 3135   Volvo B10M-61     Ikarus C53F     Toop,Dorchester 94
9003 WH   TJI 3136   Volvo B10M-61     Ikarus C53F     Toop,Dorchester 94
9004 WH   TJI 3137   Volvo B10M-61     Ikarus C53F     Toop,Dorchester 94
9005 WH   TJI 3138   Volvo B10M-61     Ikarus C53F     Toop,Dorchester 94
9007 WH   TJI 3134   Volvo B10M-61     Duple C55F      Toop,Dorchester 94
9008 MK   USV  823   Volvo B10M-61     Duple C57F      Toop,Dorchester 94
9052 MK   TJI 4683   LD TRCTL11/2R     Duple C53F      Dorset County Coun. 98
9057 TN   J732 KBC   Dennis Javelin    Plaxton C53F    Jones,Login 98
9058 BT   G804 XLO   Volvo B10M-46     Plaxton C43F    Capital,West Drayton 98
9059 BT   G803 XLO   Volvo B10M-46     Plaxton C43F    Cherrybriar,Bow 98
9060 BT   J329 LLK   Volvo B10M-46     Plaxton C43F    Capital,West Drayton 98
```
~~~~~~

OTHER VEHICLES OWNED BY THE COMPANY
* * * * * * *

```
 351 MK   C913 GYD   Ford Transit      RH B16F         Staff Bus
 362 BR   C924 GYD   Ford Transit      RH B16F         Staff Bus
 365 TN   C927 GYD   Ford Transit      RH B16F         Staff Bus
 385 YL   C947 GYD   Ford Transit      Dormobile B16F  Staff Bus
 702 -    H907 WYB   MB 709D           Carlyle B29F    Staff Bus
3301 YL   E803 MOU   MB 811D           Optare B31F     Trainer
3302 -    E815 MOU   MB 811D           Optare B31F     Trainer
3303 TN   E818 MOU   MB 811D           Optare B31F     Trainer
```
~~~~~~

N.B.:- The First Wessex fleet was taken over from First Bristol 4/01
  and all 6xxx series vehicles except 6301-4 were acquired with the
  operation.
~~~~~~

```
GIL 1684*LSK 813(5/94) & E631 UNE(4/92), IIL 2490*C90 MHG(9/92),
KDU 648*MSU 612Y(12/83), KFX 791*FNM 854Y(4/90), LIL 5851*A620 ATV(5/96),
MBZ 7140*OTO 151R(6/95), OJI 8786*E475 FWV(6/92),
RIL 1053*40 FER(2/99) & F576 AEL(11/96) & RJI 8602(9/96) & F131 TRU(2/94),
RIL 1056*RFP 6(2/99) & B904 SPR(10/94),
RIL 1069*10 HR(2/99) & G115 JBO(5/94),
TJI 3134*A600 LJT(2/99) & TJI 3134(7/97) & A600 LJT(3/95),
TJI 3135*E221 GCG(5/95), TJI 3136*E222 GCG(4/95), TJI 3137*E223 GCG(4/95),
TJI 3138*E224 GCG(5/95), TJI 4683*YPD 116Y(1/00), TPR 354*CYA 614X(11/84),
UFX 330*H229 CFJ(7/97) & H226 CFJ(12/91), UFX 940*A696 OHJ(7/98),
USV 821*A679 KDV(1/92), USV 823*ENF 560Y(11/95), 8683 LJ*E474 FWV(1/91),
620 HOD*A897 KCL(3/92), 595 JPU*H228 CFJ(7/97) & H227 CFJ(12/91),
D875 ELL*810 DYE(2/98) & D106 NDW(3/90),
E814 XHS*865 GAT(3/01) & E814 XHS(5/97),
J185 LGE*IIB 1618(6/97) & J259 WFS(4/94), M19 ABC*M496 JRY(2/95),
M802 UYA*M805 UYA(7/95), M804 UYA*M802 UYA(7/95),
M805 UYA*M804 UYA(6/95) & N633 ACF*133 CLT(10/99) & N633 ACF(11/96)
```
~~~~~~

3   FIRST WESTERN NATIONAL BUSES LTD

Garages:
BE BARNSTAPLE(Coney Avenue)	LISKEARD(Moorswater Road:8 ex PH)
BODMIN(Cummings,Liskeard Rd:4)	NEWQUAY(Tolcarne Street:15 SL)
CALLINGTON(New Road:5 PH)	PADSTOW(Trecerus IE:3 ex CE)
CE CAMBORNE(Union Street)	PENZANCE(Long Rock IE:20 ex CE)
DARTMOUTH(Little Cotton Farm:8)	PH PLYMOUTH(Laira Bridge Road)
DELABOLE(Quarry:3 ex CE)	ST JUST(Warrens,Boswedden Rd:2)
FALMOUTH(Tregoniggie IE:15 CE)	SL ST AUSTELL(Elliot Road)
HELSTON(Flambards:8 ex CE)	TAVISTOCK(Crowndale Rd:15 ex PH)
ILFRACOMBE(Ropery Road)(ex BE)	TORPOINT(Trevol Road:8 ex PH)
KINGSBRIDGE(Station Yard IE:6)	TOTNES(Wills Road IE:10 ex PH)
LAUNCESTON(Hurdon Road:4 ex PH)	TRURO(Lemon Quay:10 ex CE)

```
1003 CE  VDV 141S   BL VRT/SL3/6LXB   ECW CO43/31F    New 78
1007 PH  URS 320X   Leyland AN68C/1R AR H45/29F       First Aberdeen 320 01
1008 PH  NRS 313X   Leyland AN68C/1R AR H45/29D       First Aberdeen 313 00
1009 BE  URS 327X   Leyland AN68C/1R AR H45/29D       First Aberdeen 327 01
1010 BE  URS 328X   Leyland AN68C/1R AR H45/29D       First Aberdeen 328 01
1011 BE  NRS 307X   Leyland AN68C/1R AR H45/29D       First Aberdeen(Mair) 01
1013 PH  XSS 333Y   Leyland AN68D/1R AR H45/29D       First Aberdeen 333 01
1014 BE  XSS 334Y   Leyland AN68D/1R AR H45/29D       First Aberdeen 334 01
1015 BE  XSS 338Y   Leyland AN68D/1R AR H45/29D       First Aberdeen 338 01
1016 BE  XSS 340Y   Leyland AN68D/1R AR H45/29D       First Aberdeen 340 01
1017 BE  XSS 341Y   Leyland AN68D/1R AR H45/29D       First Aberdeen 341 01
1106 SL  SFJ 106R   BL VRT/SL3/6LXB   ECW H43/31F     New 77
                        * * * * * * *
```

1114-83 Bristol VRT/SL3/6LXB ECW H43/31F New 77-80
    VDV 114/6-8/21S,XDV 608/9/1S,AFJ 697-701/3-6/44/5/7/9-51/60-2T,
    FDV 807/8/14/5V.
```
1114 SL   1121 SL   1132 SL   1136 CE   1141 SL   1147 CE   1154 SL   1176 PH
1116 SL   1128 CE   1133 SL   1138 SL   1142 SL   1148 CE   1155 PH   1182 CE
1117 SL   1129 SL   1134 SL   1139 SL   1143 SL   1149 CE   1175 PH   1183 PH
1118 SL   1131 CE   1135 CE   1140 SL   1145 CE   1153 CE
                        * * * * * * *
1187 SL  BEP 968V   BL VRT/SL3/501    ECW H43/31F     South Wales 968 89
                        * * * * * * *
```

1197-1226 Bristol VRT/SL3/6LXB or 6LXC(1224-6) ECW H43/31F New 80/1
    LFJ 841-7/71-3W.
```
1197 PH   1199 PH   1201 PH   1202 PH   1203 PH   1224 SL   1225 SL   1226 SL
1198 PH   1200 PH
                        * * * * * * *
1227 PH  EWS 747W   BL VRT/SL3/680    ECW CH43/31F    Badgerline 5539 90
                        * * * * * * *
```

1228-37 Bristol VRT/SL3/501 ECW H43/31F South Wales 929etc 90
    RTH 929S,TWN 936S,VTH 942T,WTH 943/6/50/61T,BEP 966V.
```
1228 PH   1229 PH   1230 SL   1231 SL   1233 CE   1234 SL   1236 SL   1237 PH
                        * * * * * * *
```

1238-51 *BL VRT/SL3/6LXB ECW H43/31F Thamesway 3067/120/3/096/9,107/0
                    *1238 is H39/31F   3118/5/25 91/2
          KOO 785V,XHK 225/8X,UAR 586/9/97/0W,XHK 223/0/30X.
1238 CE   1242 CE   1244 CE   1246 SL   1248 PH   1249 CE   1250 SL   1251 CE
1240 CE   1243 CE
                              * * * * * * * *
1252 PH   PHY 697S   BL VRT/SL3/6LXB   ECW H43/31F   Bristol 5103 94
1253 SL   TWS 915T   BL VRT/SL3/6LXB   ECW H43/31F   Bristol 5134 94
1254 SL   AHU 516V   BL VRT/SL3/6LXB   ECW H43/31F   Bristol 5139 94
1256 CE   JWT 758V   BL VRT/SL3/6LXB   ECW H43/31F   Yorkshire Rider 725 96
1257 SL   PWY 38W   BL VRT/SL3/6LXB   ECW H43/31F   Yorkshire Rider 752 96
1258 CE   STW 34W   BL VRT/SL3/6LXB   ECW H39/31F   Bristol 5561 96
1260 CE   PEU 518R   BL VRT/SL3/6LXB   ECW H43/31F   Bristol 5523 98
1261 CE   RHT 503S   BL VRT/SL3/6LXB   ECW H43/31F   Provincial 503 98
1262 PH   NTC 573R   BL VRT/SL3/6LXB   ECW H43/31F   Provincial 502 99
1263 CE   VEX 288X   BL VRT/SL3/6LXB   ECW H43/31F   Provincial 502 99
1265 PH   UAR 588W   BL VRT/SL3/6LXB   ECW H43/31F   Provincial 502 99
1304 SL   XAN 431T   BL VRT/SL3/6LXB   ECW H43/31F   Berry,Taunton 98
1305 CE   AJH 855T   BL VRT/SL3/6LXB   ECW H43/31F   Berry,Taunton 98
1306 CE   RAH 267W   BL VRT/SL3/6LXB   ECW H43/31F   Eastern Counties 267 02
1307 CE   WWY 123S   BL VRT/SL3/6LXB   ECW H43/31F   Eastern Counties 213 02
1308 SL   VEX 297X   BL VRT/SL3/6LXB   ECW H43/31F   Eastern Counties 297 02
1309 SL   VEX 287X   BL VRT/SL3/6LXB   ECW CH41/25F Eastern Counties 287 02
1501 BE   X501 BFJ   Dennis Trident   EL H49/30F   New 00
1502 BE   X502 BFJ   Dennis Trident   EL H49/30F   New 00
1503 BE   X503 BFJ   Dennis Trident   EL H49/30F   New 00
1504 BE   X504 BFJ   Dennis Trident   EL H49/30F   New 00
1750 PH   A750 VAF   Leyland ONLXB/1R ECW CH45/32F   New 83
1751 CE   A751 VAF   Leyland ONLXB/1R ECW CH45/32F   New 83
1752 PH   A752 VAF   Leyland ONLXB/1R ECW CH45/32F   New 83
1753 CE   A753 VAF   Leyland ONLXB/1R ECW CH45/32F   New 83
1754 CE   A754 VAF   Leyland ONLXB/1R ECW CH45/32F   New 83
1755 PH   A755 VAF   Leyland ONLXB/1R ECW CH45/32F   New 83
1756 PH   L155 UNS   Leyland ON2R   AR H47/31F   First Glasgow LO55 00
1757 PH   D513 HUB   LD ONTL11/1RH   OE H43/27F   Yorkshire Rider 5513 00
1758 PH   D514 HUB   LD ONTL11/1RH   OE H47/27F   Yorkshire Rider 5514 00
1759 PH   F158 XYG   LD ONCL10/1RZ   NC H45/29F   First Manchester 01
1760 PH   FUM 499Y   Leyland ONLXB/1R ECW H45/32F   Yorkshire Rider 5193 01
1761 PH   FUM 492Y   Leyland ONLXB/1R ECW H45/32F   Yorkshire Rider 5189 01
1762 PH   FUM 491Y   Leyland ONLXB/1R ECW H45/32F   Yorkshire Rider 5188 01
1763 -   FUM 487Y   Leyland ONLXB/1R ECW H45/32F   Yorkshire Rider 5187 01
1764 -   FUM 486Y   Leyland ONLXB/1R ECW H45/32F   Yorkshire Rider 5186 01
1790 PH   E215 BTA   Volvo B10M-50   AR CH45/35F   Bristol 5712 97
1791 PH   E216 BTA   Volvo B10M-50   AR CH47/35F   Bristol 5713 97
1801 PH   K801 ORL   Volvo YN2RV   NC CH39/30F   New 93
1802 PH   K802 ORL   Volvo YN2RV   NC CH39/30F   New 93
1803 PH   K803 ORL   Volvo YN2RV   NC CH39/30F   New 93
1804 PH   K804 ORL   Volvo YN2RV   NC CH39/30F   New 93
1815 BE   L815 CFJ   Volvo YN2RV   NC H47/29F   New 93
1816 BE   L816 CFJ   Volvo YN2RV   NC H47/29F   New 93
1817 BE   L817 CFJ   Volvo YN2RV   NC H47/29F   New 93
1818 PH   P187 TGD   Volvo YN2RV   AR H47/32F   First Leicester 187 01
1819 PH   P189 TGD   Volvo YN2RV   AR H47/32F   First Leicester 189 02
2102 CE   M102 ECV   Volvo B12T   VH CH57/14CT New 95
2103 CE   M103 ECV   Volvo B12T   VH CH57/14CT New 95
2104 CE   N319 BYA   Volvo B12T   VH CH57/14CT Trathens,Plymouth 01
2202 PH   894 GUO   LD TRCTL11/3R   Plaxton C55F Grampian(Mair) 718 97
2207 PH   VOO 273   LD TRCTL11/3R   Plaxton C57F Ford,Gunnislake 97
2209 PH   530 OHU   LD TRCTL11/3R   Plaxton C53F Badgerline 2205 96
2211 PH   WSV 408   LD TRCTL11/3R   Plaxton C53F Yorkshire Rider 1604 96
2213 CE   HVJ 716   LD TRCTL11/3R   Plaxton C50FT Midland Red W. 1016 97
2215 SL   FNR 923   LD TRCTL11/3RH   Plaxton C51F Wealden,Five Oak Grn 96
2216 PH   NER 621   LD TRCTL11/3RH   Plaxton C51F Wealden,Five Oak Grn 96
2217 SL   B194 BAF   LD TRCTL11/3RH   Plaxton C46FT New 85
2218 -   B195 BAF   LD TRCTL11/3RH   Plaxton C46FT New 85
2219 SL   B196 BAF   LD TRCTL11/3RH   Plaxton C46FT New 85
2220 CE   B197 BAF   LD TRCTL11/3RH   Plaxton C46FT New 85
2223 SL   A206 SAE   LD TRCTL11/3R   Plaxton C53F Bristol 2206 97
2224 PH   HHJ 373Y   LD TRCTL11/2R   Alexander C53F Essex Buses 1112 98

```
2226 SL  TJI 4838  LD TRCTL11/3ARZA Plaxton C53F   Berks Bucks 768 98
2227 PH  A665 KUM  LD TRBTL11/2R    Duple DP47F    Essex Buses 1006 98
2247 CE  HFN  769   Volvo B10M-60    Plaxton C48FT  Wallace Arnold 92
2248 PH  FNJ  905   Volvo B10M-60    Plaxton C48FT  Wallace Arnold 92
2252 CE  TJY  761   Volvo B10M-60    Plaxton C51FT  Wallace Arnold 93
2253 PH  WNN  734   Volvo B10M-60    Plaxton C51FT  Wallace Arnold 93
2258 PH  H613 UWR  Volvo B10M-60    Plaxton C46FT  Wallace Arnold 94
2259 PH  H614 UWR  Volvo B10M-60    Plaxton C46FT  Wallace Arnold 94
2260 PH  H615 UWR  Volvo B10M-60    Plaxton C46FT  Wallace Arnold 94
2261 PH  FDZ  980   Volvo B10M-60    Plaxton C46FT  Wallace Arnold 94
                    * * * * * * *
```

2301-15 *Volvo B10M-62 Plaxton C44FT or C46FT(2301-3) New 94-9
                    *2314 is C51F & 2315 is C57F
          M301-3 BRL,R304/5/7-10 JAF,S311-3 SCV,S314/5 SRL,T316 KCV.
```
2301 CE  2303 CE  2305 BE  2308 CE  2310 CE  2312 CE  2314 PH  2316 CE
2302 CE  2304 BE  2307 CE  2309 CE  2311 CE  2313 CE  2315 PH
                    * * * * * * *
2401 CE  J701 CWT  Volvo B10M-60    Plaxton C48FT  Wallace Arnold 95
2402 CE  J703 CWT  Volvo B10M-60    Plaxton C46FT  Wallace Arnold 95
2505 CE  XFF  283   Volvo B10M-61    Van Hool C48FT Badgerline 2505 95
2506 PH  EWV  665   Volvo B10M-61    Van Hool C48FT Badgerline 2506 95
2507 PH  RUH  346   Volvo B10M-61    Van Hool C48FT Badgerline 2507 95
2508 PH  UWB  183   Volvo B10M-61    Van Hool C53F  Badgerline 2508 91
2511 PH  UHW  661   Volvo B10M-61    Van Hool C48FT Badgerline 2511 91
2521 PH  P521 PRL  Volvo B10M-62    Van Hool C44FT New 96
2522 PH  P522 PRL  Volvo B10M-62    Van Hool C44FT New 96
2600 PH  E200 BOD  Leyland LX112    B51F           New 88
2601 PH  E201 BOD  Leyland LX112    B51F           New 88
2602 PH  E202 BOD  Leyland LX112    B51F           New 88
2603 PH  E203 BOD  Leyland LX112    B51F           New 88
2605 PH  E205 BOD  Leyland LX112    B51F           New 88
2606 BE  G261 LUG  Leyland LX112    B51F           Brewers 507 96
2607 BE  F101 GRM  Leyland LX112    DP47F          First Beeline 800 99
2608 BE  F604 RTC  Leyland LX2R     B47F           First Bristol 1604 00
2609 BE  F605 RTC  Leyland LX2R     B47F           First Bristol 1605 00
2610 -   F606 RTC  Leyland LX2R     B47F           First Bristol 1606 00
2611 PH  F607 RTC  Leyland LX2R     B47F           First Bristol 1607 00
2612 CE  F608 RTC  Leyland LX2R     B47F           First Bristol 1608 00
2613 BE  J375 WWK  Leyland LX2R     B51F           First Cymru 839 01
2614 PH  K 10 BMS  Leyland LX2R     B47F           First Cymru 840 02
2820 -   RIL 1172  LD TRCTL11/3RH   Plaxton C51F   New 86
2821 BE  G326 PEW  Volvo B10M-60    Plaxton C49FT  Premier Travel 383 93
2822 CE  GIL 2967  Volvo B10M-61    Van Hool C53F  Philp,Dunfermline 94
2850 BE  N232 WFJ  Dennis Javelin   Plaxton C44FT  New 96
2851 BE  N233 WFJ  Dennis Javelin   Plaxton C44FT  New 96
2852 CE  P234 BFJ  Volvo B10M-62    Plaxton C49FT  New 96
2853 BE  P235 CTA  Dennis Javelin   Plaxton C44FT  New 97
2854 BE  P236 CTA  Dennis Javelin   Plaxton C44FT  New 97
2855 BE  R298 AYB  Dennis Javelin   Plaxton C49FT  First Bristol 298 02
2856 BE  M292 FAE  Dennis Javelin   Plaxton C49FT  First Bristol 292 02
3550 PH  JTH  44W   Leyland PSU3F/5R Plaxton DP53F  Brewers 159 94
4000 CE  H801 GDV  Dennis Dart      Carlyle B40F   New 91
4001 BE  J803 PFJ  Dennis Dart      Wright B39F    New 92
4002 BE  K804 WTT  Dennis Dart      Wright B39F    New 93
4003 BE  K805 WTT  Dennis Dart      Wright B39F    New 93
4004 CE  M809 FTT  Dennis Dart      Marshall B40F  New 94
4005 BE  N810 VOD  Dennis Dart SLF  Plaxton B36F   New 96
4006 BE  N811 VOD  Dennis Dart SLF  Plaxton B36F   New 96
4007 CE  P853 DTT  Dennis Dart SLF  Plaxton B37F   New 97
4008 BE  N 22 BLU  Dennis Dart      Marshall B40F  Dunstan,Middleton 22 97
4009 BE  N608 WND  Dennis Dart      Plaxton DP39F  Swanbrook,Cheltenham 98
4010 BE  N610 WND  Dennis Dart      Plaxton DP39F  Dodds,Ayr 406 98
4011 BE  N612 WND  Dennis Dart      Plaxton B39F   Dodds,Ayr 408 98
                    * * * * * * *
```

4401-26 Dennis Dart Plaxton B38F, B40F(401-6) or B37F(422-6) New 94/5
      L401-6 VCV,M407-26 CCV.

4401 BE	4405 PH	4409 PH	4412 CE	4415 CE	4418 CE	4421 CE	4424 CE
4402 BE	4406 PH	4410 CE	4413 CE	4416 CE	4419 CE	4422 CE	4425 CE
4403 BE	4407 PH	4411 CE	4414 CE	4417 CE	4420 CE	4423 CE	4426 CE
4404 BE	4408 PH						

* * * * * * *

4427-64 Dennis Dart SLF Plaxton B35F New 96/7
      P427-40 ORL,P441-6 TCV,R447-64 CCV.

4427 PH	4432 PH	4437 PH	4442 PH	4447 PH	4452 PH	4457 CE	4461 PH
4428 PH	4433 PH	4438 PH	4443 PH	4448 PH	4453 PH	4458 PH	4462 PH
4429 PH	4434 PH	4439 PH	4444 PH	4449 PH	4454 CE	4459 PH	4463 PH
4430 PH	4435 PH	4440 PH	4445 PH	4450 PH	4455 CE	4460 PH	4464 PH
4431 PH	4436 PH	4441 PH	4446 PH	4451 PH	4456 CE		

* * * * * * *

4465 PH	N561 LHU	Dennis Dart	Plaxton B35F	Bristol 1561 98
4466 PH	N562 LHU	Dennis Dart	Plaxton B35F	Bristol 1562 98
4467 PH	N563 LHU	Dennis Dart	Plaxton B35F	Bristol 1563 98
4468 PH	N564 LHU	Dennis Dart	Plaxton B35F	Bristol 1564 98

* * * * * * *

4469-78 Dennis Dart SLF Alexander B37F New 99/00
      T469-71 JCV,T472/3 YTT,X474-8 SCY.

4469 CE	4471 CE	4473 CE	4474 BE	4475 BE	4476 BE	4477 BE	4478 BE
4470 CE	4472 CE						

* * * * * * *

4479 CE	P409 MLA	Dennis Dart	Plaxton B37F	First London D39 02
4480 SL	P408 MLA	Dennis Dart	Plaxton B37F	First London D38 02
4481 SL	P410 MLA	Dennis Dart	Plaxton B37F	First London D40 02
4482 SL	P411 MLA	Dennis Dart	Plaxton B37F	First London D41 02
4483 CE	L670 SMC	Dennis Dart	NC B31F	First London DN670 02
4484 CE	K901 CVW	Dennis Dart	Plaxton B35F	First London DR691 02
4485 CE	K902 CVW	Dennis Dart	Plaxton B35F	First London DR692 02
4486 CE	J459 JOW	Dennis Dart	WS B37F	First London DS669 02
4487 SL	NDZ 3167	Dennis Dart	Wright B29F	First London DW167 02
4488 SL	NDZ 3168	Dennis Dart	Wright B29F	First London DW168 02
4490 CE	NDZ 3166	Dennis Dart	Wright B29F	First London DW166 02
4491 CE	K905 CVW	Dennis Dart	Plaxton B35F	First London DR695 02
4501 PH	M501 CCV	Dennis Dart	Plaxton B35F	New 95
4502 PH	M502 CCV	Dennis Dart	Plaxton B35F	New 95
4503 PH	M503 CCV	Dennis Dart	Plaxton B35F	New 95

* * * * * * *

4601-12 Volvo B6BLE Wright B37F or B38F(4610-2) New 00/2
      W601-9 PAF,WK02 TYH/F/D.

4601 PH	4603 PH	4605 PH	4607 PH	4609 PH	4610 CE	4611 CE	4612 CE
4602 PH	4604 PH	4606 PH	4608 PH				

* * * * * * *

4613 CE	YG02 DLV	Volvo B6BLE	Wright B38F	Yorkshire Rider 3049 02

* * * * * * *

6271-92 *Mercedes-Benz 811D Alexander B28F Centrewest 98
                *6276 is DP28F & 6278/81/4/5 are B33F
      F666,706,668 XMS,F455 TOY,F948 BMS,F680/4/3/2/43 XMS,
      F949/54 BMS,F657/67 XMS,F946/52/3 BMS,F669 XMS.

6271 CE	6276 CE	6279 CE	6281 CE	6284 CE	6286 CE	6289 CE	6291 CE
6273 CE	6277 CE	6280 CE	6283 CE	6285 CE	6287 CE	6290 CE	6292 CE
6275 CE	6278 CE						

* * * * * * *

6301-26 Mercedes-Benz 811D Carlyle B31F or DP31F(6301/2/11) New 90/1
      G151/2 GOL,H893-6 LOX,H718/23/6 HGL.

6301 SL	6308 SL	6309 SL	6310 SL	6311 SL	6318 SL	6323 SL	6326 SL
6302 SL							

* * * * * * *

6331-60 *Mercedes-Benz 811D Plaxton B31F or DP31F(6351/4) New 92-4
                *6355/7 are DP33F
      K331-43 OAF,K344-54 ORL,L355-60 VCV.

6331 SL	6335 CE	6339 CE	6343 CE	6347 CE	6351 PH	6355 PH	6358 CE
6332 SL	6336 CE	6340 CE	6344 PH	6348 PH	6352 PH	6356 PH	6359 CE
6333 SL	6337 CE	6341 CE	6345 PH	6349 PH	6353 PH	6357 PH	6360 CE
6334 SL	6338 CE	6342 CE	6346 PH	6350 PH	6354 PH		

```
6370 BE   J610 PTA   MB 811D            Carlyle B33F     New 92
6371 BE   K752 XTA   MB 811D            Wright B33F      New 93
6372 BE   K753 XTA   MB 811D            Wright B33F      New 93
6373 BE   K754 XTA   MB 811D            Wright B33F      New 93
6374 BE   K755 XTA   MB 811D            Wright B33F      New 93
6375 PH   L 69 EPR   MB 811D            Wright B33F      New 94
6376 BE   M764 FTT   MB 811D            Marshall B33F    New 94
6377 BE   M765 FTT   MB 811D            Marshall B33F    New 94
6379 BE   M768 FTT   MB 811D            Marshall DP33F   New 94
6380 BE   M769 FTT   MB 811D            Marshall DP33F   New 94
6382 CE   F800 RHK   MB 811D            RB B31F          First Capital 600 00
6383 -    G337 XRE   MB 811D            PMT B28F         PMT 337 00
6386 CE   F802 RHK   MB 811D            RB B31F          First Capital 607 00
6387 CE   J610 HMF   MB 811D            RB B28F          Mainline 177 01
                           * * * * * * *
```

6520-8 Mercedes-Benz 709D Wright B29F New 92
       J140-6/8 SJT.
```
6520 BE   6521 BE   6522 BE   6523 BE   6524 BE   6526 PH   6527 BE   6528 BE
                           * * * * * * *
6529 BE   K723 WTT   MB 709D            Wright B29F      New 93
6530 BE   L649 CJT   MB 709D            Wright B29F      New 93
6531 SL   M901 LTT   MB 609D            Frank Guy B19F   New 95
6532 SL   M902 LTT   MB 609D            Frank Guy B19F   New 95
6533 BE   M676 RAJ   MB 709D            ARB B25F         Go Ahead(OK) 476 98
6534 BE   M677 RAJ   MB 709D            ARB B25F         Go Ahead(OK) 477 98
6535 BE   M678 RAJ   MB 709D            ARB B25F         Go Ahead 478 98
                           * * * * * * *
```

6601-51 Mercedes-Benz 709D Plaxton B23F New 93/4
       K601-25 ORL,L628-51 VCV.
```
6601 PH   6608 PH   6614 PH   6620 PH   6628 SL   6634 SL   6640 SL   6646 CE
6602 PH   6609 SL   6615 SL   6621 PH   6629 PH   6635 SL   6641 CE   6647 CE
6603 PH   6610 PH   6616 -    6622 PH   6630 SL   6636 SL   6642 PH   6648 CE
6604 PH   6611 PH   6617 SL   6623 PH   6631 SL   6637 SL   6643 CE   6649 PH
6605 PH   6612 SL   6618 SL   6624 CE   6632 SL   6638 SL   6644 CE   6650 PH
6606 PH   6613 PH   6619 SL   6625 CE   6633 SL   6639 SL   6645 CE   6651 PH
6607 PH
                           * * * * * * *
6652 BE   M246 VWU   MB 709D            Plaxton B23F     Yorkshire Rider 2246 96
6653 BE   M226 VWU   MB 709D            Plaxton B23F     Yorkshire Rider 2226 96
6659 PH   N719 GRV   MB 709D            Plaxton B27F     Provincial 719 99
6662 CE   H346 LJN   MB 709D            RB B23F          First Capital 937 99
6663 CE   K435 XRF   MB 709D            Plaxton B24F     PMT 435 99
6664 CE   K443 XRF   MB 709D            Plaxton B24F     PMT 443 00
6665 CE   K432 XRF   MB 709D            Plaxton B24F     PMT 432 00
6666 CE   H481 JRE   MB 709D            PMT B25F         PMT 481 00
6667 CE   K433 XRF   MB 709D            Plaxton B24F     PMT 433 00
6668 CE   H180 JRE   MB 709D            PMT B25F         PMT 480 00
6669 CE   K447 XRF   MB 709D            Plaxton B24F     PMT 447 00
6670 CE   H345 LJN   MB 709D            RB B23F          First Capital 936 00
6700 BE   R650 TDV   MB O810D           Plaxton B29F     New 97
6701 BE   R851 YDV   MB O810D           Plaxton B29F     New 97
                           * * * * * * *
```

6702-11 *Mercedes-Benz O814D Plaxton B29F or B33F(6704) New 98/9
                  *6702/3/7 are B27F
       R852/3 TFJ,S865-72 NOD.
```
6702 BE   6704 BE   6706 BE   6707 BE   6708 BE   6709 BE   6710 BE   6711 BE
6703 BE   6705 BE
                           * * * * * * *
```

6801-15 Optare Solo M850 B27F New 99/00
       V801-3 KAF,W804-9/11-5 PAF.
```
6801 BE   6803 BE   6805 PH   6807 PH   6809 PH   6812 PH   6814 PH   6815 PH
6802 BE   6804 PH   6806 PH   6808 PH   6811 PH   6813 BE
```
~~~~~~

OTHER VEHICLES OWNED BY THE COMPANY
                           * * * * * * *
```
6054 CE   B 41 AAF   MB L608D           G & M B15FL      Recruitment Bus
6099 CE   C796 FRL   MB L608D           RB B20F          Staff Bus(Delabole)
6328 PH   E808 MOU   MB 811D            Optare B33F      Trainer
```

```
6329 PH  E812 MOU  MB 811D          Optare B33F     Trainer
6500 PH  H324 HVT  MB 609D          PMT C24F        Staff Bus
9702 BE  L548 CDV  Dennis Dart      Wright B28FL    Operated for Devon CC
9712 BE  T789 RDV  LDV Convoy       CSM B18F        Operated for Devon CC
9719 PH  N428 FOW  Dennis Dart      UVG B40F        loan from Dawsons
9720 PH  N762 SAV  Dennis Dart      Marshall B40F   loan from Dawsons
9725 BE  WJ02 HYW  LDV Convoy       CSM B16F        Operated for Devon CC
```
~~~~~~

N.B.:- Western National took over the running of Red Bus from First
Southern National 6/99 and the following vehicles were taken into
stock with that operation:- 1304/5/815-7,2820-54,4000-11,6370-80,
6520-35,6700-11 & 9702.

~~~~~~

EWV 665*D506 GHY(8/95), FDZ 980*G521 LWU(1/95), FNJ 905*F446 DUG(3/96),
FNR 923*B291 KPF(5/96), GIL 2967*LSK 819(5/94) & E634 UNE(4/92),
HFN 769*F444 DUG(3/96), HVJ 716*A658 VDA(8/97), NER 621*B295 KPF(6/96),
RIL 1172*7 ACL(2/99) & C923 HYA(7/93), RUH 346*D507 GHY(10/95),
TJI 4838*E322 OMG(12/95), TJY 761*F445 DUG(3/96), UHW 661*D511 HHW(8/95),
UWB 183*D508 HHW(6/95), VOO 273*A101 JJT(9/97), WNN 734*G541 LWU(3/96),
WSV 408*HUA 604Y(9/86), XFF 283*D505 GHY(9/95),
894 GUO*CSO 544Y(8/97) & JSV 426(2/97) & FNM 863Y(11/86),
530 OHU*A205 SAE(10/88), JTH 44W*948 RJO(8/92) & GTH 536W(10/89),
A206 SAE*CSV 231(8/97) & A206 SAE(6/87),
F455 TOY*VLT 31(4/98) & F903 CMS(6/89) & F701 XMS(4/89) &
G326 PEW*920 GTA(7/99) & G326 PEW(7/95)

~~~~~~

4   PLYMOUTH CITYBUS LTD

Garage:PLYMOUTH(Milehouse Road)

1-27 Dennis Dart SLF Plaxton B39F New 96/8
      N101-5/7-10/2 UTT,R113-26 OFJ,S127 FTA.

```
1       5       9       13      16      19      22      25
2       7       10      14      17      20      23      26
3       8       12      15      18      21      24      27
4
```
                        * * * * * * *
28-48 Dennis Dart SPD Plaxton B43F or B41F(43-8) New 99/00
      T128-40 EFJ,X141/2 CDV,X143 CFJ,Y644-8 NYD.
```
28      31      34      37      40      43      45      47
29      32      35      38      41      44      46      48
30      33      36      39      42
```
                        * * * * * * *
```
51  M 51 HOD   Volvo B6              Plaxton B40F     New 94
52  M 52 HOD   Volvo B6              Plaxton B40F     New 94
53  M 53 HOD   Volvo B6              Plaxton B40F     New 94
55  WA51 ACO   Dennis Dart SPD      Plaxton B41F     New 01
56  WA51 ACU   Dennis Dart SPD      Plaxton B41F     New 01
57  WA51 ACV   Dennis Dart SPD      Plaxton B41F     New 01
58  WA51 ACX   Dennis Dart SPD      Plaxton B41F     New 01
59  WA51 ACY   Dennis Dart SPD      Plaxton B41F     New 01
```
                        * * * * * * *
101-32 Dennis Dart Plaxton B40F New 92-4
      K101-5/7-10 SFJ,L112-26 YOD,M127-32 HOD.
```
101     105     110     115     119     123     127     130
102     107     112     116     120     124     128     131
103     108     113     117     121     125     129     132
104     109     114     118     122     126
```
                        * * * * * * *
```
159  ODV 203W  Leyland AN68A/1R EL O43/28D     New 81
160  ATK 160W  Leyland AN68A/1R EL O43/28D     New 80
161  ATK 161W  Leyland AN68A/1R EL O43/28D     New 80
```
                        * * * * * * *
162-71 Leyland AN68C/1R East Lancs H43/31F New 81
      TTT 162-71X.
```
162     164     166     167     168     169     170     171
163     165
```

```
173  G643 CHF  Volvo B10M-50   EL H49/39F    Arriva Surrey 643 00
174  G640 CHF  Volvo B10M-50   EL H49/39F    Arriva Surrey 640 00
175  B175 VDV  Volvo B10M-50   EL H42/35F    New 84
176  B176 VDV  Volvo B10M-50   EL H42/35F    New 84
177  H177 GTT  Volvo B10M-50   EL CH48/30F   New 91
178  H178 GTT  Volvo B10M-50   EL CH48/30F   New 91
                    * * * * * * *
```
179-90 Volvo B10M-50 Alexander H47/37F Trent 612etc 99/00
```
     G612/4/5/21 OTV,F600-7 GVO.
179     181     183     185     187     188     189     190
180     182     184     186
                    * * * * * * *
195  F 50 ACL  Volvo B10M-50   AR H45/37F    Chambers,Bures 00
196  F 51 ACL  Volvo B10M-50   AR H45/37F    Chambers,Bures 00
197  G623 OTV  Volvo B10M-50   AR H47/37F    Chambers,Bures 00
201  X201 CDV  Dennis Dart MPD Plaxton B29F  New 00
202  X202 CDV  Dennis Dart MPD Plaxton B29F  New 00
203  X203 CDV  Dennis Dart MPD Plaxton B29F  New 00
204  X204 CDV  Dennis Dart MPD Plaxton B29F  New 00
                    * * * * * * *
```
241-89 Mercedes-Benz 709D Plaxton B25F New 92-5
```
     K241-7 SFJ,L248-60 YOD,M261-74 HOD,N275-9/81-9 PDV.
241   247   253   259   265   271   277   284
242   248   254   260   266   272   278   285
243   249   255   261   267   273   279   286
244   250   256   262   268   274   281   287
245   251   257   263   269   275   282   288
246   252   258   264   270   276   283   289
                    * * * * * * *
301  K301 WTA  Volvo B10M-60   Plaxton C51F  New 93
302  L302 YOD  Volvo B10M-60   Plaxton C51F  New 93
                    * * * * * * *
```
304-14 Volvo B10M-62 Plaxton C49FT or C53F(311-4) New 95-01
```
     M304/5 KOD,N307 UTT,P308 CTT,R309 STA,W311/2 SDV,Y313/4 NYD.
304     307     308     309     311     312     313     314
305
                    * * * * * * *
340  JSK 261  Volvo B10M-60   Plaxton C53F   Fishwick,Leyland 92
341  JSK 262  Volvo B10M-60   Plaxton C53F   Park,Hamilton 92
346  JSK 264  Volvo B10M-60   Plaxton C53F   Park,Hamilton 90
350  JSK 265  Volvo B10M-61   Van Hool C49FT Park,Hamilton 88
```
~~~~~~
JSK 261*F973 HGE(1/93), JSK 262*F968 HGE(1/93), JSK 264*F988 HGE(1/93) &
JSK 265*UJY 932(1/93) & MCO 658(4/92) & A602 UGD(6/88)
~~~~~~

STAGECOACH GROUP

5   **CHELTENHAM DISTRICT TRACTION COMPANY LTD(CM)**
CHELTENHAM & GLOUCESTER OMNIBUS COMPANY LTD
SWINDON & DISTRICT BUS COMPANY LTD(SN)

Garages:
CH CHIPPENHAM(?)(ex SN)   *RS ROSS-ON-WYE(Station Approach)*
CM CHELTENHAM(Lansdown IE)   *SD STROUD(London Road)*
CR CIRENCESTER(Love Lane IE)(ex SN) SN SWINDON(Eastcott Road)
GR GLOUCESTER(London Road)

```
101 SN  G101 AAD  LD ONLXB/2RZ         AR H51/36F   New 90
102 SN  G102 AAD  LD ONLXB/2RZ         AR H51/36F   New 90
103 SD  G103 AAD  LD ONLXB/2RZ         AR H51/36F   New 90
104 SD  G104 AAD  LD ONLXB/2RZ         AR H51/36F   New 90
105 SD  G105 AAD  LD ONLXB/2RZ         AR H51/36F   New 90
112 SD  JHU 899X  Leyland ONLXB/1R Roe H47/29F  Bristol 9500 83
113 SN  UWW   7X  Leyland ONLXB/1R Roe H47/29F  W Yorkshire PTE 5007 87
                  * * * * * * *
```

114-24 Leyland ONLXB/1R Roe H47/29F Bristol 9513/7-25/33 83
            JHU 912X,LWS 33-41Y,NTC 132Y.
```
114 GR   116 SD   118 SD   120 GR   121 SN   122 GR   123 SD   124 SN
115 GR   117 SN   119 GR
                  * * * * * * *
125 RS  R203 DHB  Volvo Olympian    AR CH47/32F  Red & White 903 99
126 RS  R204 DHB  Volvo Olympian    AR CH47/32F  Red & White 904 99
127 RS  R205 DHB  Volvo Olympian    AR CH47/32F  Red & White 905 99
129 SN  A854 SUL  LD TNLXB/2RR      LD H44/29F   Stagecoach London 99
130 GR  C610 LFT  Leyland ONLXB/1R AR H45/31F   Busways 610 99
131 CM  C659 LFT  Leyland ONLXB/1R AR H45/31F   Busways 659 99
132 CM  C650 LFT  Leyland ONLXB/1R AR H45/31F   Busways 650 99
133 CM  C641 LFT  Leyland ONLXB/1R AR H45/31F   Busways 641 00
134 CM  C624 LFT  Leyland ONLXB/1R AR H45/31F   Busways 624 99
135 CM  C609 LFT  Leyland ONLXB/1R AR H45/31F   Busways 609 01
138 SN  MHS   4P  LD ONLXB/1RV      AR CH43/27F  Bluebird Buses 064 01
139 SN  MHS   5P  LD ONLXB/1RV      AR CH43/27F  Bluebird Buses 065 01
141 RS  R206 DHB  Volvo Olympian    AR H51/36F   Red & White 906 00
142 RS  R207 DHB  Volvo Olympian    AR H51/36F   Red & White 907 00
143 RS  R208 DHB  Volvo Olympian    AR H51/36F   Red & White 908 00
150 -   N350 HGK  Volvo YN2RC       NC H45/23D   Stagecoach London 02
151 -   N351 HGK  Volvo YN2RC       NC H45/23D   Stagecoach London 02
156 -   N349 HGK  Volvo YN2RC       NC H45/23D   Stagecoach London 02
160 GR  E500 LFL  LD ON6LXCT/1RH    OE CH43/27F  Cambus 500 02
161 GR  E501 LFL  LD ON6LXCT/1RH    Optare H43/27F Cambus 501 02
162 RS  E502 LFL  LD ON6LXCT/1RH    OE CH43/27F  Cambus 502 02
163 GR  UWW   3X  Leyland ONLXB/1R Roe H47/29F  Cambus 503 02
                  * * * * * * *
```

401-9 Volvo B10M-55 Alexander DP48F New 95
           N401-9 LDF.
```
401 CR   403 CR   404 CR   405 SN   406 CH   407 CH   408 CH   409 SN
402 CR
                  * * * * * * *
410 SN  P317 EFL  Volvo B10M-55     Alexander B49F Cambus 317 00
411 SN  P318 EFL  Volvo B10M-55     Alexander B49F Cambus 318 00
412 SN  P319 EFL  Volvo B10M-55     Alexander B49F Cambus 319 00
                  * * * * * * *
```

417-28 Volvo B10M-55 Alexander B49F Stagecoach Manchester 817-28 99
            N817/8 DNE,P819/20 GNC,P821-8 FVU.
```
417 GR   419 GR   421 SN   423 SN   425 SD   426 SD   427 SD   428 SD
418 GR   420 GR   422 SN   424 SD
                  * * * * * * *
464 GR  NDZ 3134  Dennis Dart       Wright B29F  Red & White 464 01
466 RS  NDZ 3136  Dennis Dart       Wright B29F  Red & White 466 02
                  * * * * * * *
```

501-13 Dennis Dart SLF Plaxton B41F New 00
W501 VDD,X502/3 ADF,W504,805 VDD,X506/7 ADF,W508/9 VDD,X518/1-3 ADF

501 CM	503 CM	505 CM	507 CM	509 CM	511 CM	512 CM	513 CM
502 CM	504 CM	506 CM	508 CM	510 CM			

* * * * * * *

550 CM	R550 JDF	Volvo B10M-62	Plaxton C49FT	New 97	
551 CM	R551 JDF	Volvo B10M-62	Plaxton C49FT	New 97	
552 CM	R552 JDF	Volvo B10M-62	Plaxton C49FT	New 97	
553 CM	R553 JDF	Volvo B10M-62	Plaxton C49FT	New 97	
554 CM	R554 JDF	Volvo B10M-62	Plaxton C49FT	New 97	
562 CM	P 92 URG	Volvo B10M-62	Plaxton C47FT	Busways 92 01	
570 GR	P110 FRS	Volvo B10M-62	Plaxton C51F	Western Buses 110 02	

* * * * * * *

718-35 Mercedes-Benz 709D ARB B25F or DP25F(731-5) New 96
N718-35 RDD.

718 CM	721 SD	724 CM	726 SD	728 CM	730 CM	732 CM	734 GR
719 CM	722 SD	725 SD	727 SD	729 CM	731 CM	733 GR	735 SD
720 -	723 CM						

* * * * * * *

736 -	N644 VSS	MB 709D	ARB B25F	Cambus 211 99	
803 -	L803 XDG	MB 811D	Marshall B33F	New 93	
804 SD	L804 XDG	MB 811D	Marshall B33F	New 93	
805 SD	L805 XDG	MB 811D	Marshall B33F	New 93	
806 SD	L806 XDG	MB 811D	Marshall B33F	New 93	
807 SD	L330 CHB	MB 811D	Marshall B33F	Red & White 330 94	
808 SD	K308 YKG	MB 811D	Wright B33F	Red & White 308 95	
816 GR	K311 YKG	MB 811D	Wright B33F	Red & White 311 00	
817 GR	N152 MTG	MB 711D	UVG B27F	Red & White 152 02	
818 GR	N153 MTG	MB 711D	UVG B27F	Red & White 153 02	
820 GR	P167 TNY	MB 711D	Plaxton B27F	Red & White 167 02	
821 GR	P171 TNY	MB 711D	Plaxton B27F	Red & White 171 02	
822 GR	P161 TDW	MB 711D	Plaxton B27F	Red & White 161 02	
839 -	L839 CDG	Volvo B6	Alexander B40F	New 94	
840 -	L840 CDG	Volvo B6	Alexander B40F	New 94	
841 -	L841 CDG	Volvo B6	Alexander B40F	New 94	
843 -	M843 EMW	Volvo B6	Alexander B40F	New 95	
844 CM	M844 EMW	Volvo B6	Alexander B40F	New 95	
845 GR	M845 EMW	Volvo B6	Alexander B40F	New 95	
846 RS	L248 CCK	Volvo B6	AR DP40F	Ribble 248 95	
847 -	M847 HDF	Volvo B6	Alexander B40F	New 95	
848 RS	L709 FWO	Volvo B6	Alexander B40F	Red & White 709 95	
850 GR	L711 FWO	Volvo B6	Alexander B40F	Red & White 711 95	
851 GR	L712 FWO	Volvo B6	Alexander B40F	Red & White 712 95	
885 SN	M 85 WBW	Dennis Dart	Plaxton B43F	Stagecoach London 02	
886 SN	M 86 WBW	Dennis Dart	Plaxton B43F	Stagecoach London 02	
901 SD	P901 SMR	Dennis Dart	Alexander B40F	New 97	
902 SD	P902 SMR	Dennis Dart	Alexander B40F	New 97	
903 SD	P903 SMR	Dennis Dart	Alexander B40F	New 97	

* * * * * * *

904-18 Dennis Dart SLF Alexander B36F or B37F(915-8) New 97
P904-14 SMR,R915-8 GMW.

904 SN	906 SN	908 SN	910 SN	912 SN	914 SN	916 SN	918 SN
905 SN	907 SN	909 SN	911 SN	913 SN	915 SN	917 SN	

* * * * * * *

920 SN	N319 AMC	Dennis Dart	Alexander B36F	Stagecoach London 98	
921 SN	N320 AMC	Dennis Dart	Alexander B36F	Stagecoach London 98	
922 SN	N313 AMC	Dennis Dart	Alexander B36F	Stagecoach London 98	
923 SN	N317 AMC	Dennis Dart	Alexander B36F	Stagecoach London 98	
924 SN	S924 PDD	Dennis Dart SLF	Alexander B37F	New 98	
925 GR	S925 PDD	Dennis Dart SLF	Alexander B37F	New 98	
926 CM	S926 PDD	Dennis Dart SLF	Alexander B37F	New 98	
927 CM	S927 PDD	Dennis Dart SLF	Alexander B37F	New 98	
928 CM	S928 PDD	Dennis Dart SLF	Alexander B37F	New 98	
929 CM	S929 PDD	Dennis Dart SLF	Alexander B37F	New 98	
930 CM	S930 PDD	Dennis Dart SLF	Alexander B37F	New 98	
931 SN	R808 YUD	Dennis Dart SLF	Alexander B37F	Stagecoach Oxford 98	
932 SD	R809 YUD	Dennis Dart SLF	Alexander B37F	Stagecoach Oxford 98	
933 SD	R810 YUD	Dennis Dart SLF	Alexander B37F	Stagecoach Oxford 98	
934 SD	R811 YUD	Dennis Dart SLF	Alexander B37F	Stagecoach Oxford 98	

```
935 SD  R812 YUD  Dennis Dart SLF  Alexander B37F  Stagecoach Oxford 98
936 SD  M 85 DEW  Dennis Dart      Marshall B40F   Stagecoach Manchestr 99
937 SD  M 86 DEW  Dennis Dart      Marshall B40F   Stagecoach Manchestr 99
                         * * * * * * *
```

938-62 Dennis Dart SLF Alexander B37F New 99
         V938-47 DFH,V948-60 DDG,V961/2 DFH.

```
938 GR   942 SN   945 GR   948 GR   951 GR   954 CM   957 CM   960 GR
939 GR   943 SN   946 GR   949 GR   952 GR   955 CM   958 CM   961 CM
940 CM   944 GR   947 GR   950 GR   953 CM   956 CM   959 CM   962 CM
941 GR
                         * * * * * * *
963 GR  R601 SWO  Dennis Dart SLF  Alexander B37F  Red & White 601 00
964 GR  R602 SWO  Dennis Dart SLF  Alexander B37F  Red & White 602 00
965 GR  R603 SWO  Dennis Dart SLF  Alexander B37F  Red & White 603 00
                         * * * * * * *
```

966-80 Dennis Dart SLF Alexander B38F or B37F(978-80) New 00/1
         X966-9/78/1-7 AFH,VX51 NXR-T.

```
966 GR   968 GR   970 GR   972 GR   974 GR   976 GR   978 RS   980 GR
967 GR   969 GR   971 GR   973 GR   975 GR   977 GR   979 RS
                         * * * * * * *
1108 SN  B108 WUV  LD TNLXB/2RR  LD H44/29F   Stagecoach London 98
1112 SN  B112 WUV  LD TNLXB/2RR  LD H44/29F   Stagecoach London 99
1403 SD  H403 MRW  MB 811D       Wright B33F  Midland Red Sth 403 98
1416 SD  J416 PRW  MB 811D       Wright B33F  Midland Red Sth 416 98
1838 SN  A838 SUL  LD TNLXB/2RR  LD H44/29F   Stagecoach London 99
```
~~~~~~

OTHER VEHICLES OWNED BY THE COMPANY
                         * * * * * * *

```
 842 GR  L842 CDG  Volvo B6          Alexander B40F  Trainer
 919 SN  N318 AMC  Dennis Dart       Alexander B36F  Trainer
CG 6 SN  R606 KDD  Iveco 49-10       Mellor B-F      Engineers Van
CG 7 SD  R607 KDD  Iveco 49-10       Mellor B-F      Engineers Van
CG10 CM  R610 KDD  Iveco 49-10       Mellor B-F      Engineers Van
DT 7 SD  511  OHU  Dodge G13         WS B39F         Trainer
DT 8 GR  HIL 6075  Renault G13       WS B39F         Trainer
DT10 CM  HIL 8410  Dodge G13         WS B39F         Trainer
DT11 CM  D891 DWP  Dodge G13         WS B13F         Trainer
DT12 SN  EJV  32Y  Dennis Falcon H   WS B6F          Trainer
DT14 GR  EJV  34Y  Dennis Falcon H   WS B6F          Trainer
RM 1 GR  JSK  492  Bristol FLF6LW    ECW O-F         Tree Lopper
```
~~~~~~
JSK 492*511 OHU(2/92), 511 OHU*E789 CHS(12/99), MHS 4P*C464 SSO(7/90) &
MHS 5P*C465 SSO(7/90)
~~~~~~

6   **STAGECOACH DEVON**

BAYLINE LTD   **DEVON GENERAL LTD**

Garages:
*   CULLOMPTON(Meadow IE)(ex EX)   OTTERY ST MARY(Finnimore IE)(EX)*
EM EXMOUTH(Imperial Road)(ex EX)   SIDMOUTH(?)(5 ex EX)
EX EXETER(Belgrave Road)   TIVERTON(Safeway,Kennedy Way)(EX)
*   OKEHAMPTON(Market St CP)(ex EX) TQ TORQUAY(Regent Close)*

101-18 Mercedes-Benz O814D Alexander B29F New 98
         R101-5/7-10/2-6 NTA,S117/8 JFJ.

```
101 EX   103 EX   105 EX   108 EX   110 EX   113 EX   115 EX   117 EX
102 EX   104 EX   107 EX   109 EX   112 EX   114 EX   116 EX   118 EX
                         * * * * * * *
200 EX  W102 PMS  Dennis Dart SLF  Alexander B28F Thames Transit 01
201 EX  WA51 OSE  Dennis Dart SLF  Alexander B28F New 01
202 EX  WA51 OSF  Dennis Dart SLF  Alexander B28F New 01
                         * * * * * * *
```

300-14 Iveco 59-12 Mellor B21D Devon General 1000-12/4 96
         L929-41/3 CTT.

```
300 EX   302 EX   304 EX   306 EX   308 EX   310 EX   312 EX   314 EX
301 EX   303 EX   305 EX   307 EX   309 EX   311 EX
```

315-33 Iveco 59-12 Wadham Stringer B21D Devon General 1015-33 96
    M638/40/37/6/9/29/4/3/5/8/6 HDV,M192 HTT,M630 HDV,M193 HTT,
    M627/2 HDV,M194/1 HTT,M641 HDV.

315 EX	318 TQ	321 EX	324 EM	326 EM	328 EM	330 EM	332 EX
316 EX	319 TQ	322 EM	325 EM	327 EX	329 EX	331 EX	333 EX
317 EX	320 EM	323 EM					

* * * * * * *

335 TQ	K711 UTT	Iveco 59-12	Mellor B29F	Bayline 2010 96
339 TQ	K719 UTT	Iveco 59-12	Mellor B29F	Bayline 2018 96
344 TQ	K725 UTT	Iveco 59-12	Mellor B29F	Bayline 2024 96
352 EX	K926 VDV	Iveco 59-12	Mellor B29F	Bayline 2071 96
363 TQ	K816 WFJ	Iveco 59-12	Mellor B29F	Bayline 2083 96

* * * * * * *

365-77 Iveco 59-12 Marshall B29F Bayline 2091-3/5/8/100/1/4-9 96
    L193-5/7/201/3/4/8-12/4 FDV.

365 TQ	367 TQ	369 TQ	371 TQ	373 TQ	375 TQ	376 TQ	377 TQ
366 TQ	368 TQ	370 TQ	372 TQ	374 TQ			

* * * * * * *

378 EX	N182 CMJ	Iveco 59-12	ARB B29F	Midland Red S. 832 97
379 EX	N183 CMJ	Iveco 59-12	ARB B29F	Midland Red S. 833 98
381 TQ	N190 GFR	Iveco 59-12	Mellor B27F	Ribble 716 98
382 TQ	N463 HRN	Iveco 59-12	Mellor B27F	Ribble 717 98
383 TQ	K171 CAV	Iveco 59-12	Marshall B25F	Cambus 951 99
385 TQ	K173 CAV	Iveco 59-12	Marshall B25F	Cambus 953 99
389 TQ	L945 EOD	Iveco 59-12	Mellor B29F	Thames Transit 2085 97
390 TQ	K718 UTT	Iveco 59-12	Mellor B29F	Thames Transit 2017 97
391 TQ	L947 EOD	Iveco 59-12	Mellor B29F	Thames Transit 2087 97
392 TQ	L948 EOD	Iveco 59-12	Mellor B29F	Thames Transit 2088 97
393 TQ	L949 EOD	Iveco 59-12	Mellor B29F	Thames Transit 2089 97
396 TQ	N189 GFR	Iveco 59-12	Mellor B27F	Ribble 715 98
397 TQ	L447 FFR	Iveco 59-12	Mellor B27F	Ribble 723 98
398 TQ	N188 GFR	Iveco 59-12	Mellor B27F	Ribble 714 98
399 TQ	N464 HRN	Iveco 59-12	Mellor B27F	Ribble 718 98
401 TQ	M701 EDD	MB 709D	ARB B25F	Cheltenham & G. 701 01
402 TQ	M702 EDD	MB 709D	ARB B25F	Cheltenham & G. 702 01
403 TQ	M703 EDD	MB 709D	ARB B25F	Cheltenham & G. 703 01
404 TQ	M704 EDD	MB 709D	ARB B25F	Cheltenham & G. 704 01
405 TQ	M705 EDD	MB 709D	ARB B25F	Cheltenham & G. 705 01
406 TQ	M706 JDG	MB 709D	ARB B25F	Cheltenham & G. 706 01
407 TQ	M707 JDG	MB 709D	ARB B25F	Cheltenham & G. 707 01

* * * * * * *

444-68 MB 709D Marshall B21D or B23F(461/4-8) Devon General 1034-58 96
    M226-50 UTM.

444 EX	448 EX	451 EX	454 EX	457 EX	460 EX	463 EX	466 EX
445 EX	449 EX	452 EX	455 EX	458 EX	461 EX	464 EX	467 EX
446 EX	450 EX	453 EX	456 EX	459 EX	462 EX	465 EX	468 EX
447 EX							

* * * * * * *

470-87 Mercedes-Benz 709D Alexander B23F New 96
    N978-82 NAP,N506-18 BJA.

470 TQ	473 EX	476 TQ	478 TQ	480 TQ	482 TQ	484 EX	486 EX
471 EX	474 TQ	477 EX	479 EX	481 EX	483 EX	485 EX	487 EX
472 TQ	475 TQ						

* * * * * * *

488 TQ	L685 CDD	MB 709D	ARB B25F	Red & White 330 99
489 TQ	M345 JBO	MB 709D	ARB B25F	Red & White 345 99
490 TQ	M360 JBO	MB 709D	ARB B25F	Red & White 360 99

* * * * * * *

491-9 Mercedes-Benz 709D ARB B25F Cheltenham & Gloucester 691-9 00
    L691-6 CDD,M697-9 EDD.

491 TQ	493 TQ	494 TQ	495 TQ	496 TQ	497 TQ	498 TQ	499 TQ
492 TQ							

* * * * * * *

700 EX	M343 NOD	Volvo B6	Alexander B39F Overseas(Hong Kong) 01

* * * * * * *

701-14 Volvo B6LE Alexander B35F New 97
    P701-14 BTA.
701 EX   703 EX   705 EX   707 TQ   709 EX   711 TQ   713 EX   714 TQ
702 EX   704 EX   706 EX   708 EX   710 EX   712 EX
                              * * * * * * *
715-24 Dennis Dart Plaxton B43F Stagecoach London PD715etc 02
    L715-22/14 JUD.
715 EX   717 EX   718 EX   719 EX   720 EX   721 EX   722 EX   724 EX
716 EX
                              * * * * * * *
726 EX   P636 PGP Dennis Dart   Alexander B36F Stagecoach London 02
727 EX   P619 PGP Dennis Dart   Alexander B36F Stagecoach London 02
728 EX   P618 PGP Dennis Dart   Alexander B36F Stagecoach London 02
729 EX   P639 PGP Dennis Dart   Alexander B36F Stagecoach London 02
730 EX   P640 PGP Dennis Dart   Alexander B36F Stagecoach London 02
731 EX   M103 WBW Dennis Dart   Plaxton B43F   Stagecoach London 01
                              * * * * * * *
732-44 Dennis Dart Plaxton DP37F Overseas(Hong Kong) 99/00
    N732-40/31/42-4 XDV.
732 TQ   734 TQ   736 TQ   738 TQ   740 EX   742 EX   743 EX   744 EX
733 TQ   735 TQ   737 TQ   739 EX   741 EX
                              * * * * * * *
745 EX   L139 VRH Dennis Dart   Plaxton B34F   Stagecoach London 99
746 EX   L140 VRH Dennis Dart   Plaxton B34F   Stagecoach London 99
747 EX   L141 VRH Dennis Dart   Plaxton B34F   Stagecoach London 99
748 EX   N411 MBW Dennis Dart   Plaxton B40F   Stagecoach London 99
749 EX   N410 MBW Dennis Dart   Plaxton B40F   Stagecoach London 99
750 EX   N599 DWY Dennis Dart   Plaxton B40F   Holladay,Aylesbeare 97
751 EX   R751 BDV Dennis Dart SLF   Alexander B37F New 97
752 EM   T575 KGB Dennis Dart SLF   Marshall B43F Western Buses 420 02
753 EM   R807 YUD Dennis Dart SLF   Alexander B37F Thames Transit 807 98
754 EM   R801 YUD Dennis Dart SLF   Alexander B37F Thames Transit 801 98
755 EM   R803 YUD Dennis Dart SLF   Alexander B37F Thames Transit 803 98
756 EM   R804 YUD Dennis Dart SLF   Alexander B37F Thames Transit 804 98
757 EM   R805 YUD Dennis Dart SLF   Alexander B37F Thames Transit 805 98
758 EX   P758 FOD Dennis Dart SLF   Plaxton B37F   Overseas(Hong Kong) 00
759 EX   P762 FOD Dennis Dart SLF   Plaxton B37F   Overseas(Hong Kong) 00
760 EX   P760 FOD Dennis Dart SLF   Plaxton B37F   Overseas(Hong Kong) 00
761 EX   R823 YUD Dennis Dart SLF   Alexander B37F Western Buses 474 02
762 EX   R824 YUD Dennis Dart SLF   Alexander B37F Western Buses 475 02
763 EX   T404 UCS Dennis Dart SLF   Alexander B37F Western Buses 404 02
764 EX   T131 MGB Dennis Dart SLF   Marshall B43F Western Buses 418 02
765 EX   T132 MGB Dennis Dart SLF   Marshall B43F Western Buses 419 02
778 EM   NDZ 3152 Dennis Dart   Wright B29F   Stagecoach London 98
779 EM   NDZ 3153 Dennis Dart   Wright B29F   Stagecoach London 98
780 EM   JDZ 2360 Dennis Dart   Wright B28F   Stagecoach London 98
781 EX   JDZ 2361 Dennis Dart   Wright B28F   Stagecoach London 98
784 EX   JDZ 2364 Dennis Dart   Wright B28F   Stagecoach London 98
785 EX   JDZ 2365 Dennis Dart   Wright B28F   Stagecoach London 98
786 EX   JDZ 2371 Dennis Dart   Wright B28F   Stagecoach London 98
789 EX   F706 CAG Scania N112CRB   EL B50F   Cleveland Transit 01
790 EX   F705 BAT Scania N112CRB   EL B50F   Cleveland Transit 01
791 EX   F701 BAT Scania N112CRB   EL B50F   Cleveland Transit 01
792 EX   F702 BAT Scania N112CRB   EL B50F   Cleveland Transit 01
793 EX   XIA 857 LN 11351A/1R   B48F   Stagecoach South 99
801 EX   P801 XTA Volvo B10M-62   Plaxton C51F   New 96
802 EX   P802 XTA Volvo B10M-62   Plaxton C51F   New 96
803 EX   P803 XTA Volvo B10M-62   Plaxton C51F   New 96
804 EX   P804 XTA Volvo B10M-62   Plaxton C51F   New 96
805 EX   P805 XTA Volvo B10M-62   Plaxton C51F   New 96
806 EX   P806 XTA Volvo B10M-62   Plaxton C51F   New 96
807 EM   R807 JDV Volvo B10M-55   Alexander B49F New 98
808 EX   R479 MCW Volvo B10M-55   Alexander B49F Stagecoach NW 479 01
809 EX   CSU 978 Volvo B10M-62   Plaxton C53F   Stagecoach South 00
810 EX   R480 MCW Volvo B10M-55   Alexander B49F Stagecoach NW 480 01
811 EX   R481 MCW Volvo B10M-55   Alexander B49F Stagecoach NW 481 01
812 EX   R482 MCW Volvo B10M-55   Alexander B49F Stagecoach NW 482 01
813 EX   N801 DNE Volvo B10M-55   Alexander B49F Stagecoach NW 483 01
814 EX   N802 DNE Volvo B10M-55   Alexander B49F Stagecoach NW 484 01

```
830 EX   M950 JBO   Dennis Javelin    Plaxton C47F    Red & White 950 99
831 EX   M105 CCD   Dennis Javelin    Plaxton C47F    Stagecoach London J5 01
832 EX   M106 CCD   Dennis Javelin    Plaxton C47F    Stagecoach London J6 01
833 EX   M108 CCD   Dennis Javelin    Plaxton C47F    Stagecoach London J8 01
851 EX   P563 MSX   Volvo B10M-55     Plaxton AC71F   Fife Scottish 563 01
852 EX   P564 MSX   Volvo B10M-55     Plaxton AC71F   Fife Scottish 564 01
901 TQ   R901 FDV   Volvo Olympian    AR H51/36F      New 97
902 EX   R902 JDV   Volvo Olympian    AR H51/36F      New 98
903 EX   R903 JDV   Volvo Olympian    AR H51/36F      New 98
904 EX   R904 JDV   Volvo Olympian    AR H51/36F      New 98
905 EX   R164 HHK   Volvo Olympian    NC H49/30F      Stagecoach London 01
906 EX   P816 GMU   Volvo YN2RV       NC H49/31F      Stagecoach London 01
907 EX   P817 GMU   Volvo YN2RV       NC H49/31F      Stagecoach London 01
922 EX   J822 HMC   Scania N113DRB    AR CO47/31F     Stagecoach London 00
923 EX   J823 HMC   Scania N113DRB    AR CO47/31F     Stagecoach London 00
924 EX   J824 HMC   Scania N113DRB    AR CO47/31F     Stagecoach London 00
925 EX   J825 HMC   Scania N113DRB    AR CO47/31F     Stagecoach London 00
926 EX   J826 HMC   Scania N113DRB    AR CO47/31F     Stagecoach London 00
927 EX   J827 HMC   Scania N113DRB    AR CO47/31F     Stagecoach London 00
928 EX   J828 HMC   Scania N113DRB    AR H47/31F      Stagecoach South 01
929 EX   J829 HMC   Scania N113DRB    AR H47/31F      Stagecoach South 00
                          * * * * * * *
```

931-51 Volvo YN2RC NC H45/27F Stagecoach London V301etc 01/2
            M301-20 DGP,N348 HGK.

```
931 EX    934 TQ   937 TQ   940 TQ   943 TQ   946 TQ   948 TQ   950 TQ
932 EX    935 TQ   938 TQ   941 TQ   944 TQ   947 TQ   949 TQ   951 TQ
933 EX    936 TQ   939 TQ   942 TQ   945 TQ
                          * * * * * * *
```

955-67 *Leyland TNLXB/2RR LD H44/27F Stagecoach London T660,1067/32,
           *956/7/60 are H44/29F   976,585,444/62/9/73 98/00
           NUW 660Y,A67 THX,A632 THV,A976 SYE,NUW 585Y,KYV 444/62/9/73X.

```
955 -     957 EM   960 EX   963 EX   964 EX   965 EX   966 EX   967 -
956 EX
```

~~~~~~

OTHER VEHICLES OWNED BY THE COMPANY
                    * * * * * * *

```
 20 EX   G806 YTA   Renault G13    WS B17F     Trainer
 21 EX   G818 YTA   Renault G13    WS B17F     Trainer
 22 EX   G847 LNP   Renault G13    WS B21F     Trainer
313 TQ   L942 CTT   Iveco 59-12    Mellor B21D  Staff Bus
395 TQ   L448 FFR   Iveco 59-12    Mellor B27F  Staff Bus
615 TQ   R615 KDD   Iveco 49-10    Mellor B17F  Staff Bus
```
~~~~~~

CSU 978*M408 BFG(10/98) & XIA 857*XIA 256(2/96) & PKP 548R(2/96)
~~~~~~

7   THAMESDOWN TRANSPORT LTD

Garage:SWINDON(Corporation Street)

```
61   A 61 WMW   Dennis DDA174    NC H43/31F    New 84
63   A 63 WMW   Dennis DDA174    NC H43/31F    New 84
65   B 65 GHR   Dennis DDA909    NC CH43/31F   New 85
66   B 66 GHR   Dennis DDA909    NC CH43/31F   New 85
67   B 67 GHR   Dennis DDA909    NC CH43/31F   New 85
68   B 68 GHR   Dennis DDA909    NC CH43/31F   New 85
69   H969 XHR   Dennis DDA1033   EL H45/31F    New 90
70   H970 XHR   Dennis DDA1033   EL H45/31F    New 90
71   H971 XHR   Dennis DDA1033   EL H45/31F    New 90
72   H972 XHR   Dennis DDA1033   EL H45/31F    New 90
73   H973 XHR   Dennis DDA1033   EL H45/31F    New 90
74   F602 RPG   Dennis DDA1026   EL H45/30F    Arriva Surrey DD2 98
75   F603 RPG   Dennis DDA1026   EL H45/30F    Arriva Surrey DD3 98
76   F604 RPG   Dennis DDA1026   EL H45/30F    Arriva Surrey DD4 98
77   F606 RPG   Dennis DDA1026   EL H45/30F    Arriva Surrey DD6 98
78   F608 RPG   Dennis DDA1026   EL H45/30F    Arriva Surrey DD8 99
79   F605 RPG   Dennis DDA1026   EL H45/30F    Arriva Surrey DD5 99
                          * * * * * * *
```

101-28 Dennis Dart Plaxton B40F or B33F(101-10) New 93-6
      K101-6/8-10 OMW,M711,112-9 BMR,XMW 120,N121-4 JHR,N125-8 LMW.

101	105	110	114	117	120	123	126
102	106	111	115	118	121	124	127
103	108	112	116	119	122	125	128
104	109	113					

* * * * * * *

129	XBZ 7729	Dennis Dart		Plaxton B40F	Isle of Man 14 00
130	XBZ 7730	Dennis Dart		Plaxton B40F	Isle of Man 15 00
131	XBZ 7731	Dennis Dart		Plaxton B40F	Isle of Man 76 00
132	XBZ 7732	Dennis Dart		Plaxton B40F	Isle of Man 78 00
141	R314 NGM	Dennis Dart SLF		Plaxton B37F	Kings Ferry,Gillingham 00
142	R315 NGM	Dennis Dart SLF		Plaxton B37F	Kings Ferry,Gillingham 00
143	R317 NGM	Dennis Dart SLF		Plaxton B37F	Kings Ferry,Gillingham 00
144	R319 NGM	Dennis Dart SLF		Plaxton B37F	Johnson,Newingreen 00

* * * * * * *

151-65 Dennis Dart SLF Plaxton B41F or B40F(162-5) New 96-9
      P151-8 SMW,P159-61 VHR,S162 BMR,T163-5 RMR.

| 151 | 153 | 155 | 157 | 159 | 161 | 163 | 165 |
| 152 | 154 | 156 | 158 | 160 | 162 | 164 | |

* * * * * * *

| 175 | KMW 175P | Daimler CRG6LX | ECW O43/31F | New 76 |
| 180 | S838 VAG | Dennis Dart SPD | Plaxton B45F | Plaxton(Demonstrator) 00 |

* * * * * * *

181-205 Dennis Dart SPD Plaxton B45F or B41F(184-6/92-200) New 98-02
      S181-6 BMR,V187-91 EAM,Y192-7 VMR,WV02 NNA-C, oo .

181	185	188	191	194	197	200	203
182	186	189	192	195	198	201	204
183	187	190	193	196	199	202	205
184							

* * * * * * *

218	TWH 698T	Leyland FE30AGR	NC H43/32F	GM Buses 6939 89
219	TWH 699T	Leyland FE30AGR	NC H43/32F	GM Buses 6940 89
221	ANA 21T	Leyland FE30AGR	NC H43/34F	GM Buses South 4021 96
222	BVR 98T	Leyland FE30AGR	NC H43/34F	GM Buses South 4098 96
262	GRU 162V	Leyland FE30AGR	AR H43/31F	Bournemouth 162 00
263	GRU 163V	Leyland FE30AGR	AR H43/31F	Bournemouth 163 00
264	GRU 164V	Leyland FE30AGR	AR H43/31F	Bournemouth 164 00
265	GRU 165V	Leyland FE30AGR	AR H43/31F	Bournemouth 165 00
266	GRU 166V	Leyland FE30AGR	AR H43/31F	Bournemouth 166 00
299	UMR 199T	Leyland FE30AGR	ECW H43/31F	New 78
300	UMR 200T	Leyland FE30AGR	ECW H43/31F	New 78
301	BMR 201V	Leyland FE30AGR	ECW H43/31F	New 80
302	BMR 202V	Leyland FE30AGR	ECW H43/31F	New 80
303	BMR 203V	Leyland FE30AGR	ECW H43/31F	New 80
304	BMR 204V	Leyland FE30AGR	ECW H43/31F	New 80
305	BMR 205V	Leyland FE30AGR	ECW H43/31F	New 80

~~~~~~

OTHER VEHICLES OWNED BY THE COMPANY
* * * * * * *

317	DCZ 2317	LD TRCTL11/2RH	Plaxton C53F	Trainer
318	DCZ 2318	LD TRCTL11/2RH	Plaxton C53F	Trainer
319	DCZ 2319	LD TRCTL11/2RH	Plaxton C53F	Trainer
383	OHR 183R	Leyland FE30AGR	ECW O-F	Tree Lopper/Workshop

~~~~~~

DCZ 2317*A127 EPA(3/00), DCZ 2318*A103 EPA(3/00), DCZ 2319*A126 EPA(3/00),
XBZ 7729*M410 XTC(7/00) & MAN 14A(5/00),
XBZ 7730*M409 XTC(7/00) & MAN 15D(5/00),
XBZ 7731*M505 XTC(7/00) & CMN 76X(5/00) &
XBZ 7732*M506 XTC(7/00) & CMN 78X(5/00)

~~~~~~

8   A B COACHES LTD

Depot:The Garage,Wills Road Industrial Estate,TOTNES,Devon.

```
ABZ 5780   26   DAF MB200DKFL600     Plaxton C53F        Garrett,Newton Abbot 02
IAZ 3454   28   Dennis Javelin       Duple C53FT         Stolzenberg,Maesteg 96
IIL 8694   23   Dennis Javelin       Duple C57F          Stolzenberg,Maesteg 96
JIW  297   31   Duple 425            C57F                Rons,Lancing 99
LIL 7234   22   DAF SB2300DHS585     Jonckheere C53F     Nichols,Carlton 00
MIL 1031   33   Duple 425            C59F                Day &,Chatteris 97
NBZ 1639   36   Van Hool T815H       C41FT               Nightingale,Langley 02
NIL 1095   30   Duple 425            C59F                Snell,Newton Abbot 96
NIL 1787   25   Scania K112CRS       Jonckheere C57F     Head,Lutton 99
NIL 6094   32   Duple 425            C53FT               Ferris &,Senghenydd 97
PJI 5861   18   Ford R1114           Plaxton C53F        Parkin,Paignton 93
RIL 1279   35   Scania K93CRB        Van Hool C55F       Snell,Newton Abbot 98
RIL 4472   24   Volvo B10M-61        Jonckheere C51FT    Head,Lutton 99
UFH  277   17   Volvo B10M-61        Caetano C51FT       Endicott,Totnes 01
WIB 4393   34   Scania K92CRB        Duple C55F          Wilfreda,Adwick-le-St 98
FBC   1C   37   Van Hool T815        C49FT               Lavoie,Yate 02
```
~~~~~~
```
ABZ 5780*THB 442Y(5/95), IAZ 3454*F240 OFP(5/96), IIL 8694*H576 OTH(7/96),
JIW 297*F129 TDF(4/95) & JIW 21(8/94) & F129 TDF(8/94),
LIL 7234*B555 XEG(10/96), MIL 1031*E855 CTT(3/97),
NBZ 1639*E448 MMM(9/96), NIL 1095*F906 KOD(11/96),
NIL 1787*RBD 536Y(12/96) & AEF 368A(4/96) & DLX 33Y(8/88),
NIL 6094*F871 CNY(5/97), PJI 5861*YDM 864W(5/93), RIL 1279*G800 FJX(1/99),
RIL 4472*JNV 631Y(11/99) & 7195 BY(8/99) & JNV 631Y(12/86),
UFH 277*C665 MTY(9/01), WIB 4393*F90 CWG(5/96) & FBC 1C*F547 TJF(12/89)
```
~~~~~~

9   ABBOT COACH TRAVEL LTD

Depot:Jetty Marsh Lane,NEWTON ABBOT,Devon.

```
C 17 ACT   Scania K112CRB       Plaxton C49FT       Expert,Grimsby 99
C 18 ACT   Scania K113TRB       Van Hool C48FT      First Aberdeen 00
C 19 ACT   Scania K113TRB       Van Hool C49FT      Smith,Rayne 01
C286 DFJ   Scania K112CRS       Plaxton C57F        Snell,Newton Abbot 99
```
~~~~~~
```
C17 ACT*F166 DET(6/01), C18 ACT*K24 GVC(9/01) & C19 ACT*L399 LHE(7/01)
```
~~~~~~

10   ALANSWAY COACHES LTD

Depot:King Charles 1st Business Park,Old Newton Road,HEATHFIELD,Devon.

```
CCZ 3164   Ford Transit            Mellor B16F         Southern National 189 99
CCZ 3165   Ford Transit            Mellor B16F         Southern National 181 99
CCZ 8927   Ford Transit            Dormobile B16F      Landylines,Wellington 00
C694 FFJ   Ford Transit            Carlyle B16F        Stagecoach Devon 87 97
C705 FFJ   Ford Transit            Robin Hood B16F     Stagecoach Devon 91 96
C745 FFJ   Ford Transit            Carlyle B16F        Stagecoach Devon 119 97
C752 FFJ   Ford Transit            Carlyle B16F        Stagecoach Devon 125 98
C759 FFJ   Ford Transit            Carlyle B16F        Stagecoach Devon 128 98
D910 HOU   Fiat 49-10              Robin Hood B19F     Bristol 7910 95
D914 HOU   Fiat 49-10              Robin Hood B19F     Non-PSV(Filton) 96
D779 PTU   Freight Rover Sherpa    Dormobile B16F      Harratt,Kingsteignton 98
E215 BDV   Ford Transit            Mellor B16F         Southern National 185 01
E203 HRY   Fiat 49-10              Carlyle B25F        Arriva Fox M203 98
E963 HTP   Fiat 49-10              Robin Hood B25F     Southern National 522 01
E815 WDV   Ford Transit            Mellor B16F         Preserved 02
F892 BCY   Mercedes-Benz 709D      G & M C25F          Duchy,Newton Abbot 01
F751 FDV   Ford Transit            Mellor B16F         Southern National 155 00
G833 CVX   Fiat 49-10              Dormobile B16FL     Non-PSV 98
G230 EOA   Fiat 49-10              Carlyle B25F        Arriva Fox M230 98
G222 KWE   Mercedes-Benz 811D      RB B26F             Bell,Southwick 01
H132 CDB   Mercedes-Benz 811D      LHE B33F            Arriva Midlands Nth 432 01
H133 CDB   Mercedes-Benz 811D      LHE B31F            Arriva Midlands Nth 433 01
```

```
J140 KPX   Fiat 49-10        Marshall B23F    Southern National 8140 01
J141 KPX   Fiat 49-10        Marshall B23F    Southern National 8141 01
J145 KPX   Fiat 49-10        Marshall B23F    Southern National 8345 01
```
~~~~~~
```
CCZ 3164*E219 BDV(11/99), CCZ 3165*D788 NDV(11/99),
CCZ 8927*D92 CFA(11/00) & F892 BCY*JJI 5614(7/01) & F892 BCY(4/98)
```
~~~~~~

11   ALEXCARS LTD

Depot:Unit 11,Love Lane Trading Estate,CIRENCESTER,Gloucestershire.

```
LUI 5601   Dennis Javelin    WS DP70FA         MOD 01
ODW  459   Dennis Javelin    Auwaerter C49FT   Hopes,Leigh-on-Sea 00
RIL 3702   Duple 425         C57F              Markham,Birmingham 99
TIL 1898   Toyota HDB30R     Caetano C21F      Peruffo,Kimbolton 00
516  ACH   MAN 18.310        Noge C49FT        Torquay Travel 02
672  DYA   Toyota HDB30R     Caetano C21F      Hearn,Harrow Weald 01
ACH  53A   MAN 10.180        Caetano C35F      Wray,Harrogate 99
ACH  69A   Bedford YNV       Plaxton C57F      Rowland &,St Leonards 92
E901 LVE   Volkswagen LT55   Optare B25F       Baird,Prestwood 98
H 39 VNH   MAN 10.180        Jonckheere C37F   Taylor,Sutton Scotney 95
M887 WWB   Dennis Javelin    Plaxton C43F      Clegg &,Middle Wallop 01
M549 XHC   Dennis Javelin    Plaxton C57F      Gatwick Parking,Horley 02
N 4  RDC   Dennis Javelin    Berkhof C55F      Mitchell,Plean 02
P505 VUS   Dennis Javelin    Marcopolo C53F    Hutchison,Overtown 02
P506 VUS   Dennis Javelin    Marcopolo C53F    Hutchison,Overtown 02
R851 SDT   MAN 11.220        Irizar C35F       Cherrybriar,Bow 01
T446 HRV   Dennis Dart SLF   SCC B44F          New 99
W312 SBC   Toyota BB50R      Caetano C26F      New 00
Y 69 HHE   Scania L94IB      Irizar C53F       New 01
```
~~~~~~
```
LUI 5601*K279 PHT(10/01), ODW 459*P969 HWF(1/00), RIL 3702*C152 PAB(3/99),
TIL 1898*J990 JKN(3/01) & FIW 748(2/97) & J303 KFP(12/92),
516 ACH*T810 RDL(3/02), 672 DYA*J310 KFP(12/94), ACH 53A*H172 EJF(11/99),
ACH 69A*B888 PDY(5/95), E901 LVE*ACH 80A(?/02) & E901 LVE(6/98) &
M549 XHC*A15 GPS(9/01) & M785 NBA(1/00)
```
~~~~~~

12   T.J. ALLEN.t/a ALLENS TRAVEL

Depot:36 Woodland Road,ST AUSTELL,Cornwall.

```
M 5  BUS   LDV 400            Jubilee C16F     New 94
M684 PDA   LDV 400            LDV B16F         Non-PSV(Kenning) 97
P845 BJF   LDV Convoy         Crystals C16F    Dalgleish,Annan 01
P690 FUJ   LDV Convoy         LDV B16F         Non-PSV(Tipton) 98
P900 TCC   Mercedes-Benz 711D Crest C24F       Streamline,Maidstone 01
R 46 BYG   LDV Convoy         Concept C16FL    Main,High Barnet 01
Y341 XAG   LDV Convoy         Excel C16F       New 01
```
~~~~~~
```
P900 TCC*P2 SET(5/01)
```
~~~~~~

13   I.V.,P.D. & L.P. ANDREWS

Depot:Lawns Farm,TRUDOXHILL,Somerset.

```
USU  487   Kassbohrer S215H   C53F             Jason,Cranford 98
D817 LWX   Volkswagen LT55    Optare C21F      Non-PSV(Bath) 01
F814 RJF   TAZ D3200          C53F             New 89
G891 VNA   Mercedes-Benz O303 Plaxton C51F     Shearings 891 95
```
~~~~~~
```
USU 487*C313 UPC(4/90)
```
~~~~~~

14   J.M. & H.T. ANDREWS.t/a ANDREWS COACHES

Depot:142 High Street,MARSHFIELD,Gloucestershire.

AHZ 1250	DAF SB2300DHS585	Plaxton C55F	Bennett &,Gloucester 00
BHZ 1260	DAF SB2305DHS585	Caetano C53F	Bennett &,Gloucester 02
IAZ 4022	Volvo B10M-61	Plaxton C53F	Knowles,Paignton 99
A735 HFP	Bova EL26/581	C53FT	Central Coachways 93
A817 LEL	Quest VM	Plaxton C53F	Bird,North Hykeham 90
D290 XCX	DAF SB2300DHS585	Plaxton C53F	Bennett &,Gloucester 97
F765 TLB	Fiat 49-10	Carlyle DP21F	Hoskins &,Eastington 98

AHZ 1250*B7 BEN(3/00) & B368 YDE(9/96) & 817 FKH(8/87),
BHZ 1260*F607 JSS(1/02) &
IAZ 4022*D478 DWP(5/96) & A1 FRP(1/96) & D874 EEH(2/93)

15   APL TRAVEL LTD

Depots:Coach Station,CHRISTIAN MALFORD & Pickwick Motors,CORSHAM,Wiltshire

VYU 454	Toyota HB31R	Caetano C19F	MC Travel,Melksham 02
A 10 APL	Toyota HDB30R	Caetano C21F	Webb,Barham 01
F152 GVO	Mercedes-Benz 709D	RB B29F	MC Travel,Melksham 00
G150 GOL	Iveco 49-10	Carlyle B25F	Midland Red North 300 98
G154 NRC	Renault S56	RB B25F	MC Travel,Melksham 02
K527 EFL	Iveco 49-10	Marshall B23F	Midland Red South 827 99
K727 UTT	Iveco 59-12	Mellor B29F	Stagecoach Devon 346 02
K730 UTT	Iveco 59-12	Mellor B29F	Stagecoach Devon 347 02
M259 CDE	Mercedes-Benz 811D	Mellor DP31F	Curtis,Brislington 01
P 76 VWO	Mercedes-Benz 814D	ACL DP33F	Bebb,Llantwit Fardre 99
R 87 EDW	Mercedes-Benz O814D	ACL DP33F	Bebb,Llantwit Fardre 00

VYU 454*E735 LHX(8/99) & A10 APL*H390 CFT(3/01)

16   E.F. APPLEGATE.t/a APPLEGATES INTERNATIONAL

Depot:Heathfield Garage,NEWPORT,Gloucestershire.

YPL 420T	LN 10351B/1R	B41F	Arriva Surrey SNB420 00
GYE 277W	Leyland TNLXB/2RR	LD H44/28F	Sovereign T277 97
BFR 958Y	Mercedes-Benz L307D	Cheshire C12F	Grantley &,Sharpness 96
OHV 707Y	Leyland TNLXB/2RR	LD H44/26D	Go Ahead London T707 98
OHV 768Y	Leyland TNLXB/2RR	LD H44/26D	Wilkinson,Staines 00
PHT 885Y	Kassbohrer S215H	C49FT	Ball,Felixstowe 94
A 16 EFA	LAG Panoramic	C49FT	Streets,Chivenor 01
A 18 EFA	Scania K113TRB	Irizar C51FT	Gardiner,East Kilbride 97
A 19 EFA	Auwaerter N722/3	PN CH53/18CT	Durham Travel,Hetton 95
A610 THV	Leyland TNLXB/2RR	LD H44/26D	Go Ahead London T1010 01
G340 KWE	Auwaerter N122/3	CH57/18CT	Home James,Totton 00
N862 RFU	Kassbohrer S250	C48FT	Allied,Uxbridge 02
R477 CKN	Mercedes-Benz O814D	Robin Hood C24F	New 97
V 2 EFA	Mercedes-Benz O814D	Robin Hood C24F	New 99

PHT 885Y*6348 ED(5/01) & CPA 477Y(9/85),
A16 EFA*G485 KBD(4/02) & WJI 3814(9/00) & G485 KBD(3/98),
A18 EFA*M26 XSC(7/97), A19 EFA*RIB 4320(10/97) & C220 CWW(2/92),
G340 KWE*HJI 8686(2/00) & G340 KWE(10/96) &
N862 RFU*243 CUW(3/02) & N862 RFU(3/00)

17   <u>**ARLEEN COACH & HIRE SERVICES LTD**</u>

Depot:14 Bath Road,PEASEDOWN ST JOHN,Somerset.

CLZ 8307	Mercedes-Benz O303	C49FT	New 90
RIL 2102	DAF MB230LB615	Plaxton C53F	Ryan,Bath 02
RIL 4022	DAF MB200DKFL600	Duple C53F	Adams,Walsall 99
RIL 7643	Leyland TRCTL11/3LZ	WS DP68FA	MOD 99
RIL 7644	Dennis Javelin	Plaxton C53F	Martin,Kettering 00
XBZ 4253	Bova EL28/581	Duple C53F	Park,Hamilton 86
XBZ 4254	Mercedes-Benz 811D	Optare C29F	New 88
XBZ 4256	DAF SB2305DHS585	Van Hool C51FT	Cropper,Kirkstall 00
YBZ 9558	EOS E180Z	C49FT	Berkeley,H. Hempstead 01
152 EKH	EOS E180Z	C49FT	Collis,Bristol 00
660 FHU	DAF SB2300DHS585	Plaxton C53F	Clapton,Haydon 01
BYC 828B	Leyland TRCTL11/3R	Plaxton C53F	Chivers,Stratton-on-F. 88
NYC 398V	Bedford YMT	Duple C53F	South West,Yeovil 021 02
RYD 51V	Bedford YMT	Plaxton C53F	Bodman,Worton 02
XYC 249W	Bedford YMT	Duple C53F	South West,Yeovil 033 02
G449 VEE	Mercedes-Benz 408D	? C16F	Maggs,Paulton 01
P 7 ARL	Mercedes-Benz 814D	ACL C29F	New 96
V689 OJW	Mercedes-Benz 410D	Excel C16F	Non-PSV 01
W506 EOL	Mercedes-Benz 410D	Excel C16F	Woods,Tillicoultry 01
WP51 WXY	Volvo B10M-62	Berkhof C49FT	New 02
YR02 UNY	Auwaerter N316SHD	C51FT	New 02

~~~~~~
CLZ 8307*G884 WHY(?/98), RIL 2102*E647 KCX(4/99),
RIL 4022*B915 TKV(10/99) & PSV 483(8/88) & B809 YRH(6/85),
RIL 7644*G411 YAY(3/00), XBZ 4253*A800 JAY(6/01), XBZ 4254*E468 VUM(6/01),
XBZ 4256*F256 RJX(3/01), YBZ 9558*M604 RCP(7/01),
152 EKH*M801 RCP(10/00) & ROI 1417(9/00) & M801 RCP(5/97),
660 FHU*SIB 7515(6/01) & C310 UFP(3/94), BYC 828B*SND 711X(9/88),
RYD 51V*217 NYA(10/93) & HNT 539V(9/90) & XYC 249W*SYD 2W(12/99)
~~~~~~

18   <u>**J.A. ARNELL.t/a BATH TRAVEL SERVICES**</u>

Depots:Unit 7,Victoria Business Centre,Midland Road,BATH,Somerset &
Station Car Park,TROWBRIDGE,Wiltshire.

LUI 9675	Mercedes-Benz 811D	Carlyle B25F	First Cymru 454 02
LUI 9676	Mercedes-Benz 811D	Carlyle B25F	? 02
B164 VHG	Mercedes-Benz L307D	Imperial C12F	Freeway,Devizes 02
C239 BWS	Mercedes-Benz L307D	RB C8F	Stone,Bath 01
N351 HBX	Renault Master	Cymric C16F	Towey & Day,Keynsham 00

~~~~~~
LUI 9675*H788 GTA(?/02) & LUI 9676* ? (?/02)
~~~~~~

19   <u>**B.J. ASTON.t/a KWT COACHES**</u>

Depot:Station Road,MILKWALL,Gloucestershire.

NIW 2235	AEC Reliance	Plaxton C57F	Heyfordian,Upr. Heyford 93
DUP 143S	Leyland PSU3E/4R	Plaxton C53F	Bevan,Lydney 01
AKK 175T	Bedford YMT	Duple B61F	Hancock,Sheffield 01
DJB 865V	Volvo B58-56	Plaxton C53F	Berkeley,Paulton 00
LDG 700V	Bedford YMT	Plaxton C53F	Bevan,Lydney 94
XRT 685X	Volvo B10M-56	Plaxton C53F	Rodger,Weldon 97
SGC 970Y	Volvo B10M-61	Jonckheere C51FT	Baker,Chiswick 98
A 11 MSN	Mercedes-Benz 609D	MM C24F	Nash,Milkwall 99
H996 TAK	Mercedes-Benz 609D	Whittaker C23F	Frome Minibuses 00
L945 NWW	Volvo B10M-60	Jonckheere C51FT	Cherrybriar,Bow 01
L946 NWW	Volvo B10M-60	Jonckheere C51FT	Cherrybriar,Bow 01

~~~~~~
NIW 2235*6595 KV(1/94) & TBW 300P(5/83),
AKK 175T*794 SKO(10/01) & AKK 175T(10/91),
DJB 865V*704 BYL(8/00) & DJB 865V(9/84),
XRT 685X*229 LRB(4/88) & VGV 445X(6/85),

SGC 970Y*341 LTL(5/98) & EOF 341(12/95) & LAG 236Y(6/93) & GNT 708(4/93) &
    UTN 940Y(9/87), All MSN*F443 ENB(4/96) &
H996 TAK*A17 ABU(11/99) & H996 TAK(8/95)

20   ASTRA COACH TRAVEL LTD.t/a EAGLE LINE

Depot:Andoversford Trading Estate,ANDOVERSFORD,Gloucestershire.

ESU 980	Auwaerter N122/3	CH57/20CT	Davies,Shipton Oliffe 97
LBZ 2936	DAF MB200DKFL600	Van Hool C55F	Lawman & Bull,Pytchley 00
LIL 8556	Volvo B10M-50	Van Hool C49FT	West,Belmont 99
PJI 5625	Auwaerter N122/2	CH48/12CT	Davies,Shipton Oliffe 97
SIL 4456	Volvo B10M-60	Van Hool C49FT	Wood,Buckfastleigh 99
SIL 4457	DAF MB230LB615	Van Hool C53F	Arriva London Nth East 98
SIL 4458	DAF SBR3000DKZ570	PN CH55/19CT	Field,Newent 99
G 84 NUX	Scania K93CRB	Duple C55F	Leons,Stafford 98
G690 UHU	Mercedes-Benz 408D	MM C15F	Clevedon Motorways 98
J212 XKY	Scania K93CRB	Plaxton C53F	Thomas,Porth 01
N462 CBU	Mercedes-Benz 412D	? C16F	Payne & Cole,Gloucester 01
N789 NYS	Toyota HZB50R	Caetano C21F	Morrow,Glasgow 00
S969 RDG	Mercedes-Benz O814D	Plaxton C29F	New 98
V744 EJF	Toyota BB50R	Caetano C26F	New 99
Y434 RDG	Mercedes-Benz O814D	Plaxton C33F	New 01
WA51 JYH	Mercedes-Benz O815L	Sitcar C33F	New 02

ESU 980*B380 PAJ(4/88),
LBZ 2936*A803 WSU(7/94) & GIL 3271(11/93) & A976 ESF(5/90),
LIL 8556*G500 CVC(6/99) & LIB 378(6/99) & G500 CVC(5/97),
PJI 5625*MVL 610Y(1/93),
SIL 4456*K102 VJT(3/00) & A4 EKW(3/98) & K102 VJT(1/98) & A3 XCL(12/97) &
    K102 VJT(10/93), SIL 4457*G909 TYR(2/00),
SIL 4458*E125 NHY(2/00) & 110 LHW(8/98) & E125 NHY(1/94) & HHF 15(8/91) &
    E639 KCX(4/90) & G84 NUX*8636 PL(1/98) & G655 EFA(5/94)

21   A.L.,C.P. & J.I. BAILEY.t/a AXE VALE COACHES

Depot:Apple Tree Cottage,A38,BIDDISHAM,Somerset.

IIL 2949	12	DAF MB200DKFL600	Plaxton C53F	Glowbelle,W. Bromwich 92
LKW 13	14	Fiat 60-10	Caetano C22F	Goodman,Culmhead 93
PIL 6831		Bova FHD12-340	C51F	Heaton,Mayford 02
PJI 8324	4	DAF MB200DKTL600	Plaxton C51F	Bennett,Beedon 90
RJI 8581		Bova FHD12-290	C49FT	Smith,Ford 00
RJI 8615	1	Bova FHD12-280	C49FT	Day,North Common 97
28 XYB		Bova FHD12-340	C51FT	Alfa,Euxton 02
EUE 338T	9	Ford R1114	Plaxton C53F	Lapage,Basildon 88
M312 EEA	12	LDV 400	WMB C16F	New 94
P 12 BSL		Bova FHD12-340	C51FT	Alfa,Euxton 02
P970 OAK		MB 814D	Plaxton C32F	Powell,Hellaby 00
W154 RYB		Bova FHD12-340	C49FT	New 00
WJ02 VRP		Bova FHD12-340	C51FT	New 02

IIL 2949*A262 GUE(8/92), LKW 13*C403 NAW(10/93), PIL 6831*L792 EOD(3/99),
PJI 8324*TND 424X(5/93), RJI 8581*F433 XEG(3/94),
RJI 8615*578 DAF(12/96) & A576 KFP(7/94) & 3253 VU(3/92) &
    A197 FAY(8/88), 28 XYB*P13 BSL(5/02) & P970 OAK*P2 BUS(12/99)

22   K.E.,R.A. & T. BAKER.t/a KTM COACHES

Depot:The Garage,DULOE,Cornwall.

LIL 3287	Volvo B58-56	Plaxton C53F	Hayball,Warminster 98
RBZ 2675	Volvo B10M-61	Plaxton C53F	Claremont,Worcester Pk 99
TXI 9303	Mercedes-Benz 609D	G & M C20F	Charman,Polruan-b-Fowey 01
XSU 761	Volvo B10M-60	Plaxton C53F	Isaac,Gunn 00
F681 CYC	Dennis Javelin	Duple C53F	Hazell,Northlew 01

```
G434 NGE  Mercedes-Benz 609D    Scott C24F      Hambly,Pelynt 98
N908 EWD  Volvo B10M-62         Plaxton C55F    Wickson,Walsall Wood 01
P476 NCR  LDV Convoy            LDV B15F        Non-PSV(Kenning) 00
```
~~~~~~
```
LIL 3287*JOU 522X(4/97),
RBZ 2675*D572 KJT(6/97) & XEL 941(3/89) & D265 HFX(10/87),
TXI 9303*H906 GGL(1/91),
XSU 761*G64 RGG(8/00) & 90KY 2605(6/97) & G64 RGG(3/92) &
N908 EWD*WT 8590(7/01) & N684 YUJ(3/01) & 3601 RU(12/00)
```
~~~~~~

23   M.S.C. BAKER.t/a CHANDLERS COACH TRAVEL

Depot:158 Chemical Road,West Wilts Trading Estate,WESTBURY,Wiltshire.

```
PIL 4420  Volvo B10M-61    Van Hool C52FT   Wood,Buckfastleigh 93
TIL 7916  Volvo B10M-61    Plaxton C57F     Edwards,Tiers Cross 01
TIL 9066  Volvo B10M       Plaxton C ?F     ? 01
XHT  48T  Bedford YMT      Plaxton C53F     Baker,Weston-super-Mare 98
YAM 897T  Bedford YMT      Duple C53F       Thomas,Calne 91
EYP  33V  Bedford YMT      Plaxton C49F     Common,Witney 92
H199 DVM  Volvo B10M-60    Van Hool C53F    Shearings 199 98
L916 NWW  Volvo B10M-60    Van Hool C48FT   Armchair,Brentford 00
M 43 HSU  Volvo B10M-62    Van Hool C49FT   Holmeswood Coaches 02
```
~~~~~~
```
PIL 4420*C336 FSU(7/98),
TIL 7916*B264 YBX(6/01) & 526 NDE(4/01) & B229 PEY(1/00) & WSV 552(9/99) &
         B201 PEY(3/99) & 8214 VC(2/99) & B533 BML(8/93),
TIL 9066*   ?   (?/??), XHT 48T*612 TYB(6/86) & DYA 979T(3/84),
YAM 897T*XPM 516(12/90) & BMJ 508T(10/87),
L916 NWW*B16 APT(2/00) & L916 NWW(4/98) & M43 HSU*LSK 514(1/98)
```
~~~~~~

24   BAKERS COACHES LTD.t/a BAKERS DOLPHIN

Depots:Cattle Market,BRIDGWATER & Locking Road,WESTON-SUPER-MARE,Somerset.

```
IUI 4360  75  MB 609D          Olympus C24F      MCH,Uxbridge 97
NIL 4981  18  Volvo B10M-61    Van Hool C49FT    Edwards,Tiers Cross 97
NIL 4982  23  Volvo B10M-61    Van Hool C53F     Clarke,Lower Sydenham 97
NIL 4983  31  Volvo B10M-61    Plaxton C53F      Shearings 345 93
NIL 4984  32  Volvo B10M-61    Plaxton C53F      Whitehead,Conisbrough 93
NIL 4985  33  Volvo B10M-61    Plaxton C53F      East Surrey,Godstone 93
NIL 4986  34  Volvo B10M-61    Plaxton C53F      Shearings 355 93
NIL 5381  39  Volvo B10M-61    Van Hool C53F     Clarke,Lower Sydenham 97
NIL 5382  25  Volvo B10M-61    Van Hool C53F     Clarke,Lower Sydenham 97
RJI 5716  61  Volvo B10M-53    VH CH51/29CT      New 85
SIL 6715   9  Volvo B10M-60    Jonckheere C49FT  Wallace Arnold 99
SIL 6716   8  Volvo B10M-60    Jonckheere C49FT  Wallace Arnold 99
UJI 3791  15  Volvo B10M-61    Van Hool C49FT    Phillips,Crediton 97
UPV  487  16  Volvo B10M-62    Van Hool C46FT    New 96
WJI 2321  21  Volvo B10M-60    Van Hool C53F     Clarke,Lower Sydenham 98
WJI 3490  44  LD TRCTL11/3LZ   Plaxton DP52FA    MOD 97
WJI 3491  41  LD TRCTL11/3LZ   Plaxton DP52FA    MOD 98
WJI 3492  42  LD TRCTL11/3LZ   Plaxton DP52FA    MOD 98
WJI 3493  43  LD TRCTL11/3LZ   Plaxton DP52FA    MOD 98
WJI 3494  58  LD TRCTL11/3LZ   Plaxton DP68FA    MOD 98
WJI 3495  59  LD TRCTL11/3LZ   Plaxton DP68FA    MOD 98
WJI 3496  46  LD TRCTL11/3LZ   Plaxton DP68FA    MOD 98
WJI 3497  60  LD TRCTL11/3LZ   Plaxton DP68FA    MOD 98
WJI 6879  29  Volvo B10M-60    Van Hool C53F     Silcox,Pembroke Dock 98
WJI 6880  17  Volvo B10M-60    Van Hool C49FT    Metroline(Brents) 96
XJI 5457  47  LD TRCTL11/3RZ   Plaxton DP52FA    MOD 99
XJI 5458  53  LD TRCTL11/3LZ   Plaxton DP68FA    MOD 99
XJI 5459  52  LD TRCTL11/3LZ   Plaxton DP68FA    MOD 99
XJI 6330  48  LD TRCTL11/3RZ   Plaxton DP52FA    MOD 99
XJI 6331  45  LD TRCTL11/3LZ   Plaxton DP54FA    Hayball,Warminster 99
XJI 6332  54  LD TRCTL11/3LZM  Plaxton DP68FA    Munden,Bristol 98
XJI 6333  55  LD TRCTL11/3LZ   Plaxton DP68FA    MOD 99
```

Reg	Fleet	Chassis	Body	Operator
XLH 570	102	Volvo B10M-61	Van Hool C53F	Park,Hamilton 94
YXI 2730	26	Volvo B10M-61	Van Hool C53F	Shearings 730 96
YXI 2732	27	Volvo B10M-61	Van Hool C53F	Shearings 732 96
7740 KO	11	Volvo B10M-61	Van Hool C57F	Rowe,Muirkirk 86
315 MWL	105	Volvo B10M-62	Van Hool C57F	New 96
340 MYA	7	Volvo B10M-60	Van Hool C49FT	Shearings 868 93
958 VKM	22	Volvo B10M-61	Van Hool C53F	Park,Hamilton 94
791 WHT	14	Volvo B10M-62	Van Hool C46FT	New 96
VNT 18S	99	Bedford YLQ	Duple C45F	Herring,Burnham-o-Sea 86
ERB 548T	84	Bedford YMT	Plaxton C53F	Barnes,Puriton 91
FTO 552V	94	Bedford YMT	Plaxton C53F	Barton 552 88
HHU 31V	106	Volvo B58-61	Plaxton C57F	New 80
HHU 146V	83	Bedford YMT	Plaxton C53F	Barnes,Puriton 91
HPL 422V	107	Volvo B58-61	Plaxton C57F	Syway,Cranleigh 83
VJY 921V	108	Volvo B58-61	Plaxton C57F	Smith,Buntingford 91
LNU 578W	96	Bedford YMT	Plaxton C53F	Barton 578 88
LNU 579W	97	Bedford YMT	Plaxton C53F	Barton 579 88
LNU 582W	98	Bedford YMT	Plaxton C53F	Barton 582 88
OUF 359W	109	Volvo B58-61	Plaxton C57F	Brown,Horley 91
SLH 42W	89	Bedford YMT	Plaxton C53F	Capital,West Drayton 92
SLH 43W	90	Bedford YMT	Plaxton C53F	Capital,West Drayton 92
LTY 551X	91	Bedford YNT	Plaxton C53F	R & M,Gt Whittington 90
LTY 552X	92	Bedford YNT	Plaxton C53F	R & M,Gt Whittington 90
TAY 888X	82	Bedford YMT	Plaxton C53F	King of Road,Worthing 91
VBC 984X	88	Bedford YNT	Plaxton C53F	Mountford,Manchester 92
XEL 542X	87	Bedford YNT	Plaxton C53F	Hayball,Warminster 92
PHT 114Y	85	Bedford YNT	Plaxton C53F	Palmer,Dunstable 92
YRY 1Y	81	Bedford YMT	Plaxton C53F	King of Road,Worthing 91
C432 VGX	73	MB L608D	Rootes C19F	Springham,Dartford 90
P725 JYA	1	Volvo B10M-62	Van Hool C44FT	New 97
P726 JYA	65	Volvo B12T	VH CH53/14CT	New 97
R778 MFH	72	MB O1120L	Ferqui C35F	New 98
R632 VYB	66	Volvo B12T	VH CH53/14CT	New 98
R372 XYD	2	Volvo B10M-62	Van Hool C46FT	New 98
R373 XYD	3	Volvo B10M-62	Van Hool C46FT	New 98
T761 JYB	5	Volvo B10M-62	Van Hool C48FT	New 99
T762 JYB	6	Volvo B10M-62	Van Hool C48FT	New 99
T920 UEU	104	Volvo B7R	Plaxton C57F	New 99
Y227 NYA	4	Volvo B10M-62	Van Hool C48FT	New 01
Y228 NYA	10	Volvo B10M-62	Van Hool C48FT	New 01
Y229 NYA	12	Bova FHD12-370	C48FT	New 01

~~~~~~
```
IUI 4360*N697 SPK(6/98),
NIL 4981*E86 ODE(5/97) & 3432 RE(2/96) & E956 CBU(12/93) &
       WSV 528(12/91) & E622 UNE(9/90), NIL 4982*E220 JJF(8/97),
NIL 4983*C345 DND(4/97), NIL 4984*C347 DND(4/97), NIL 4985*C349 DND(4/97),
NIL 4986*C355 DND(5/97), NIL 5381*E222 LBC(8/97), NIL 5382*E223 LBC(8/97),
RJI 5716*340 MYA(12/99) & C342 GSD(11/92), SIL 6715*L962 NWW(5/00),
SIL 6716*L956 NWW(5/00), UJI 3791*E634 BFJ(3/96), UPV 487*N205 DYB(9/00),
WJI 2321*F672 TFH(2/98),
WJI 6879*F552 TMH(4/98) & A3 WLS(2/98) & F552 TMH(11/94),
WJI 6880*J690 LGA(6/98) & LSK 501(11/94) & J461 HDS(2/93),
XJI 6331*G514 XWS(2/99), XJI 6332*D76 JHY(5/99),
XLH 570*F276 MGB(4/96) & LSK 510(11/94) & F753 ENE(2/93),
YXI 2730*F730 ENE(12/93), YXI 2732*F732 ENE(12/93),
7740 KO*USD 224Y(5/86), 315 MWL*N203 DYB(9/00),
340 MYA*G868 RNC(9/00) & RJI 5716(12/99) & G868 RNC(2/94),
958 VKM*F279 MGB(4/96) & LSK 514(11/94) & F758 ENE(2/93),
791 WHT*N204 DYB(9/00), HHU 31V*340 MYA(10/92) & BEU 817V(6/84),
HHU 146V*315 MWL(2/96) & DKG 271V(2/83),
HPL 422V*UPV 487(4/96) & HPL 422V(5/84),
VJY 921V*958 VKM(4/96) & VJY 921V(7/85),
OUF 359W*789 CLC(3/92) & FTH 991W(12/87),
XEL 542X*YBK 605(5/92) & WFX 74X(5/91),
PHT 114Y*6108 BT(10/92) & DNK 107Y(9/82) &
C432 VGX*CSU 907(4/90) & C390 CKK(4/89)
```
~~~~~~

25   A.J. & J.A. BALL.t/a EAGLE COACHES

Depot:Fireclay House,Netham Road,St. George,BRISTOL.

```
FIL 9370   DAF MB230LB615      Van Hool C51F      Ribblesdale,Gt Harwood 96
VWF  328   DAF SB2305DHTD585    Plaxton C57F       New 88
6130  EL   DAF MB230LT615      Van Hool C53F      Parry,Blaen. Ffestiniog 95
2411  KR   MAN 10-180          Caetano C35F       New 90
931  DHT   DAF MB230LT615      Van Hool C53F      New 88
863  EKX   Leyland RT          Van Hool C53F      New 86
 94  SHU   DAF SB3000DKV601    Van Hool C45FT     Smith,Alcester 92
 24  THU   DAF SB3000DKV601    Van Hool C49FT     Norman,Keynsham 99
613  WHT   DAF SB3000DKV601    Van Hool C51FT     Austin,Earlston 92
WPW 202S   Bristol VRT/SL3/6LXB  ECW H43/31F      Eurotaxis,Harry Stoke 97
VCA 463W   Bristol VRT/SL3/6LXB  ECW H43/31F      Eastville,Bristol 99
TPD 112X   Leyland ONTL11/1R   Roe H43/29F        Eastville,Bristol 02
A379 UNH   DAF MB200DKFL600    Jonckheere C53F    Roman City,Bath 86
E718 LOU   Freight Rover Sherpa CD C16F           Pugh,Chipping Sodbury 95
G651 ORR   Leyland LBM6T/2RS   RB C37F            Ingleby,York 94
H731 BHW   DAF SB2305DHTD585   Plaxton C53F       New 90
J888 ALL   Leyland TRCL10/3RZM Plaxton C57F       New 91
J811 FOU   DAF 400             Carlyle C20F       New 91
J693 GTC   DAF MB230LB615      Van Hool C53F      New 92
K518 RJX   DAF MB230LTF615     Van Hool C57F      New 93
M738 OKK   Iveco 49-10         ? DP19F            Staines,Brentwood 01
M775 RCP   DAF MB230LT615      Van Hool C55F      New 95
N993 FWT   DAF DE33WSSB3000    Van Hool C51FT     New 96
N780 LHY   Mercedes-Benz 814D  ACL C29F           New 96
R990 EHU   Mercedes-Benz O814D Plaxton C29F       New 97
T 54 AUA   Mercedes-Benz O814D ACL C29F           New 99
V801 LWT   DAF DE23RSSB2750    Smit C36FT         New 99
W201 CDN   DAF DE33WSSB3000    Van Hool C49FT     New 00
Y151 XAE   Mercedes-Benz O814D Plaxton C29F       New 01
WX51 YGN   Iveco 50-13         ? C16F             New 02
```
```
FIL 9370*G233 NCW(11/00), VWF 328*E589 LTC(6/94), 6130 EL*G999 KJX(11/00),
2411 KR*G158 XJF(8/97), 931 DHT*E638 KCX(12/91), 863 EKX*C320 CWS(4/89),
94 SHU*E351 EVH(1/94), 24 THU*G539 LWU(6/00), 613 WHT*E347 EVH(1/94),
A379 UNH*FIL 9370(8/01) & A379 UNH(2/90),
G651 ORR*6130 EL(8/00) & G651 ORR(12/95) &
H731 BHW*OO 1290(1/99) & H731 BHW(1/95)
```

26   K.A. BALL.t/a PLYM COACHES

Depot:Plymstock Commercials,Central Avenue,Lee Mill IE,IVYBRIDGE,Devon.

```
IIL 8918   Ford R1114          Duple C53F          AB Coaches,Paignton 29 99
JBZ 4909   Leyland TRCTL11/3R  Plaxton C53F        Barnes &,Birmingham 02
KAD 352V   Leyland PSU5C/4R    Plaxton C57F        Millmans,Newton Abbot 01
E354 KRP   Freight Rover Sherpa Mellor B8FL        Pointmost,Plymouth 02
E968 SVU   Mercedes-Benz 609D  Dixon Lomas C27F    Campbell,East Kilbride 00
G485 ANM   Freight Rover Sherpa G & M B11FL        Pointmost,Plymouth 02
```
```
IIL 8918*SYG 437W(9/96) &
JBZ 4909*JUB 675Y(8/93) & VFN 53(3/90) & RNY 309Y(5/88)
```

27   BARRYS COACHES LTD

Depot:9 Cambridge Road,Granby Industrial Estate,WEYMOUTH,Dorset.

```
LAZ 2370   Leyland TRCTL11/3RZ Plaxton C53F        Dorset County Council 00
LEN  616   Auwaerter N722/3    PN CH53/18DT         Amberline 91
LUI 1519   Mercedes-Benz 811D  Optare C29F          Gatwick Airport 01
LUI 4653   Volvo B10M-60       Van Hool C49FT       Chambers,Bures 01
LUI 5812   Dennis Javelin      Plaxton C51F         Whittle,Kidderminster 01
OIL 5267   Leyland TRCTL11/3R  Plaxton C57F         Dorset County Council 98
SBZ 8075   Volvo B10M-60       Van Hool C49FT       Smith,Rayne 02
```

```
TIL 2506   Dennis Javelin          Plaxton C49FT    Windsorian,Bedfont 00
YHA  320   Scania L94IB            Irizar C49FT     Bus Eireann SI17 01
YSV  645   Dennis Javelin          Plaxton C35F     Dewar,Falkirk 97
4708  RU   Dennis Javelin          Plaxton C51FT    Mayne,Buckie 00
471 BET    Volvo B12T              VH CH57/14CT     Trathens,Plymouth 01
AMJ 191X   Ford R1114              Plaxton C53F     Wheelband,Weymouth 02
YPD 119Y   Leyland TRCTL11/2R      Duple C53F       Cudlipp,Sturminster 99
A523 MJK   Bedford YMP             Plaxton C45F     Non-PSV(Brighton) 00
B919 BGA   Ford R1115              Plaxton C35F     Evans,Stokenchurch 00
G517 MYD   Dennis Javelin          Caetano C53F     Redwood,Hemyock 02
G861 VAY   Dennis Javelin          Duple C35F       Non-PSV(Norwood) 96
G501 VRV   Leyland TRCL10/3ARZM    Plaxton C53F     Clements,Nailsea 01
G165 XOR   Fiat 49-10              Dormobile C24FL  Non-PSV(High Wycombe) 98
H672 ATN   Toyota HB31R            Caetano C21F     Safeguard,Guildford 01
H655 DKO   Ford Transit            Dormobile B16F   Devon County Council 98
N860 XMO   Dennis Javelin          Berkhof C53F     Q Drive,Battersea 99
N862 XMO   Dennis Javelin          Berkhof C53F     Q Drive,Battersea 99
P644 MSC   Mercedes-Benz 711D      Mellor C25F      Curness,Blantyre 00
```

LAZ 2370*D153 HML(3/00), LEN 616*C174 KHG(8/91), LUI 1519*G590 SNJ(4/01),
LUI 4653*K103 VJT(8/01) & A4 XEL(12/97) & K103 VJT(10/93),
LUI 5812*G111 JNP(10/01) & URH 341(1/00) & G111 JNP(8/97),
OIL 5267*B89 XBA(6/98) & BUI 1133(11/92) & B592 SNC(7/90),
SBZ 8075*H166 DVM(5/00), TIL 2506*E509 JWP(11/00),
YHA 320*R474 YDT(?/02) & 98D 41101(11/01), YSV 645*F902 BLS(2/00),
4708 RU*F797 GFD(2/00) & XXI 8950(2/00) & F797 GFD(9/97),
471 BET*M865 TYC(4/02) & G517 MYD*USV 562(2/02) & G517 MYD(9/95)

28   BATH BUS COMPANY LTD

Depot:Burnett Business Park,Gypsy Lane,BURNETT,Somerset.

```
BBZ 6818   Leyland-DAB             ADP67D           Mainline 2013 00
BBZ 8027   Leyland-DAB             ADP67D           Mainline 2012 00
BBZ 8051   Leyland-DAB             ADP67D           Mainline 2011 00
WOI 8022   Bristol VRT/SL3/501     ECW O43/31F      Lamcote,Nottingham 97
783  DYE   AEC Routemaster         PR O36/26R       London Coaches RM1783 97
NFB 115R   Bristol VRT/SL3/6LXB    ECW O43/27F      Stringer,Pontefract 97
UFX 857S   Bristol VRT/SL3/6LXB    ECW CO43/31F     Southern Vectis 505 98
BCL 213T   Bristol VRT/SL3/6LXB    ECW O43/29F      Thorne,Rayleigh 97
WTG 360T   Bristol VRT/SL3/6LXB    AR CO44/31F      Cardiff 360 99
A931 SUL   MCW Metrobus DR101      O43/32F          Go Ahead London M931 01
A947 SUL   MCW Metrobus DR101      O43/32F          Go Ahead London M947 01
A740 THV   MCW Metrobus DR101      H43/28D          Metroline M1040 01
C 42 CHM   Leyland ONLXB/1RH       ECW H42/26D      loan from Ensign
C 48 CHM   Leyland ONLXB/1RH       ECW H42/26D      loan from Ensign
E461 CGM   Mercedes-Benz 609D      Robin Hood B20F  Express Travel,Speke 99
E477 CGM   Mercedes-Benz 609D      Robin Hood B20F  Express Travel,Speke 99
E678 DCU   Leyland LX112           B51F             Blue Triangle,Rainham 01
J624 KCU   Dennis Dart             Wright B40F      Go North East 8024 02
J632 KCU   Dennis Dart             Wright B40F      Go North East 8032 02
J637 KCU   Dennis Dart             Wright B40F      Go North East 8037 02
J601 WHJ   Mercedes-Benz 811D      Plaxton B28F     North Star,Kirkby 01
J608 WHJ   Mercedes-Benz 811D      Plaxton B28F     Arriva London MD608 01
K861 PCN   Dennis Dart             Wright B40F      Go North East 8061 02
K862 PCN   Dennis Dart             Wright B40F      Go North East 8062 02
K370 RTY   Dennis Dart             Wright B40F      Go North East 8070 02
```

BBZ 6818*C113 HDT(9/00), BBZ 8027*C112 HDT(9/00),
BBZ 8051*C111 HDT(9/00) & WOI 8022*PVO 818R(9/94)

29   K.W. BEARD LTD

Depot:Valley Road,CINDERFORD,Gloucestershire.

CHZ 4714	Volvo B10M-61	Plaxton C51FT	Ashton,St Helens 95
RIL 9864	Leyland TRCTL11/3RZ	Plaxton C53F	Smith-Shearings 502 90
RIL 9865	DAF MB230DKVL615	Duple C49FT	Yorkshire Euro,Harrogte 97
VEU 231T	LN 11351A/1R	B52F	Cheltenham & G. 310 01
YFB 972V	LN 11351A/1R	B52F	Cheltenham & G. 314 01
WDD 17X	Bedford YNT	Plaxton C53F	New 82
F715 RDG	Freight Rover Sherpa	Crystals C16F	New 88
F167 UDG	Leyland TRCTL11/3RZ	Plaxton C53F	New 89
G897 NYC	Bova FHD12-290	C55F	Dawlish Coaches 02
J813 KHD	DAF SB3000DKV601	Van Hool C51FT	Moxon,Oldcotes 01
K321 AUX	Volvo B10M-60	Jonckheere C51FT	Elcock,Madeley 00
X564 CUY	Mercedes-Benz O814D	Onyx C24F	New 00

CHZ 4714*E318 UUB(3/02), RIL 9864*B502 UNB(9/00),
RIL 9865*C604 FWW(9/00) & A2 YET(10/97) & C645 LVH(5/92) &
J813 KHD*5711 MT(6/01) & J813 KHD(9/97)

30   B.E.W. BEAVIS & A.M. BAXTER.t/a BEAVIS HOLIDAYS

Depot:The Garage,BUSSAGE,Gloucestershire.

ALP 2	Auwaerter N116/2	C44FT	New 98
111 ALP	Auwaerter N116/3	C49FT	New 90
267 ALP	Toyota HZB50R	Caetano C21F	New 94
684 ALP	Scania K113CRB	Irizar C48FT	New 94
A 5 ALP	Volkswagen LT35	Crystals C15F	New 97
H 15 ALP	Auwaerter N116/3	C49FT	New 91
M 7 ALP	EOS E180Z	C55F	New 95
WU51 OMB	Auwaerter N313SHD	C36FT	New 01

111 ALP*ALP 2(4/98), 684 ALP*L11 ALP(3/98) & A5 ALP*P257 BDF(2/98)

31   R.J. BELFITT.t/a BELFITT MINIBUS HIRE

Depot:Steam Mills Industrial Park,CINDERFORD,Gloucestershire.

RAZ 3998	Mercedes-Benz 709D	Whittaker C24F	Myrtle Tree,Bristol 02
J597 MNA	DAF 400	Deansgate C16F	Smith,Kennford 96
J106 SOE	DAF 400	DAF B16FL	Non-PSV(Birmingham) 01
J132 SRE	Fiat 49-10	Mellor B16FL	Birmingham City Council 01
J133 SRE	Fiat 49-10	Mellor B16FL	Birmingham City Council 01
L435 CND	DAF 400	Kirkham C16F	Hoare,Wardle 00
L511 YHA	DAF 400	Jubilee C16F	Barratt,Crich 99
P 3 SMS	LDV Convoy	Jubilee C16F	Simpson,Towcester 01
W592 AAY	LDV Convoy	? C16F	Simpson,Towcester 02

RAZ 3998*F609 EWB(?/02)

32   P.,R.A. & D. BENNETT & P.A. LANE.t/a BENNETTS COACHES

Depot:Eastern Avenue,GLOUCESTER,Gloucestershire.

RUA 458W	Bristol VRT/SL3/6LXB	ECW H43/31F	West Riding 908 93
EEH 902Y	Leyland ONLXB/1R	ECW H45/32F	Arriva Midlands N. 1902 01
OFS 701Y	Leyland ONTL11/2R	ECW H50/31D	Lothian 701 00
OFS 702Y	Leyland ONTL11/2R	ECW H50/31D	Lothian 702 00
SJR 617Y	Leyland ONLXB/1R	ECW H43/32F	Go North East 3617 00
B 7 BEN	Leyland ONLXB/1R	ECW H45/32F	Arriva North East 7256 00
F318 EWF	DAF SB220LC550	Optare DP51F	Wall,Sharston 95
G247 CLE	DAF SB220LC590	Hispano B45D	Capital,West Drayton 99
G293 CLE	DAF SB220LC590	Hispano B66F	Capital,West Drayton 99

```
J 21 GCX   DAF SB2305DHS585     Plaxton C53F      Yorkshire,Harrogate 92
J518 LRY   DAF SB2305DHS585     Caetano C53F      Bland,Cottesmore 97
K 2  BCC   DAF MB230LT615       Plaxton C53F      New 92
K712 RNR   DAF SB2700HS585      Caetano C53F      Perrett,Shipton Oliffe 00
K 34 VFV   DAF SB2700HS585      Van Hool C51FT    J Jackson,Blackpool 98
K424 WUT   DAF SB2700HS585      Caetano C53F      Winson,Loughborough 97
L519 EHD   DAF SB2700HS585      Van Hool C53F     Enfield Transport(Ire) 98
L463 RDN   DAF SB2700HS585      Van Hool C53F     O'Sullivan,Killarney(I) 95
M809 RCP   DAF SB3000WS601      Van Hool C51FT    Redwood,Hemyock 96
R400 BEN   Optare Excel L1150   B40F              New 98
R500 BEN   Optare Excel L1150   B40F              New 98
R600 BEN   Optare Excel L1150   B40F              New 98
T 59 AUA   DAF DE33WSSB3000     Van Hool C49FT    New 99
T419 PDG   DAF DE02GSSB220      Ikarus B43F       New 99
X 83 AAK   MAN 18.220           Ikarus B42F       MAN(Demonstrator) 01
Y200 BCC   Auwaerter N316SHD    C49FT             New 01
Y300 BCC   Auwaerter N316SHD    C49FT             New 01
Y400 BCC   Auwaerter N316SHD    C49FT             New 01
YR02 UMU   Auwaerter N316SHD    C49FT             New 02
```

B7 BEN*B256 RAJ(3/00), G247 CLE*CAP 11(2/00) & G247 CLE(1/98),
G293 CLE*CAP 21(6/99) & G293 CLE(3/99), K424 WUT*K10 PSW(7/95),
L519 EHD*94MH 3061(3/98) & L519 EHD(1/95) & L463 RDN*94KY 1609(12/95)

33   BERKELEY COACH & TRAVEL LTD

Depot:Berkeley Garage,Ham Lane,PAULTON,Somerset.

```
BAZ 7901   Volvo B10M-61        Van Hool C49FT    loan from Dawsons
LIB 6445   Volvo B10M-60        Duple C57F        Skill,Nottingham 28 96
C110 DWR   Volvo B10M-61        Plaxton C53F      Rapsons 99
C112 DWR   Volvo B10M-61        Plaxton C53F      Rapsons 99
E339 MHU   Mercedes-Benz 609D   RB B25F           Streamline,Bath 92
E 42 ODE   Volvo B10M-61        Plaxton C53F      Jones,Login 94
L 2  POW   Volvo B10M-60        Van Hool C53F     New 94
M725 LYP   Dennis Javelin       Plaxton C53F      loan from Dawsons
N527 PYS   Volvo B10M-62        Van Hool C49FT    loan from Dawsons
N556 SJF   Volvo B10M-62        Plaxton C49FT     New 96
P 2  POW   Volvo B10M-62        Plaxton C49FT     New 97
R 2  POW   Volvo B10M-62        Plaxton C43FT     New 98
R 3  POW   Mercedes-Benz O814D  Plaxton C33F      New 98
R 4  POW   Volvo B10M-62        Plaxton C49FT     New 98
T 4  POW   Volvo B10M-62        Plaxton C43FT     New 99
W107 RTC   Volvo B10M-62        Plaxton C49FT     New 00
WR02 RVX   Volvo B12M           Plaxton C43FT     New 02
```

BAZ 7901*G861 RNC(1/94), LIB 6445*F28 LTO(4/90),
C110 DWR*ESK 930(10/97) & C110 DWR(5/91),
C112 DWR*ESK 932(10/97) & C112 DWR(5/91),
E42 ODE*834 TDE(3/94) & E327 UUB(5/91) &
N527 PYS*LSK 473(5/01) & LSK 875(8/96)

34   E.G. & G.A. BERRY.t/a COACHMANS TRAVELS

Depots:Northfield Close,SHRIVENHAM &
Stratton Close,STRATTON ST MARY,Wiltshire.

```
SDZ 3017   DAF MB200DKFL600     Plaxton C53F      O'Donnell,Portglenone 97
900  HGG   MAN SR280            C53F              Cotterell,Torquay 02
VOD 597S   Bristol VRT/SL3/6LXB ECW H43/31F       Cheltenham & Glou. 219 99
GSC 644X   Leyland AN68C/1R     AR H45/30D        Lothian 644 00
F165 AWO   MCW Metrorider MF154 B31F              Greatley,Warminster 01
G706 LKW   Scania K93CRB        Duple C57F        Talbot &,Portsmouth 99
L201 BPL   Toyota HDB30R        Caetano C21F      Horseman,Reading 98
```

SDZ 3017*C959 MWB(12/96) & 893 KM(12/89) & C793 GHD(3/88) &
900 HGG*B161 FHR(3/86)

35   BERRYS COACHES (TAUNTON) LTD

Depot:Cornishway West,New Wellington Road,TAUNTON,Somerset.

PIB 2470	Volvo B10M-53	VH CH51/13DT	New 88
PIB 3360	Volvo B10M-61	Van Hool C53F	New 88
PIB 4019	Volvo B10M-61	Van Hool C53F	New 87
PIB 5767	Volvo B10M-61	Van Hool C53F	New 82
SIB 8398	Volvo B10M-61	Van Hool C55F	Foster,Glastonbury 95
SIB 9309	Volvo B10M-60	Van Hool C49FT	New 89
SIB 9313	Volvo B10M-61	Jonckheere C53F	New 86
PYA 646P	AEC Reliance	Plaxton C51F	New 76
TVD 862R	Bedford YLQ	Duple C45F	Non-PSV(Yeovil) 99
UYC 860R	Bedford YLQ	Plaxton C45F	New 77
AYA 912S	Bedford YLQ	Plaxton C45F	New 78
B910 SPR	Volvo B10M-61	Plaxton C53F	Excelsior,Bournemouth 87
C219 FMF	Volvo B10M-46	Plaxton C41F	Richmond,Barley 02
D260 HFX	Volvo B10M-61	Plaxton C53F	Excelsior,Bournemouth 89
E131 KGM	Volvo B10M-46	Plaxton C41F	Gerry,Plymouth 01
F476 WFX	Volvo B10M-60	Plaxton C53F	Excelsior,Bournemouth 89
J819 EYC	Volvo B10M-60	Jonckheere C53F	New 92
L920 NWW	Volvo B10M-60	Van Hool C49FT	Wallace Arnold 97
L238 OYC	Volvo B10M-60	Van Hool C49FT	New 93
M201 TYB	Volvo B12T	VH CH57/14CT	New 94
N320 BYA	Volvo B12T	VH CH57/14CT	New 95
N758 CYA	Volvo B10M-62	Van Hool C49FT	New 96
N199 DYB	Volvo B10M-62	Van Hool C49FT	New 96
P727 JYA	Volvo B12T	VH CH57/14CT	New 97
R199 WYD	Volvo B10M-62	Van Hool C49FT	New 98
R202 WYD	Volvo B10M-62	Van Hool C49FT	New 98
R380 XYD	Volvo B12T	VH CH57/14CT	New 98
T766 JYB	Volvo B10M-62	Van Hool C49FT	New 99
W161 RYB	Volvo B10M-62	Van Hool C49FT	New 00
YN51 WGX	Volvo B10M-62	Plaxton C49FT	New 01

~~~~~~

PIB 2470*E22 XYD(2/97), PIB 3360*E63 XYC(3/95), PIB 4019*D547 OYD(5/94),
PIB 5767*JYC 794Y(7/91), SIB 8398*E272 XYA(5/01),
SIB 9309*F121 GYB(11/99), SIB 9313*C785 HYA(4/93),
C219 FMF*851 FYD(1/02) & C219 FMF(5/86) & E131 KGM*WSV 478(8/97)

~~~~~~

36   JAMES BEVAN (LYDNEY) LTD

Depot:The Bus Station,Hams Road,LYDNEY,Gloucestershire.

A 20 JAB	Leyland TRCTL11/3ARZ	Plaxton C51FT	Thorpe,North Kensington 97
E323 UUB	Volvo B10M-61	Plaxton C53F	Wallace Arnold 91
K216 SUY	Dennis Javelin	WS C53F	MOD 01
K237 SUY	Dennis Javelin	WS C53F	MOD 01
N653 THO	Volvo B10M-62	Plaxton C49F	Excelsior,Bournemouth 99
P590 CFH	MAN ?	Caetano C ?F	? (Ire) 02
R170 SUT	Volvo B7R-63	Plaxton C53F	New 98
W678 DDN	Optare Solo M850	B30F	New 00

~~~~~~

A20 JAB*E217 RDW(5/99), N653 THO*XEL 254(11/98) & P590 CFH* ? (?/02)

~~~~~~

37   BLAGDON LIONESS COACHES LTD

Depot:Mendip Garage,Street End,BLAGDON,Somerset.

D771 GTC	Leyland TRCTL11/3RZ	Plaxton C57F	New 87
H644 UWR	Volvo B10M-60	Plaxton C53F	Wallace Arnold 96
N 11 BLC	Volvo B10M-62	Plaxton C53F	? (Ire) 00
P466 XHW	Toyota BB50R	Caetano C21F	New 97
S 11 BLC	Mercedes-Benz O814D	Plaxton DP25F	New 98
X 11 BLC	Volvo B10M-62	Plaxton C53F	New 00

~~~~~~

N11 BLC* ? (?/??)

38   BLUEBIRD COACHES (WEYMOUTH) LTD

Depot:450a Chickerell Road,CHICKERELL,Dorset.

HIL 2146	Leyland PSU3G/2R	Duple B53F	Court,Fillongley 98
UCT 838	Volvo B10M-61	Duple C57F	Jacobs,Horton Heath 99
YJI 8595	Volvo B10M-61	Plaxton C53F	Limebourne,Battersea 95
YJI 8596	Volvo B10M-62	Plaxton C49F	New 94
654 JHU	Volvo B10M-61	Van Hool C53F	Tellings-GM,Byfleet 88
CEL 919T	Bedford YMT	Plaxton C53F	New 79
LUA 287V	Leyland PSU3F/4R	Plaxton C53F	Newton,Guildford 99
URU 650X	Volvo B10M-56	Plaxton C53F	Westbus,Hounslow 02
A 14 FRX	Volvo B10M-62	Plaxton C53F	Frames Rickard,Victoria 01
A 15 FRX	Volvo B10M-62	Plaxton C53F	Frames Rickard,Victoria 01
A191 MNE	Volvo B10M-61	Van Hool C53F	Crowther,Morley 91
A693 TPO	Volvo B10M-56	Plaxton C53F	Tillingbourne,Cranleigh 00
C680 KDS	Volvo B10M-61	Caetano C49FT	Non-PSV(Winfrith) 93
E768 HJF	Dennis Javelin	Plaxton C35F	Luckett,Fareham 92
G 38 KAK	Mercedes-Benz 609D	Whittaker C19F	Andrews,Watford 01
M590 GRY	Toyota HZB50R	Caetano C21F	Venture,Harrow 02
M740 RCP	DAF DE33WSSB3000	Van Hool C55F	London,Northfleet 01
M741 RCP	DAF DE33WSSB3000	Van Hool C55F	London,Northfleet 01
P 4 BBC	Volvo B10M-62	Van Hool C49FT	New 97
R 9 BBC	Volvo B10M-62	Van Hool C49F	New 98
S659 ETT	LDV Convoy	G & M C16F	New 98
T 7 BBC	Bova FHD12-340	C49FT	New 99
W 2 BBC	MAN 18.350	Auwaerter C53F	New 00
BC51 BBC	Auwaerter N316SHD	C53F	New 02

HIL 2146*OWO 233Y(12/91), UCT 838*KRV 878Y(12/86),
YJI 8595*E310 OMG(2/00), YJI 8596*L948 CRU(2/00), 654 JHU*C335 FSU(12/88),
A14 FRX*M428 WAK(2/96), A15 FRX*M429 WAK(2/96) &
A693 TPO*MIL 4687(8/99) & HFB 89(6/96) & A475 JPB(7/95) & TBC 658(5/94) &
     A489 YGL(8/90) & 353 TPF(6/90) & A298 XUK(11/89)

R.J.,C.J. & D.W. BODMAN & K.G. HEATH.t/a C. BODMAN & SONS

Depot:The Old Forge Garage,88 High Street,WORTON,Wiltshire.

ALZ 6244	Leyland TRCL10/3ARZM	Plaxton C53F	Holmeswood Coaches 01
BHZ 9620	Mercedes-Benz 814D	Plaxton C33F	Forsyth,Glasgow 02
IIL 4579	Dennis Javelin	Duple C53F	Stone,Aldershot 97
IIL 4580	Dennis Javelin	Duple C53F	Stone,Aldershot 97
UJI 1778	Volvo B10M-61	Jonckheere C51F	Londoners,Nunhead 96
UJI 4519	DAF MB200DKFL600	Van Hool C51F	McCulloch,Stoneykirk 96
WIB 2951	Volvo B10M-61	Plaxton C53F	Glenvic,Stanton Wick 02
XUD 367	Volvo B10M-61	Plaxton C53F	Jackson,Castleford 99
YSU 987	Volvo B10M-60	Plaxton C57F	Wickson,Clayhanger 01
A 2 NBT	Volvo B10M-60	Caetano C49FT	O'Neill,Gillingham 4.19 93
E145 WKK	Bedford YNV	Plaxton C53F	Camden,Sevenoaks 94
F357 MUT	Dennis Javelin	Plaxton C57F	Ferrers,South Woodham 99
F325 SHU	Volvo B10M-61	Plaxton C57F	Wickson,Walsall Wood 01
F630 XMS	Mercedes-Benz 811D	Alexander B28F	Curtis,Brislington 99
G220 LGK	Dennis Dart	Duple B36F	Metroline DC220 02
G 41 SSR	Fiat 49-10	Phoenix B25F	APL,Crudwell 00
H508 KSG	Iveco 49-10	Carlyle C25F	Cowan,Ratho 01
H141 UUA	Optare MR03	B31F	Dukes,Berry Hill 01
J933 JJR	Optare MR03	B26F	Go North East 333 01
K356 SCN	Optare MR03	B26F	Go North East 356 01
K357 SCN	Optare MR03	B26F	Go North East 357 01
L193 DDW	Optare MR15	B31F	Cardiff 193 01
L194 DDW	Optare MR15	B31F	Cardiff 194 01
L196 DDW	Optare MR15	B31F	Cardiff 196 01
L780 GMJ	Dennis Javelin	Plaxton C57F	Q Drive,Battersea 98
L625 RPX	Iveco 59-12	ECC B29F	Williams,Crosskeys 14 98
M 93 JHB	Mercedes-Benz 811D	WS B33F	Anslow,Pontypool 00
M510 JRY	Mercedes-Benz 814D	Dormobile C33F	Williamson,Rutherglen 00
M153 LPL	Iveco 59-10	WS B24FL	Metrobus,Orpington 53 98

```
N911 DWJ   Dennis Javelin        Berkhof C49FT    Buddens,Romsey 99
N435 MGF   Mercedes-Benz 711D    Crystals C25F    Thomas,Cheltenham 01
N890 SBB   Mercedes-Benz 811D    Plaxton B31F     Docklands,Sth Woodford 00
P 73 VWO   Mercedes-Benz 814D    ACL DP33F        Bebb,Llantwit Fardre 99
R708 NJH   Dennis Javelin        Berkhof C49FT    New 97
S762 XYA   Iveco 59-12           Marshall B27F    New 98
```

```
ALZ 6244*F713 ENE(2/01) & IIL 7077(5/00) & F713 ENE(7/93),
BHZ 9620*M292 XSF(1/02), IIL 4579*E33 SBO(3/93), IIL 4580*E37 SBO(4/93),
UJI 1778*E693 NNH(12/96), UJI 4519*HUG 643Y(2/96),
XUD 367*D709 XJL(10/99) & HVL 611(5/93) & D915 TBM(6/87),
YSU 987*H497 BGE(7/01) & WT 8355(1/01) & H497 BGE(1/99),
A2 NBT*G997 RKN(3/93), F325 SHU*6486 LJ(7/96) & F325 SHU(7/93) &
F630 XMS*8426 MU(9/99) & F630 XMS(8/98)
```

40   BOOMERANG BUS COMPANY LTD

Depot:Oldbury Buildings,Northway Lane,TEWKESBURY,Gloucestershire.

```
LIL 9267   Mercedes-Benz 811D       Phoenix B31F       Solent Blue Line 209 95
LIL 9270   Leyland TRCTL11/3R        Plaxton C53F       Yorkshire Rider 1625 95
LIL 9271   Leyland TRCTL10/3RZA      Plaxton C53F       Blackpool 00
RIL 9772   Dennis Dart              Plaxton B40F       Hylton Castle,E. Boldon 98
RIL 9773   Dennis Dart              Carlyle B28F       Metroline DT135 98
RIL 9774   Dennis Dart              Duple DP28F        London United DT6 99
RIL 9775   Dennis Dart              Carlyle DP28F      London United DT44 99
RIL 9776   Dennis Dart              Duple DP28F        London United DT8 99
WLT  713   Leyland ONLXB/1R          EL H43/31F         Cardiff 516 99
AAL 520A   Freight Rover Sherpa      Carlyle B20F       Carlyle(Demonstrator) 91
A101 FPL   Leyland ONTL11/2R         ECW CH45/27F       Isle of Wight CC 5802 01
G399 PNN   Leyland TRBL10/2RZA       East Lancs DP53F   Southlands,Swanley 02
H639 XGX   DAF 400                   Warner B8F         Non-PSV(Van) 98
L838 UCD   DAF 400                   ? B ?FL            Non-PSV(Cheadle) 02
```

R.C. & N.J. WARNER LTD.t/a WARNERS BUS & COACH CO(Associated)

```
BAZ 7386   Mercedes-Benz 814D    ACL C29F         School Mule,Chiswick 02
4529  WF   Leyland TRCTL11/3R     Van Hool C48FT   Leyland(Demonstrator) 84
5904  WF   Leyland TRCTL11/3RH    Berkhof C53F     County 96
G100 VMM   Leyland TRCL10/3ARZA   Plaxton C57F     Reading 262 00
```

```
BAZ 7386*P938 EHN(?/02), LIL 9267*G209 YDL(2/96), LIL 9270*EWW 947Y(2/96),
LIL 9271*F700 ENE(3/00), RIL 9772*L881 YVK(11/99),
RIL 9773*H135 MOB(12/99), RIL 9774*G506 VYE(1/00), RIL 9775*G44 TGW(9/01),
RIL 9776*G508 VYE(12/99), WLT 713*A516 VKG(12/99),
4529 WF*8921 WF(10/96) & 6449 WF(9/92) & WBV 541Y(7/84),
5904 WF*BAZ 7386(7/98) & B110 KPF(5/94),
AAL 520A*F418 BOP(7/98) & 4529 WF(10/96) & F418 BOP(7/91) &
G399 PNN*A13 RBL(5/00) & G399 PNN(1/96reb)
```

41   R.S. BORKOWSKI.t/a ALPHA COACHES

Depot:Smithers Pit Farm,SHUTE,Devon.

```
HIL 6571   DAF MB200DKTL600      Jonckheere C53FT   Crudge,Honiton 01
HIL 7670   Volvo B58-61          Duple C57F         Redwood,Hemyock 01
DYA 221A   Volkswagen LT55       Optare C25F        McCouid,Burghfield 98
EPD 530V   LN 10351B/1R          B41F               Arriva Surrey SNB530 99
```

```
HIL 6571*JSV 374(3/92) & WRK 26X(12/86),
HIL 7670*USV 676(3/01) & MTV 19W(8/96) & DYA 221A*D164 KDN(1/92)
```

42   K.G. BOULTON.t/a KB COACHES

Depot:Hillview Garage,CLAYPITS,Gloucestershire.

JIL 5361	DAF MB200DKFL600	Van Hool C53F	Clews,Wolverhampton 97
KBC 431	Volvo B10M-61	Van Hool C53FT	Silver Knight,Malmesbry 95
KFX 863	Volvo B10M-61	Van Hool C53F	Leese,Crewe 99
RIL 5087	Duple 425	C54FT	Jones & Levitt,Ebley 99
984 FJB	Volvo B10M-61	Van Hool C53F	Leese,Crewe 01
MSF 359T	Volvo B58-56	Duple C57F	Irving,Dalston 01
E 58 YAM	Volvo B10M-61	Van Hool C53FT	Silver Knight,Malmesbry 00
K650 HNW	Mercedes-Benz 711D	ACL C23F	Hillier,Foxham 99

~~~~~~
JIL 5361*B970 SHP(3/95), KBC 431*C571 HCV(2/95),
KFX 863*E604 DMA(7/99) & 853 DKF(6/99) & E27 TCV(10/95) & 794 PAF(9/95) &
      E617 CDS(5/94) & LSK 845(11/93) & E657 UNE(5/92),
RIL 5087*A6 ECS(8/99) & C911 YPW(4/92), 984 FJB*C531 DND(7/92) &
MSF 359T*OFJ 870(9/00) & MSF 359T(7/88)
~~~~~~

43   D. & D. BRIGGS.t/a DIAL A BUS

Depot:Hyperion Hotel,Cinderford Road,TORQUAY,Devon.

F319 LOD	Mercedes-Benz 308D	DC C12F	New 89
H354 BDV	Mercedes-Benz 308D	DC B12F	New 90
L267 BFJ	Mercedes-Benz 308D	G & M B12F	New 93
P950 KVP	LDV Convoy	G & M B12F	Non-PSV(Van) 00

~~~~~~
~~~~~~

44   CITY OF BRISTOL

Main Depot:Bath Road,Brislington,BRISTOL.

E371 KHT	481/ 05	MB 609D	WS B15FL	Avon County Council 96
E372 KHT	481/ 06	MB 609D	WS B15FL	Avon County Council 96
E373 KHT	481/ 07	MB 609D	WS B15FL	Avon County Council 96
E378 KHT	481/ 12	MB 609D	WS B15FL	Avon County Council 96
E 51 KWS	481/ 18	MB 609D	RH B15FL	Avon County Council 96
E 53 KWS	481/ 16	MB 609D	RH B15FL	Avon County Council 96
E 55 KWS	481/ 14	MB 609D	RH B15FL	Avon County Council 96
F923 OHW	482/ 23	Leyland RR8-13R	WS B24FL	Avon County Council 96
F394 RHT	483/ 16	Leyland RR9-13R	WS B32FL	Avon County Council 96
F405 RHT	482/ 27	Leyland RR8-13R	WS B24FL	Avon County Council 96
F 30 TMP	482/ 29	LD LBM6T/1RS	RB B24FL	Avon County Council 96
F 31 TMP	482/ 30	LD LBM6T/1RS	RB B24FL	Avon County Council 96
F 32 TMP	483/ 18	LD LBM6T/2RS	RB B32FL	Avon County Council 96
F 34 TMP	483/ 20	LD LBM6T/2RS	RB B32FL	Avon County Council 96
F 35 TMP	483/ 21	LD LBM6T/2RS	RB B32FL	Avon County Council 96
G466 ODT	482/ 32	LD LBM6T/1RS	RB B28FL	Avon County Council 96
G467 ODT	482/ 33	LD LBM6T/1RS	RB B28FL	Avon County Council 96
G469 ODT	482/ 34	Leyland ST2R	RB B28FL	Avon County Council 96
H887 AAE	481/ 23	MB 609D	SE B15FL	Avon County Council 96
H889 AAE	481/ 25	MB 609D	SE B15FL	Avon County Council 96
H890 AAE	481/ 26	MB 609D	SE B15FL	Avon County Council 96
H368 YHY	481/ 24	MB 609D	SE B13FL	Avon County Council 96
J 71 FEU	410/ 78	DAF 400	Whittaker B16F	Avon County Council 96
J581 FFB	481/ 28	MB 609D	Oatia B15FL	Avon County Council 96
K969 OEU	481/ 36	MB 609D	FGY B15FL	Avon County Council 96
L998 TEU	483/ 27	MB 814D	Mellor B32FL	Avon County Council 96
L973 TFB	482/ 36	MB 711D	Mellor B24FL	Avon County Council 96
L978 TFB	483/ 30	MB 814D	Mellor B32FL	Avon County Council 96
L988 TFB	483/ 28	MB 814D	Mellor B32FL	Avon County Council 96
L991 TFB	482/ 37	MB 711D	Mellor B24FL	Avon County Council 96
L998 TFB	482/ 38	MB 711D	Mellor B24FL	Avon County Council 96
L 24 THU	483/ 29	MB 814D	Mellor B32FL	Avon County Council 96
L113 TOU	483/ 34	MB 814D	Mellor B32FL	Avon County Council 96
L944 UEU	481/ 38	MB 609D	FGY B15FL	Avon County Council 96

```
L945 UEU   481/ 37   MB 609D            FGY B15FL        Avon County Council 96
L701 VHY   483/ 36   MB 814D            Mellor B32FL     Avon County Council 96
L702 VHY   483/ 37   MB 814D            Mellor B32FL     Avon County Council 96
L704 VHY   483/ 38   MB 814D            Mellor B32FL     Avon County Council 96
L708 VHY   482/ 45   MB 711D            Mellor B24FL     Avon County Council 96
L712 VHY   482/ 44   MB 711D            Mellor B24FL     Avon County Council 96
N239 HHT   411/ 63   LDV 400            Crystals B16FL   Avon County Council 96
N393 JWS   481/ 41   MB 609D            TBP B15FL        Avon County Council 96
N394 JWS   481/ 42   MB 609D            TBP B15FL        Avon County Council 96
N392 KHT   410/ 31   LDV 400            Crystals B16F    Avon County Council 96
N814 KHW   482/ 50   MB 814D            Mellor B24FL     Avon County Council 96
N930 LEU   481/ 44   MB 609D            TBP B15FL        Avon County Council 96
P340 RTC   482/ 51   MB 811D            Mellor B24FL     New 97
P341 RTC   482/ 52   MB 811D            Mellor B24FL     New 97
P342 RTC   482/ 54   MB 811D            Mellor B24FL     New 97
P343 RTC   482/ 53   MB 811D            Mellor B24FL     New 97
P344 RTC   482/ 56   MB 811D            Mellor B24FL     New 97
P345 RTC   482/ 58   MB 811D            Mellor B24FL     New 97
P346 RTC   482/ 55   MB 811D            Mellor B24FL     New 97
R101 DTC   810/ 01   Gulliver Tecnobus B9F              First Bristol 8101 00
R102 DTC   810/ 02   Gulliver Tecnobus B9F              First Bristol 8102 00
R865 WHY   410/ 25   LDV Convoy         LDV B16F         New 98
R866 WHY   410/ 26   LDV Convoy         LDV B14F         New 98
R867 WHY   410/ 22   LDV Convoy         LDV B16F         New 98
S538 FTA   410/100   Ford Transit       G & M B11F       New 98
T975 BHY   481/ 46   Iveco 49-10        FGY B15FL        New 99
T198 VAE   481/ 45   Iveco 52-10        FGY B15FL        New 99
V318 EEU   410/103   LDV Convoy         LDV B16F         New 99
V319 EEU   410/104   LDV Convoy         LDV B16F         New 99
V761 EFB   481/ 47   Iveco 49-10        FGY B15FL        New 99
W401 LDV   410/105   Ford Transit       G & M B14F       New 00
W449 LDV   410/106   Ford Transit       G & M B15F       New 00
W347 PFB   747/ 11   LDV Convoy         LDV B16F         New 00
X996 AHT   481/ 48   MB 413CDI          UVG B16FL        New 00
X997 AHT   481/ 49   MB 413CDI          UVG B16FL        New 00
X998 AHT   481/ 50   MB 413CDI          UVG B16FL        New 00
X468 AHY   410/110   LDV Convoy         LDV B16F         New 00
Y208 GEU   410/113   LDV Convoy         LDV B16F         New 01
Y209 GEU   410/114   LDV Convoy         LDV B16F         New 01
Y226 GEU   410/116   LDV Convoy         G & M B16F       New 01
WA51 EOT   481/ 51   MB 413CDI          UVG B16FL        New 02
WU51 VAX   410/119   LDV Convoy         G & M B16FL      New 02
WV02 NJK   481/ 52   MB 413CDI          UVG B16FL        New 02
```

~~~~~~

45   BRISTOL INTERNATIONAL AIRPORT LTD

Depot:Bristol Airport,LULSGATE,Somerset.

```
K 51 NEU   91   MB 709D           Frank Guy DP21F   New 93
M920 ATC   89   MB 709D           Frank Guy DP9FL   New 95
P115 GHE   86   Scania L113CRL    Wright B31D       New 97
P116 GHE   87   Scania L113CRL    Wright B32D       New 97
P932 VAE   90   MB 811D           ? DP12C           New 97
R677 MEW   121  Dennis Dart SLF   Marshall B24D     Centrewest DML249 99
R678 MEW   123  Dennis Dart SLF   Marshall B24D     Centrewest DML250 99
R679 MEW   122  Dennis Dart SLF   Marshall B24D     Centrewest DML251 99
R680 MEW   120  Dennis Dart SLF   Marshall B24D     Centrewest DML252 99
V215 FEU   84   Dennis Dart SLF   Marshall B29D     New 00
V216 FEU   85   Dennis Dart SLF   Marshall B29D     New 00
Y 38 UEU   94   MB O814D          Plaxton B17F      New 01
```

~~~~~~

N.B.:- Also operated airside are 4x Cobus 2700/B ?D registered C1/2/3/4.

~~~~~~

```
R677 MEW*809 DYE(10/99) & R677 MEW(7/98),
R678 MEW*810 DYE(10/99) & R678 MEW(7/98),
R679 MEW*811 DYE(10/99) & R679 MEW(7/98) &
R680 MEW*292 CLT(10/99) & R680 MEW(7/98)
```

46   **R.S. BROWN.t/a SHAFTESBURY & DISTRICT**

Depots:Mayo Farm &
Unit 2,Melbury Motors,Higher Blandford Road,SHAFTESBURY,Dorset.

```
GDZ  795  Leyland TRCTL11/3RH   Duple C51F        Dunn-Line,Nottingham 01
HIL 8518  Leyland TRCTL11/3ARZ  Plaxton C57F      Hearn,Harrow Weald 02
POI 4905  DAF SB2300DHS585      Berkhof C57F      Edwards,High Wycombe 98
RIL 6390  Bristol LH6L          Plaxton C41F      Millman,Newton Abbot 99
RIL 9429  Freight Rover Sherpa  Carlyle B20F      Roberts,Rhandir 00
YAZ 6391  Leyland TRCTL11/2R    Duple C53F        Dorset County Council 99
YAZ 6392  Mercedes-Benz 811D    Optare C29F       Atkinson,Kirkby Malzrd. 97
YAZ 6393  AEC Reliance          Plaxton C53F      Barrys,Weymouth 98
YAZ 6394  Leyland TRCTL11/2RH   Alexander C53F    Fife Scottish 441 00
KGJ 603D  AEC Routemaster       PR H40/32F        Western Scottish W1088 92
AFJ 733T  Bristol LH6L          Plaxton C41F      Guernseybus 170 01
G221 VDX  Optare MR01           B33F              Ipswich 221 01
H913 FTT  Volvo B10M-60         Ikarus C51FT      G & A Travel,Caerphilly 01
```
```
GDZ 795*C249 SPC(12/96), HIL 8518*E318 OMG(6/92),
POI 4905*7947 RU(1/94) & B690 BTW(11/89), RIL 6390*AFJ 734T(7/99),
RIL 9429*E166 TWO(12/00), YAZ 6391*YPD 138Y(5/99),
YAZ 6392*E872 EHK(5/99) & MXX 481(4/98) & E872 EHK(12/97),
YAZ 6393*FCX 576W(5/99),
YAZ 6394*B207 FFS(12/00) & GSU 341(9/99) & B207 FFS(9/94),
AFJ 733T*31920(?/02) & AFJ 733T(5/95) &
H913 FTT*NIL 8645(2/98) & H913 FTT(10/97)
```

47   **N.E.G. BRYANT & L.M. CLARKE.t/a BRYANTS COACHES**

Depot:1 Station Road,WILLITON,Somerset.

```
JIL 2018  Volvo B10M-60         Plaxton C53F      Ideal,Watford 94
UJI 3793  Volvo B10M-61         Van Hool C53F     Phillips,Crediton 99
YXI 7381  Volvo B10M-61         Van Hool C53F     Skill,Nottingham 55 99
A888 FFP  Bedford YNT           Plaxton C53F      Keebur &,Leicester 86
B655 BYB  Bedford YNT           Plaxton C53F      New 85
D970 RNC  Volvo B10M-61         Plaxton C53F      Clarke,Lower Sydenham 96
D 73 RYA  Bedford YNT           Plaxton C53F      New 87
E133 PLJ  Bedford YNT           Plaxton C53F      Buckland,Hurst 89
E331 UYC  Mercedes-Benz 609D    RB C25F           New 87
E574 WOK  Dodge G10             WS B38F           MOD 98
H123 TYD  Dennis Javelin        Plaxton C53F      New 90
H124 TYD  Dennis Javelin        Plaxton C53F      New 90
J173 BYD  Leyland TRCL10/3RZ    Plaxton C53F      New 91
J 41 EYB  Volvo B10M-60         Plaxton C53F      Denslow,Chard 95
P532 CLJ  Volvo B10M-62         Plaxton C49FT     Excelsior,Bournemouth 98
```
```
JIL 2018*G83 RGG(2/94), UJI 3793*E443 RCV(2/96),
YXI 7381*F743 ENE(12/93) & P532 CLJ*A8 EXC(11/97)
```

48   **J.T. BUCKINGHAM.t/a WESTERN PRIVATE HIRE**

Depot:Co-op Business Park,Recreation Road,Beacon Park,PLYMOUTH,Devon.

```
D910 MVU  Freight Rover Sherpa  MM C16F           Marks,Plymouth 96
D915 PGB  Freight Rover Sherpa  Deansgate C16F    Luke,Northallerton 88
G552 BSJ  Mercedes-Benz 408D    DC C15F           Marks,Plymouth 98
G685 LYG  Freight Rover Sherpa  Optare C16F       Graham &,Edwinstowe 94
G732 PGA  Mercedes-Benz 407D    DC C15F           New 89
K370 LWS  DAF 400               G & M C16F        Marks,Plymouth 02
```

49   R.A. & S.J. BUGLER.t/a BUGLERS

Depot:100 School Road,Brislington,BRISTOL.

HAZ 2963	Dennis Javelin	Plaxton C57DL	Guideissue,Biddulph 94
HIL 3471	Dennis Javelin	Plaxton C53DL	Mayne,Buckie 91
TAZ 6963	Volvo B10M-60	Van Hool C53F	Clarke,Lower Sydenham 98
TRX 615	Dennis Javelin	Plaxton C53F	Snowdon,Easington 90
WDR 145	Volvo B10M-62	Van Hool C53FL	Hallmark,Luton 99
280 OHT	Leyland ST2R	Elme C37DL	Gosling,Redbourn 91
586 PHU	Mercedes-Benz 811D	Robin Hood C29F	New 88
426 VNU	Dennis Javelin	Plaxton C53DL	Denslow,Chard 92
YDL 673T	Bristol VRT/SL3/6LXB	ECW H43/34F	Southern Vectis 673 95
XWY 475X	Leyland ONLXB/1R	ECW H43/32F	Isle of Man 81 01
F432 OBK	Mercedes-Benz 811D	RH DP16FL	New 88
M845 CWS	Mercedes-Benz 711D	Marshall DP18FL	New 95
P536 YEU	Dennis Javelin	UVG C47F	Western W.,Ystradowen 01
R814 LFV	Mercedes-Benz O810D	Plaxton B18FL	Fitzsimons,Harker 01
T565 RFS	Mercedes-Benz O810D	Plaxton B27F	New 99

HAZ 2963*G143 FRF(10/95) & 3379 RU(2/94) & G653 EBF(?/91),
HIL 3471*F640 PSE(5/91), TAZ 6963*F167 RJF(5/98), TRX 615*E843 EUT(2/90),
WDR 145*M210 UYD(11/00), 280 OHT*G647 KBV(2/94), 586 PHU*F251 OPX(5/99),
426 VNU*G366 PYB(7/93) & XWY 475X*DMN 81H(7/01) & XWY 475X(3/96)

50   M.J. BULEY.t/a AYREVILLE COACHES

Depot:Aspley Yard,Aspley Road,PLYMOUTH,Devon.

E223 DMV	Freight Rover Sherpa	Crystals C16F	Cotton,Saltash 01
E343 TYD	Mercedes-Benz 609D	RB C25F	Owen,Nefyn 97
F731 JTT	Mercedes-Benz 407D	DC B9FL	Cotton,Saltash 00
J759 YWA	Iveco 49-10	Carlyle DP12FL	Non-PSV(Taunton) 99
R103 MEH	Mercedes-Benz 612D	Central C18FL	Non-PSV 01

51   C. BULL.t/a CB's ILLOGAN COACHES

Depot:3 Druids Lodge,ILLOGAN HIGHWAY,Cornwall.

C724 FFJ	Ford Transit	Robin Hood B16F	Petes,West Bromwich 00
E515 PWR	Volkswagen LT55	Optare B25F	Huggins &,Wallasey 97
E 44 RDW	Volkswagen LT55	Optare DP25F	Hanson,Wordsley 98
F258 DKG	Freight Rover Sherpa	Carlyle B20F	Crocker,St Austell 00

ARL 997T*883 VCV(12/97) & KYA 839T(11/94) & XFJ 379(11/88) &
    MCG 990T(8/85)

52   B. CAINEY.t/a MIKES TRAVEL

Depot:Brynderie Farm,Oldbury Naite,OLDBURY ON SEVERN,Gloucestershire.

SRY 759R	4	AEC Reliance	Plaxton C53F	Pugh,Chipping Sodbury 91
DAD 600Y	14	Leyland TRCTL11/3R	Plaxton C57F	Pulham,Bourton-Water 98
A707 GPR	7	Leyland TRCTL11/2R	Duple C53F	Martin,West End 93
E458 CGM	16	Mercedes-Benz 609D	Robin Hood B19F	Bugler,Bristol 99
E995 KJF	17	MB 0303/15R	C53F	Talbott,Moreton-Marsh 00
M569 SRE	20	Mercedes-Benz 709D	Plaxton DP25F	PMT 569 02

DAD 600Y*VDF 365(4/98) & DAD 600Y(3/94)

53 CAMELOT LEISURE CORPORATION UK LTD.t/a UNICORN TRAVEL

Depot:Jubilee Garage,Station Road,BRUTON,Somerset.

IUI 2128	DAF SB2300DHS585	Plaxton C53F	Holt,Swinefleet 97
IUI 2129	DAF SB2300DHS585	Jonckheere C53F	Norman,Keynsham 94
926 FRH	LAG Panoramic	C49FT	Amberline,Speke 98
EAM 418V	Bedford YMT	Plaxton C53F	Cooper,Maiden Bradley 94
H 49 ECW	Kassbohrer S210H	C28FT	Holmeswood Coaches 01
J 61 GCX	DAF SB3000DKV601	Van Hool C53F	Sanders,Holt 00
J 62 GCX	DAF SB3000DKV601	Van Hool C53F	Armchair,Brentford 98

IUI 2128*D167 WRC(4/97), IUI 2129*A583 XRP(4/97), 926 FRH*F99 UNV(7/98),
EAM 418V*XMR 558(1/94) & HFX 7V(11/88),
H49 ECW*ESK 807(4/99) & H478 FLD(12/97) &
J61 GCX*3990 ME(5/01) & J61 GCX(8/96)

54   D. CARRIE-CARGILL.t/a DAVRON COACHES

Depot:The Old Worksop,LONGBRIDGE DEVERILL,Wiltshire.

FOR 398	Leyland TRCTL11/3R	Duple C45FL	Thamesdown 308 00
XAD 761	Mercedes-Benz 811D	Alexander B28F	Curtis,Burnett 01
F578 OOU	Fiat 49-10	Dormobile B20F	Bristol 7578 96
F579 OOU	Fiat 49-10	Dormobile B20F	Bristol 7579 96
G412 OAM	Renault S56	NC B25F	Thamesdown 412 00
G413 OAM	Renault S56	NC B25F	Thamesdown 413 00
G414 OAM	Renault S56	NC B25F	Thamesdown 414 00
H932 UWX	Mercedes-Benz 811D	Dormobile C33F	Coachstyle,Nettleton 00
L917 UGA	Mercedes-Benz 709D	Dormobile B29F	Ryder,West Bromwich 00
R943 AMB	Mercedes-Benz O810D	Plaxton B31F	Somerset Rider,Minehead 01

FOR 398*UOB 124Y(2/95) & CIB 1535(12/94) & WCN 963Y(4/93) &
     491 JVX(2/93) & TTN 11Y(5/87) & XAD 761*F615 XMS(11/98)

55   CASTLEWAYS (WINCHCOMBE) LTD

Depot:Castle House,Greet Road,WINCHCOMBE,Gloucestershire.

TJF 757	Kassbohrer S250	C53F	Pullmanor,Camberwell 00
86 JBF	Kassbohrer S210H	C35F	New 95
LFH 719V	Leyland PSU3E/4R	Plaxton C49F	New 80
LFH 720V	Leyland PSU3E/4R	Plaxton C49F	New 80
G 82 BHP	Talbot Pullman	C20F	Dobson,Lostock Gralam 93
J934 CYK	Leyland TRCL10/3ARZA	Plaxton C57F	Metropolitan Police 97
J688 MFE	Kassbohrer S215HR	C53F	New 92
J689 MFE	Kassbohrer S215HR	C53F	New 92
M139 LNP	Mercedes-Benz 814D	Plaxton C33F	Rose,Broadway 99
P200 TCC	Kassbohrer S250	C48F	Brelaton,Hounslow 97
V200 OCC	Kassbohrer S315GTHD	C48FT	New 00
W391 JOG	Toyota BB50R	Caetano C22F	New 00
BX02 CME	Mercedes-Benz O530	B38F	New 02
VU02 UVM	Dennis Dart SLF	Plaxton B26F	New 02

TJF 757*N205 PUL(1/01) & 86 JBF*N325 MFE(8/00)

56   CATHEDRAL COACHES LTD

Depot:18 Quay Street,GLOUCESTER,Gloucestershire.

PFH 90W	Bedford YMT	Duple C53F	New 81
TND 403X	DAF MB200DKTL600	Plaxton C53F	Craiggs,Radcliffe 88
A689 CWP	Mercedes-Benz L608D	RB C25F	Fletcher,Studley 86
A337 VHB	DAF MB200DKFL600	Caetano C53F	Thomas,Tonypandy 87
B549 NDG	Bedford YNT	Plaxton C53F	Perrett,Shipton Oliffe 93

```
B395 UPO  Fiat 79-14        Robin Hood C31F  Russell,Strathaven 88
G114 APC  Toyota HB31R      Caetano C21F     Lutterworth Coaches 01
G410 USE  Dennis Javelin    Plaxton C53F     Ellison,Ashton Keynes 00
```

OTHER VEHICLE OWNED BY THE COMPANY
* * * * * * *
```
224 HUM  Bedford VAL14      Plaxton C-F      Office
```

57   D.R.,N.D. & I.R. CATTERMOLE.t/a Z-CARS OF BRISTOL

Depot:24 Brookgate,South Liberty Lane,Ashton Vale,BRISTOL.

```
DXI  84  Scania K113TRB        Irizar C38FT   Dunn-Line,Nottingham 01
A 10 FRX  Scania K93CRB        Plaxton C53F   Frames Rickard,Victoria 00
N614 LEU  Scania K113CRB       Irizar C48FT   New 96
P104 GHE  Scania K113CRB       Irizar C48FT   New 97
R470 YDT  Scania L94IB         Irizar C53F    New 98
T850 JWB  Auwaerter N116/2     C48FT          New 99
V 91 EAK  Auwaerter N116/3H    C48FT          New 99
BU51 AYE  Mercedes-Benz 413CDI Excel C16F     New 01
YN51 MFZ  Scania K114IB        Irizar C53F    New 01
WJ02 UVV  Toyota BB50R         Caetano C ?F   New 02
```
DXI 84*P26 RGO(8/01) & A10 FRX*H925 DRJ(2/96)

58   CENTURION TRAVEL LTD.t/a ECONOMY TRAVEL

Depot:West Road Garage,WELTON,Somerset.

```
RIB 8809  Bedford YRT          Duple C53F     Arleen,Peasedown St J. 92
RIB 8816  Bedford YMT          Duple C53F     Arleen,Peasedown St J. 90
RIB 8817  Bedford YMT          Duple C53F     Arleen,Peasedown St J. 90
RIB 8819  Bedford YMT          Plaxton C53F   Arleen,Peasedown St J. 90
TTL  262  Sanos S315-21        C49FT          TW,South Molton 00
XIB 8380  Bova FHD12-280       C49F           Arleen,Peasedown St J. 95
XIB 8381  DAF MB200DKTL600     Plaxton C57F   Arleen,Peasedown St J. 96
XIB 8385  Bedford YNT          Duple C53F     Metrobus,Orpington 93
XIB 8387  Bedford YNT          Duple C53F     Metrobus,Orpington 93
BYC 802B  Bedford YMT          Plaxton C53F   Arleen,Peasedown St J. 98
JKV 415V  Bedford YMT          Plaxton C53F   Arleen,Peasedown St J. 98
B991 YTC  Bedford YNT          Plaxton C53F   Cole,Winford 98
D801 GHU  DAF MB230DKFL615     Duple C61F     Arleen,Peasedown St J. 98
F251 RJX  DAF MB230LT615       Van Hool C49FT Moxon,Oldcotes 00
F252 RJX  DAF MB230LT615       Van Hool C49FT Moxon,Oldcotes 00
G793 RNC  Leyland TRCTL11/3ARZ Duple C53F     Arleen,Peasedown St J. 01
J211 DYL  MB OH1628L           Jonckheere C53F Curtis,Brislington 00
J471 MDB  DAF 400              MM C16F        Cunningham,Daventry 95
L667 PWT  Mercedes-Benz 814D   Optare C29F    James,Tetbury 99
R627 VNN  Dennis Javelin       Marcopolo C53F New 98
WV02 ANX  Mercedes-Benz O814D  ACL C29F       New 02
```
RIB 8809*KPC 211P(2/93), RIB 8816*DHT 666W(6/92), RIB 8817*DHT 665W(6/92),
RIB 8819*UPH 571S(6/92), TTL 262*B10 MSH(8/97) & J412 LLK(5/97),
XIB 8380*B720 MBC(7/96), XIB 8381*VBC 469X(7/96), XIB 8385*B47 DNY(7/96),
XIB 8387*B43 DNY(7/96), BYC 802B*XHE 759T(5/88), B991 YTC*B115 NSS(7/01),
F251 RJX*166 YHK(3/98) & F251 RJX(4/94) &
F252 RJX*FIL 7887(4/99) & F252 RJX(4/94)

48

59   A.J. CHIVERS.t/a JVA SUNSEEKER TOURS & HOLIDAYS

Depot:Coombend Garage,Coombend,RADSTOCK,Somerset.

```
NJI 3653   Bova EL28/581      Duple C55F      Muse,Hockley 00
PJI 6084   Bedford YNT        Plaxton C44FT   Banks,Sandiacre 90
RJI 1648   Auwaerter N116     C49FT           Davies,Slough 97
WJI 8913   Auwaerter N116     C49FT           Hall,Coventry 01
A 9  JVA   Bova EL28/581      Duple C53F      Gray,Hoyland Common 00
E589 CFW   Mercedes-Benz 507D ? B16F          Non-PSV(Leeds) 01
```
```
NJI 3653*A533 KRT(1/91) & 5516 PP(5/89) & A215 YAB(3/86),
PJI 6084*JVA 1(3/99) & PJI 6084(8/96) & JVA 1(10/95) & PJI 6084(3/94) &
      YDP 396X(7/93) & 194 WHT(3/88) & TPN 750X(4/82),
RJI 1648*C179 KET(5/93),
WJI 8913*TWG 561Y(5/02) & UYB 649(9/99) & TWG 561Y(7/87) &
A9 JVA*B999 MAY(10/00)
```

60   P.D. CHIVERS.t/a PAUL CHIVERS COACHING

Depot:Town Mill,Mill Road,RADSTOCK,Somerset.

```
RIJ  579   Mercedes-Benz 709D  RB C19F        Rigby,Lathom 00
RIL 5288   Scania K113CRB      Plaxton C49FT   Voel,Dyserth 01
RIL 9671   Mercedes-Benz 609D  North West C26F Rigby,Lathom 00
206  EJO   DAF ?               Caetano C49FT   ? 02
G906 RHH   LAG Panoramic       C49FT           McDermott,Barlestone 00
J470 NJU   Toyota HDB30R       Caetano C18F    Zamir,Khan &,Burton 00
```
```
RIJ 579*D305 JJD(9/96),
RIL 5288*G158 TJF(9/01) & 8868 VC(3/01) & G998 HKW(3/95),
RIL 9671*F762 DCC(5/00) & RIJ 397(5/00) & F762 DCC(10/96),
206 EJO*   ?  (?/??) & G906 RHH*368 SHX(1/99) & G39 ORM(2/97)
```

61   CLAPTON HOLIDAYS LTD

Depot:Unit 1,Haydon Industrial Estate,RADSTOCK,Somerset.

```
DSK  660   Volvo B10M-60       Van Hool C49FT  Armchair,Brentford 00
HIB  660   Bova FHD12-340      C49FT           New 98
PIJ  660   Mercedes-Benz 410D  Concept C8F     Non-PSV 94
VDJ  660   Bova FHD12-340      C49FT           New 97
R650 RKX   Mercedes-Benz 412D  ? C16F          Neighbour,High Wycombe 02
V210 EAL   Iveco 391E          Beulas C48FT    New 00
V 36 YJV   Mercedes-Benz 208D  Concept C8F     Non-PSV 02
W804 AAY   Iveco 391E          Beulas C48FT    New 00
```
```
DSK 660*B12 APT(2/00) & K291 GDT(4/98) & PIJ 660*L897 UKB(2/95)
```

62   G.R. CLEMENTS.t/a NORTH SOMERSET COACHES

Depot:Southfield Road,NAILSEA,Somerset.

```
VHY  437   LN 11351A/1R        B52F           Stagecoach South 100 99
307  WHT   Volvo B10M-60       Plaxton C57F    Rowe,Muirkirk 01
F218 BHF   TAZ D3200           C53F            O'Sullivan,Huyton 96
F 90 KDS   Volvo B10M-61       Ikarus C53F     Warren,Neath 01
G283 FKD   TAZ D3200           C53F            O'Sullivan,Huyton 96
J 98 UBL   Dennis Javelin      Berkhof C53F    Glenvic,Stanton Wick 01
```
```
VHY 437*AYJ 100T(7/99),
307 WHT*F652 ASJ(1/01) & VJI 9412(10/00) & F47 LRA(9/97),
F218 BHF*NSU 572(2/94) & F881 ONR(11/89),
G283 FKD*NSU 573(8/93) & G702 UNR(11/89) &
J98 UBL*UFX 567(3/01) & J98 UBL(2/98)
```

63   COACH HOUSE TRAVEL LTD/L. WATTS

Depots:Marabout IE & Unit 16a,Poundbury West IE,DORCHESTER,Dorset.

PNT 825X	Bedford YNT	Duple C53F	Hutchings,Kilmington 98
F891 BCY	Mercedes-Benz 709D	Robin Hood B24FL	Curtis,Brislington 01
F425 DUG	Volvo B10M-60	Plaxton C50F	Hearn,Harrow Weald 01
F254 MGB	Volvo B10M-60	Van Hool C49FT	Courtney,Bracknell 00
F875 RFP	Dennis Javelin	Duple C53F	McDougall,Bayswater 99
G250 CPS	Dennis Javelin	Plaxton C53F	Windsorian,Bedfont 01
G902 VKJ	Ford Transit	Crystals B8FL	Kent County Council 96
G907 VKJ	Ford Transit	Crystals B8FL	East Sussex County Coun 96
H347 CKP	Ford Transit	Crystals B8FL	Kent County Council 96
J 61 NJT	Volvo B10M-60	Plaxton C47F	Jones,Market Drayton 97
J571 PRU	Ford Transit	Dormobile B16F	West Dorset HA 94
J 93 UBL	Dennis Javelin	Berkhof C35FT	Hughes,Ashford 02
K526 EFL	Iveco 49-10	Marshall DP23F	Midland Red South 826 99
M 39 LOA	Iveco 49-10	Jubilee C19F	New 95
N232 HWX	Volvo B10M-62	Plaxton C53F	Sunline,Flimwell 02
N791 WNE	LDV 400	Concept C16F	New 95
R974 MGB	Mercedes-Benz O814D	Mellor C33F	New 98
V600 CBC	Mercedes-Benz O814D	Marshall B31F	Coakley,Motherwell 02

F254 MGB*LSK 507(11/94) & F767 ENE(2/93), J61 NJT*A4 XEL(11/95) &
N232 HWX*969 LKE(?/02) & N232 HWX(3/01)

64   COACHSTYLE LTD

Depot:Horsdown Garage,NETTLETON,Wiltshire.

KIB 2101	DAF MB200DKFL600	Van Hool C49FT	Tague,Grantown 96
MJI 3833	DAF MB200DKFL600	Van Hool C50F	Tague,Grantown 96
OIB 3510	Leyland TRCTL11/3R	Plaxton C53F	County TPL510 96
RIL 3148	Volvo B10M-62	Jonckheere C53F	Pullmanor,Camberwell 98
SIL 5960	Scania K113CRB	Irizar C49FT	Happy Days,Woodseaves 00
SIL 5970	Scania K113CRB	Irizar C49FT	Astons,Worcester 00
UPP 938	Volvo B10M-61	Plaxton C53FT	Collins,Cliffe 98
5970 FH	DAF SB3000DKV601	Van Hool C49FT	Harris,West Thurrock 97
7968 FH	DAF SB3000DKV601	Van Hool C48FT	Harris,West Thurrock 97
AFP 440Y	Bedford YNT	Plaxton C53F	Haywood &,Bedworth 98
A342 MWD	Leyland TRCTL11/3R	Plaxton C53F	DeCourcey,Coventry 99
B299 AMG	Bedford YNT	Plaxton C53F	Robillard,Harlow 91
J 46 SNY	Leyland TRCL10/3ARZM	Duple C70F	Watts,Old Tupton 02
J 28 UNY	Leyland TRCL10/3ARZM	Duple C70F	Moffat &,Gauldry 02
N230 MUS	Mercedes-Benz 811D	Marshall B33F	Lochs,Leurbost 02
T 2 ALJ	Volvo B10M-62	Berkhof C51FT	New 99

KIB 2101*FCX 943Y(3/89), MJI 3833*DDF 729Y(12/89),
OIB 3510*EWW 944Y(3/93), RIL 3148*L753 YGE(3/01), SIL 5960*N11 HDC(7/00),
SIL 5970*N915 DWJ(3/01), UPP 938*B368 HNL(8/88), 5970 FH*E96 EVW(5/93),
7968 FH*E95 EVW(2/93),
A342 MWD*MJI 3751(8/98) & A224 NAC(4/97) & 420 GAC(6/95) &
        A211 SAE(5/93) & J28 UNY*121 ASV(2/99) & J28 UNY(2/97)

65   D. COCKS.t/a DANNY COCKS COACHES

Depot:Three Dees,Tremevan,TREWOON,Cornwall.

IIL 2945	Quest VM	Plaxton C53F	James,Wilnecote 00
KOU 427P	Ford R1114	Duple C53F	Stoneman,Nanpean 98
OHE 933R	Ford R1014	Duple C45F	Collins,Rame 90
MBT 676T	Ford R1114	Plaxton C53F	Crocker,St Austell 97
OUH 770X	Ford R1114	Duple C53F	Stoneman,Nanpean 99
A684 KCP	Ford R1114	Duple C53F	McLaughlin,Penwortham 01
B934 CGL	Fiat 60-10	Caetano C18F	Fry,Tintagel 99

IIL 2945*A815 LEL(8/92) & OUH 770X*PNK 1M(6/94) & NBO 996X(11/93)

66   **D.B. & A.D. COLE.t/a WINFORD QUEEN COACHES**

Depot:Orchard Leigh,WINFORD,Somerset.

ESK 931	Volvo B10M-61	Van Hool C53F	Filer,Stanton Wick 93
D516 ODV	Ford R1115	Plaxton C53F	Nightingale,Exmouth 88
F339 YTG	Dennis Javelin	Duple C53F	Down,Ottery St Mary 00
J200 OMP	DAF SB2305DHTD585	Plaxton C53F	Pearce,Berinsfield 98

ESK 931*C332 DND(4/93)

67   **COLEFORDIAN WILLETTS LTD**

Depot:Crown Park Estate,Edenwall Road,COALWAY,Gloucestershire.

HIL 5389	Volvo B10M-61	Plaxton C49F	Aston,Kempsey 94
RHV 462	Volvo B10M-61	Jonckheere C49FT	Brice,Four Marks 97
4221 BY	Volvo B10M-61	Plaxton C53FT	Smith-Shearings 390 89
BAT 54T	Volvo B10M-60	Van Hool C53F	Whitelaw,Stonehouse 99
BUD 57Y	Volvo B10M-60	Van Hool C46FT	Shearings 451 00
C345 VNR	Bedford YNV	Duple C57F	Buley,Plymouth 95
P304 VWR	Volvo B10M-62	Plaxton C48FT	Wallace Arnold 02

HIL 5389*RHV 462(10/98) & D362 DWP(9/95) & RDU 4(12/94) & D111 HMH(5/92),
RHV 462*F953 RNV(10/98), 4221 BY*E590 VTH(11/91),
BAT 54T*L647 PSB(11/00) & 9201 WW(3/99) & L256 AHS(3/95) & LSK 444(6/94) &
BUD 57Y*K451 VVR(7/01)

68   **P.F. COLLIS.t/a PETER CAROL**

Depot:Bamfield House,Bamfield,Whitchurch,BRISTOL.

ROI 1229	MAN 11.190	Caetano C15FT	New 96
ROI 1417	Auwaerter N122/3	CH57/22CT	New 97
ROI 1913	Auwaerter N116/3	C48FT	Parry,Cheslyn Hay 01
ROI 2929	Scania K113CRB	Berkhof C30FT	Jones,Pontypridd 99
ROI 6774	MAN 18.350	Auwaerter C42FT	New 97
ROI 7435	Auwaerter N122/3	CH57/22DT	New 99
ROI 8235	Scania K124IB	Van Hool C49FT	New 01
ROI 8358	DAF DE33WSSB3000	Van Hool C ?FT	New 99
TJI 6925	DAF DE33WSSB3000	Van Hool C ?FT	New 99
800 XPC	Auwaerter N116/2	C27FT	New 98
Y218 NYA	Bova FHD10-340	C ?FT	New 01
FJ51 JXX	Toyota BB50R	Caetano C12FT	New 02

ROI 1229*N790 ORY(9/97), ROI 1417*R262 THL(9/00), ROI 1913*T774 JWA(2/01),
ROI 2929*R83 RBY(1/00), ROI 6774*R265 THL(10/99),
ROI 7435*S150 SET(10/00), ROI 8235*Y989 HET(3/02),
ROI 8358*T117 AUA(5/01), TJI 6925*T118 AUA(5/01) & 800 XPC*R275 THL(6/99)

69   **B.F. COOMBS/BRC ENTERPRISES LTD.t/a COOMBS COACHES**

Depots:Pound Yard,TOCKINGTON,Gloucestershire &
*   Searle Crescent,Winterstoke Road,WESTON-SUPER-MARE,Somerset.*

KAZ 4504	Dennis Lancet	Alexander B53F	Redby,Sunderland 96
KAZ 4505	Dennis Lancet	Alexander B53F	Redby,Sunderland 96
UPK 138S	Leyland AN68A/1R	PR H43/30F	North Western 728 97
A158 EPA	Leyland TRCTL11/3R	Plaxton C57F	London & Country TPL58 97
B289 KPF	Leyland TRCTL11/3RH	Plaxton C53F	London & Country TPL89 97
D 21 CTR	Bedford YMT	WS B53F	Cambus 401 92
D 22 CTR	Bedford YMT	WS B53F	Somerbus,Paulton 92
D 23 CTR	Bedford YMT	WS B53F	Cambus 403 92
D327 TRN	Mercedes-Benz 709D	RB C19F	Miles,Stratton St Mar. 99
G693 NUB	Renault S56	Optare B13FL	Leeds City Council 98

```
G699 NUB   Renault S56          Optare B8FL        Leeds City Council 98
H642 GRO   Leyland TRCL10/3ARZA Plaxton C53F       East London TPL7 96
J272 NNC   Scania K93CRB        Plaxton C53F       Shearings 272 97
J275 NNC   Scania K93CRB        Plaxton C53F       Shearings 275 97
J278 NNC   Scania K93CRB        Plaxton C53F       Shearings 278 97
K721 HYA   Mercedes-Benz 709D   Dormobile DP29F    New 92
K722 HYA   Scania K93CRB        Plaxton C53F       New 93
L882 MWB   Mercedes-Benz 609D   Cunliffe DP15FL    Derbyshire County Coun 02
L103 SKB   Ford Transit         Whitacre B8F       Meteor,Heathrow 3 96
L104 SKB   Ford Transit         Whitacre B8F       Meteor,Heathrow 4 96
L106 SKB   Ford Transit         Whitacre B8F       Meteor,Heathrow 6 96
L102 UHF   Ford Transit         Whitacre B6FL      Meteor,Heathrow 2 96
L110 UHF   Ford Transit         Whitacre B8FL      Meteor,Heathrow 10 96
M572 TYB   Scania K93CRB        Van Hool C57F      New 95
M573 TYB   Scania K93CRB        Van Hool C57F      New 95
N967 BYC   Dennis Javelin       UVG C57F           New 96
N970 BYC   Scania K113CRB       Van Hool C57F      New 96
N541 CYA   Ford Transit         G & M B8FL         Non-PSV(Van) 00
N605 DOR   Ford Transit         Robin Hood B8FL    Meteor,Mayfair 05 98
N410 WJL   Mercedes-Benz 814D   ACL C29F           Myrtle Tree,Bristol 98
P 87 JYC   Toyota HZB50R        Caetano C21F       New 96
P 89 JYC   Dennis Javelin       Plaxton C55F       New 97
V448 DYB   LDV Convoy           Concept C16F       New 99
W371 PHY   Mercedes-Benz O814D  ACL DP31F          New 00
W372 PHY   Scania N113DRB       EL CH47/31F        New 00
Y621 HHU   LDV Convoy           ? C16FL            New 01
WV02 OGG   LDV Convoy           LDV B14FL          New 02
WV02 OGH   Scania K114IB        Irizar C57F        New 02
```

OTHER VEHICLES OWNED BY THE COMPANY
* * * * * * *

```
300  AYG   Bedford VAS1         Plaxton C-F        Storeshed
D308 SDS   Dodge S56            Alexander B-F      Storeshed
```

```
KAZ 4504*A504 FSS(6/96), KAZ 4505*A505 FSS(6/96),
L102 UHF*L102 SKB(12/94) & L110 UHF*L110 SKB(12/94)
```

70   A.K. COTTON

Depot:The Gables,147 Old Ferry Road,SALTASH,Cornwall.

```
SIB 8941   Mercedes-Benz 609D   Coachcraft C16F    Booth,Andover 98
E707 WKC   Mercedes-Benz 507D   RH DP15FL          Conway,Kirkby-Ashfield 00
G110 OGA   Mercedes-Benz 709D   North West C20FL   Brenton,Plymouth 99
G249 XDV   Mercedes-Benz 507D   DC B12FL           Brenton,Plymouth 00
H251 FDV   Ford Transit         G & M B12F         Non-PSV(Plymouth) 97
L819 WMM   Mercedes-Benz 410D   G & M B16F         Brenton,Plymouth 00
M386 EDH   Toyota HZB50R        Caetano C21F       Meadway,Birmingham 01
```

```
SIB 8941*G795 WTR(8/01)
```

71   COTTRELLS COACHES LTD

Depot:St Michaels Close,Mill End,MITCHELDEAN,Gloucestershire.

```
GBU   2V   MCW Metrobus DR101   H43/30F            G. Manchester PTE 5002 86
GBU   6V   MCW Metrobus DR101   H43/34F            G. Manchester PTE 5006 86
GBU   7V   MCW Metrobus DR101   H43/34F            Stevensons 78 96
NDE 147Y   Leyland TRCTL11/2R   Plaxton C53F       Horlock,Northfleet 88
C474 CAP   Leyland TRCTL11/3RH  Plaxton C53F       Thames Transit 1016 91
D803 NBO   Leyland TRCTL11/3RH  Plaxton C51FT      Munden,Bristol 89
D160 UGA   Leyland LDTL11/1R    AR CH49/37F        Clydeside 2000 165 94
E478 AFJ   Leyland TRCTL11/3RZ  Plaxton C53F       Loverings,Combe Martin 95
F309 RMH   Leyland TRBTL11/2RP  Duple B55F         Dell,Chesham 93
F183 UFH   Leyland TRCTL11/3ARZ Plaxton C57F       New 89
H932 DRJ   Volvo B10M-60        Plaxton C53F       Capital,West Drayton 97
H651 UWR   Volvo B10M-60        Plaxton C53F       Machin,Ashby-d-l-Zouch 98
```

```
M 9  FUG  Dennis Dart           WS B43F           Fuggles,Benenden 9 99
```
~~~~~~
```
C474 CAP*YDG 616(11/90) & D160 UGA*705 DYE(6/94) & D852 RDS(12/92)
```
~~~~~~

72   B.M. COUCH.t/a PARAMOUNT MINI COACHES

Depot:Unit 18,Wolseley Business Park,Ford,PLYMOUTH,Devon.

```
E478 XTT  Mercedes-Benz 507D   PG C16F           Thompson,Plymouth 98
H155 UYC  DAF 400              Deansgate C16F    Foster,Glastonbury 95
L889 GYH  DAF 400              Jubilee C14FL     Brenton,Plymouth 00
M465 KFJ  LDV 400              G & M C15FL       Brenton,Plymouth 00
R566 BAF  Mercedes-Benz 612D   G & M C20FL       New 97
V155 EFV  Mercedes-Benz 412D   G & M C16FL       New 99
```
~~~~~~

73   A.J. CRIDLAND.t/a TAUNTON COACHES

Depot:Taunton Trading Estate,NORTON FITZWARREN,Somerset.

```
GSU  372  DAF MB200DKVL600      Van Hool C48FT    Dunne,Fintona(Ire) 97
JUI 9791  Volvo B10M-61         Van Hool C49FT    Parnham,Ludgershall 87
UOP  948  DAF SB2300DHS585      Plaxton C49FT     Broadwest,Ogmore Vale 98
XLF  622  Volvo B10M-61         Caetano C53F      Deeble,Darleyford 93
B533 TEO  DAF SB2300DHS585      Plaxton C55F      Hann,Wimborne 00
```
~~~~~~
```
GSU 372*OIW 1461(8/97) & 87KK 1315(4/93) & GSU 372(3/89) &
        D864 EFS(12/87), JIL 9791*UUS 373(9/00) & STT 606X(7/85),
UOP 948*C336 UFP(12/98), XLF 622*E665 RGL(7/96) &
B533 TEO*TTK 597(12/00) & B533 TEO(12/98)
```
~~~~~~

74   J.R. CROCKER.t/a JC TOURS

Depots:32 Symons Close,BOSCOPPA &
               Garsue Lodge,High Street,ST AUSTELL,Cornwall.

```
SIB 8357  Volvo B10M-61         Van Hool C53F     Bugler,Bristol 01
WUO 612V  Ford R1114            Duple C53F        Thomas,Relubbus 96
ENF 571Y  Volvo B10M-61         Duple C53F        Crabbe,Stockton-on-Tees 94
G201 PAO  Mercedes-Benz 709D    Alexander DP25F   Bluebird Buses 312 01
G860 VAY  Toyota HB31R          Caetano C21F      Webber,St Austell 01
S326 UEW  LDV Convoy            Central C16F      Non-PSV 01
```
~~~~~~
```
SIB 8357*D344 KVE(5/93)
```
~~~~~~

75   CROSS COUNTRY LTD

Depot:Blackford Lane Garage,CASTLE EATON,Wiltshire.

```
DSU  405  Kassbohrer S228DT     CH54/20CT         Silver Knight,Malmesbry 98
NJI 9479  DAF MB230DKFL615      Van Hool C55F     London Northern VH2 97
TIL 7910  DAF SB3000DKV601      Van Hool C51FT    Aztecbird,Guiseley 01
TIL 7915  DAF SB3000DKV601      Van Hool C51FT    Aztecbird,Guiseley 01
WJI 7690  DAF MB230LT615        Van Hool C49F     London Northern VH3 97
115  CLT  Kassbohrer S228DT     CH54/20CT         Silver Knight,Malmesbry 98
964  FXM  Leyland TRCTL11/3R    Plaxton C57F      Thamesdown 300 01
XBU  19S  Leyland FE30AGR       NC H43/32F        Thamesdown 217 02
BVR  89T  Leyland FE30AGR       NC H43/32F        Thamesdown 211 02
HDB 101V  Leyland FE30AGR       NC H43/32F        G Manchester South 4101 95
KDB 138V  Leyland FE30AGR       NC H43/32F        G Manchester South 4138 95
RVW  89W  Leyland AN68A/1R      ECW H43/31F       Court,Fillongley 01
G116 APC  Toyota HB31R          Caetano C21F      Nesbeth & Rowe,Thatcham 02
```
~~~~~~
```
DSU 405*A414 GPY(12/88), NJI 9479*D276 XCX(3/92), TIL 7910*J821 KHD(2/01),
```

TIL 7915*J824 KHD(2/01), WJI 7690*G260 EHD(5/98),
115 CLT*SWH 67(2/91) & B149 NPE(2/88) & 964 FXM*VPR 861X(9/87)

76   K.W. & S. CRUDGE.t/a STAMPS COACHES

Depot:Slade Barton,PAYHEMBURY,Devon.

NIW 8793	Volvo B10M-61	Duple C53F	Kingdom,Tiverton 01
TIL 6880	Bedford YMP	Plaxton C35F	Wills,Bow 01
UMS 394	Bova FHD12-280	C49FT	Jackman,Willand 02
WSV 728	Bedford YNT	Duple C53F	Forward,Tiverton 02
1560 KX	DAF MB200DKFL600	Van Hool C53F	Warren,Neath 99
D 22 NWO	Leyland TRCTL11/3R	Duple C55F	Baker,Trowbridge 01
D510 OTA	Fiat 49-10	Robin Hood DP21F	Southern Nat.(Smiths) 98
E244 FLD	Bedford YNV	Plaxton C53F	Smith,Pylle 01
F309 RVT	Freight Rover Sherpa	PMT B20F	Trotter,Stoney Stoke 99
H287 AHU	DAF 400	Zodiac C16F	Williams,Charmouth 01
L800 RAG	Toyota HZB50R	Caetano C21F	Forward,Tiverton 02

NIW 8793*GTT 417Y(4/93),
TIL 6880*VWB 866Y(10/01) & MIL 6684(9/01) & VWB 866Y(8/00) &
      RIB 3195(11/99) & VWB 866Y(1/96), UMS 394*A732 HFP(2/88),
WSV 728*B390 HEW(12/00) & MCT 612(1/95) & B634 YVL(4/92),
1560 KX*CPD 670Y(4/92) & 665 GJF(2/92) &
E244 FLD*505 AYB(4/01) & E244 FLD(11/97)

77   G.H. CUDLIPP.t/a LINCO TRAVEL

Depot:The Air Raid Shelter,Henstridge Airfield,HENSTRIDGE,Somerset.

FIL 2294	DAF SB2300DHS585	Berkhof C49FT	Hill,Hersham 01
NBZ 1286	Toyota HB31R	Caetano C21F	Barrys,Weymouth 01
298 HPK	Ford R1014	Duple C32FL	Russell,Wall 00
362 KHT	Leyland TRCTL11/2R	Duple C53F	Dorset County Council 98
DNT 717T	Leyland PSU3E/4R	Plaxton C53F	Royds,Rochdale 01
JLS 5V	MAN SR280	C40FL	Barrys,Weymouth 00
KDL 204W	Bristol LHS6L	ECW DP31F	Brown,Shaftesbury 97
C311 SPL	Mercedes-Benz L608D	RB B20F	Weaver,Weymouth 01
K809 WPF	Talbot Pullman	B20F	Barrys,Weymouth 01

FIL 2294*JVW 159Y(1/88), NBZ 1286*E701 MTC(12/01), 298 HPK*OJX 21T(6/02),
362 KHT*YPD 135Y(10/00), DNT 717T*289 MPU(2/01) & PGR 961T(5/00) &
JLS 5V*4708 RU(2/00) & JLS 5V(10/83)

78   J.A.R. CURTIS.t/a COURTESY COACHES

Depot:38 Speculation Road,Forest Vale IE,CINDERFORD,Gloucestershire.

A624 HNF	Ford Transit	Mellor B3FL	Couch,Plymouth 96
D784 JUB	Freight Rover Sherpa	Dormobile B16F	Webber,Bodmin 97
E492 CPE	DAF MB230LB615	Caetano C53F	Cowdrey,Gosport 01
E732 YBH	Freight Rover Sherpa	RB B8FL	Buckinghamshire CC 97

E492 CPE*HIL 5682(1/97) & E178 KNH(4/92)

79   DAC COACHES LTD

Depot:Rylands Garage,St Anns Chapel,GUNNISLAKE,Cornwall.

CLZ 3681	Mercedes-Benz O814D	Plaxton B27F	Hardie,Port Glasgow 01
LUI 5603	Leyland ONTL11/2R	ECW CH45/28F	McColl,Balloch 02
NIL 5651	Volvo B10M-46	Plaxton C43F	Docherty,Auchterarder 00
NIL 5652	Volvo B10M-60	Van Hool C49FT	Wood,Buckfastleigh 99
WSV 529	Volvo B58-56	Plaxton C53C	Monetgrange,Codnor 92

```
228  FHT   Volvo B10M-61         Van Hool C50FT       Phillips,Crediton 99
TWS 914T   Bristol VRT/SL3/6LXB  ECW H45/29F          Munden,Bristol 01
RUE 300W   Bedford YMQ           Plaxton C35F         Dalybus,Eccles 95
ANA 158Y   MCW Metrobus DR102    H43/30F              Blazefield Lancashire 02
ENF 573Y   Volvo B10M-61         Duple C57F           West Dorset 9012 98
D930 LYC   Bedford YNV           Duple C57F           Evans,St Athan 98
G165 NAG   Mercedes-Benz 609D    Coachcraft C24F      Sands,Shepshed 94
H437 BVU   Mercedes-Benz 709D    Cunliffe B24FL       Webber &,Wheddon Cross 99
M345 TDO   Mercedes-Benz 609D    ACL C23F             Witte,Calne 01
P558 BAY   Dennis Javelin        Marcopolo C50FT      Solent,Wootton 02
V 54 MOD   Toyota BB50R          Caetano C24F         New 00
W348 XEE   Mercedes-Benz 1223L   Ferqui C39F          Abbeyways,Halifax 02
SF51 PVY   Mercedes-Benz O814D   Plaxton B27F         New 01
WJ02 KDX   Bova FHD12-340        C51FT                New 02
```

```
CLZ 3681*V384 HGG(12/01), LUI 5603*C449 BKM(10/01),
NIL 5651*H717 FLD(9/00),
NIL 5652*H487 FGL(3/00) & WIA 69(7/99) & H487 FGL(12/98),
WSV 529*DYW 169V(4/87), 228 FHT*A239 LFH(4/90) & YWD 687(11/89) &
D930 LYC*PIL 7046(12/00) & D930 LYC(10/98) & A16 BCG(2/98) &
        D930 LYC(11/97)
```

80   DANGERFIELDS CAR HIRE SERVICE LTD

Depot:Isis TE,Marshfield TE,Stratton Rd,Upper Stratton,SWINDON,Wiltshire.

```
C451 GGT   Ford Transit          Dormobile B8FL       RB Kingston 445 95
L959 GOP   Renault Master        SLS B11F             West Midlands Ambulance 02
M 79 VAK   Ford Transit          Bedwas DP16FL        Non-PSV(Thryburgh) 98
N145 NFB   Iveco 49-10           LCB B24FL            Non-PSV(TLS) 99
P830 ADO   Mercedes-Benz O810D   ACL C29F             Slack,Matlock 00
P937 EOP   Iveco 49-10           Jubilee C19F         New 96
P798 FCF   LDV Convoy            LDV B16F             New 97
P799 FCF   LDV Convoy            LDV B16F             New 97
R667 OJM   LDV Convoy            LDV B14F             New 98
R668 OJM   LDV Convoy            LDV B14F             New 98
V328 XDO   Mercedes-Benz O814D   ACL C29F             New 99
W599 KFE   Mercedes-Benz 410D    ACL C12F             On Time,Wandsworth 02
X212 AWB   Mercedes-Benz O814D   Plaxton C33F         New 00
X412 KRD   LDV Convoy            LDV B16F             New 00
X413 KRD   LDV Convoy            LDV B16F             New 00
Y847 LDP   LDV Convoy            LDV B16F             New 01
Y848 LDP   LDV Convoy            LDV B16F             New 01
YN51 WHJ   Volvo B7R             Plaxton C57F         New 01
YN51 WHK   Volvo B7R             Plaxton C57F         New 01
```

81   DART PLEASURE CRAFT LTD

Depot:Baltic Wharf Boatyard,St Peters Quay,TOTNES,Devon.

```
UWV 604S  2   Bristol VRT/SL3/6LXB ECW CO43/31F    Stagecoach Devon 936 00
UWV 614S  1   Bristol VRT/SL3/6LXB ECW CO43/31F    Stagecoach Devon 937 00
WTU 467W  3   Bristol VRT/SL3/6LXB ECW O43/31F     Arriva Cymru OVG467 02
F301 RUT  4   Mercedes-Benz 709D   Robin Hood B26F Thorn,Rayleigh 02
```

82   C.M. & K.S. DAVIS

Depot:Hilltop Garage,Cuckoo Row,MINCHINHAMPTON,Gloucestershire.

```
1092  AD   Volvo B10M-60         Van Hool C46FT       Shearings 483 99
3134  AD   Volvo B10M-61         Van Hool C53F        New 89
3672  AD   Volvo B10M-48         Van Hool C28FT       Armchair,Brentford 01
5469  AD   Volvo B10M            Van Hool C ?F        ? 02
6501  AD   Volvo B10M-60         Van Hool C46FT       Shearings 478 99
```

```
8727  AD   DAF MB200DKFL600      Van Hool C53F    Ardenvale,Knowle 89
9210  AD   DAF MB230LT615        Van Hool C51FT   Ribblesdale,Gt Harwood 97
2052  NF   Mercedes-Benz L608D   RB C19F          Foster,Glastonbury 93
KUM 533L   Leyland PSU3B/4R      Plaxton C53F     Wallace Arnold 80
XUY 289V   Leyland PSU3E/4R      Plaxton C53F     Pulham,Bourton-on-Water 96
T993 PFH   Toyota BB50R          Caetano C21F     New 99
Y707 KNC   LDV Convoy            Concept C16F     New 01
```
~~~~~~
```
1092 AD*K483 VVR(3/99), 3134 AD*F719 SML(7/99), 3672 AD*L117 OWF(7/01),
5469 AD*    ?   (?/02), 6501 AD*K478 VVR(3/99), 8727 AD*B971 SHP(5/89),
9210 AD*F223 YHG(7/99) & 3672 AD(10/97) & F223 YHG(2/97),
2052 NF*B494 BYA(7/01) & 2052 NF(7/01) & B494 BYA(2/01) & 3672 AD(7/00) &
       2052 NF(10/97) & B494 BYA(6/95),
KUM 533L*9210 AD(7/99) & KUM 533L(7/84) &
XUY 289V*3134 AD(7/99) & MNN 33V(4/96)
```
~~~~~~

83   M.H. DAVIS.t/a MICHAELS TRAVEL

Depot:c/o Colins Transport,Plump Hill,MITCHELDEAN,Gloucestershire.

```
JAZ 9910   Toyota HDB30R         Caetano C21F     Ryder,West Bromwich 98
A 18 MHD   Mercedes-Benz L307D   PMT B12FL        WMSNT,Birmingham 97
J261 TDA   Mercedes-Benz 410D    DC B8FL          WMSNT,Birmingham 00
P785 KRW   Mercedes-Benz 312D    ? C16FL          Non-PSV(Van) 00
FX51 AXP   LDV Convoy            Excel C16FL      New 01
```
~~~~~~
```
JAZ 9910*J133 CWJ(4/96) & J2 JBT(11/94) & A18 MHD*F343 SEH(2/00)
```
~~~~~~

84   DAWLISH COACHES LTD

Depot:Shutterton Industrial Estate,Exeter Road,DAWLISH,Devon.

```
  8 RDV   Van Hool T815H        C49FT            Brighton 121 93
A168 PAE  Volvo B10M-61         Duple C57F       Turner,Bristol 92
A169 PAE  Volvo B10M-61         Duple C57F       Turner,Bristol 92
E296 OMG  Volvo B10M-61         Van Hool C49FT   North Mymms Coaches 92
F512 LTT  Volvo B10M-60         Van Hool C49FT   New 89
F 77 MFJ  Volvo B10M-60         Van Hool C53F    New 89
H920 BPN  Van Hool T815H        C53F             Brighton 120 93
K922 UFX  Mercedes-Benz 811D    Plaxton C33F     Tedd,Thruxton 94
L796 DTT  Bova FHD12-340        C53F             New 94
L182 PMX  Bova FHD12-340        C53F             Q Drive,Battersea 99
M 12 BUS  Volvo B10M-62         Van Hool C53F    Irving,Carlisle 00
M587 KTT  Bova FHD12-340        C53F             New 95
M421 VYD  Volvo B10M-62         Van Hool C55F    Foster,Glastonbury 01
N201 DYB  Bova FHD12-340        C53F             New 96
N202 DYB  Bova FHD12-340        C53F             New 96
N231 YCT  Mercedes-Benz 814D    ACL C29F         New 96
P928 KYC  Bova FHD12-340        C49FT            New 97
P929 KYC  Bova FHD12-340        C49FT            New 97
P344 VWR  Volvo B10M-62         Plaxton C50F     Wallace Arnold 02
R 2 AVC   Bova FHD12-340        C53F             Bailey,Biddisham 8 02
R913 ULA  Volvo B10M-62         Berkhof C49FT    Q Drive,Battersea 98
R920 ULA  Volvo B10M-62         Berkhof C49FT    Q Drive,Battersea 98
R208 WYD  Bova FHD12-330        C49FT            New 98
R209 WYD  Bova FHD12-330        C49FT            New 98
V483 XJV  Mercedes-Benz O814D   ACL C29F         New 00
W157 RYB  Bova FHD12-370        C53F             New 00
W562 RYC  Bova FHD12-370        C49FT            New 00
X424 CFJ  Mercedes-Benz O814D   Plaxton B27F     New 00
Y818 NAY  Iveco 391E            Beulas C49FT     New 01
Y835 NAY  Iveco 391E            Beulas C49FT     New 01
WJ02 KDF  Bova FHD12-340        C49FT            New 02
WK02 YYK  Toyota BB50R          Caetano C22F     New 02
```
~~~~~~
```
8 RDV*H921 BPN(3/99), A168 PAE*3138 DP(3/92) & A879 UHY(6/85) &
A169 PAE*2170 MV(3/92) & A880 UHY(1/86)
```

85   R.S. DAY.t/a SWALLOW COACHES

Depot:Palm Grove Hotel,Meadfoot Sea Road,TORQUAY,Devon.

```
FIL 4138   Bedford YMP          Plaxton C28F    Sault &,Sth Bermondsey 98
137  DAF   Bova FHD12-290       C49FT           Q Drive,Battersea 99
578  DAF   Bova FHD12-340       C53F            Weaver,Newbury 99
927  DAF   Bova FHD12-290       C53F            New 90
```
~~~~~~
```
FIL 4138*B409 CMC(11/88), 137 DAF*G826 YJF(9/99),
578 DAF*B10 MST(9/99) & B10 MWT(6/98) & J5 PAG(5/97) &
927 DAF*G151 WHT(4/97)
```
~~~~~~

86   DEALTOP LTD.t/a DARTLINE

Depot:Langdons Business Park,Oil Mill Lane,CLYST ST MARY,Devon.

```
CSU  926   Volvo B10M-61        Duple C49FT     Park,Hamilton 87
KIW 4489   Mercedes-Benz 709D   Robin Hood C24FL West Glamorgan SS 97
LBZ 2571   DAF SB3000DKV601     Van Hool C53F   Phillips,Crediton 99
LIL 6537   Volvo B10M-61        Plaxton C53F    Shearings 568 93
LIL 6538   Volvo B10M-60        Plaxton C53F    St Buryan Garage 94
LIL 7802   Volvo B10M-61        Van Hool C53F   Leon,Stafford 39 96
LIL 8052   Volvo B10M-61        Plaxton C53F    Phillips,Crediton 99
LIL 8823   Volvo B10M-61        Van Hool C53F   Shearings 738 96
LIL 8876   Volvo B10M-60        Plaxton C48FT   Wray,Harrogate 98
LIL 9017   Volvo B10M-60        Plaxton C49FT   Cheltenham & Glou. 548 98
LIL 9990   Volvo B10M-60        Caetano C53FT   Goodere,Melbourne 96
UJI 3794   Van Hool T815H       C51FT           Phillips,Crediton 99
XFJ  466   Volvo B10M-61        Plaxton C53F    Docherty,Auchterarder 98
G958 VBC   DAF SB2305DHS585     Caetano C49FT   Phillips,Crediton 99
J870 FGX   Mercedes-Benz 609D   Crystals C24F   Crystals(Demonstr.) 91
J824 MOD   Mercedes-Benz 609D   Crystals C24F   New 91
J825 MOD   Mercedes-Benz 609D   Crystals C24F   New 91
K775 UTT   Mercedes-Benz 609D   Crystals C24F   New 92
L345 ATA   Mercedes-Benz 609D   G & M C24F      New 93
L858 COD   Mercedes-Benz 811D   Marshall B33F   New 94
L422 WHR   Mercedes-Benz 609D   ACL C19F        Shayler,Blunsden 94
M752 GDV   LDV 400              Coachsmith B7FL Non-PSV(Plymouth) 98
M158 KOD   Mercedes-Benz 609D   G & M C24F      New 95
N 40 TCC   Dennis Javelin       Plaxton C53F    Stort Valley,Stansted 01
P429 JDT   Dennis Javelin       Plaxton C53F    Silver Coach,Edinburgh 01
P934 KYC   Bova FHD12-340       C51FT           Phillips,Crediton 99
S671 ETT   LDV Convoy           G & M C16F      New 98
S923 KOD   Iveco 59-12          Marshall B29F   New 98
S924 KOD   Iveco 59-12          Marshall B29F   New 98
S925 KOD   Iveco 59-12          Marshall B29F   New 98
S926 KOD   Iveco 59-12          Marshall B29F   New 98
S944 WYB   Volvo B10M-62        Jonckheere C51FT New 98
W259 WRV   Mercedes-Benz O814D  Robin Hood C25F New 00
Y 14 DLC   Bova FHD12-370       C49FT           New 01
WJ02 KDZ   Bova FHD12-340       C51FT           New 02
WJ02 KUE   Mercedes-Benz O815DT Sitcar C27F     New 02
```
~~~~~~
```
CSU 926*A728 HFP(3/92), KIW 4489*F896 BCY(2/98), LBZ 2571*E341 EVH(9/94),
LIL 6537*D568 MVR(10/95), LIL 6538*F23 HGG(10/95),
LIL 7802*A149 MFA(11/96) & LOI 9772(11/96) & A644 UGD(6/87),
LIL 8052*UJI 3792(3/01) & E556 UHS(3/96),
LIL 8823*YXI 4971(7/98) & F738 ENE(12/93),
LIL 8876*G293 PUB(10/98) & A20 MCW(12/95) & G503 LWU(3/95),
LIL 9017*G548 LWU(6/98), LIL 9990*491 NFC(1/97) & D304 KFP(1/95),
UJI 3794*E22 MMM(3/96) & XFJ 466*913 EWC(8/98) & D573 MVR(5/92)
```
~~~~~~

87   A.J. DEEBLE.t/a DARLEY FORD TRAVEL

Depot:Darley Ford Garage,Darley Ford,UPTON CROSS,Cornwall.

OIL 6847	Volvo B10M-61	Duple C49FT	Non-PSV(Kelvedon Hatch) 97
OIL 6849	Volvo B58-61	Plaxton C46FT	Hughes,Sunderland 98
RAZ 7203	Volvo B10M-60	Ikarus C49FT	Chariots,Stanford-le-H. 00
RAZ 7349	Volvo B10M-61	Van Hool C49FT	Ward & Keith,Bedfont 98
RAZ 8723	Volvo B10M-60	Plaxton C47FT	Heyfordian,Upr Heyford 98
RAZ 9649	Volvo B10M	Ikarus C ?F	? 02
VAN 524	Scania K112CRS	Plaxton C46FT	Scriven,Street 93
8909 DF	Scania K112TRS	JE CH55/19CT	Mandale,Greystoke 87
ODJ 584W	Volvo B58-61	Duple C53F	Lianswood,St Austell 99
G277 BEL	Toyota HB31R	Caetano C21F	Smith,Millbrook 99
G932 HRN	Leyland LBM6T/1RS	Elme C31F	Gregory,Netherton 00
P985 LKL	Scania K113TRB	Irizar C51FT	Kings Ferry,Gillingham 01

```
OIL 6847*YFJ 49X(5/98) & YXL 947(1/87) & FHS 731X(5/85),
OIL 6849*GGD 666T(5/98) & PJI 2409(9/97) & GGD 666T(10/92),
RAZ 7203*G432 SNN(3/02),
RAZ 7349*C275 LBH(5/98) & MSK 286(5/96) & C238 GBH(7/92),
RAZ 8723*L43 CNY(3/02), RAZ 9649*  ?  (?/02), VAN 524*VWB 845Y(4/85) &
8909 DF*C384 KGG(3/92)
```

88   J.K. DEEBLE.t/a CARADON RIVIERA TOURS

Depots:Culverland Rd,Trevecca,LISKEARD & The Garage,UPTON CROSS,Cornwall.

GSU 344	Leyland TRCTL11/2RH	Alexander C47F	Fife Scottish 444 99
HIL 2379	Leyland TRCTL11/3R	Duple C57F	Monaghan &,Liskeard 01
HIL 7621	Leyland TRCTL11/3R	Duple C57F	Liskeard & District 01
LUI 9952	Leyland PSU3E/4R	Plaxton C53F	Ford,Street 94
LUI 9953	Leyland TRBTL11/2RP	Alexander C53F	Bluebird Buses 441 01
VJI 8683	Bedford YMT	Plaxton C53F	Edwards,High Wycombe 02
VJI 8684	Bedford YMT	Plaxton C53F	East Midland 1013 01
751 CRT	MCW Metrorider MF154	C29F	Meyers,Llanpumsaint 02
761 CRT	Leyland TRCTL11/2RP	Alexander C51F	Bluebird Buses 442 01
924 CRT	Leyland TRCTL11/1RH	RB C35F	Chambers,Stevenage 99
PHN 570R	Leyland PSU3D/2R	Duple B53F	Ross,Featherstone 02
SCN 276S	Leyland AN68A/2R	AR H49/37F	Helms,Bootle 02
DAD 256T	Leyland PSU5C/4R	Plaxton C57F	Millmans,Newton Abbot 01
AVK 150V	Leyland AN68A/2R	AR H49/37F	Travelspeed,Burnley 02
BVA 787V	Leyland PSU3F/5R	Plaxton C49F	Millmans,Newton Abbot 01
B330 LSA	Leyland TRCTL11/2RP	Alexander C49F	Bluebird Buses 444 01
C849 CSN	Leyland RT	Leyland C49FT	Martin,Bootle 01
D241 OOJ	Freight Rover Sherpa	Carlyle B20F	Henderson,Penygraig 98
D309 PEJ	Freight Rover Sherpa	Optare C16F	Childs,Kiveton Park 01
E402 TCV	MCW Metrorider MF150	B23F	Stolzenberg,Maesteg 97
F 92 XBV	Leyland TRBTL11/2RP	East Lancs DP47F	Rossendale 92 01
F 93 XBV	Leyland TRBTL11/2RP	East Lancs B51F	Boseley,Widnes 01
F 94 XBV	Leyland TRBTL11/2RP	East Lancs B51F	Rossendale 94 01
F 95 XBV	Leyland TRBTL11/2RP	East Lancs B51F	Rossendale 95 01
L778 XCV	Dennis Javelin	WS C36FA	MOD 01
L779 XCV	Dennis Javelin	WS C36FA	Collison,Stonehouse 01

```
GSU 344*B210 FFS(9/94), HIL 2379*ARE 508Y(3/91), HIL 7621*WFA 210X(5/92),
LUI 9952*751 CRT(6/02) & LUA 276V(6/94),
LUI 9953*A663 WSU(6/02) & WLT 976(4/93) & A120 GLS(3/87),
VJI 8683*TER 4S(3/02), VJI 8684*FTO 550V(12/01),
751 CRT*F481 WFA(6/02) & 565 LON(8/94) & F114 UEH(12/93),
761 CRT*B328 LSA(4/02) & TSV 718(12/99) & B328 LSA(7/90),
924 CRT*B276 YSL(5/99) & EUE 489(8/96) & B833 VSR(5/86),
BVA 787V*LIL 3066(7/98) & BVA 787V(3/95),
B330 LSA*TSV 720(12/99) & B330 LSA(7/90),
C849 CSN*WLT 784(8/91) & C816 BTS(9/86),
D309 PEJ*TJI 6875(8/00) & D309 PEJ(10/95),
E402 TCV*VJI 8684(6/99) & E142 TBO(1/98), L778 XCV*L519 KRS(12/01) &
L779 XCV*L166 XUS(12/01)
```

89 DENWELL TRANSPORT LTD

*Depots:Norton Garage,Tewkesbury Road,NORTON &
                    Station Road,TEWKESBURY,Gloucestershire.*

B304 WTP	Ford Transit	Dormobile B8F	Sussex County Council 90
F627 GKM	Ford Transit	Dormobile B16F	Welwyn-Hatfield CVS 98
G639 UKL	Ford Transit	Dormobile B8F	Non-PSV 98
J290 HJX	DAF 400	Crystals B15FL	Telling,Norcote 99
M817 LNC	LDV 400	Concept C16F	Telsons,Kings Cross 99
N184 HBX	Renault Master	Cymric C16F	New 95
P420 EOX	LDV Convoy	WJW C16F	Non-PSV 99
P107 MOV	LDV Convoy	WJW C16F	Non-PSV 99
P256 PBX	Renault Master	Cymric C16F	New 96
R376 EBX	Renault Master	Cymric C16F	New 97

J290 HJX*XIB 51(6/99) & J290 HJX(11/98)

90 DHM TAXIS & MINI COACHES LTD

Depot:Kingsland Road Sidings,St Philips,BRISTOL.

G 90 KTH	DAF 400	DAF B16F	Moore,Bedminster 98
J662 HFW	DAF 400	Cunliffe B8FL	Richens,Bristol 01
K275 DSG	DAF 400	POW B16F	Post Office 2750039 99
K393 PVL	DAF 400	Cunliffe B4FL	Translinc,Lincoln 00

91 A.G. DONALD.t/a HIGHWAY TRAVEL

Depot:c/o FBG Auction Centre,Henstridge Airfield,HENSTRIDGE,Somerset.

HIL 7982	DAF MB200DKFL600	Plaxton C49FT	Expertpoint,Stratford 00
HUI 6824	Volvo B10M-61	Duple C55FT	Worrall,Stourport 00
1256 RU	Leyland TRCTL11/3R	Duple C50FT	Duchy,Newton Abbot 01
STK 133T	Leyland AN68A/1R	Roe H43/31F	North Birmingham 00
CRL 917V	Bedford YMT	Plaxton C53F	Thorne,Pewsey 00
BRT 787Y	Ford R1114	Duple C53F	Suffolk County Council 98
B111 ORU	Ford Transit	CD C16F	North Dorset,Hazlebury 00
C 68 BFX	Leyland RT	Leyland C47FT	Bonfield,Leyton 99
C744 JYA	Leyland TRCTL11/3RZ	Willowbrook C55F	Gunn,South Petherton 02

HIL 7982*C903 REW(10/92),
HUI 6824*EJC 466X(2/01) & XSU 653(9/98) & YFJ 759X(1/96) & NDO 856(9/95) &
        FHS 745X(6/91) &
1256 RU*PES 87Y(3/94) & HOI 2319(4/93) & SFS 581Y(7/92)

92 DORSET COUNTY COUNCIL

Main Depot:Grove Trading Estate,DORCHESTER,Dorset.

3408 WY	2564	LD TRCTL11/3ARZ	Plaxton C53F	Summerfld,Southmpton 90
A820 RTP	9066	Leyland CU435	WS B32FL	New 84
F770 GNA	2567	LD TRCL10/3ARZM	Plaxton C53F	Shearings 770 97
G559 CEF	9015	CVE Omni	B16F	New 89
G560 CEF	9016	CVE Omni	B16F	New 89
G746 CEF	9025	CVE Omni	B16F	New 89
G747 CEF	9017	CVE Omni	B16F	New 89
G828 CEF	9021	CVE Omni	B14F	New 89
G829 CEF	9019	CVE Omni	B16F	New 89
G830 CEF	9018	CVE Omni	B16F	New 89
G831 CEF	9023	CVE Omni	B16F	New 89
G607 EDC	9096	CVE Omni	B14F	New 90
G609 EDC	9098	CVE Omni	B14F	New 90
G650 EVN	9029	CVE Omni	B14F	New 90

```
G900 NHG  2566  LD TRCTL11/3ARZ      Plaxton C53F       Walls,Higher Ince 97
G983 TSE  2565  LD TRCL10/3RZM       Plaxton C53F       Keir,Glass 96
G176 UWS  6503  Renault Master       Steedrive B16FL    New 89
J170 MNX  9077  Talbot Freeway       B16FL              New 91
K576 AVP  9036  Talbot Freeway       B16FL              New 93
K578 AVP  9049  Talbot Freeway       B16FL              New 93
K579 AVP  9053  Talbot Freeway       B16FL              New 93
K583 AVP  9055  Talbot Freeway       B16FL              New 93
K586 AVP  9059  Talbot Freeway       B16FL              New 93
K589 AVP  9065  Talbot Freeway       B9FL               New 93
L466 DOA  9152  Talbot Freeway       B9FL               New 94
L484 DOA  9151  Talbot Freeway       B9FL               New 94
L139 FOJ  9156  Talbot Freeway       B16FL              New 94
L618 VEU  6499  Renault Master       Atlas B14FL        New 94
M781 OOM  2651  Mercedes-Benz 609D   TBP B10FL          New 95
M782 OOM  2652  Mercedes-Benz 609D   TBP B8FL           New 95
N958 PCG  9159  Mercedes-Benz 609D   DC B16FL           New 95
N959 PCG  9160  Mercedes-Benz 609D   DC B16FL           New 95
N622 SOP  9158  Mercedes-Benz 609D   TBP B16FL          New 95
N626 SOP  9162  Mercedes-Benz 609D   TBP B16FL          New 95
N628 SOP  9106  Mercedes-Benz 609D   TBP B16FL          New 95
N631 SOP  9164  Mercedes-Benz 609D   TBP B16FL          New 95
N210 UFX  9174  Mercedes-Benz 609D   DC B15FL           New 96
N211 UFX  9172  Mercedes-Benz 609D   DC B15FL           New 96
N212 UFX  9173  Mercedes-Benz 609D   DC B15FL           New 96
N197 UUK  9165  Mercedes-Benz 609D   TBP B16FL          New 95
N208 UUK  9166  Mercedes-Benz 609D   TBP B16FL          New 95
N501 WOE  9167  Mercedes-Benz 609D   TBP B16FL          New 95
N502 WOE  9168  Mercedes-Benz 609D   TBP B16FL          New 95
N503 WOE  9169  Mercedes-Benz 609D   TBP B16FL          New 96
N504 WOE  9170  Mercedes-Benz 609D   TBP B16FL          New 96
N505 WOE  9171  Mercedes-Benz 609D   TBP B16FL          New 96
P389 BEL  9192  Mercedes-Benz 611D   Frank Guy B15FL New 97
P390 BEL  9190  Mercedes-Benz 611D   Frank Guy B15FL New 97
P391 BEL  9191  Mercedes-Benz 611D   Frank Guy B15FL New 97
P392 BEL  9193  Mercedes-Benz 611D   Frank Guy B15FL New 97
P393 BEL  9194  Mercedes-Benz 611D   Frank Guy B15FL New 97
P394 BEL  9195  Mercedes-Benz 611D   Frank Guy B15FL New 97
P395 BEL  9196  Mercedes-Benz 611D   Frank Guy B15FL New 97
P396 BEL  9199  Mercedes-Benz 611D   Frank Guy B15FL New 97
P341 DOF  9175  Mercedes-Benz 609D   TBP B16FL          New 96
P562 FDA  9176  Mercedes-Benz 609D   Frank Guy B15FL New 96
P563 FDA  9177  Mercedes-Benz 609D   Frank Guy B15FL New 96
P565 FDA  9179  Mercedes-Benz 609D   Frank Guy B15FL New 96
P567 FDA  9181  Mercedes-Benz 609D   Frank Guy B15FL New 96
P568 FDA  9182  Mercedes-Benz 609D   Frank Guy B15FL New 96
P777 TCC  2579  Dennis Javelin       Plaxton C53F       Memories,Stansted 01
P687 XLJ  9184  Mercedes-Benz 609D   DC B15FL           New 96
P688 XLJ  9185  Mercedes-Benz 609D   DC B15FL           New 96
P689 XLJ  9186  Mercedes-Benz 609D   DC B15FL           New 96
P690 XLJ  9187  Mercedes-Benz 609D   DC B15FL           New 96
P691 XLJ  9183  Mercedes-Benz 609D   DC B15FL           New 96
P692 XLJ  9188  Mercedes-Benz 609D   DC B15FL           New 96
P693 XLJ  9189  Mercedes-Benz 609D   DC B15FL           New 96
R179 TKU  2580  Dennis Javelin       Plaxton C53F       Memories,Stansted 01
T501 JEL  9130  Mercedes-Benz 310D   Frank Guy B10FL New 99
V968 DFX  9200  Mercedes-Benz 614D   Frank Guy B15FL New 99
V969 DFX  9201  Mercedes-Benz 614D   Frank Guy B15FL New 99
W253 RHT  6527  Renault Master       Atlas B14FL        New 00
HF51 AWA  9209  Fiat Ducato          Rohill B14F        New 01
HF51 AWC  9208  Fiat Ducato          Rohill B14F        New 01
HF51 AWG  9207  Fiat Ducato          Rohill B14F        New 01
HF51 AWH  9206  Fiat Ducato          Rohill B14F        New 01
HF51 AWM  9204  Fiat Ducato          Rohill B14F        New 01
HF51 AWN  9203  Fiat Ducato          Rohill B14F        New 01
HF51 AWO  9202  Fiat Ducato          Rohill B14F        New 01
HF51 AWS  9205  Fiat Ducato          Rohill B14F        New 01
```
~~~~~~
~~~~~~

93 DORSET QUEEN COACHES LTD

Depot:EAST CHALDON,Dorset.

TIL 3383	Bedford YNT	Plaxton C57F	R & R,Warminster 02
XAA 27V	Bedford YMT	Plaxton C53F	New 79
B184 TRU	Bedford YNT	Plaxton C53F	New 85
C195 CYO	Volvo B10M-61	Plaxton C53F	Tellings-GM,Byfleet 90
D280 JME	Volvo B10M-61	Plaxton C53F	Kim,Sandown 89
E753 WKB	Mercedes-Benz 609D	Coachcraft C20F	Cooper,Woolston 97
J511 LRY	Volvo B10M-60	Caetano C51FT	Harley &,Wednesford 93
P 8 RJH	Volvo B10M-62	Plaxton C49FT	New 97
W931 PPT	Volvo B10M-62	Plaxton C49FT	Dodds,Ashington 02
Y223 NYA	Mercedes-Benz O815D	Sitcar C27F	Moseley(Demonstrator) 02
HJ02 HCG	Volvo B10M-62	Plaxton C49FT	New 02

TIL 3383*B22 NKB(8/00) & LIL 9666(6/00) & B22 NKB(6/96) &
       A18 ALS(10/93) & B448 CMC(1/92)

94 G.A. DOUGLASS.t/a WESSEX BUS & WEYMOUTH BUS COMPANY

Depot:Unit 2,Class Body Works,Surrey Close,Granby Ind Est,WEYMOUTH,Dorset.

D463 CKV	Freight Rover Sherpa	Rootes B16F	Charlton,Weymouth 98
E654 DGW	Freight Rover Sherpa	Crystals B16F	Charlton,Weymouth 99
F949 CUA	Freight Rover Sherpa	Carlyle B20F	Charlton,Weymouth 98
G106 KUB	Mercedes-Benz 811D	Optare B31F	Stagecoach London SR106 01
J234 KDL	Iveco 49-10	CarChairs B22F	Southern Vectis 234 01
J238 KDL	Iveco 49-10	CarChairs B22F	Southern Vectis 238 01
J112 LKO	Iveco 49-10	Carlyle B25F	Turner,Chesham 01
K712 FNO	Iveco 59-12	Dormobile B31F	Arriva Shires 2332 01
K803 SKN	Ford Transit	CarChairs B10FL	LB Brent 484 02
K715 VNH	DAF 400	LCB B16F	Hall,Kennoway 02
L289 SEM	Iveco 49-10	WS B16FL	Liverpool City Council 01
L292 SEM	Iveco 49-10	WS B16FL	Liverpool City Council 01
L293 SEM	Iveco 49-10	WS B16FL	Liverpool City Council 01
P786 VYS	LDV Convoy	? B16F	Non-PSV 02

K712 FNO*K811 JKH(8/93)

95 C.J. & J.A. DOWN

Depot:Mary Tavy Garage,MARY TAVY,Devon.

IIL 6567	Bedford YMP	Plaxton C35F	Astra,Andoversford 01
JIL 3967	Bedford YRT	Duple C53F	Heard,Hartland 96
MIL 7609	Volvo B10M-61	Plaxton C57F	Richmond,Barley 99
MIL 7610	Bedford YMP	Plaxton C45F	Crudge,Honiton 98
NIL 4987	Ford R1115	Plaxton C35F	Redwood,Hemyock 01
NIL 4988	Volvo B58-56	Plaxton C49F	Crowther,Morley 87
RIB 5086	Volvo B10M-61	Plaxton C53F	Jackson,Castleford 01
RIL 4958	Volvo B10M-61	Duple C53F	Friend,Harrowbarrow 99
RIL 4960	Volvo B58-61	Duple C57F	Longstaff,Broomhill 86
RJI 4563	Volvo B10M-61	Plaxton C49FT	Expertpoint,Stratford 01
3271 CD	Volvo B10M-61	Plaxton C57F	Ford,Gunnislake 90
3504 CD	Volvo B10M-60	Plaxton C53F	MTL London VP332 97
3594 CD	Volvo B10M-61	Plaxton C53F	Kingdom,Tiverton 93
5448 CD	Volvo B10M-60	Plaxton C53F	Cambridge Coach Service 99
8405 CD	Volvo B10M-60	Plaxton C53F	MTL London VP336 97
8515 CD	Volvo B10M-61	Duple C57F	Wansbeck,Ashington 87
9891 CD	Volvo B10M-61	Plaxton C51F	Jennings,Bude 98
562 PTU	Bedford YMT	Duple C46FT	Friend,Harrowbarrow 99

IIL 6567*C441 WFO(9/93), JIL 3967*RTT 860N(8/96), MIL 7610*B560 DSE(1/98),
MIL 7609*RMH 868Y(11/99) & 668 PTM(11/99) & RMH 868Y(3/85),
NIL 4987*A35 AWA(10/01) & USV 620(9/01) & A35 AWA(9/96),
NIL 4988*KTA 630V(6/97) & 8405 CD(6/92) & DAX 451V(6/87),

```
RIB 5086*A652 UGD(6/01) & PJI 8364(10/98) & A652 UGD(10/94),
RIL 4958*HTT 225Y(9/99) & 3504 CD(4/95) & UCV 144Y(3/89) &
         EFH 295Y(9/88) & PSV 111(4/88) & DDD 311Y(2/85),
RIL 4960*KTA 953V(9/99) & 9891 CD(4/98) & KTA 565V(6/91) & 9891 CD(5/91) &
         LGB 851V(10/86), RJI 4563*E992 MHY(2/94),
3271 CD*A568 YGL(6/91) & 794 PAF(5/91) & A796 TGG(3/88),
3504 CD*43 FJF(1/98) & G43 RGG(12/94), 3594 CD*A653 UGD(5/93),
5448 CD*G97 RGG(2/00), 8405 CD*RIB 5086(10/97) & G86 RGG(10/94),
8515 CD*MCN 238X(10/97) & 8515 CD(9/97) & MCN 238X(4/87),
9891 CD*D808 SGB(4/98) & 562 PTU*NED 762W(8/83)
```

96   W.J.,W.M.,A.,V.F. & C. DOWN.t/a OTTER COACHES

Depot:1 Mill Street,OTTERY ST MARY,Devon.

EAZ 9056	Bedford YNT	Duple C53F	New 84
IUI 4166	Bedford YNT	Plaxton C53F	Cowdrey,Gosport 97
UIB 3169	Dennis Javelin	Plaxton C53F	Logan,Dunloy(NI) 94
VIL 1486	Dennis Javelin	Plaxton C53F	Richmond,Epsom 02
VJI 2997	Bedford YNT	Caetano C51F	New 87
F468 UPB	Toyota HB31R	Caetano C21F	Hodge,Sandhurst 95
G215 XOD	Dennis Javelin	Duple C39F	Yeates(Demonstrator) 90
P 32 EDV	Dennis Javelin	Caetano C53F	New 97
P470 JWB	Bova FLD12-270	C53F	Welsh,Upton 99
P964 YTA	Toyota HZB50R	Caetano C21F	New 96

```
EAZ 9056*B879 OLJ(5/95), IUI 4166*C563 DDV(3/98),
UIB 3169*MDZ 5489(4/94) & F385 MUT(9/92), VIL 1486*M332 MPG(4/02),
VJI 2997*E167 WOD(5/97) & F468 UPB*7107 PH(4/95)
```

97   A.P. DOWNTON.t/a DOWNTON TRAVEL

Address:5 Ackerman Road,DORCHESTER,Dorset.

D613 KJT	Volvo B10M-61	Plaxton C53F	Dorset Q.,East Chaldon 01
G301 CPL	Mercedes-Benz 811D	Optare DP29F	Pickford,Chippenham 02
G803 RDB	Ford Transit	Cunliffe DP16FL	Watts,Dorchester 95
R501 WJF	LDV Convoy	LDV B16F	Non-PSV(BCR) 00

```
D613 KJT*XEL 14(3/89) & D269 HFX(10/87) &
G301 CPL*PSV 444(10/01) & G301 CPL(9/00)
```

98   DUCHY TRAVEL LTD/TOWN & COUNTRY COACHES LTD

Depot:Unit 8b,Decoy Industrial Estate,Silverhills Road,NEWTON ABBOT,Devon.

JJI 5614	Volvo B10M-60	Van Hool C49FT	Chariots,Stanford-le-H. 00
LIL 6536	LAG Panoramic	C49FT	Redwood,Hemyock 99
MIJ 9795	Bova EL26/581	C53F	Cowdrey,Gosport 99
MIL 3292	Volvo B10M-61	Plaxton C49FT	Expertpoint,Stratford 00
PBZ 9154	Leyland PSU5C/4R	Duple C57F	Folland,Paignton 02
WDZ 5236	LAG Panoramic	C49FT	AJC,Leeds 00
XIB 5178	DAF MB200DKFL600	Caetano C53F	Pulham,Newton Abbot 99
MOU 739R	Bristol VRT/SL3/6LXB	ECW H43/28F	Cheltenham & Glou. 204 01
RAN 646R	Bristol VRT/SL3/6LXB	ECW H44/30F	Millmans,Newton Abbot 02
ESC 847S	Seddon Pennine 7	Alexander B51F	Millmans,Newton Abbot 98
ETA 874T	Ford R1114	Van Hool C53F	Coyne,Redruth 01
XCT 251T	Bedford YLQ	Plaxton C45F	Millward,Newton Abbot 99
DYW 167V	Volvo B58-56	Plaxton C53C	Edgecumbe,Sidmouth 02
LAK 304W	Leyland PSU3E/4R	Duple C53F	Treneary,Paignton 99
D101 PTT	Ford Transit	Mellor B16F	Patakis,Torquay 01
G265 GKG	Freight Rover Sherpa	Carlyle B20F	Sassarini,Wemyss Bay 96
G113 PGT	Mercedes-Benz 811D	Alexander B28F	Arriva Cymru MMM113 00
G837 UDV	Mercedes-Benz 811D	Carlyle B33F	Thames Transit 361 01
H652 DOD	Ford Transit	DC B8FL	LB Hammersmith & Fulham 98
H177 DVM	Volvo B10M-60	Van Hool C49FT	Ashby,Chingford 01

```
H987 FTT   Mercedes-Benz 811D   Carlyle B29F      Bluebird Buses 238 01
H989 FTT   Mercedes-Benz 811D   Carlyle B29F      Bluebird Buses 239 01
K597 EKU   Iveco 49-10          G & M B24FL       Non-PSV(Thrybergh) 97
M829 HNS   Volvo B10M-62        Van Hool C53F     Wood,Buckfastleigh 00
N  2 WKC   Kassbohrer S250      C48FT             Ashby,Chadwell Heath 01
```

```
JJI 5614*H176 DVM(7/01),
LIL 6536*F864 OFJ(7/99) & USV 577(11/97) & A8 SOL(3/97) & F618 VNH(12/91),
MIJ 9795*CAY 212Y(8/99),
MIL 3292*D100 GSG(4/96) & LS 8411(11/89) & D450 CSH(11/87),
PBZ 9154*HHG 193W(4/97), WDZ 5236*G957 GRP(3/00),
XIB 5178*B670 GBD(10/00),
ETA 874T*KIW 8606(4/02) & HVW 991T(7/90) & 214 TRT(11/87) &
          FHK 496T(2/84), DYW 167V*MIB 2963(1/00) & DYW 167V(7/89) &
M829 HNS*LSK 495(10/97)
```

99   DUKES TRAVEL LTD

Depot:Lakers Road,BERRY HILL,Gloucestershire.

```
FSU  803   Volvo B10M-61        Van Hool C53F     Barratt,Nantwich 95
666  VHU   Leyland RT           Van Hool C53F     Tellings-GM,Byfleet 92
WUH 171T   LN 11351A/1R         B52F              Jones,Llandeilo 01
B  6 GBD   Volvo B10M-61        Jonckheere C51FT  Morrow,Glasgow 95
F293 AWW   Leyland LX112        B49F              Arriva Cymru SLC293 00
H  4 GBD   Volvo B10M-62        Jonckheere C53F   Landtourers,Farnham 98
H  5 GBD   Volvo B10M-60        Plaxton C49FT     Shaw & Duffelen,Maxey 00
H  6 GBD   Volvo B12T           Jonckheere C53FT  Rossendale 01
H  7 GBD   Volvo B12T           Jonckheere C53FT  Rossendale 01
H  8 GBD   Volvo B10M-60        Berkhof C50FT     Cantabrica,St Albans 01
H  9 GBD   Mercedes-Benz 811D   ACL C33F          Taylor,Nine Wells 99
J302 BVO   DAF SB220LC550       Optare B49F       Trent 302 01
J303 BVO   DAF SB220LC550       Optare B49F       Trent 303 01
J304 BVO   DAF SB220LC550       Optare B49F       Trent 304 01
J305 BVO   DAF SB220LC550       Optare B49F       Trent 305 01
J177 MCW   Optare MR09          B26F              Ribble 677 98
K859 ODY   Mercedes-Benz 709D   Alexander B25F    Stagecoach South 859 02
K882 UDB   Mercedes-Benz 709D   Plaxton B27F      Arriva Cymru MMM782 01
K884 UDB   Mercedes-Benz 709D   Plaxton B27F      Arriva Cymru MMM784 01
Y201 KNB   Dennis Dart SLF      Alexander B38F    loan from Mistral
VX51 AMB   Optare Solo M920     B29F              loan from Mistral
```

```
FSU 803*A643 UGD(1/88), 666 VHU*B551 TWR(6/92),
WUH 171T*MIL 9313(2/99) & WUH 171T(12/96),
B6 GBD*216 TYC(3/00) & E218 GNV(8/95),
H4 GBD*676 GBD(1/01) & L754 YGE(3/98), H5 GBD*J427 HDS(4/00),
H6 GBD*M26 HNY(1/01), H7 GBD*M27 HNY(2/01), H8 GBD*K900 CCH(10/01) &
H9 GBD*J673 MFH(9/99)
```

J.R. & B.M. DURBIN.t/a SOUTH GLOUCESTERSHIRE BUS & COACH

Depot:Station Road,PATCHWAY,Gloucestershire.

```
BHZ 6984   Dennis Lance         NC B48F           Tayside 106 01
BHZ 6985   Dennis Lance         Plaxton B47F      Tayside 107 01
BHZ 6986   Leyland LX112        B47F              Brighton & Hove 186 00
BHZ 6987   Leyland LX112        B47F              Brighton & Hove 185 00
ENH  634   Volvo B10M-61        Van Hool C53F     Eastville,Bristol 96
ESK  812   Volvo B10M-61        Van Hool C48FT    First Bristol 2502 01
OIL 9262   Leyland TRCTL11/3RH  Plaxton C53F      First Bristol 8212 01
OIL 9263   Leyland TRCTL11/3RH  Plaxton C53F      First Bristol 8213 01
OIL 9264   Leyland TRCTL11/3RH  Plaxton C53F      First Bristol 8214 01
PSU  527   Volvo B10M-61        Van Hool C49FT    First Bristol 2510 01
YYD  699   Volvo B10M-61        Plaxton C51F      Eastville,Bristol 96
FFR 165S   Bristol VRT/SL3/6LXB ECW H43/34F       Eastville,Bristol 98
GYE 261W   Leyland TNLXB/2RR    Leyland H44/26D   Baldock,Five Oak Green 00
OFS 668Y   Leyland ONTL11/2R    ECW H50/31D       Lothian 668 00
```

```
OHV 766Y   Leyland TNLXB/2RR    Leyland H44/23D    Go Ahead London T766 00
OHV 798Y   Leyland TNLXB/2RR    Leyland H44/24D    Trustline,Potters Bar 00
A892 SYE   Leyland TNLXB/2RR    Leyland H44/26D    Go Ahead London T892 00
A943 SYE   Leyland TNLXB/2RR    Leyland H44/26D    Go Ahead London T943 00
B883 YTC   Leyland TRCTL11/3LZ  WS DP68FA          MOD 99
C681 EHU   Leyland TRCTL11/3LZ  WS DP54FA          MOD 98
C822 EHU   Leyland TRCTL11/3LZ  WS DP68FA          MOD 99
C 28 EUH   Leyland ONTL11/2R    EL CH47/31F        First Bristol 5000 01
C 29 EUH   Leyland ONTL11/2R    EL CH47/31F        First Bristol 5001 01
F538 LUF   Leyland LX112        B47F               Brighton & Hove 178 00
F544 LUF   Leyland LX112        B47F               Brighton & Hove 184 00
G107 EOG   Leyland LX2R         B49F               West Midlands 1107 01
G174 EOG   Leyland LX2R         B49F               West Midlands 1174 01
G177 EOG   Leyland LX2R         B49F               West Midlands 1177 01
G296 EOG   Leyland LX2R         B49F               West Midlands 1296 01
G823 KWF   Mercedes-Benz 811D   RB B31F            East Midland 723 01
G827 KWF   Mercedes-Benz 811D   RB B31F            East Midland 727 01
G900 TJA   Mercedes-Benz 811D   Mellor B16FL       Arriva Midlands Nth 450 00
G840 UDV   Mercedes-Benz 811D   Carlyle B33F       Thames Transit 364 00
G992 VWV   Leyland LX112        B47F               Brighton & Hove 192 01
G993 VWV   Leyland LX112        B47F               Brighton & Hove 193 01
H544 FWM   Leyland LX2R         B51F               Halton 51 00
H422 GPM   Mercedes-Benz 709D   Phoenix B27F       Tillingbourne,Cranleigh 00
H 34 HBG   Leyland LX2R         B51F               Halton 11 00
J297 NNB   Mercedes-Benz 709D   Plaxton B27F       Arriva Cymru MMM297 01
J236 NNC   Volvo B10M-60        Van Hool C49FT     Shearings 236 99
J237 NNC   Volvo B10M-60        Van Hool C49FT     Shearings 237 99
J430 PPF   Mercedes-Benz 709D   Dormobile B29F     Tillingbourne,Cranleigh 00
J988 TVU   Mercedes-Benz 709D   Plaxton B23F       Crichton,Felling 02
J606 WHJ   Mercedes-Benz 811D   Plaxton B28F       Arriva London MD606 00
K239 FAW   Mercedes-Benz 811D   Plaxton B31F       Arriva North West 171 01
K326 PHT   Dennis Javelin       WS DP54FA          MOD 00
K327 PHT   Dennis Javelin       WS DP70FA          MOD 00
K329 PHT   Dennis Javelin       WS DP70FA          MOD 00
K695 RNR   Toyota HDB30R        Caetano C21F       First Bristol 8316 01
K371 RTY   Dennis Dart          Wright B40F        Go North East 8071 02
K879 UDB   Mercedes-Benz 709D   Plaxton B27F       Arriva Cymru MMM879 01
L778 RWW   Mercedes-Benz 811D   Plaxton B31F       Arriva North West 118 02
L779 RWW   Mercedes-Benz 811D   Plaxton B31F       Arriva North West 119 02
M 87 DEW   Dennis Dart          Marshall B40F      Halton 66 00
M 46 POL   Mercedes-Benz 811D   Plaxton B31F       Chambers,Bures 02
```
~~~~~~

EASTVILLE COACHES LTD(Associated Company)

Depot:Albert Crescent,St Phillips,BRISTOL.

```
HIL 3188   Leyland ONTL11/2RH   EL CH47/31F        Shuttle,Kilwinning 98
KUI 8150   Volvo B12T           VH CH57/16CT       Bakers,Weston-s-Mare 01
PJI 5013   Volvo B10M-60        Van Hool C57F      Ede,Par 92
PJI 5016   Volvo B10M-60        Van Hool C57F      New 89
TPD 120X   Leyland ONTL11/1R    Roe H43/29F        Londonlinks LR20 97
TPD 125X   Leyland ONTL11/1R    Roe H43/29F        Londonlinks LR25 97
BPF 131Y   Leyland ONTL11/1R    Roe H43/29F        Sovereign 31 98
C 30 EUH   Leyland ONTL11/2R    EL CH47/31F        Stephenson,Rochford 98
M861 TYC   Volvo B10M-62        Van Hool C53F      Chalfont,Southall 98
M862 TYC   Volvo B10M-62        Van Hool C53F      Chalfont,Southall 01
M419 VYD   Volvo B10M-62        Van Hool C53F      New 95
N 24 EYB   Volvo B10M-62        Van Hool C53F      New 96
```
~~~~~~
```
BHZ 6984*J215 OCW(7/01), BHZ 6985*J120 SPF(7/01), BHZ 6986*F546 LUF(7/01),
BHZ 6987*F545 LUF(12/01), ENH 634*MSU 613Y(6/85), ESK 812*D502 GHY(8/00),
HIL 3188*D888 YHG(6/91), KUI 8150*M415 VYD(?/01), OIL 9262*F615 XWY(5/98),
OIL 9263*F617 XWY(5/98), OIL 9264*F620 XWY(5/98), PJI 5013*F533 WGL(3/93),
PJI 5016*G965 UHU(4/93), PSU 527*D510 HHW(8/95), YYD 699*E576 UHS(12/95),
H544 FWM*BHZ 6987(12/01) & H544 FWM(7/01),
J988 TVU*J7 SLT(2/96) & J58 MHF(8/92), K239 FAW*K1 SLT(10/01),
K695 RNR*SSU 437(9/01) & K695 RNR(8/99) &
M87 DEW*BHZ 6988(10/01) & M87 DEW(7/01)
```
~~~~~~

A2   N.A. EASTWOOD

Depot:r/o Becks Fish & Chip Shop,Longstone Hill,CARBIS BAY,Cornwall.

```
JIL 7714   Mercedes-Benz 609D    North West C24F   Perry,Bromyard 142 01
G713 HOP   Mercedes-Benz 709D    Carlyle B29F      Perry,Bromyard 158 01
G717 HOP   Mercedes-Benz 709D    Carlyle B25F      Perry,Bromyard 156 01
L189 DDW   Optare MR15           B31F              Cardiff 189 01
L611 WCC   Volkswagen LT55       Optare B25F       Monetgrange,Nottingham 98
L612 WCC   Volkswagen LT55       Optare B25F       Monetgrange,Nottingham 98
```
JIL 7714*E900 ASU(7/00)

M.N.,J.P.,A.B. & P.D. EDE & K.A. PARAMOR.t/a ROSELYN COACHES

Depot:Middleway Garage,St Blazey Road,PAR,Cornwall.

```
YOR  456   DAF MB200DKTL600       Plaxton C57F       Ford,Gunnislake 95
237  AJB   Volvo B10M-61          Van Hool C57F      New 88
239  AJB   Volvo B58-56           Plaxton C53F       New 81
241  AJB   Volvo B10M-61          Plaxton C53F       Guideissue,Biddulph 11 95
244  AJB   Volvo B10M-60          Plaxton C50F       Turner,Bristol 01
728  FDV   Volvo B10M-61          Plaxton C53F       Moffat &,Gauldry 96
AFH 390T   Bedford YMT            Duple C53F         Prout,Port Isaac 95
AJH 854T   Bristol VRT/SL3/6LXB   ECW H41/34F        Berry,Taunton 01
BCV  91T   Bristol VRT/SL3/6LXB   ECW H43/31F        Stagecoach South 786 95
BKH 981T   Bristol VRT/SL3/501    ECW H43/31F        East Yorkshire 981 96
BKH 983T   Bristol VRT/SL3/501    ECW H43/31F        East Yorkshire 983 96
XAN  48T   Bristol VRT/SL3/6LXB   ECW H43/34F        Berry,Taunton 99
ATK 153W   Leyland AN68B/1R       EL H43/28D         Plymouth 153 01
ATK 156W   Leyland AN68B/1R       EL H43/28D         Plymouth 156 00
ATK 157W   Leyland AN68B/1R       EL H43/28D         Plymouth 157 00
HUD 495W   Bristol VRT/SL3/6LXB   ECW H43/27D        Arriva Cymru DVG495 98
HUD 501W   Bristol VRT/SL3/6LXB   ECW H43/27D        Arriva Cymru DVG501 98
M325 KRY   Volvo B10M-62          Jonckheere C51FT   Clarke,Lower Sydenham 01
M 34 TRR   Volvo B10M-62          Plaxton C49FT      Skill,Nottingham 34 02
```
YOR 456*LWS 116Y(3/96) & 6130 EL(9/95) & LWS 116Y(9/84),
237 AJB*E44 SAF(2/94), 239 AJB*KAF 129W(8/88),
241 AJB*E803 NVT(9/96) & 9995 RU(10/95), 244 AJB*L939 NWW(1/02),
728 FDV*B211 YSL(9/96) & BSK 789(11/95) & B706 WUA(7/91) &
BCV 91T*AET 186T(2/98)

A4   A.A. & M.G. ELLISON

Depot:High Road,ASHTON KEYNES,Wiltshire.

```
PE  4134   Dennis Javelin        Auwaerter C53F     New 98
PIW 5455   Bova EL26/581         C53F               Byles,Kidlington 02
OMR 221R   Bedford YLQ           Duple C45F         New 77
VCG 127R   Bedford YMT           Duple C53F         Budden,Woodfalls 88
WAM 519T   Bedford YMT           Duple C53F         New 78
NJT 123W   Bedford YMT           Duple C53F         New 81
UJT 987X   Bedford YMT           Plaxton C53F       New 82
FYD 523Y   Bedford YNT           Duple C53F         Vince,Burghclere 95
B205 FMW   Leyland TRCTL11/3R     Duple C53F         New 84
D 12 ELL   Duple 425             C57F               New 90
D 14 ELL   Duple 425             C55FT              Chapman,Airdrie 95
E941 BHR   Dennis Javelin        Duple C57F         New 88
H202 TCP   DAF SB2305DHS585      Duple C53FT        Hallam,Newthorpe 93
M 85 FMR   Dennis Javelin        Plaxton C36FT      New 95
N  8 HMC   Dennis Javelin        Auwaerter C50FT    Camden,West Kingsdown 01
P212 RWR   Dennis Dart           Plaxton B40F       Barwick &,Cawood 98
T 14 ELL   Dennis Javelin        Auwaerter C53F     New 99
W 14 ELL   Dennis Javelin        Auwaerter C48FT    New 00
OO02 ELL   Dennis Javelin        Auwaerter C53F     New 02
```

```
PE 4134*R271 THL(4/98),
PIW 5545*EGV 587Y(2/95) & 5611 PP(10/94) & FUA 400Y(3/88),
D12 ELL*G477 THR(5/02), D14 ELL*G471 OGG(5/02), W14 ELL*W393 PHU(3/00) &
OO02 ELL*YR02 UOH(4/02)
```

E. & C.M. ENDICOTT.t/a DARTINGTON & TOTNES OMNIBUS COMPANY

Depot:Station Yard,TOTNES,Devon.

```
RIL 1841   DAF SB2300DHS585   Jonckheere C51FT  Wilkinson,Easteigh 02
URL 375Y   DAF SB2300DHS585   Berkhof C53F      Baker,Duloe 00
E276 DDV   Dennis Javelin     Duple C53FT       Wellington,Kingsbridge 99
H236 RUX   Duple 425          C55F              Williamson,Oswestry 01
```
```
RIL 1841*E500 KNV(12/98) & SIW 1936(10/98) & E500 KNV(6/96) &
URL 375Y*XSU 761(8/00) & KNO 220Y(1/92)
```

A6   EUROTAXIS (BRISTOL) LTD

Depot:Jorrocks Industrial Estate,WESTERLEIGH,Gloucestershire.

```
A513 VKG   Leyland ONLXB/1R       EL H43/31F      L Munden,Bristol 99
D215 GHY   Leyland TRCTL11/3RZ    Plaxton DP55FA  MOD 99
E954 YGA   Mercedes-Benz 609D     Robin Hood C24F Manchester City Council 96
F425 JFT   Mercedes-Benz 507D     Cunliffe B16FL  Manchester City Council 98
F278 LND   Mercedes-Benz L307D    NC B12FL        G. Manchester D-a-R 98
G 90 HJC   Mercedes-Benz 609D     MM C24F         Jones,Bontnewydd 96
G258 UFB   Mercedes-Benz 408D     DC C15F         New 88
G629 XWS   Leyland TRCTL11/3LZM   Plaxton DP68FA  MOD 97
G783 XWS   Leyland TRCTL11/3RZM   Plaxton DP55FA  MOD 98
G828 XWS   Leyland TRCTL11/3RZM   Plaxton DP54FA  MOD 98
G524 YAE   Leyland TRCTL11/3RZM   Plaxton DP68FA  MOD 00
G525 YAE   Leyland TRCTL11/3RZM   Plaxton DP68FA  MOD 00
H338 FLH   Mercedes-Benz 308D     PG B10FL        London Dial A Ride 98
H606 GLT   Mercedes-Benz 308D     PG B6FL         London Dial A Ride 98
H 82 PTG   Mercedes-Benz 811D     Optare B33F     Walsh,Middleton 97
H476 VDM   Mercedes-Benz 408D     ? B8FL          Cresswell,Castleford 99
J321 MLF   Mercedes-Benz 308D     PG B8FL         Beeston,Hadleigh 01
J253 TDA   Mercedes-Benz 410D     DC B8FL         WMSNT,Birmingham 01
K271 BRJ   Dennis Javelin         WS DP36FA       Bennett,Hayes End 00
K497 OSU   Mercedes-Benz 709D     LCB B24FL       E Dunbartonshire Coun. 01
K998 WNC   Mercedes-Benz 410D     MM C16F         New 92
L 24 FNC   Mercedes-Benz 410D     DC B14FL        G. Manchester D-a-R 01
L703 JSC   Mercedes-Benz 410D     DC B16FL        Ferguson,East Whitburn 00
L340 NMV   Mercedes-Benz 308D     PG B8F          Non-PSV(Gatwick) 97
L 3 RDC    Mercedes-Benz 814D     ACL C33F        Reynolds &,Bushey 98
M 45 GRY   Mercedes-Benz 811D     Mellor DP33F    New 94
M 46 GRY   Mercedes-Benz 811D     Mellor DP33F    New 94
M 47 GRY   Mercedes-Benz 811D     Mellor DP33F    New 94
M 48 GRY   Mercedes-Benz 811D     Mellor DP33F    New 94
M646 OOM   Mercedes-Benz 410D     TBP B12FL       WMSNT,Birmingham 02
M778 PDC   Mercedes-Benz 609D     ACL DP24F       Bradshaw,Heywood 98
M675 TNA   Mercedes-Benz 709D     Mellor B27F     New 95
M676 TNA   Mercedes-Benz 709D     Mellor B27F     New 94
N990 AEF   Mercedes-Benz 814L     Buscraft C31F   Fairley,Tudhoe 01
N541 BFY   Mercedes-Benz 410D     Concept C15F    New 96
N542 BFY   Mercedes-Benz 410D     Concept C15F    New 96
N543 BFY   Mercedes-Benz 410D     Concept C15F    New 96
P473 MNA   Mercedes-Benz 312D     Mellor B12F     Non-PSV(Staines) 00
P474 MNA   Mercedes-Benz 312D     Mellor B12F     Non-PSV(Staines) 00
P183 RSC   Mercedes-Benz 614D     Aitken C24F     Haggis,Edinburgh 99
R583 DYG   Mercedes-Benz 614D     Crest C24F      Haggis,Edinburgh 00
R 35 WDA   Mercedes-Benz O814D    ACL C33F        British Telecom 98
S234 FGD   Mercedes-Benz 614D     Crest C24F      Haggis,Edinburgh 99
W953 WDS   Mercedes-Benz 412D     Stuart C16F     Collison,Stonehouse 01
X314 HOU   Mercedes-Benz O814D    Eurocoach C24F  McGinn,Ballycastle(NI) 01
```

A7   D.O. FIELD.t/a DAVID FIELD TRAVEL & FIELDS OF NEWPORT

Depot:Stoney Road Garage,KILCOT,Gloucestershire.

```
  2  DOF   Kassbohrer S215H        C48F              Tellings-GM,Byfleet 94
  4  DOF   Leyland TRCTL11/3RZ     Plaxton C53F      Tate,Markyate 99
ABM 470A   Leyland PSU3D/4R        Plaxton C47DL     Hadley,West Bridgford 94
DOF   1V   Mercedes-Benz 609D      RB C23F           Welcome,Stratford 94
CAB   2W   Bedford VAS5            Plaxton C29FL     James,Sherston 96
KBM  14Y   Leyland TRCTL11/3R      Plaxton C57F      Cottrell,Mitcheldean 95
F898 XOE   Fiat 49-10              Carlyle C25F      Davies,Ebbw Vale 90
```
~~~~~~
```
2 DOF*B52 MPM(4/94),
4 DOF*CAZ 3687(4/99) & RJI 6239(1/96) & B508 UNB(4/94),
ABM 470A*SDD 147R(4/85), DOF 1V*E670 HWK(3/94) & CAB 2W*A763 YAB(4/92)
```
~~~~~~

A8   P.M. & V. FILER

Depot:The Old Colliery,Wick Lane,STANTON WICK,Somerset.

```
PJI 8360   DAF MB200DKFL600         Duple C57F        Corfield,Ashton-U-Lyne 94
PJI 8361   Volvo B10M-61           Van Hool C57F     Smith-Shearings 316 90
PJI 8362   Volvo B10M-61           Van Hool C53F     Smith-Shearings 272 90
XYC  561   Volvo B10M-60           Jonckheere C51FT  Taylor,Sutton Scotney 96
G426 NGE   Mercedes-Benz 408D      Scott C16F        Irvine,Glenluce 99
H633 UWR   Volvo B10M-60           Plaxton C53F      Woodstone,Kidderminster 98
L530 XUT   Volvo B10M-60           Jonckheere C51FT  Q Drive,Battersea 99
M822 HNS   Volvo B10M-62           Van Hool C57F     Armchair,Brentford 02
```
~~~~~~
```
PJI 8360*B295 DYS(9/95), PJI 8361*B316 UNB(8/94), PJI 8362*A193 MNE(4/93),
XYC 561*H47 VNH(8/95) & M822 HNS*LSK 501(10/97)
```
~~~~~~

A9   R.J. & I.H. FILER.t/a FILERS TRAVEL

Depot:Slade Lodge,Slade Road,ILFRACOMBE,Devon.

```
MIL 9750   Volvo B10M-61           Caetano C53F      Jennings,Bude 98
MIL 9751   Volvo B10M-56           Plaxton C53F      Harding,Bagborough 95
RJI 8606   Volvo B10M-60           Plaxton C53F      Baker,Weston-S-Mare 17 98
946  WAE   Bedford SB5             Farrar O16/18RO   Farrar,Fraddon 93
D128 HML   Mercedes-Benz 709D      RB B24F           Skinner & Harvey,Oxted 94
K537 CWN   DAF SB3000DKVF601       Caetano C49FT     D Coaches,Morriston 02
K539 CWN   DAF SB3000DKVF601       Caetano C49FT     Pointmost,Plymouth 02
K339 EJV   Mercedes-Benz 609D      ACL C21F          Harvey,North Bovey 95
K332 YDW   Bova FHD12-290          C53FT             Thomas,Porth 99
L336 DTG   Bova FHD12-290          C53FT             Thomas,Porth 99
M823 HNS   Volvo B10M-62           Van Hool C53F     Armchair,Brentford 01
M825 HNS   Volvo B10M-62           Van Hool C53F     Armchair,Brentford 01
N751 DAK   Bova FHD12-340          C49FT             Dunn-Line,Nottingham 01
T825 OBL   Volkswagen LT35         ? B ?F            Non-PSV 01
V957 EOD   Mercedes-Benz 614D      G & M C24F        New 99
```
~~~~~~
```
N.B.:- 946 WAE has a replica London General 'B' Type body built in 1990
```
~~~~~~
```
MIL 9750*C681 KDS(12/01), MIL 9751*JYD 877Y(3/02),
RJI 8606*G261 JCY(2/94), M823 HNS*LSK 497(10/97) & M825 HNS*LSK 498(10/97)
```
~~~~~~

C1   D.J. FOLLAND.t/a RIVIERA COACH & MINIBUS HIRE

Depot:Unit 11,Castleport Industrial Estate,Alders Way,PAIGNTON,Devon.

```
C631 BEX   Freight Rover Sherpa    Dormobile B16F    Facey,Torquay 98
C911 DVF   Ford R1115              Plaxton C35F      Andrews,Trudoxhill 97
C708 FFJ   Ford Transit            Robin Hood B16F   Hearn,Stibb Cross 01
D586 EWS   Freight Rover Sherpa    Dormobile B16F    Searle,Seaton 01
```

```
D 75 YRF   Freight Rover Sherpa Dormobile B16F    Facey,Torquay 98
G264 GKG   Freight Rover Sherpa Carlyle B20F      Duchy,Newton Abbot 01
```
~~~~~~
```
C911 DVF*KAC 1(8/88)
```
~~~~~~

C2   B.A. FORWARD.t/a FORWARD TRAVEL

Depot:r/o Texaco Garage,SAMPFORD PEVERELL,Devon.

```
MIL 9574   Dennis Javelin        Plaxton C53FT      Brighton & Hove 504 99
VPH  900   Kassbohrer S215HR     C49FT              National Holidays 01
VJT 458S   Bedford YLQ           Plaxton C45F       Wellington,Kingsbridge 02
TND 125X   Volvo B58-61          Duple C53F         Jackman,Willand 02
D101 LTA   Dodge S56             RB DP25F           Goodwin,Witheridge 01
D753 RTT   Fiat 49-10            Robin Hood B25F    Edgecumbe,Sidmouth 02
G526 PDH   DAF 400               Commercial C16F    Non-PSV(Exbridge) 01
K771 MAE   Toyota HDB30R         Caetano C18F       Halford,Bridport 99
```
~~~~~~
```
MIL 9574*F504 LAP(10/96), VPH 900*G715 TTY(4/02) &
TND 125X*585 RCV(4/02) & TND 125X(5/88)
```
~~~~~~

C3   R.A.F. & M. FOSTER.t/a AVALON COACHES

Depot:Northload Garage,Northload Road,GLASTONBURY,Somerset.

```
F542 HYD   Dennis Javelin        Plaxton C53F       New 89
G519 EFX   Volvo B10M-60         Plaxton C53F       Excelsior,Bournemouth 92
M215 UYD   Volvo B10M-62         Van Hool C53F      New 95
N132 BYD   LDV 400               ACL C16F           New 95
N757 CYA   Volvo B10M-62         Van Hool C53F      New 96
P403 CTA   Volvo B10M-62         Van Hool C57F      New 97
P719 JYA   Bova FLD12-270        C49FT              New 96
R355 AYC   Mercedes-Benz O814D   Plaxton C33F       New 98
R526 WYB   Dennis Javelin        Plaxton C57F       New 97
V543 DYA   Volvo B10M-62         Van Hool C53F      New 00
X584 BYD   Bova FHD12-340        C53F               New 00
AV51 AVA   Volvo B12M            Van Hool C57F      New 02
```
~~~~~~
~~~~~~

C4   FROME MINIBUSES LTD

Depot:Georges Ground,FROME,Somerset.

```
G217 EOA   Freight Rover Sherpa  Carlyle B20F       Halford,Bridport 01
H402 XTU   Mercedes-Benz 609D    North West C19F    Rimmer,Runcorn 97
L108 UHF   Ford Transit          Whitacre B11F      Coombs,Weston-s-Mare 99
M851 RAW   LDV 400               LDV B16F           Non-PSV 96
M349 XHY   Mercedes-Benz 711D    ACL C24F           James,Tetbury 98
N617 ESN   Mercedes-Benz 711D    Plaxton C25F       Logan,Dunloy(NI) 01
T 46 KYB   Mercedes-Benz 614D    Onyx C24F          New 99
W631 SYC   Mercedes-Benz O814D   ACL DP31F          New 00
WU51 CZC   Mercedes-Benz 413CDI  Onyx C16F          New 01
WV02 BEY   Mercedes-Benz 413CDI  Onyx C16F          New 02
```
~~~~~~
```
L108 UHF*L108 SKB(12/94) & M349 XHY*M30 ARJ(6/98)
```
~~~~~~

C5   GARRETTS COACHES LTD

Depot:Silverwood Garage,St. Marychurch Road,Milber,NEWTON ABBOT,Devon.

```
F545 HTA   Mercedes-Benz L307D   DC C12F            Millmans,Newton Abbot 99
T 91 EFJ   Bova FHD12-340        C49FT              New 99
W646 STA   Bova FHD12-370        C49FT              New 00
Y626 FOD   Bova FHD12-370        C49FT              New 01
```

```
PG51 GAR  Bova FHD12-340        C49FT          New 02
```
~~~~~~
```
PG51 GAR*WA51 JYN(3/02)
```
~~~~~~

C6   R.J. & Y. GERRY.t/a RAYS COACHES

Depot:32 Recreation Road Business Park,Beacon Park,PLYMOUTH,Devon.

```
PRF 361W  Fiat 60-10             Harwin C25F          Battams,Teignmouth 98
SWW 187W  Fiat 55-10             Caetano C18F         Western National 563 89
C875 ARJ  Freight Rover Sherpa   Dixon Lomas C16F     Evans,Tregaron 96
D947 ARE  Mercedes-Benz 609D     PMT C26F             Trollope,Salisbury 99
D509 MJA  Fiat 49-10             Robin Hood B21F      Evans,Tregaron 01
D572 MNK  Fiat 35-8              G & M C16F           Wood,Buckfastleigh 96
D915 MVU  Freight Rover Sherpa   Dixon Lomas C16F     Kerswell,Plymouth 97
D809 PUK  Freight Rover Sherpa   Carlyle B18F         Evans,Tregaron 95
G216 EOA  Freight Rover Sherpa   Carlyle B20F         Evans,Tregaron 00
H491 BND  Mercedes-Benz 811D     MM C26F              Browne,Yiewsley 98
J573 JUY  MAN 10.180             Jonckheere C32FT     Davis,Minchinhampton 01
```
~~~~~~
OTHER VEHICLE OWNED BY THE COMPANY
* * * * * * *
```
KMW 361X  Fiat 60-10             Caetano C-F          Office
```
~~~~~~
```
J573 JUY*2052 NF(7/01) & 3672 AD(7/01) & J695 LPX(7/00) & HIL 7978(8/99)
```
~~~~~~

C7   GLENVIC OF BRISTOL LTD

Depot:The Old Colliery,Wick Lane,STANTON WICK,Somerset.

```
NIL 8254  Leyland AN68B/1R       NC H43/32F           Mayne,Clayton 7 99
NIL 8255  Leyland ONLXB/1R       ECW H45/32F          East Midland 301 01
NIL 8259  Leyland ONLXB/1R       ECW H45/32F          East Midland 304 01
SAZ 3952  Leyland TRCTL11/3RH    Plaxton C53F         James,Tetbury 96
TIL 3866  Mercedes-Benz 709D     Alexander DP25F      Bevan,Lydney 02
TIL 4679  Leyland TRCTL11/3R     Plaxton C53F         Blagdon Lioness 01
NHL 305X  Leyland ONLXB/1R       ECW H45/32F          East Midland 305 01
SND 489X  Leyland AN68A/1R       NC H43/32F           Mayne,Clayton 18 99
A 16 GVC  Mercedes-Benz 609D     Whittaker C24F       Bevan,Lydney 96
M272 POS  Volvo B10M-62          Jonckheere C51FT     MCT,Motherwell 02
Y153 EAY  Volvo B7R              Plaxton C55F         New 01
```
~~~~~~
```
NIL 8254*SND 476X(9/97), NIL 8255*NHL 301X(?/02), NIL 8259*NHL 304X(?/02),
SAZ 3952*A112 TRP(8/98), TIL 3866*G71 APO(2/02), TIL 4679*A443 RYC(6/01),
SND 489X*NIL 8255(?/02) & SND 489X(9/97), A16 GVC*E735 VWJ(11/96) &
M272 POS*M1 MCT(3/02) & M272 POS(5/99)
```
~~~~~~

C8   J.W.G. GODDARD & D.R. TWEEDIE.t/a A-LINE COACHES

Depot:Gallows Park,MILLBROOK,Cornwall.

```
SUJ 434X  DAF MB200DKTL600       Jonckheere C49FT     Ellis & Swain,Coventry 95
C344 FTT  Bedford YNV            Caetano C53F         Keech,Rousdon 01
D397 SGS  Freight Rover Sherpa   Dormobile B16F       Country Bus,Atherington 89
E510 TOV  Fiat 49-10             Carlyle B25F         Lawrence,Weston-s-Mare 01
E801 WDV  Ford Transit           Mellor B16F          Stagecoach Devon 262 97
```
~~~~~~
```
SUJ 434X*FO 8933(6/93) & XAY 858X(1/88) & 6037 PP(10/86)
```
~~~~~~

C9   R. GOULDEN.t/a COASTLINE COACHES

Depot:Unit 1,Kings Hill Industrial Estate,BUDE,Cornwall.

D102 LTA	Dodge S56	RB B23F	Filer,Ilfracombe 97
D103 LTA	Dodge S56	RB B23F	Filer,Ilfracombe 97
D114 LTA	Dodge S56	RB B23F	Pickford,Chippenham 98
G182 PAO	Mercedes-Benz 709D	Alexander B23F	Ribble 582 01
H162 DAP	DAF 400	Dormobile B20F	Halford,Bridport 01

D1   A.K. GRIFFITHS.t/a AD-RAINS

Address:Lynton,Washpool,BRINKWORTH,Wiltshire.

LUI 4655	Leyland TRCTL11/3RZ	Plaxton C53F	Taylor,Meppershall 01
PIB 8117	Leyland LBM	RB B39F	Derbyshire CC 01
RIL 4961	Leyland TRCTL	Plaxton C53F	? 01
TIB 4947	MAN SR280	C53F	Stoneman,Nanpean 00
BTX 182T	Leyland PSU5C/4R	Plaxton C57F	Anslow,Pontypool 97
NCW 151T	Leyland PSU3E/2R	Duple B55F	Warstone,Great Wyrley 1 98
E667 JAD	MCW Metrorider MF150	B23F	APL,Crudwell 01
E200 TUE	MCW Metrorider MF150	B23F	Perry,Bromyard 137 00

LUI 4655*C806 FMC(?/02) & 93 JNM(8/01) & C806 FMC(3/90),
PIB 8117*   ? (?/01), RIL 4961* ? (?/01),
TIB 4947*KTA 665V(4/94) & 7646 RU(4/94) & JLS 3V(3/93) &
BTX 182T*IIB 9140(2/97) & DDG 260T(4/88)

D2   G.N.F. GRIGG

Depot:Old Pottery Garage,Shave Lane,HORTON,Somerset.

LUI 4658	Volvo B10M-61	Berkhof C53F	Heath,Wem 02
SJI 7467	Bova FLD12-250	C53F	Cowdrey,Gosport 94
F590 PSE	Dennis Javelin	Duple C57F	Mayne,Buckie 90
G423 WFP	Bova FHD12-290	C55F	Cowdrey,Gosport 01
P915 KKY	Mercedes-Benz 412D	Crest C15F	Non-PSV(Van) 98

OTHER VEHICLE OWNED BY THE COMPANY
* * * * * * *

JUR 599G	Bedford VAM70	Duple C-F	Storeshed

LUI 4658*A583 RVW(?/02) & MIB 899(5/01) & A583 RVW(2/89) &
SJI 7467*C550 WAC(11/94)

D3   GRINDLES COACHES LTD

Depot:Forest Vale Road,CINDERFORD,Gloucestershire.

NJI 8067	DAF MB200DKFL600	Plaxton C53F	Rowland &,Hastings 21 91
EPC 909V	Bedford YMT	Plaxton C53F	Hollowell,Yielden 86
GHE 844V	Bedford YMT	Plaxton C53F	Scott,Ravenfield 98
D217 YCW	DAF MB230DKFL615	Van Hool C51FT	Ribblesdale,Gt. Harwood 93
F225 YHG	DAF MB230LT615	Van Hool C51FT	Ribblesdale,Gt. Harwood 97
N119 FHK	Kassbohrer S250	C48FT	Staines,Clacton 02

NIJ 8067*KDY 888Y(6/90), GHE 844V*893 KM(5/93) & JTM 110V(12/89) &
D217 YCW*3935 PG(4/98) & D217 YCW(5/97)

D4   V.L. GUNN.t/a SAFEWAY SERVICES

Depot:North Street Garage,North Street,SOUTH PETHERTON,Somerset.

```
GIB 5970  Leyland PSU3E/4R    Willowbrook B48F  Kellett,Barnoldswick 92
HIL 7772  Leyland PSU3E/4R    Willowbrook B48F  Alexcars,Cirencester 00
NIB 8459  Volvo B10M-61       East Lancs B55F   Bornyard,Flitwick 02
RJI 3046  Volvo B10M-61       Duple C51F        Kingdom,Tiverton 01
YXI 9258  Volvo B10M-61       Van Hool C53F     Skills,Nottingham 58 02
NPA 228W  Leyland PSU3E/4R    Plaxton C49F      London Country PL28 86
VYC 852W  Leyland PSU3F/5R    Duple C53F        New 81
YYA 122X  Leyland PSU3F/5R    Plaxton C53F      New 82
GTT 417Y  Volvo B10M-61       Duple C53F        Kingdom,Tiverton 01
A983 NYC  Leyland TRCTL11/2R  Plaxton C53F      New 83
E565 YYA  Leyland TRCTL11/3RZ Duple C55F        New 88
F202 HSO  Leyland TRCTL11/3ARZ Plaxton C53F     Park,Hamilton 93
G997 OKK  Volvo B10M-60       Caetano C53F      Wilson,Strathaven 00
J601 KCU  Dennis Dart         Wright B40F       Go North East 8001 01
K835 HUM  Volvo B10M-60       Jonckheere C50F   Burton,Haverhill 00
```

```
GIB 5970*XCW 153R(4/92reb), HIL 7772*TPT 25V(11/91reb),
NIB 8459*E637 NEL(7/90reb), RJI 3046*RMU 967Y(12/93),
YXI 9258*F751 ENE(12/93) & GTT 417Y*NIW 8793(10/01) & GTT 417Y(4/93)
```

D5   GUSCOTTS COACHES LTD

Depot:The Garage,Croft Gate,HALWILL,Devon.

```
ALZ 4582  Bedford YNT          Duple C53F      Hayball,Warminster 96
ALZ 4583  Leyland TRCTL11/3R   Plaxton C55F    North Devon 2221 94
ALZ 4584  Bedford YMT          Plaxton C53F    Hayball,Warminster 97
IIW  670  Leyland TRCTL11/3R   Duple C55F      Boyle,Longfield 99
RIW 4963  DAF MB200DKTL600     Plaxton C57F    D Coaches,Morriston 97
RJI 8725  DAF MB200DKFL600     Plaxton C50FT   Forward,Tiverton 01
TJI 4681  Leyland TRCTL11/3RH  Berkhof C51FT   Southern National 6000 01
CYH 800V  Ford R1014           Duple C35F      Goulden,Bude 98
LUA 239V  Volvo B58-61         Plaxton C57F    Shearer,Mayford 97
VUO 455V  Ford R1114           Duple C45F      Forward,Tiverton 99
RTT 693W  DAF MB200DKTL600     Plaxton C52F    Helmore,Torquay 99
HAV   1Y  Volvo B10M-61        LAG C49FT       Long,Lake 99
HTT 672Y  Volvo B10M-61        Duple C53F      Forward,Tiverton 01
A114 ACV  Volvo B10M-61        Duple C52FT     Lawrence,St Anns Chapel 00
C708 FDV  Mercedes-Benz 307D   ? B12F          Non-PSV(Tavistock) 99
C308 GOC  Mercedes-Benz L608D  DC C21F         Angela,Bursledon 94
D212 VVV  Fiat 79-14           Caetano C25F    Smiths,Liskeard 00
```

```
ALZ 4582*OAL 788W(4/97),
ALZ 4583*HTT 204Y(11/94) & 925 GTA(11/94) & FWH 41Y(11/92),
ALZ 4584*HBT 147W(4/97),
IIW 670*UUY 142Y(11/96) & 50 ABK(12/94) & LCA 181Y(9/90),
RIW 4963*6927 LJ(7/95) & GWN 909W(3/84),
RJI 8725*UJW 539Y(3/94) & OJI 4363(6/92) & EDH 541Y(1/92),
TJI 4681*C137 SPB(5/95),
RTT 693W*HIW 993(9/99) & RUT 927W(7/93) & 917 ETV(11/91) &
                RJU 310W(6/81),
HTT 672Y*VPH 900(7/01) & UOB 428Y(5/98) & CIB 8623(2/96) &
          CIB 9623(1/96) & KUR 859Y(5/95) & 54 FS(10/92) &
          ACK 710Y(12/85) &
A114 ACV*NIL 5652(3/00) & A599 LJT(5/98) & UFX 330(7/97) & A599 LJT(5/95)
```

D6   M.G. HALFORD

Depot:Kisem,North Mills Road,BRIDPORT,Dorset.

LIL 5930	Mercedes-Benz 814D	Optare C28F	Ralphs,Langley 98
TAZ 6696	Mercedes-Benz O1120L	Eurocoach C33F	Dorgan,Dublin(Ire) 02
E461 ANC	Mercedes-Benz 609D	MM C20F	Male & Graham,Yeovil 89
E756 CCA	Mercedes-Benz 609D	PMT C24F	PMT(Demonstrator) 88
E908 KBF	Ford Transit	Dormobile B16F	Western,Exeter 01
E469 YTA	Ford Transit	Dormobile B16F	Couch,Plymouth 01
F221 DDY	Leyland LBM6T/2RS	RB C33F	Goulding,Knottingley 02
F169 SMT	Leyland LBM6T/2RS	WS B43F	LB Redbridge 01
S726 LEF	Mercedes-Benz 412D	Crest C16F	Kent,Guisborough 01
T713 YDV	Toyota BB50R	Caetano C26F	New 99

LIL 5930*K939 GWR(9/96), TAZ 6696*98D 21565(5/02) &
F221 DDY*A15 GPS(7/97) & F997 UME(11/92)

D7   P.A. & A.F. HAMBLY.t/a HAMBLYS OF KERNOW

Depot:The Garage,PELYNT,Cornwall.

WAF 156	Volvo B10M-61	Van Hool C48F	Stagecoach North West 99
YCV 500	Volvo B10M-61	Van Hool C53F	Cridland,Taunton 2 98
645 UCV	Volvo B58-61	Plaxton C57F	Ford,Gunnislake 96
710 VCV	Volvo B10M-61	Plaxton C53F	Prout,Port Isaac 95
539 WCV	Volvo B58-61	Plaxton C57F	Filer,Ilfracombe 96
H362 BDV	Mercedes-Benz 709D	WS B27F	Plymouth 202 98
S100 PAF	Mercedes-Benz O814D	Plaxton B31F	New 98

WAF 156*URM 141X(6/99) & LJC 800(5/99),
YCV 500*XFJ 379(2/99) & B319 UNB(6/92),
645 UCV*WUF 955(7/96) & CEB 135V(9/95),
710 VCV*BYJ 967Y(12/92) & 710 VCV(2/91) & 800 GTR(9/88) & LTR 444Y(1/85) &
539 WCV*PJI 2417(2/96) & SFH 694W(9/92) & 29 DRH(5/88) & PFH 5W(6/83)

D8   D.R. HAND.t/a ROVER

Depots:The Garage,HORSLEY &
*   Spring Mill Industrial Estate,NAILSWORTH,Gloucestershire.*

29 DRH	Bedford YNT	Plaxton C53F	Brooks,Ryarsh 99
74 DRH	Bova FHD12-340	C49FT	Ellison,St Helens 00
904 DRH	Bova FHD12-290	C55F	Bennett,Chieveley 95
B 7 AND	Mercedes-Benz L307D	Whittaker B14F	Hawkins,Walthamstow 96
B 8 AND	Bova FLD12-250	C55F	Burton,Fellbeck 95
B 9 AND	Bedford YNT	Duple C53F	Joplin,Tittleshall 01
B436 RJU	Dodge G13	RB B39F	Sworder,Walkern 00
H 19 AND	MAN 11.220	Berkhof C33FT	Mayne,Buckie 00
K 18 AND	Bova FHD12-370	C51F	New 01
P 50 AND	Bova FHD12-340	C49FT	New 97
R 12 AND	Dennis Javelin	Berkhof C51FT	New 98
DR02 DRH	Bova FHD12-340	C55F	New 02

29 DRH*APF 617Y(?/02), 74 DRH*P100 VWX(1/00), 904 DRH*F212 TAN(4/95),
B7 AND*E169 XWF(4/97), B8 AND*E121 KRP(2/96), B9 AND*C810 FMC(?/02) &
H19 AND*R500 GSM(8/00)

D9   A.M. & C. HARDING.t/a PALM TREE TRAVEL

Depots:Trawler PH,North Boundary Road,BRIXHAM &
Torre Station Yard,TORQUAY,Devon.

```
ESK  988  Leyland TRCTL11/3RH  Duple C50F       Brands,Guildford 02
RIL 4411  DAF MB200DKTL600      Van Hool C52FT   Curtis,Burnett 00
SJI 1969  DAF MB200DKTL600      Jonckheere C49F  Smith,Liskeard 00
F128 KAO  Mercedes-Benz 609D    RB B20F          Hayball,Warminster 00
H874 MHB  DAF 400               Pearl C16F       Stirk,Torquay 01
```
```
ESK  988*B815 JPN(3/92),
RIL 4411*OHU 874Y(5/00) & 8426 MU(8/98) & 458 VHT(7/95) & OHU 874Y(3/86) &
SJI 1969*XYB 654W(6/94) & 28 XYB(2/90) & GEU 77W(4/88) & 927 DAF(3/88) &
          RLA 837W(7/83)
```

E1   HARTPURY COLLEGE

Depot:Hartpury House,HARTPURY,Gloucestershire.

```
R727 KDD  Mercedes-Benz O814D  UVG B33F  New 97
S584 RDG  LDV Convoy           LDV B16F  New 99
V287 ENT  LDV Convoy           LDV B16F  New 00
V288 ENT  LDV Convoy           LDV B16F  New 00
X377 ADF  LDV Convoy           LDV B16F  New 00
```

E2   H.J. HARVEY.t/a HARVEYS MINI BUS SERVICES

Depot:Old Gas Works,Station Road,MORETONHAMPSTEAD,Devon.

```
J517 LRL  Mercedes-Benz 410D    G & M C15F  Downderry & District CB 95
J764 YWA  Iveco 49-10           G & M C24F  Sheffield City Council 98
K153 LHT  DAF 400               G & M C16F  Non-PSV(Van) 96
K373 LWS  DAF 400               G & M C16F  Non-PSV 96
K760 UVR  DAF 400               MM C16F     New 92
M830 DRL  Mercedes-Benz 410D    G & M C15F  Downderry & District CB 98
N167 UTA  Iveco 49-10           G & M B19F  Western,Exeter 01
Y  2 BUS  Mercedes-Benz 416CDI  G & M C16F  New 01
```

E3   L. HAYWARD.t/a EMERALD TRAVEL

Depot:Unit 21,S & H Buildings,Deep Pit Road,Fishponds,BRISTOL.

```
RJI 8716  LAG Panoramic       C49FT          Richens,Bristol 01
AFJ 712T  Leyland PSU3E/4R     Plaxton C53F   Millmans,Newton Abbot 01
B 94 PLU  Bedford VAS5         Plaxton C29F   Thomas,Relubbus 01
C 86 NNV  Fiat 79-14           Caetano C19F   Dodd &,Haydon Bridge 02
```
```
RJI 8716*RPP 734(4/94) & HIL 3432(10/93) & YJF 505(2/92) &
B94 PLU*SIJ 1673(3/01) & B94 PLU(7/00)
```

E4   A.G. HAZELL.t/a CARMEL COACHES

Depot:Station Road,NORTHLEW,Devon.

```
PIL 6501  Duple 425        C53FT         Redwood,Hemyock 99
RJI 8611  Dennis Javelin   Plaxton C53F  Baker,Weston-s-Mare 18 96
UJI 1765  Toyota HDB30R    Caetano C21F  Nelson,Glyn Neath 00
F680 CYC  Dennis Javelin   Duple C53F    Coombs,Weston-s-Mare 96
F487 WPR  Dennis Javelin   Duple C53F    Vince,Burghclere 00
G218 SWL  Dennis Javelin   Duple C57F    Grey,Witchford 00
J  2 EST  Duple 425        C55FT         Bailey,Hucknall 99
```

```
K807 EET  Bova FHD12-290        C49FT           Cowdrey,Gosport 00
K555 GSM  Dennis Javelin        Plaxton C57F    Benjamin,Llanrhystyd 02
L225 BUT  Dennis Javelin        Plaxton C53F    Non-PSV(Fleggburgh) 00
M505 XFY  Mercedes-Benz 814L    North West C35F Jordan,Stourport 124 99
N998 KUS  Mercedes-Benz 814D    Mellor C33F     Lawrence,St Anns Chapel 02
N 76 KVS  Mercedes-Benz 811D    Plaxton DP31F   Bunyan,Hemel Hempstead 01
N205 OAE  Dennis Javelin        WS C47F         MOD 01
P100 SYD  Iveco 59-12           UVG B27F        Crockernwell,Cheriton B 02
S 18 RED  Mercedes-Benz O814D   Plaxton B27F    Nuttall,Penwortham 00
```

PIL 6501*USV 630(10/99) & G981 OGJ(9/95), RJI 8611*F129 TRU(8/94),
UJI 1765*K999 GSM(11/96) & G218 SWL*ESU 320(1/00) & G218 SWL(3/92)

E5   W.L. HEARD & SONS LTD.t/a HEARDS COACHES

Depots:Kingsley Road,BIDEFORD & Heards Garage,Fore Street,HARTLAND,Devon.

```
DAZ 2283  Volvo B10M-61         Van Hool C51FT  Walton,Stockton 94
LIW 3221  Volvo B10M-61         Caetano C53F    Windsorian,Windsor 95
LXI 4455  Fiat 315              Robin Hood C28F Marton,West Drayton 90
NJI 8874  Duple 425             C57F            Daish,Shanklin 97
RJI 4668  Volvo B10M-61         Van Hool C51FT  Redwood,Hemyock 98
UDL  718  Volvo B10M-61         VR C49F         Seaview,Parkstone 86
UTA  199  Volvo B10M-61         Berkhof C49FT   McLellan,Perranporth 93
VOT  762  Volvo B10M-61         Berkhof C49FT   Wadman,Throwleigh 93
WIA 4122  Kassbohrer S215HR     C49FT           National Holidays 122 99
797  ONU  Volvo B58-56          Plaxton C53F    Windsorian,Windsor 96
635  UNU  Volvo B58-56          Plaxton C53F    Windsorian,Windsor 95
LHC 427P  Bedford VAS5          Duple C29F      Windsorian,Windsor 86
STG 345S  Bedford YMT           Duple C53F      Terraneau,South Molton 98
XFJ 843X  Bedford YLQ           Plaxton C45F    New 82
GTA 528Y  Volvo B58-56          Plaxton C53F    New 83
LOU 437Y  Bedford YNT           Plaxton C53F    Windsorian,Windsor 97
A162 OOT  Mercedes-Benz L608D   Robin Hood C19F Windsorian,Windsor 95
A188 OOT  Mercedes-Benz L608D   Robin Hood C19F Windsorian,Windsor 95
B156 YFJ  MAN SR280             C53F            Tearall,West Buckland 01
E200 FCF  Volvo B10M-61         Ikarus C49FT    Windsorian,Windsor 95
F 28 NLE  Volvo B10M-46         Plaxton C39F    Capital,West Drayton 98
G226 DGM  Mercedes-Benz 814D    Phoenix C24F    Windsorian,Windsor 95
P887 FMO  Dennis Javelin        Berkhof C53F    Q Drive,Battersea 99
```

DAZ 2283*MIW 9046(11/94) & E307 OPR(8/92), LIW 3221*C705 KDS(9/90),
LXI 4455*B874 MLN(4/97) & B788 VPO(4/85), NJI 8874*C107 PAB(8/91),
RJI 4668*USV 330(9/98) & NIB 7615(7/97) & 570 PRR(8/90),
UDL 718*B24 NPE(2/88), UTA 199*JVW 158Y(8/93), VOT 762*A142 JTA(6/85),
WIA 4122*G181 VBB(8/95), 797 ONU*YJB 332T(3/85) & 635 UNU*YJB 333T(3/85)

E6   W.J.,M.E. & D.J. HEARN.t/a HILLS SERVICES

Depot:The Garage,STIBB CROSS,Devon.

```
FIL 5120  Volvo B58-61          Plaxton C50F       Hansons,Wordsley 02
FIL 7659  DAF SB2300DHS585      Jonckheere C49FT   Mutch,Loughborough 01
HIL 3487  Volvo B58-61          Duple C57F         Newey,Bognor Regis 95
HIL 3858  Volvo B58-56          Plaxton C51C       Kingdom,Tiverton 93
HIL 3891  DAF MB200DKTL600      Jonckheere C57F    Jenkins,Abersychan 99
HIL 3981  DAF MB200DKTL600      Jonckheere C57F    Randall,Willesden 85
HIL 7908  Volvo B58-61          Plaxton C51F       Kim,Sandown 94
HIL 8224  Volvo B10M-60         Jonckheere C51FT   Ashall,Clayton 01
KSU  476  Bova FHD12-280        C49FT              Jones,Newtown 96
LAZ 5827  Bova FHD12-290        C51FT              City Cars,Norwich 01
TJI 5813  Volvo B58-61          Jonckheere C51F    Denning,Enfield 01
YIA  258  Volvo B58-61          Plaxton C57F       Ashall,Clayton 00
385  UFM  Volvo B58-61          Duple C57F         Webber,Blisland 99
LUA 240V  Volvo B58-61          Plaxton C51F       Safford,Little Gransden 00
WRP 225W  Volvo B58-61          Plaxton C53F       Premiereshow,Heywood 01
NDW  39X  Ford R1114            Duple C51F         Forward,Tiverton 02
```

```
C713 FFJ   Ford Transit          Robin Hood B16F  Stagecoach Devon 97 97
C894 GYD   Ford Transit          Robin Hood B16F  First Cawlett 332 00
F 95 OYO   Freight Rover Sherpa  Dormobile B15FL  LB Lambeth 01
H429 DVM   Ford Transit          MM DP20F         McKenna,Bedford 01
S311 KNR   LDV Convoy            LDV B16F         Non-PSV 01
```

FIL 5120*MTB 516W(7/89),
FIL 7659*LHO 491Y(4/89) & 8998 LJ(10/87) & BLJ 702Y(7/86),
HIL 3487*LHS 187V(7/01), HIL 3858*HYR 177W(11/94),
HIL 3891*OUH 959X(10/99) & TJI 1680(7/98) & WRK 5X(5/96),
HIL 3981*HIB 5277(3/95) & WRK 1X(2/88),
HIL 7908*GIL 8940(1/95) & LUA 246V(3/91),
HIL 8224*UJI 1764(4/01) & G234 YVL(5/96), KSU 476*A422 CUJ(7/88),
LAZ 5827*H624 FUT(2/98), TJI 5813*VBD 569W(5/95),
YIA 258*SIB 7359(11/94) & 386 BUO(3/93) & FAA 358W(6/87),
385 UFM*YPX 113V(1/86) & WRP 225W*SYK 901(9/89) & SNV 74W(4/86)

E7   K.A. & L.A. HEMMINGS.t/a HEMMINGS COACHES

Depot:Little Collingsdown,BUCKLAND BREWER,Devon.

```
KSU 468    Volvo B10M-61          Jonckheere C49FT  Johnson,Upton Park 00
RIL 5090   Scania K113TRB         Irizar C51FT      Newby,Backbarrow 01
RIL 8182   Volvo B10M-60          Van Hool C46FT    Courtney,Bracknell 02
RIL 9343   Bova FHD12-290         C49FT             Bowen,Birmingham 01
EFX 336T   Leyland PSU3A/4R       Plaxton C53F      Sluggett,Holsworthy 99
F439 LTU   Volvo B10M-60          Plaxton C53F      Weardale,Stanhope 02
```

KSU 468*JBM 18Y(6/88), RIL 5090*N94 WVC(8/01),
RIL 8182*K16 CCL(2/02) & K485 VVR(4/99), RIL 9343*F30 COM(3/01),
EFX 336T*TTK 584(3/91) & EHJ 76T(12/88) & MED 270F(2/79reb) &
F439 LTU*NIL 9777(5/02) & F439 LTU(3/02) & 3810 VT(10/97) &
       7052 VT(6/97) & 9975 VT(4/94) & F994 KFM(2/91)

N.K.,M.W.,E.K. & A.C. HILLIER/HATTS EUROPA LTD.t/a HATTS COACHES

Depot:The Coach House,FOXHAM,Wiltshire.

```
ACZ 1133   Volvo B10M-61          Van Hool C49DLT  Sovereign 350 99
AHZ 1257   MAN 16.290             JE C42DLT        Hallmark,Luton 93
BAZ 6170   Volvo B10M-60          Van Hool C53F    Shearings 850 97
BAZ 6516   Volvo B10M-60          Van Hool C53F    Shearings 846 97
JAZ 4886   Leyland TRCTL11/3RZ    Van Hool C53F    Shearings 340 94
JIL 3959   DAF MB200DKFL600       Van Hool C48FT   Williamson,Knockin Hth. 94
LIL 3060   Leyland TRCTL11/3RZ    Plaxton C57F     Harker,South Shields 94
LJI 3799   MAN 18.370             Berkhof C51FT    Henshaw,Jacksdale 02
OIL 3924   DAF MB230LT615         Van Hool C53FT   Staffordian,Stafford 90
OIL 3927   DAF SB2300DHTD585      Plaxton C57F     Seward,Dalwood 93
PJI 6909   Leyland TRCTL11/3R     Plaxton C57F     Evans,Senghenydd 89
SIW 2778   Leyland TRCTL11/3RZ    Van Hool C51FL   Hedingham & Dist. L155 96
YPD 144Y   Leyland TRCTL11/2R     Duple C53F       Dorset County Council 98
B514 OEH   Leyland TRCTL11/3RH    Duple C51F       PMT CTL54 90
D272 BJB   Leyland TRCTL11/3RZ    Plaxton C53F     Weaver,Newbury 02
H139 TAB   Iveco 49-10            Mellor C18FL     Calderdale MBC 648 00
J853 KHD   DAF SB2305DHTD585      Van Hool C53F    Kent County Council 02
J762 YWA   Iveco 49-10            Carlyle DP15FL   Thacker,Westcliff-o-Sea 97
K505 RJX   DAF SB2700HS585        Van Hool C55F    Reading 233 01
K104 TCP   DAF SB3000DKS601       Van Hool C51FT   Murray,St Helens 96
K714 UTT   Iveco 59-12            Mellor B29F      Stagecoach Devon 337 02
K726 UTT   Iveco 59-12            Mellor B29F      Stagecoach Devon 345 02
K732 UTT   Iveco 59-12            Mellor B29F      Stagecoach Devon 349 01
K622 XOD   Iveco 59-12            Mellor B26D      First Hampshire 241 02
L471 DOA   Talbot Freeway         DP20FL           Staines,Brentwood 00
M657 COR   Volvo B10M-62          Van Hool C46FT   Coliseum,Southampton 02
M 6  HAT   EOS E180Z              C51F             New 95
M 8  HAT   EOS E180Z              C51FT            New 95
M153 XHW   Dennis Javelin         UVG C70F         MOD 02
```

```
N857 XMO   Dennis Javelin          Berkhof C53F       Jones,Pontypridd 99
P321 ARU   Volvo B10M-62           Berkhof C49FT      Bournemouth 321 02
P534 PLB   Mercedes-Benz O814D     ACL C18F           Central Pkg.,Heathrow 02
P 74 VWO   Mercedes-Benz 814D      ACL DP33F          Bebb,Llantwit Fardre 99
P298 WFG   Mercedes-Benz 814D      UVG C33F           University Bus,Hatfield 99
T892 LKJ   Renault Master          Rohill B14F        op for Wiltshire CC
T893 LKJ   Renault Master          Rohill B12F        op for Wiltshire CC
T894 LKJ   Renault Master          Rohill B12F        op for Wiltshire CC
W818 AAY   Iveco 391E              Beulas C49FT       New 00
W414 HOB   Mercedes-Benz O814D     Cymric C33F        New 00
W415 HOB   Mercedes-Benz O814D     Cymric C33F        New 00
W416 HOB   Mercedes-Benz O814D     Cymric C33F        New 00
W554 SJM   Volvo B10M-62           Berkhof C49FT      New 00
Y  4 HAT   Ayats A2E/AT            C51FT              New 01
Y736 OBE   Mercedes-Benz O814D     ACL B33F           New 01
```
~~~~~~
```
ACZ 1133*D350 KVE(5/99), AHZ 1257*G651 ONH(2/00), BAZ 6170*G850 RNC(2/94),
BAZ 6516*G846 RNC(1/94), JAZ 4886*C340 DND(?/96), JIL 3959*D814 PNT(8/94),
LIL 3060*B452 JVK(4/95) & A6 WEH(4/94) & B511 UNB(11/92),
LJI 3799*M717 NCY(4/98), OIL 3924*E645 KCX(4/98), OIL 3927*D302 XCX(4/98),
PJI 6909*UDW 385Y(4/93) & EEU 359(1/89) & SAX 998Y(12/86),
SIW 2778*D232 HMT(?/96),
D272 BJB*B10 MLT(2/02) & SIB 9043(5/01) & D602 MVR(6/93) &
M657 COR*MIB 650(?/02)
```
~~~~~~

E9   HOOKWAYS LTD.t/a GREENSLADES & HOOKWAYS JENNINGS

Depots:Lansdowne Road,BUDE,Cornwall,
*   Pinhoe Trading Estate,EXETER & The Garage,MEETH,Devon.*

```
CSU  938   Leyland PSU4E/4R        Plaxton C45F       Thomas,Llangadog 02
GOU  908   DAF SB2305DHS585        Jonckheere C51FT   Fairline,Glasgow 01
HIL 7541   DAF SB2305DHS585        Duple C51FT        Morris,Pencoed 94
MIL 3727   Volvo B10M-61           Plaxton C57F       Jennings,Bude 98
MIL 4680   Leyland TRCTL11/3RZ     Plaxton C57F       Ham,Flimwell 01
NIW 8290   Volvo B58-56            Plaxton C51C       Nightingale,Exeter 96
PIL 6581   Volvo B10M-61           Plaxton C48FT      Chiltern Queen,Woodcote 01
RJI 5701   Leyland TRCTL11/3R      Duple C55F         PB Garratt,Birstall 01
RJI 5702   Leyland TRCTL11/3R      Duple C55F         Viscount,Burnley 01
SJI 8117   Volvo B10M-61           Plaxton C49FT      Buddens,Romsey 97
TJI 9141   Leyland TRCTL11/3RH     Duple C55F         Reynolds,Watford 99
WXI 3860   DAF MB200DKFL600        Duple C51F         Oakland,Immingham 99
1434  HP   Volvo B10M-62           Plaxton C53F       Dodsworth,Boroughbridge 01
2603  HP   DAF SB2300DHTD585       Plaxton C57F       Seward,Dalwood 99
3315  HP   Volvo B10M-61           Plaxton C49FT      Jennings,Bude 98
3427  HP   Volvo B10M-60           Plaxton C53FT      Goode,West Bromwich 02
3785  HP   Volvo B10M-60           Plaxton C53F       Leons,Stafford 106 01
4415  HP   Volvo B10M-60           Plaxton C51F       Hill,Hanwell 01
4691  HP   LAG Panoramic           C49FT              Tarhum,Nailsea 97
4846  HP   LAG Panoramic           C49FT              Wheatley,Hetton-le-Hole 98
5351  HP   LAG Panoramic           C49FT              Farrow,Hillingdon 97
6230  HP   LAG Panoramic           C49FT              Wood,Buckfastleigh 93
6740  HP   Volvo B10M-61           Plaxton C53F       Evans,Newchurch 99
7105  HP   LAG Panoramic           C49FT              Annis,Felling 98
7346  HP   Volvo B10M-60           Plaxton C49FT      Stevens,Bristol 99
7876  HP   Volvo B10M-60           Plaxton C49FT      Leons,Stafford 96 01
9743  HP   Volvo B10M-61           Plaxton C57F       Jennings,Bude 98
9878  HP   Volvo B10M-61           Plaxton C57F       Jennings,Bude 98
9880  HP   Volvo B10M-62           Plaxton C53F       Dodsworth,Boroughbridge 01
6185  RU   DAF MB200DKFL600        Plaxton C41FLT     Reynolds,Perivale 93
789  FAY   Volvo B10M-61           Duple C57F         Jennings,Bude 98
409  FRH   Volvo B10M-61           Plaxton C57F       Jennings,Bude 98
748  JTA   Toyota HB31R            Caetano C21F       Gale,Haslemere 99
990  XYA   Volvo B58-56            Plaxton C51C       Nightingale,Exeter 96
RCV 493M   Volvo B58-56            Plaxton C53F       Jennings,Bude 98
KUY 443X   Volvo B58-61            Duple C57F         Jennings,Bude 98
OBO 631X   Leyland TRCTL11/2R      Plaxton C51F       Evans,Tregaron 98
YNW  33X   Leyland PSU3E/4R        Plaxton C53F       Lofty,Bridge Trafford 93
```

```
A 60 AFS   Leyland TRCTL11/3RH      Duple C51F        Whitehead,Rochdale 99
C942 DHT   Volvo B10M-61            Duple C57F        Warren,Alton 00
C547 MNH   Freight Rover Sherpa     RB C16F           Nightingale,Exeter 96
C248 OFE   Mercedes-Benz L608D      RB B20F           Berry,Worlingham 96
D137 LTA   Dodge S56                RB B25F           Taw & Torridge,Merton 97
D510 WNV   Fiat 79-14               Caetano C19F      Berryhurst,Vauxhall 89
D517 WNV   DAF SB2300DHS585         Caetano C21DL     Non-PSV(Chigwell) 01
E716 CPC   Mercedes-Benz 811D       Robin Hood C24F   Warren,Alton 00
F215 DCC   Mercedes-Benz 709D       Robin Hood B25F   Campbell,Port Glasgow 01
F221 DCC   Mercedes-Benz 709D       Robin Hood B27F   Arriva Cymru MMM221 01
F714 EUG   Toyota HB31R             Caetano C21F      Rehill &,Thornbury 00
F554 MBC   Toyota HB31R             Caetano C21F      Gosling,Redbourn 99
G105 APC   Toyota HB31R             Caetano C21F      Chariots,Stanford-le-H. 00
G992 WLU   Renault Master           Smith B8F         Non-PSV(Ashburton) 01
H346 JFX   Volvo B10M-60            Plaxton C46FT     Mikes,Gravesend 01
H348 JFX   Volvo B10M-60            Plaxton C46FT     Rest & Ride,Smethwick 01
J135 LLK   Toyota HDB30R            Caetano C18F      Richmond,Barley 01
J 42 VWO   Volvo B10M-60            Plaxton C49FT     Ferris,Nantgarw 01
```

```
CSU 938*WUG 128S(5/87reb),
GOU 908*F921 YNV(2/02) & XIW 1184(10/00) & F921 YNV(9/99),
HIL 7541*D90 NHB(5/92), MIL 3727*SGL 498Y(4/98),
MIL 4680*AEF 315A(2/02) & B542 HAM(1/01) & AEF 315A(8/93) &
        C331 PEW(4/89), NIW 8290*HYR 175W(8/93), PIL 6581*E533 PRU(9/98),
RJI 5701*XEC 347Y(3/02) & GSU 554(9/99) & ANA 52Y(4/89),
RJI 5702*XEC 348Y(3/02) & XSU 905(9/99) & XFK 305(4/90) & ANA 53Y(4/89),
SJI 8117*F308 URU(1/95),
TJI 9141*B157 WRN(2/02) & 927 GTA(4/99) & B157 WRN(6/90),
WXI 3860*B512 HFE(6/99) & NBZ 1680(4/99) & B32 RJU(9/95) & YNR 778(7/93) &
        B901 KAU(11/91), 1434 HP*M740 YNW(3/02), 2603 HP*D490 RUS(2/00),
3315 HP*D809 SGB(3/99), 3427 HP*L160 EOG(3/02),
3785 HP*H891 JVR(8/01) & 972 SYD(9/00) & H168 EJU(11/97),
4415 HP*H660 UWR(5/01) & GSU 382(3/01) & H660 UWR(3/96) & H658 UWR(2/92),
4691 HP*GOU 908(3/98) & E399 MVV(3/94), 4846 HP*F774 PFF(9/00),
5351 HP*G487 KBD(5/97), 6230 HP*F631 SRP(3/97),
6740 HP*E857 WEP(2/00) & DSU 772(9/99) & E565 UHS(4/98) & FSU 375(12/97) &
        E565 UHS(6/93), 7105 HP*WXI 3860(6/99) & F680 BBD(2/94),
7346 HP*H834 AHS(1/00),
7876 HP*H912 JVR(6/01) & 5888 EH(4/01) & H169 EJU(10/96),
9743 HP*D275 MCV(9/99), 9878 HP*E561 RRL(4/00), 9880 HP*P741 YUM(3/02),
6185 RU*ANA 447Y(3/94), 789 FAY*D36 LRL(4/00), 409 FRH*URU 651X(3/02),
748 JTA*G604 YUT(3/02),
990 XYA*FGL 249V(10/92) & WSV 530(8/92) & DYW 170V(4/87),
C942 DHT*244 SYA(1/94) & C942 DHT(1/93),
E716 CPC*KXI 599(8/93) & E81 LLO(8/93) & WET 590(5/90) & E480 JLK(3/89) &
J135 LLK*577 HTX(6/01) & J135 LLK(3/97)
```

F1   B.,D.R. & N.A. HOPLEY

Depot:Sunic,Rope Walk,MOUNT HAWKE,Cornwall.

```
IAZ 2314   Leyland ONLXB/1R         ECW H45/32F         Arriva Shires 5067 02
TSV 302    Volvo B10M-61            Jonckheere C49FT    Hand,Horsley 98
508 AHU    Volvo B10M-56            Plaxton C53F        Tillingbourne,Cranleigh 94
640 UAF    Volvo B10M-60            Jonckheere C51FT    Vale Llangollen,Cefn M. 01
NNK 808P   Bedford YRT              Duple B63F          Ede,Par 89
KVF 248V   Bristol VRT/SL3/6LXB     ECW H43/31F         Red & White 860 99
P 87 SAF   Volvo B10B-58            Wright B60F         New 97
Y922 DCY   Mercedes-Benz O814D      Cymric C24F         New 01
```

```
IAZ 2314*MUH 288X(12/95), TSV 302*ONV 653Y(3/85), 508 AHU*NUH 262X(5/89) &
640 UAF*VLT 280(3/01) & VLT 293(4/00) & VLT 149(3/97) & J986 GLG(3/96)
```

F2   **C.E. INMAN & T.R. COMPTON.t/a C & B**

Depot:Station Approach,FROME,Somerset.

```
CCZ 2217  Volvo B10M-61            Plaxton C53F      Castell,Trethomas 01
ATH  4V   Ford R1114               Plaxton C53F      Elcock,Madeley 01
A673 RWL  DAF MB200DKFL600         Caetano C48FT     Johnson,Newingreen 00
C149 LJR  Mercedes-Benz L608D      Mellor C19F       Miles,Coventry 00
D221 GLJ  Freight Rover Sherpa     Dormobile B16F    Price,Halesowen 99
```
CCZ 2217*D787 SGB(5/01) & A673 RWL*KIB 7026(2/90) & A462 NJF(2/88)

F3   **D.J. ISAAC.t/a DENE VALLEY COACHES**

Depot:Sandick Garage,GUNN,Devon.

```
JBZ 1653  Volvo B10M-61        Van Hool C53F    Weaver,Newbury 01
NIB 7615  Kassbohrer S215HR    C49F             Oates,St Ives 00
682 FUV   DAF MB200DKFL600     Plaxton C51FT    Filer,Ilfracombe 94
533 JBU   Volvo B58-61         Duple C57F       Crutwell,Ramsey 90
GWF 759N  Volvo B58-56         Plaxton C51F     Venner,Minehead 93
WDA 979T  Leyland FE30AGR      MCW H43/33F      West Midlands 6979 96
ANA 437Y  DAF MB200DKFL600     Plaxton C51F     Smith,Pylle 96
CJU 110Y  Bedford YNT          Duple C53F       Delahaye,Barnstaple 97
```
JBZ 1653*B318 UNB(1/94), NIB 7615*D977 AMY(4/00), 682 FUV*DVS 163Y(1/83) &
533 JBU*BTB 713T(2/86)

F4   **J.N. & P.J. JACKMAN.t/a SPEARINGS COACHES**

Depots:B3181 & Willand Garage,WILLAND,Devon.

```
AHZ 1258  Duple 425                 C59F             Dealtop,Clyst St Mary 00
AHZ 1259  Volvo B10M-60             Plaxton C57F     Foster,Glastonbury 00
CBZ 2894  Leyland TRCTL11/3R        Duple C51F       Ludlows,Halesowen 98
TIB 8564  Scania K112CRS            Jonckheere C53F  Snell,Newton Abbot 98
C 78 MAK  Volvo B10M-61             Caetano C53F     Smith,High Wycombe 02
C194 RVV  Fiat 79-14                Caetano C19F     Heard,Hartland 99
E953 KDP  Volvo B10M-61             Plaxton C57F     Rowland &,Hastings 21 01
F195 CEA  Bova FHD12-290            C49FT            Jarvis,Aberaman 01
G 58 KET  Freight Rover Sherpa      Crystals C16F    New 89
M534 TVH  LDV 400                   Concept C16F     Cherrybriar,Bow 98
P944 YSB  Mercedes-Benz 611D        Onyx C24F        Melvin,Dyce 01
```
AHZ 1258*D888 PGA(5/00), AHZ 1259*F967 HGE(7/00),
CBZ 2894*YWD 687(10/98) & B717 MPC(10/93), TIB 8564*B506 CBD(8/93),
C78 MAK*OIW 5800(1/97) & C145 MDS(2/96) & WIB 7193(2/96) &
         C199 RVV(10/95),
E953 KDP*ODY 395(9/00) & E953 KDP(3/97) & OVK 902(11/96) &
         E301 OMG(11/93) & F195 CEA*IIL 6244(5/00) & F195 CEA(8/93)

F5   **E.S.J. JACOBS.t/a ESJ MERLIN TOURS**

Depot:The Yard,Brunel Road,Saltash Industrial Estate,SALTASH,Cornwall.

```
TIW 2114  Bedford YMT           Unicar C53F      Hamer,Rainham 4 01
VUB 382H  Leyland PSU3A/4R      Plaxton C53F     Webber,Blisland 90
PUN 100S  Ford R1114            Plaxton C53F     Crocker,St Austell 02
LHG 438T  Bristol VRT/SL3/501   ECW H43/31F      Lawrence,Weston-s-Mare 00
```
TIW 2114*MPC 902W(12/97)

F6   A.R. JAMES.t/a ANDYBUS

Depot:Priory Industrial Estate,London Road,TETBURY,Gloucestershire.

TIL 6877	Optare Excel L1070	B36F	Tillingbourne,Cranleigh 01
UWY 83X	Leyland PSU3F/4R	Duple C49F	Harrogate & Dist. 683 94
YPD 140Y	Leyland TRCTL11/2R	Duple C53F	Dorset County Council 01
D726 VAM	Dodge G10	WS B39FA	MOD 96
E318 SYG	Mercedes-Benz 811D	Optare DP29F	Cruisers,Redhill 01
E204 YGC	Mercedes-Benz 709D	RB C25F	Hand,Horsley 00
G 42 SSR	Fiat 49-10	Phoenix B25F	Pinkney,Bransholme 01
G782 YAE	Leyland TRCTL11/3RZM	Plaxton DP70F	MOD 02
K345 PJR	Renault S75	Plaxton B31F	Somerbus,Paulton 01
K803 WFJ	Iveco 59-12	Mellor B30F	Stagecoach Devon 357 01
K806 WFJ	Iveco 59-12	Mellor B30F	Stagecoach Devon 362 01
N 3 ARJ	Bova FLC12-280	C53F	New 95
N222 LFR	MAN NL222FR	East Lancs B43F	MAN(Demonstrator) 01
R 30 ARJ	Bova FLD12-300	C53F	Gardiner,Low Prudhoe 01
R807 HWS	Mercedes-Benz O814D	Plaxton B33F	New 98
R808 HWS	Mercedes-Benz O814D	Plaxton B33F	New 98
R 57 JSG	Mercedes-Benz O810D	Plaxton B33F	New 98
T436 TEU	Mercedes-Benz O814D	ACL C29F	New 99
WR02 XXO	Bova FHD12-340	C51FT	New 02

TIL 6877*P446 SWX(9/00), R30 ARJ*R987 PFT(5/02) &
T436 TEU*T30 ARJ(9/01) & T436 TEU(3/99)

F7   G.A. JONES & C.C. LEVITT.t/a EBLEY COACH SERVICES

Depot:Unit 11,Ebley Trading Estate,EBLEY,Gloucestershire.

BUI 4646	DAF SB3000DKV601	Jonckheere C51FT	Buddens,Romsey 97
AFH 186T	Leyland PSU5C/4R	Duple C57F	Hoskins &,Eastington 00
LSJ 872W	LN NL116AL11/1R	B52F	Western Buses 765 98
JEO 587X	DAF MB200DKTL600	Duple C52FT	James,Sherston 93
OWO 37X	Leyland TRCTL11/3R	Plaxton C55F	Matthews,Goytre 02
XFG 25Y	LN NL116HLXB/1R	B52F	Bygone,Smarden 98
XFG 30Y	LN NL116HLXB/1R	B47F	Bygone,Smarden 98
A 6 ECS	DAF SB3000DKV601	Van Hool C51FT	Hallmark,Luton 99
A 9 ECS	DAF MB200DKFL600	Berkhof C53F	Watts,Gillingham 96
A523 YSD	LN NL116HLXCT/1R	B52F	Western Buses 769 98
B 21 AUS	DAF MB200DKFL600	Van Hool C50FT	Midland Red South 3021 96
D 33 FYH	Dodge S66	Locomotors B27F	Maun,Sutton-in-Ashfield 94
G115 TNL	Mercedes-Benz 814D	RB C33F	James,Tetbury 02
H 23 JMJ	Leyland TRCL10/3ARZA	Plaxton C53F	Austin,Earlston 01
J229 JJR	Renault S75	Plaxton B28F	Green Triangle,Atherton 00
J230 JJR	Renault S75	Plaxton B28F	Green Triangle,Atherton 00
M608 RCP	EOS E180Z	C51FT	Coupland &,Rossall 01

BUI 4646*F955 RNV(10/94), AFH 186T*29 DRH(8/00) & AFH 186T(2/94),
JEO 587X*2428 WW(9/85) & PFR 835X(1/82),
OWO 37X*PIL 6502(2/01) & JSV 391(9/98) & XPP 297X(1/86),
A6 ECS*J63 GCX(8/99) & HC 6422(3/99) & J63 GCX(4/96),
A9 ECS*C588 KTW(9/96) & M608 RCP*95WX 3711(11/01) & M608 RCP(1/96)

F8   P. JONES.t/a P & CJ TRAVEL

Depot:131 Hawkinge Gardens,Ernesettle,PLYMOUTH,Devon.

E382 GAB	Fiat 35-8	G & M C14F	Parsons,St Austell 97
F336 JMV	Freight Rover Sherpa	Crystals C16F	Harvey,North Bovey 00
M314 XSX	LDV 400	Deansgate C16F	Grieve,Edinburgh 01
N358 YNB	LDV 400	Concept C16F	Town Hire,Clitheroe 00

F9   T.P. JONES.t/a VISTA COACHWAYS

Depot:51 Claverham Road,YATTON,Somerset.

```
IJI 5367  Bristol RELH6L       Plaxton C49F   Girling,Plymouth 98
VCO 772   Toyota HB31R          Caetano C21F   Talbott,Moreton-Marsh 98
VCO 802   Leyland TRCTL11/3R    Plaxton C53F   United Counties 87 98
RNE 692W  Bedford CFL           Plaxton C17F   Mayo,Kings Stanley 92
```
~~~~~~
```
IJI 5367*ARU 500A(1/90) & ARU 80A(1/89) & SNJ 611(12/88) &
         HGC 233J(3/85) & 240 MT(7/84) & UFJ 229J(1/84)
VCO 772*E346 AAM(5/99) &
VCO 802*FKK 840Y(5/98) & TSU 640(11/97) & FKK 840Y(11/89)
```
~~~~~~

G1   R.C.,R.A. & C.M. KEECH.t/a SOVEREIGN COACHES

Depot:Pine Lodge,Sidmouth Road,ROUSDON,Devon.

```
G732 YAC  Volvo B10M-60         Plaxton C53F   Kent Coach,Ashford 01
J263 NNC  Volvo B10M-60         Plaxton C53F   Shearings 263 00
L967 JFU  Mercedes-Benz 814D    ACL C33F       Browne,Yiewsley 98
T 65 BCU  LDV Convoy            Crest C11F     Non-PSV(Van) 00
T 24 COF  Mercedes-Benz 614D    ? C24F         Armstrong,Birmingham 02
X216 EKK  LDV Convoy            Crest C16F     New 00
```
~~~~~~
```
G732 YAC*KCT 986(9/01) & G732 YAC(6/98)
```
~~~~~~

G2   A.D. & A.D. KINCH

Depot:Hornbury Hill Farm,MINETY,Wiltshire.

```
MIL 2529  DAF SB2300DHTD585     Plaxton C57F   Stone,Bath 98
WGR 565   Leyland TRCTL11/3R    Plaxton C53F   Silver K.,Malmesbury 00
BFX 569T  Bristol VRT/SL3/6LXB  ECW H43/31F    Hoare,Chepstow 02
FTO 555V  Bedford YMT           Plaxton C53F   Witte,Calne 98
KCK 202W  Leyland AN68C/2R      EL H50/36F     Lincolnshire 702 02
PWY 40W   Bristol VRT/SL3/6LXB  ECW H43/31F    Eurotaxis,Harry Stoke 99
JBW 211Y  Leyland PSU5/2L       Plaxton C53F   Bristol 8209 01
N383 EAK  Volvo B10M-62         Plaxton C53F   McLeans,Witney 00
T722 JHE  Scania L94IB          Irizar C49FT   Buddens,Romsey 02
```
~~~~~~
```
MIL 2529*D592 WCP(7/99), WGR 565*DVH 272Y(12/86) &
JBW 211Y*URT 682(10/94) & CJX 563Y(12/88)
```
~~~~~~

G3   KINGDOMS TOURS LTD.t/a TIVVY COACHES

Depot:Westfield Garage,Exeter Road,TIVERTON,Devon.

```
KCZ 8550  Scania K113TRB        Irizar C49FT      Hallmark,Luton 02
KYC 618   Volvo B10M-60         Van Hool C53F     Shearings 161 98
NIW 8795  Volvo B10M-61         Plaxton C53F      Park,Hamilton 87
RIL 2201  Volvo B10M-61         Plaxton C49FT     Miles,Swindon 99
RJI 3047  Volvo B58-61          Plaxton C53F      Monks,Leigh 83
TIL 8706  Mercedes-Benz 408D    Coachcraft C15F   Webb,Barham 00
TIL 8707  Mercedes-Benz 408D    Whittaker C15F    Webb,Barham 00
TIL 8708  Mercedes-Benz 811D    Optare C29F       Bodman & Heath,Worton 00
TIL 8709  Mercedes-Benz 609D    RB C19F           Wakes,Wincanton 97
TIL 9833  Volvo B10M-60         Van Hool C49FT    Guideissue,Biddulph 12 01
TIL 9834  Volvo B10M-60         Van Hool C49FT    Guideissue,Biddulph 10 01
TJI 4860  Volvo B10M-61         Van Hool C49F     Skill,Nottingham 60 97
XYD 169   Volvo B10M-61         Jonckheere C51FT  Hilo,Sandy 93
936 NTT   Volvo B10M-61         Van Hool C53F     Worthing Coaches 93
804 TYA   Volvo B10M-60         Van Hool C53F     Shearings 257 99
G916 CLV  Mercedes-Benz 609D    North West C24F   Letham,Blantyre 97
H962 LOC  Mercedes-Benz 408D    DC B12FL          Aziz,Birmingham 00
```

```
J812 FOU   Mercedes-Benz 814D   Carlyle C29F        Ball,Bristol 01
L669 PWT   Mercedes-Benz 814D   Optare C29F         Gastonia,Cranleigh 02
L966 VGE   Mercedes-Benz 709D   Dormobile DP25F     Tourex,Hinksey 02
M548 DAF   Iveco 49-10          DC B6FL             Cornwall County Council 02
P744 GOH   LDV Convoy           Jubilee C16F        Bennett,Tamworth 01
P688 LKL   LDV Convoy           Jaycas C16F         Jaycrest,Sittingbourne 01
P689 LKL   LDV Convoy           Jaycas C16F         Jaycrest,Sittingbourne 01
R629 VYB   Bova FHD12-340       C49FT               Grimmett,Minehead 02
```
~~~~~~
```
KCZ 8550*N15 CAN(2/02) & HC 6422(2/01) & N15 CAN(4/00),
KYC 618*H161 DVM(2/98), NIW 8795*A655 UGD(4/93),
RIL 2201*D558 FFL(7/99) & ESU 913(3/94) & D813 SGB(12/93),
RJI 3047*WDB 84X(9/93), TIL 8706*F183 UEE(3/01), TIL 8707*H726 THL(3/01),
TIL 8708*F313 TLU(3/01) & WET 590(1/92) & F933 AWW(5/90),
TIL 8709*E529 VYD(3/01),
TIL 9833*J774 AAW(3/01) & 8399 RU(10/00) & J218 NNC(3/99),
TIL 9834*J772 AAW(3/01) & 5946 RU(10/00) & J217 NNC(3/99),
TJI 4860*E957 CGA(11/95) & TJI 4860(7/95) & E957 CGA(5/95) &
      LSK 825(11/94) & E636 UNE(4/92), XYD 169*E217 GNV(5/93),
936 NTT*B474 UNB(11/93) & 804 TYA*J257 NNC(4/99)
```
~~~~~~

G4   KINGSBURY COACHES LTD

Depots:Withey Cutters,KINGSBURY EPISCOPI &
c/o Bridge Hauliers,THORNEY,Somerset.

```
YDZ 4234   Bova FLD12-250       C53F                Heath,Wem 01
HTU 416X   Bova EL26/581        C53F                Wellington,Kingsbridge 02
K721 GBE   Mercedes-Benz 814D   ACL C29F            Ash,Wooburn Moor 01
P696 NDX   Mercedes-Benz 814D   Robin Hood C29F     Perry,Woolpit 02
```
~~~~~~
```
YDZ 4234*C314 NNT(12/98), HTU 416X*HSV 674(6/93) & SMY 624X(9/86) &
K721 GBE*K5 JFS(3/02) & K721 GBE(5/93)
```
~~~~~~

G5   B.J. KNOWLES.t/a CLASSIC TOURS

Depot:c/o Pontins,Barton Hall Holiday Camp,KINGSKERSWELL,Devon.

```
P141 DDV   Bova FHD12-333       C49FT               Garrett,Newton Abbot 00
P270 RBX   Volvo B10M-62        Jonckheere C49FT    Burdett,Mosbrough 01
V 92 EAK   MAN 18.350           Auwaerter C49FT     New 99
Y144 HWE   MAN 18.350           Auwaerter C49FT     New 01
```
~~~~~~
```
P270 RBX*J4 KYS(8/01) & P270 RBX(9/99)
```
~~~~~~

G6   LANDYLINES LTD.t/a COOKS COACHES & KILMINGTON COACHES

Depots:Dowell St Car Park,HONITON & c/o Batten,Ottermere,MONKTON,Devon &
c/o Chard Truck Services,Millfield Trading Estate,CHARD &
Whiteball Garage,WELLINGTON,Somerset.

```
BAZ 7326   Volvo B10M-61          Plaxton C57F      Richmond,Barley 00
HAZ 3346   Leyland TRCTL11/2R     Duple C53F        Shearings 307 91
HBZ 4676   Mercedes-Benz 814D     Plaxton C33F      Cooper,Dukinfield 01
JUI 1717   Mercedes-Benz 811D     RB C25F           New 90
NIL 7228   Mercedes-Benz 308D     RB C12F           Non-PSV 95
PIL 9537   Mercedes-Benz 814D     Plaxton C33F      Farmer,Ashford 98
TXI 8761   Mercedes-Benz 609D     RB B20F           AMS,Maidenhead 98
VIB 9378   Leyland TRCTL11/3R     Plaxton C57F      Chalkwell,Sittingbourne 00
GAF  69V   Volvo B58-56           Duple C53F        Dealtop,Exeter 02
F659 NPF   Mercedes-Benz 407D     Crystals C15F     CSGB,South Newton 99
G895 HHB   Mercedes-Benz 408D     DC B7FL           Hart,Caerphilly 99
G940 TTA   Mercedes-Benz 408D     DC B15F           op for Devon County Coun
H759 CTA   Mercedes-Benz 308D     DC B8F            New 91
H112 DVM   Mercedes-Benz 609D     RB B25F           Sadler,Gloucester 00
K338 FYG   Mercedes-Benz 410D     G & M C16F        Brenton,Plymouth 99
```

```
K974 XND  Mercedes-Benz 410D    MM C16F          Luckett,Fareham 98
L360 ANR  Mercedes-Benz 410D    G & M C16F       Non-PSV(Van) 98
L543 JFS  Mercedes-Benz 609D    Crystals DP20F   Courts,Fillongley 01
L948 JFU  Mercedes-Benz 410D    ACL C16F         Anderson,Bermondsey 00
L 32 OKV  Mercedes-Benz 410D    G & M C16F       Non-PSV 97
M289 CAM  Mercedes-Benz 709D    G & M C24F       Non-PSV 99
M 91 JHB  Mercedes-Benz 709D    WS B29F          Anslow,Pontypool 01
M582 KTG  Mercedes-Benz 711D    G & M C24F       Hazell,Northlew 01
M842 TYC  LDV 400               ACL C16F         New 94
M843 TYC  Mercedes-Benz 410D    ACL C5FL         New 94
M792 TYD  LDV 400               ACL C16F         New 94
M968 TYG  Mercedes-Benz 410D    G & M C16F       Non-PSV(Wakefield) 00
M345 UVX  Mercedes-Benz 811D    Plaxton B31F     Curtis,Burnett 01
N614 DKR  Mercedes-Benz 811D    Plaxton B31F     Farmer,Ashford 01
N172 DWX  Mercedes-Benz 814D    G & M C24F       Non-PSV(Van) 00
N456 VOD  Mercedes-Benz 709D    Alexander B25F   Blazefield Lancs 647 02
N457 VOD  Mercedes-Benz 709D    Alexander B25F   Blazefield Lancs 648 02
N837 YRC  Mercedes-Benz 711D    Onyx C23F        Spencer,New Ollerton 01
P158 BFJ  LDV Convoy            G & M C16F       Non-PSV(Van) 99
P944 CEG  LDV Convoy            WMB C16F         Horn,East Finchley 00
P306 HWG  LDV Convoy            Onyx C16F        Holloway,Scunthorpe 01
P211 JKL  Mercedes-Benz 709D    Plaxton B27F     Arriva Kent 1211 02
P117 KBL  LDV Convoy            G & M C16F       Non-PSV 99
P232 NKK  Mercedes-Benz 811D    Plaxton B31F     Farmer,Ashford 01
P848 REU  LDV Convoy            WMB C16F         Horn,East Finchley 00
P494 RHU  LDV Convoy            G & M C16F       Non-PSV(Van) 98
R501 BUA  Mercedes-Benz 412D    Crest C16F       Skills,Nottingham 79 01
R667 KFE  LDV Convoy            Onyx C16F        Holloway,Scunthorpe 01
S857 BDV  LDV Convoy            Coachsmith B15FL op for Devon County Coun
S995 BTA  LDV Convoy            G & M C16F       Non-PSV(Van) 98
T788 RDV  LDV Convoy            Coachsmith B15FL op for Devon County Coun
W416 RYC  Mercedes-Benz 412D    Ferqui C16F      New 00
Y921 FDV  LDV Convoy            Coachsmith B16FL op for Devon County Coun
Y334 GFJ  LDV Convoy            Coachsmith B16FL op for Devon County Coun
```
~~~~~~
```
BAZ 7326*B29 ABH(4/01) & 729 KTO(9/00) & B29 ABH(3/86),
HAZ 3346*A159 MNE(10/95), HBZ 4676*N796 CVU(1/02),
JUI 1717*H476 UYD(12/98), NIL 7228*G825 MYB(7/01), PIL 9537*K13 KCT(7/01),
TXI 8761*D249 ABV(4/91)
VIB 9378*A541 WAV(11/94) & HSV 196(11/94) & A832 PPP(12/93) &
GAF 69V*728 FDV(9/96) & ESN 640V(2/94) & 4009 SC(10/91) & FVO 661V(5/90)
```
~~~~~~

G7   J.R. LAWRENCE.t/a HUTTON COACH HIRE

Depot:Rectors Way,WESTON-SUPER-MARE,Somerset.

```
LIL 6637  Leyland PSU5C/4R      Van Hool C55F    Jacobs,St Stephens 00
RFX   23  Volvo B10M-61         Plaxton C51F     Gilbert,St Columb 92
SIB 6741  DAF MB200DKTL600      Van Hool C49FT   Hillier,Foxham 97
TIL 2326  Leyland RT            Van Hool C53F    Smith,Ledbury 00
E 33 DSS  Mercedes-Benz 609D    DC C19F          Britton,Bristol 01
K100 OMP  Iveco 315             Lorraine C30F    Pearce,Berinsfield 99
```
~~~~~~
```
LIL 6637*MDS 241V(10/95),
RFX 23*BUA 157X(5/88) & 4120 WA(12/87) & VWX 365X(6/86),
SIB 6741*OHR 491X(10/93) & 754 DXE(12/90) & 800 XPC(8/88) &
        KHY 348X(6/85) & TIL 2326*D124 HMT(6/00)
```
~~~~~~

G8   A.T.H. LAWTON.t/a COTSWOLD EXPERIENCE TOURS

Depot:Corn Mill Yard,Ebley Corn Mill,Bridge Road,EBLEY,Gloucestershire.

```
G978 NGN  Renault Master        ? B14F           Walsh,Middleton 00
G577 PRM  Mercedes-Benz 709D    Alexander B25F   Davies,Bettws Gwerfil G 01
G274 TSL  Mercedes-Benz 709D    Alexander B25F   Bluebird Buses 274 01
K319 YKG  Mercedes-Benz 709D    ARB B25F         Bluebird Buses 322 01
M255 HVP  Renault Master        ? B14F           Non-PSV 01
```

G9   M.A. LEACH.t/a COLOMBUS & WHEELS CARE

Depots:88 Argyle Street & c/o Powdrills,West End Road,SWINDON,Wiltshire.

```
B715 FCF  Ford Transit          Mellor B16FL      McCouid,Burghfield 96
B 39 MBY  Ford Transit          Dormobile B8FL    Reynolds,Perivale 98
B678 OVU  Ford Transit          Mellor B14FL      McCouid,Burghfield 96
C453 GGT  Ford Transit          Dormobile B8F     RB Kingston 98
D982 FYR  Ford Transit          Dormobile B16F    Connor,Calne 98
E731 YBH  Freight Rover Sherpa  RB B10F           Buckinghamshire CC 98
F316 NPF  Freight Rover Sherpa  Dormobile B8FL    Surrey County Council 98
F968 XEW  Ford Transit          Dormobile B11FL   Norfolk County Council 98
```

OTHER VEHICLE OWNED BY THE COMPANY
* * * * * * *

```
B842 WYO  Ford Transit          Dormobile B-FL    Store
```

H1   LEWIS COACHES (STALBRIDGE) LTD

Depot:The Garage,Marsh Lane,HENSTRIDGE,Somerset.

```
WLJ  926  Leyland TRCTL11/3RZ  Van Hool C53F  Lodge,High Easter 96
YAF  624  Volvo B10M-61        Van Hool C53F  Chivers,Elstead 98
422  GDV  Bedford YMT          Plaxton C53F   Clarke,Wimborne 92
688  UYB  Volvo B10M-61        Plaxton C53F   Taylor,Sutton Scotney 99
AUJ 745T  Bedford YLQ          Duple C45F     Non-PSV(Plumstead) 92
SHR 638Y  Bedford YNT          Plaxton C53F   Seaview,Parkstone 95
A989 AET  Bedford YNT          Plaxton C53F   Torr,Gedling 93
```

WLJ 926*AAL 551A(9/98) & A164 MNE(10/89),
YAF 624*FJI 336(7/99) & B487 UNB(9/90),
422 GDV*GAW 455V(1/94) & 688 UYB*RJI 8921(?/02) & C354 DND(3/94)

H2   LISKEARD & DISTRICT OMNIBUS COMPANY LTD

Depot:Culverland Road,Trevecca,LISKEARD,Cornwall.

```
V956 HEB  Mercedes-Benz 412D    Eurocoach B14FL  loan from Mistral
W921 JNF  Dennis Dart SLF       Plaxton B29F     loan from Mistral
W922 JNF  Dennis Dart SLF       Plaxton B29F     loan from Mistral
X436 CDW  Mercedes-Benz 411CDI  UVG B14FL        loan from Mistral
VU02 TRV  Optare Alero          B14F             New 02
```

H3   G.W. & A.N. LITTLE & J.A. BOWYER.t/a TEDBURN COACHES

Depot:Kent Estates,TEDBURN ST. MARY,Devon.

```
GDZ 6250  Bova EL26/581     C53F             Jackman,Willand 99
HIL 5672  Bova EL26/581     C53F             Millership,Dudley 99
PAF 276X  Bova EL26/581     C51F             Tilley,Wainhouse Corner 01
AEF 203Y  Bova EL26/581     C53F             Baker,Trowbridge 98
A320 HFP  Bova EL28/581     Duple C53F       Smith,St Leonards 99
A459 JJF  Bova EL28/581     Duple C53F       Carterton Coaches 97
A126 NAC  Bova EL28/581     Duple C53F       Roberts,Clawddnewydd 98
A423 XGL  Bova EL28/581     Duple C53FT      Whitehead,Bournemouth 93
C522 BNX  MAN MT8.136       GCS C29F         Judge,Corby 97
E608 TCV  DAF SB2305DHS585  Duple C53FT      Tilley,Wainhouse Corner 02
G417 TNJ  DAF 400           Carlyle B20F     Judge,Corby 00
```

GDZ 6250*YBM 246X(7/96), HIL 5672*FUA 401Y(4/92),
PAF 276X*TIL 1260(8/01) & FSU 358(9/00) & VWX 358X(3/87),
A126 NAC*CEC 62(1/94) & A460 JJF(6/85),
C522 BNX*162 TTO(6/97) & C869 WBC(10/90) &

E608 TCV*TIL 1258(2/02) & MIL 1064(9/00) & E24 ETN(1/96)
~~~~~~

H4   LOVERINGS (COMBE MARTIN) LTD.t/a LOVERINGS COACHES

Depot:Borough Road,COMBE MARTIN,Devon.

H821 AHS	Volvo B10M-60	Plaxton C53F	Park,Hamilton 92
H822 AHS	Volvo B10M-60	Plaxton C53F	Park,Hamilton 93
J729 CWT	Volvo B10M-60	Plaxton C50F	Wallace Arnold 96
J732 CWT	Volvo B10M-60	Plaxton C50F	Wallace Arnold 96
K596 VBC	Toyota HDB30R	Caetano C18F	Viking Bland,Corringham 95
L924 NWW	Volvo B10M-60	Plaxton C50F	Wallace Arnold 98
M134 UWY	Volvo B10M-62	Plaxton C53F	Wallace Arnold 00
N219 HWX	Volvo B10M-62	Plaxton C50F	Browne,Yiewsley 02
N220 HWX	Volvo B10M-62	Plaxton C53F	Wallace Arnold 01
N226 HWX	Volvo B10M-62	Plaxton C51F	Wallace Arnold 00

~~~~~~
~~~~~~

H5   LYN VALLEY COMMUNITY TRANSPORT ASSOCIATION

Address:1 Market Flat,Queen Street,LYNTON,Devon.

F389 HTA	Renault S56	WS B22FL	Wellington,Kingsbridge 96
H650 DKO	Ford Transit	Dormobile B16FL	Devon County Council 00
H187 FDV	Ford Transit	Dormobile B13FL	New 90
K676 TTT	Ford Transit	G & M B16F	New 92

~~~~~~
~~~~~~

H6   P. McGARRY.t/a G LINE HIRE

Depot:DNR Workshops,Wroughton Airfield,WROUGHTON,Wiltshire.

E128 AAL	Ford Transit	Mellor B16FL	Nottinghamshire CC 96
E991 ANC	Talbot Freeway	B18FL	Liverpool City Council 99
E131 ANU	Ford Transit	Mellor B16FL	Nottinghamshire CC 96
G555 DLV	Fiat 49-10	Mellor B16FL	Patterson,Birmingham 00
G556 DLV	Fiat 49-10	Mellor B16FL	Patterson,Birmingham 00
J415 KEC	Mercedes-Benz 308D	DC C12F	Raxwise,Ulverston 99
J595 MVU	DAF 400	MM C16F	New 91
M104 LOA	Talbot Freeway	B10FL	SEWAT,Canton 96
M105 LOA	Talbot Freeway	B10FL	SEWAT,Canton 97
M106 LOA	Talbot Freeway	B10FL	SEWAT,Canton 96
M107 LOA	Talbot Freeway	B10FL	SEWAT,Canton 96
M108 LOA	Talbot Freeway	B10FL	SEWAT,Canton 96
M109 LOA	Talbot Freeway	B10FL	SEWAT,Canton 96
M561 VUM	Ford Transit	Cunliffe B12FL	Leeds City Council 01
M562 VUM	Ford Transit	Cunliffe B12FL	Leeds City Council 01
M563 VUM	Ford Transit	Cunliffe B12FL	Leeds City Council 01
M631 VUM	Ford Transit	Cunliffe DP12FL	Leeds City Council 01
M632 VUM	Ford Transit	Cunliffe DP12FL	Leeds City Council 01
P 86 GOF	LDV Convoy	A Line B12FL	Non-PSV 00
R962 JCU	LDV Convoy	A Line B14F	New 98
R963 JCU	LDV Convoy	A Line B14F	New 98
S916 KRG	LDV Convoy	LDV B16F	New 99
S917 KRG	LDV Convoy	A Line B12FL	New 99
S919 KRG	LDV Convoy	LDV B16F	New 99
S164 UBU	Iveco 49-10	Mellor B16FL	Non-PSV(TLS) 01
S169 UBU	Iveco 49-10	Mellor B16FL	Non-PSV(TLS) 01
S171 UBU	Iveco 49-10	Mellor B16FL	Non-PSV(TLS) 01
T615 FPY	Iveco 49-10	Mellor B16FL	Non-PSV(TLS) 02
T620 FPY	Iveco 49-10	Mellor B16FL	Non-PSV(TLS) 02
T536 JND	Iveco 49-10	Mellor B16FL	Non-PSV(TLS) 02
X615 CWN	Mercedes-Benz 614D	Cymric C24F	New 00
X616 CWN	Mercedes-Benz 614D	Cymric C24F	New 00
X617 CWN	Mercedes-Benz 614D	Cymric C14FL	New 00
X618 CWN	Mercedes-Benz 614D	Cymric C24F	New 00

H7   R.E.,A. & P. MANSFIELD

Depot:Lotmead Farm,LOWER WANBOROUGH,Wiltshire.

PIL 3215	Toyota HZB50R	Caetano C21F	New 95
PIL 3216	Mercedes-Benz 412D	Olympus C16F	MCH,Uxbridge 98
PIL 3453	MAN 10.180	Caetano C35F	Johnson,Louth 94
PIL 3454	MAN 10.180	Caetano C35F	Hughes,Slough 97

PIL 3215*M380 KFP(3/99), PIL 3216*N267 TPM(5/99),
PIL 3453*G605 YUT(?/99) & PIL 3454*H391 CJF(?/99)

H8   MARCHANTS COACHES LTD

Depot:100 Prestbury Road,CHELTENHAM,Gloucestershire.

LIL 9843	Auwaerter N122/3	CH57/20CT	Lambert,Beccles 98
KTL 25V	Bristol VRT/SL3/6LXB	ECW H43/31F	Lincolnshire 1942 96
KTL 26V	Bristol VRT/SL3/6LXB	ECW H43/31F	Lincolnshire 1943 96
RUA 451W	Bristol VRT/SL3/6LXB	ECW H43/31F	Bennett &,Gloucester 00
RUA 452W	Bristol VRT/SL3/6LXB	ECW H43/31F	Bennett &,Gloucester 00
RUA 457W	Bristol VRT/SL3/6LXB	ECW H43/31F	Bennett &,Gloucester 01
TSO 17X	Leyland ONLXB/1R	ECW H45/32F	Stringer,Pontefract 00
TSO 31X	Leyland ONLXB/1R	ECW H43/32F	Davies,Bettws Gwerfil G 00
WDF 998X	Volvo B10M-56	Plaxton C53F	New 82
WDF 999X	Volvo B10M-56	Plaxton C53F	New 82
JEY 124Y	Volvo B10M-61	Plaxton C57F	Morris,Llanrug 90
E322 PMD	Volvo B10M-46	Plaxton B31C	Capital,West Drayton 99
E323 PMD	Volvo B10M-46	Plaxton B40F	Capital,West Drayton 99
E324 PMD	Volvo B10M-46	Plaxton B40F	Capital,West Drayton 99
E325 PMD	Volvo B10M-46	Plaxton B42F	Capital,West Drayton 99
F660 RTL	Volvo B10M-60	Plaxton C53F	Appleby 94
G448 CDG	Volvo B10M-60	Plaxton C53F	New 90
G993 DDF	Volvo B10M-60	Plaxton C51FT	New 90
G 50 ONN	Volvo B10M-60	Plaxton C57F	Skill,Nottingham 50 97
G 51 ONN	Volvo B10M-60	Plaxton C57F	Skill,Nottingham 51 97
L543 YUS	Volvo B10M-60	Van Hool C49FT	National Holidays 62 98
P 10 TCC	Auwaerter N122/3	CH57/20DT	Kings Ferry,Gillingham 02
R431 FWT	Volvo B10M-62	Plaxton C48FT	Wallace Arnold 00
R432 FWT	Volvo B10M-62	Plaxton C48FT	Wallace Arnold 00
R452 FWT	Volvo B10M-62	Plaxton C53F	Wallace Arnold 00
VX51 AWO	Mercedes-Benz O814D	Plaxton C25F	New 01

LIL 9843*E214 BOD(1/96), JEY 124Y*VYB 704(11/89reb) & MSU 593Y(12/84),
F660 RTL*5517 RH(5/94) & F287 OFE(10/90),
L543 YUS*KSK 954(5/94) & XIA 257(1/94) & P10 TCC*P981 HWF(11/96)

H9   D.G. MILES.t/a BMS COACHES

Depot:104a Swindon Road,STRATTON-ST-MARGARET,Wiltshire.

C737 MEJ	Bedford VAS5	Plaxton C29F	Evans,Penrhyncoch 91
L255 XHR	Mercedes-Benz 711D	ACL C19F	New 94
N971 WJL	Mercedes-Benz 308D	ACL C12F	New 96
P613 AJL	Mercedes-Benz O814D	ACL C29F	New 97
R 91 GWO	Mercedes-Benz O814D	ACL C29F	Bebb,Llantwit Fardre 01
R 95 HUA	Mercedes-Benz O1120L	Ferqui C35F	New 98
T 58 RJL	Mercedes-Benz 614D	ACL C19F	New 99
W183 RWP	Mercedes-Benz O814D	Onyx C24F	New 00
FY02 LCT	Mercedes-Benz 614D	ACL C24F	New 02

J1   J.E.,M. & K.P. MILLER

Depots:High Street Garage,BOX & Wood Yard,MIDDLEHALL,Wiltshire.

TPG 313X	Volvo B58-56	Duple C53F	Gale,Haslemere 88
ENF 570Y	Volvo B10M-61	Duple C53F	Smith-Shearings 246 89
B112 CCS	Volvo B10M-61	Plaxton C55F	Durber,Burslem 96
E170 OMU	Volvo B10M-61	Duple C49FT	Kavanagh,Urlingford(I) 93
K 62 BAX	Volvo B10M-60	Jonckheere C48FT	CS & GB,South Newton 02
K840 HUM	Volvo B10M-60	Jonckheere C50F	Pullman,Crofty 01

B112 CCS*OYY 3(4/94) & B112 CCS(3/88)

J2   MILLMANS COACHES LTD.t/a GREY CARS

Depot:6/7 Daneheath Business Park,Heathfield Ind. Estate,HEATHFIELD,Devon.

GIL 3113	Volvo B10M-61	Plaxton C51FT	New 85
MIL 2066	Auwaerter N122/3	CH57/18CT	Premiershow,Heywood 99
MIL 2088	Auwaerter N122/3	CH57/18CT	Airport,Stansted 97
MIL 3010	Volvo B10M-61	Plaxton C49FT	Park,Hamilton 88
MIL 3012	Volvo B10M-62	Van Hool C49FT	Park,Hamilton 96
PJI 2803	Volvo B10M-60	Jonckheere C51FT	Marbill,Beith 91
PJI 2804	Volvo B10M-61	Plaxton C53F	Frames-Rickards,Brentfd 91
PJI 2805	Volvo B10M-61	Plaxton C53F	Frames-Rickards,Brentfd 91
SIL 3066	Dennis Javelin	Berkhof C53F	Q Drive,Battersea 98
SIL 4460	Leyland TRCTL11/3RZ	Plaxton C53F	Hedingham & Dist. L195 99
SIL 4466	Leyland TRCTL11/3RZ	Plaxton C53F	Hedingham & Dist. L193 99
SIL 4470	Volvo B10M-62	Van Hool C51FT	New 96
KAD 355V	Leyland PSU5C/4R	Plaxton C57F	Plymouth 355 00
PWF 240X	Volvo B58-61	Plaxton C57F	Shaw,Barnsley 83
A104 OUG	Leyland ONTL11/1R	NC H43/28F	Arriva Cymru DOL104 00
E506 CTT	Mercedes-Benz 811D	DC C19F	Non-PSV(Plymouth) 95
M582 DAF	Toyota HZB50R	Caetano C21F	Western National 582 99
S748 XYA	Volvo B10M-62	Van Hool C51FT	New 98

GIL 3113*B230 RRU(6/90),
MIL 2066*E706 CHS(4/00) & MIL 2066(3/00) & E706 CHS(12/99) &
        HGR 150(2/98) & E706 CHS(7/97) & KFK 172(5/96) & E482 YWJ(10/93),
MIL 2088*E473 YWJ(12/97),
MIL 3010*PJI 2807(3/96) & D922 UOD(12/92) & 944 JTT(4/91) &
        D819 SGB(1/91), MIL 3012*L629 AYS(8/98) & LSK 483(11/95),
PJI 2803*G842 GNV(12/92), PJI 2804*B534 BML(12/92),
PJI 2805*B535 BML(12/92), SIL 3066*P889 FMO(12/99),
SIL 4460*D584 MVR(12/99), SIL 4466*D600 MVR(4/00),
SIL 4470*N25 EYB(12/99) &
E506 CTT*MIL 1942(2/01) & E506 CTT(5/00) & MIL 3012(11/97) &
        E506 CTT(3/96)

J3   A.J. MILLNER & A.L.B. PETERS.t/a ALVAJOAN COACHES

Depot:Unit 2,Cowley Bridge Road,EXETER,Devon.

NIL 5069	Van Hool T815	C48FT	Stoneman,Nanpean 99
NIL 8237	Bova EL26/581	C53F	Alfa,Chieveley 99
UJI 1757	Scania K112CRS	Van Hool C49FT	Renown,Bexhill 00
A 7 FRX	Scania K93CRB	Plaxton C53F	Kingston,Hockley 02
J 78 VTX	Kassbohrer S215	C49FT	Pan,Friern Barnet 02
R502 WJF	LDV Convoy	LDV B16F	Non-PSV(BCR) 02

NIL 5069*URL 335Y(9/00) & XRL 923(8/99) & FIL 8695(4/92) & MSU 853Y(6/90),
NIL 8237*274 FYP(2/98) & BAR 905X(9/85),
UJI 1757*IIL 5316(3/96) & TSV 759(7/93) & A28 FUF(12/86) &
A7 FRX*H524 DVM(2/96)

J4   J.F. MILLNER.t/a BATH MINIBUSES & BATH MINI TRAVEL

Depots:Unit 9,Ferry Court,Ferry Lane,Widcombe,BATH &
                              Timsbury Road,FARMBOROUGH,Somerset.

E149 AGG	Dennis Javelin	Duple C35F	Bornyard,Flitwick 01
F200 GMR	Toyota HB31R	Caetano C21F	Perkins,Telford 00
F194 HNN	Freight Rover Sherpa	Premier C16F	Snape,Bath 98
H688 UAK	Dennis Javelin	Plaxton C35F	Gordon,Rotherham 01
J409 GFG	DAF 400	Crystals C16F	Dosanjh,Strood 98
L945 GNF	DAF 400	Crystals C16F	Peruffo,Kimbolton 00
N751 VNA	LDV 400	? C16F	Reynolds,Maerdy 01
N989 WNE	LDV 400	Concept C16F	Snape,Bath 98
P133 NVM	LDV Convoy	Concept C16F	Greenwood,Gedling 02
R305 DUA	LDV Convoy	Concept C16F	Cropper,Kirkstall 01

E149 AGG*7178 KP(6/01) & E149 AGG(5/95)

P.J. MONAGHAN & C.D. KILLEEN.t/a COUNTY LINE & LITTLE BLUE BUS

Depot:The Garage,UPTON CROSS,Cornwall.

BMS 511Y	Leyland TRBTL11/3R	Alexander C51F	Bluebird Buses 447 01
BMS 513Y	Leyland TRBTL11/3R	Alexander C51F	Bluebird Buses 448 01
B331 LSA	Leyland TRCTL11/2RP	Alexander C51F	Bluebird Buses 445 01
D 89 VCC	Mercedes-Benz L608D	RB B20F	Arriva Manchester 1972 02
E 32 NEF	MCW Metrorider MF154	DP33F	Roberts,Rhandir 02

BMS 511Y*126 ASV(12/99) & BMS 511Y(8/86),
BMS 513Y*127 ASV(12/99) & BMS 513Y(8/86) &
B331 LSA*TSV 721(12/99) & B331 LSA(7/90)

J6   MOONWAY SERVICES LTD.t/a BAKERS COACHES

Depot:8 Buckland Road,Pen Mill Trading Estate,YEOVIL,Somerset.

IIL 2947	DAF MB230DKFL615	Plaxton C53F	Bailey,Biddisham 95
IIL 4154	Volvo B58-61	Duple C53F	Warren,Neath 98
IIL 8745	Bova FHD12-290	C49FT	Cowdrey,Gosport 98
NIB 8657	DAF MB200DKFL600	Jonckheere C49FT	Bridges,Saham Toney 91
NIB 8773	DAF MB230DKFL615	Plaxton C53F	Bailey,Biddisham 95
JRU 373V	DAF MB200DKTL600	Plaxton C51FT	Marsh,Wincanton 94
JKL 942Y	DAF SB2300DHS585	Berkhof C49FT	Baker,Duloe 97
A298 SPS	Bedford VAS5	Plaxton C29F	Perry,Blackwood 02
B 85 ACX	DAF MB200DKFL600	Caetano C53F	Ford,Gunnislake 90
B608 EYB	Kassbohrer S215H	C53F	Kerry,Killarney(Ire) 00
D 42 VDV	MB O303/15RHS	C53F	Millmans,Newton Abbot 00
E343 EVH	DAF MB230LB615	Van Hool C55F	Hand,Horsley 97
J763 CWT	Mercedes-Benz 308D	DC C12F	Wallace Arnold 02

IIL 2947*D623 YCX(8/92), IIL 4154*WUO 765V(4/93), IIL 8745*E277 HRY(6/94),
NIB 8657*A371 UNH(10/91),
NIB 8773*D785 RYD(11/95) & 28 XYB(8/95) & D629 YCX(2/92),
JRU 373V*5515 LJ(1/88) & KDV 896V(3/83),
JKL 942Y*8465 LJ(2/95) & LHK 645Y(3/88), B608 EYB*890 PIP(5/00),
D42 VDV*MIL 3012(8/98) & MIL 2088(11/97) & D409 OSJ(3/96) &
         GIL 1683(12/91) & D353 CBC(4/90) &
E343 EVH*B7 AND(4/97) & E343 EVH(2/96)

J7   R.J. & K. MOORE.t/a ZOAR COACHES

Depot:Zoar Garage,ST. KEVERNE,Cornwall.

705 AOW	3	Ford R1115	Plaxton C53F	Titchen,Sth Benfleet 92
HGD 899N	2	Ford R1014	Plaxton C45F	Ede,Par 82
PYA 645P		Bedford YRQ	Plaxton C45F	Bryant &,Williton 98
FDV 787V	9	Bristol LHS6L	ECW B35F	Western National 1557 90
MPH 5W	7	Ford R1114	Plaxton C53F	Western National 2461 92
B697 WAR		LD TRCTL11/3RH	Plaxton C51F	Danter,Llangeinor 00
E680 RGL	8	FR Sherpa	MM C16F	New 88

705 AOW*BLJ 706Y(4/92)

J8   S.B. MOORE.t/a OTS MINIBUS & COACH HIRE

Depot:c/o Walker,Kerrick Business Park,Kerrick Road,PENRYN,Cornwall.

XSU 746	Mercedes-Benz 408D	DC C16F	Cornwall County Council 92
841 ERL	DAF MB200DKTL600	Plaxton C53F	Pollard,Ruan Minor 3 94
573 LCV	Toyota HB31R	Caetano C21F	Pollard,Ruan Minor 12 94
873 VRL	Leyland TRCTL11/1RH	RB C35F	Tayside 235 97

XSU 746*291 TRL(3/96) & G93 AAF(6/92),
841 ERL*XAF 900(7/94) & KYD 344Y(3/89), 573 LCV*G913 DCV(4/94) &
873 VRL*LXJ 462(8/97) & B835 VSR(6/86)

J9   T.S. MOORE.t/a TJs COACHES

Depots:HAZELBURY BRYAN & Butts Pond Ind Estate,STURMINSTER NEWTON,Dorset.

MIL 1054	Volvo B10M-61	Plaxton C51F	Monetgrange,Nottingham 97
JNM 745Y	Bedford YNT	Plaxton C53F	Bugler,Bristol 94
A646 GLD	Volvo B10M-61	Plaxton C53F	Staples,Leominster 96
K264 SSD	Volvo B10M-60	Plaxton C57F	Wickson,Walsall Wood 01

MIL 1054*WEC 761Y(3/96) & 8850 WU(10/95) & JNV 627Y(4/91reb) &
JNM 745Y*280 OHT(2/94) & JNM 745Y(6/87)

K1   MOUNTS BAY COACHES LTD

Depot:The Garage,Eastern Green,PENZANCE,Cornwall.

MIB 9068	Bedford YMT	Plaxton C53F	Herrington,Alderholt 98
OXI 483	Volvo B10M-61	Plaxton C49FT	Spring,Evesham 96
OXI 499	Volvo B58-61	Plaxton C57F	Ford,Gunnislake 89
OXI 626	DAF MB200DKTL600	Plaxton C49FT	Plumpton Coaches 90
OXI 630	Volvo B10M-61	Van Hool C49FT	Dawlish Coaches 99
OXI 725	Duple 425	C59F	Silcox,Pembroke Dock 94
OXI 726	Volvo B10M-60	Van Hool C49FT	Timeline,Bolton 973 00
OXI 7058	Mercedes-Benz 609D	RB C23F	Pollard,Ruan Minor 97
OXI 8095	Bedford YRQ	Duple C45F	Garrett,Newton Abbot 84
UTT 806	Volvo B10M-61	Van Hool C49FT	Kingdoms,Tiverton 02

MIB 9068*EMJ 991T(11/89), OXI 483*9896 EL(8/97) & A852 AUY(2/91),
OXI 499*ARL 754T(5/89) & 674 SHY(2/89) & DMJ 755T(1/88),
OXI 626*YBP 939(8/97) & YFX 183Y(6/84),
OXI 630*8 RDV(3/99) & A896 PTA(7/88),
OXI 725*D45 KDE(2/95) & A3 WLS(10/94) & D901 HBX(12/92),
OXI 726*H173 DVM(10/00), OXI 7058*F981 EYD(4/98),
OXI 8095*NDC 333P(1/90) &
UTT 806*HGR 150(1/94) & YNE 758Y(9/93) & HGR 150(7/93) & BPC 222Y(5/88)

L.C. MUNDEN & SON LTD/A.J. PETERS.t/a ABUS & CROWN COACHES

Depots:6/7 Freestone Road & Kingsland Road Sidings,St. Philips,BRISTOL.

```
TAZ 4992   Leyland RT            Leyland C49FT    Merthyr Tydfil 1 89
MOU 747R   Bristol VRT/SL3/6LXB  ECW H43/27D      First Bristol 5073 99
NFB 113R   Bristol VRT/SL3/6LXB  ECW H43/33F      Bristol 5077 93
XAK 912T   ·Bristol VRT/SL3/501  ECW H43/31F      Rennie,Dunfermline 02
AHW 198V   Bristol VRT/SL3/6LXB  ECW H43/27D      First Bristol 5147 00
KOO 791V   Bristol VRT/SL3/6LXB  ECW H39/31F      Bristol 5553 98
KOO 792V   Bristol VRT/SL3/6LXB  ECW H39/31F      Bristol 5551 00
KOO 793V   Bristol VRT/SL3/6LXB  ECW H39/31F      Bristol 5554 00
EWS 739W   Bristol VRT/SL3/680   ECW H43/31F      Bristol 5531 00
EWS 741W   Bristol VRT/SL3/680   ECW H43/31F      Bristol 5533 99
GGM  78W   Bristol VRT/SL3/6LXB  ECW H43/31F      Rennie,Dunfermline 02
GGM  79W   Bristol VRT/SL3/6LXB  ECW H43/31F      Rennie,Dunfermline 02
LFJ 862W   Bristol VRT/SL3/6LXB  ECW H43/31F      Rennie,Dunfermline 02
STW  33W   Bristol VRT/SL3/6LXB  ECW H39/31F      First Bristol 5560 00
XHK 221X   Bristol VRT/SL3/6LXB  ECW H43/31F      Bristol 5562 01
XHK 222X   Bristol VRT/SL3/6LXB  ECW H43/31F      Bristol 5563 99
RBO 506Y   Leyland ONLXB/1R      EL H43/31F       Cardiff 506 98
RBO 508Y   Leyland ONLXB/1R      EL H43/31F       Cardiff 508 98
B823 YTC   Leyland TRCTL11/3LZ   WS DP68FA        MOD 98
D283 XCX   DAF SB2305DHTD585     Plaxton C53F     Bennett,Gloucester 92
E211 JDD   DAF SB2305DHTD585     Plaxton C53F     Bennett,Gloucester 92
K474 NTP   Renault Master        Pearl B16F       S Munden,Bristol 01
R222 AJP   DAF DE02RSDB250       Optare H51/30F   New 98
S111 AJP   DAF DE02RSDB250       Optare H50/27F   New 98
V444 AJP   DAF DE02RSDB250       AR H45/24F       New 99
```

TAZ 4992*D801 NBO(2/98)

K3   MYRTLE TREE HOLDINGS LTD.t/a AZTEC

Depot:16 Emery Road,Brislington,BRISTOL.

```
F882 OHY   Mercedes-Benz 609D    RB C25F      New 88
F616 PRE   Mercedes-Benz 609D    PMT C26F     Charlesworth,Melksham 89
H715 FWD   Talbot Freeway        B16FL        Non-PSV(Bristol) 96
P913 XUG   Mercedes-Benz O814D   ACL C29F     New 97
S925 RBE   Mercedes-Benz O814D   ACL C33F     New 98
VU51 GGK   Mercedes-Benz 614D    Onyx C24F    New 02
```

K4   D. OATES.t/a OATES TRAVEL

Depot:Riverside,Rosepeath Industrial Estate,CROWLAS,Cornwall.

```
831  OCV   Volvo B10M-61      Plaxton C55F     New 87
682  VAF   Volvo B10M-60      Plaxton C47FT    Park,Hamilton 90
AAF 409T   Volvo B58-56       Plaxton C53F     New 79
A 1  DWO   Kassbohrer S250    C53F             Q Drive,Battersea 99
E400 JNR   Toyota HB31R       Caetano C21F     Beavis,Bussage 92
M662 BAF   Volvo B10M-62      Van Hool C49FT   New 94
N976 LCL   Toyota HZB50R      Caetano C21F     Sanders,Holt 11 99
S686 EAF   Volvo B10M-62      Van Hool C49FT   New 98
```

831 OCV*D756 MRL(3/93), 682 VAF*F997 HGE(7/99), A1 DWO*M975 NFU(4/99) &
N976 LCL*N11 NJS(3/99)

K5   C.E. PALMER.t/a WHEAL BRITON COACHES

Depot:Ivy Cottage,BLACKWATER,Cornwall.

CCZ 2215	Volvo B10M-60	Plaxton C57F	Castell,Trethomas 01
JIL 9410	Kassbohrer S210HD	C35FT	Buckley,Killarney(Ire) 00
RBZ 2673	Volvo B10M-61	Plaxton C53F	Claremont,Worcester Pk 00
156 FMU	Scania K112CRB	Plaxton C51FT	Woollon,Feltham 96
F127 AEL	Volvo B10M-60	Plaxton C57F	Castell,Trethomas 01
K 7 DTS	Scania K113CRB	Plaxton C51FT	Durham Travel,Hetton-H. 98
L542 JJV	Scania K113CRB	Irizar C49FT	Appleby 98
L230 RDO	Scania K113CRB	Irizar C49FT	Appleby 98

CCZ 2215*F128 AEL(9/99) & A16 EXC(1/95) & F456 WFX(3/92),
JIL 9410*B220 EGP(4/00) & 85KY 333(3/00) & B220 EGP(3/91) & OO 1942(2/90),
RBZ 2673*D570 KJT(6/97) & XEL 31(3/89) & D268 HFX(10/87),
156 FMU*F87 CWG(11/97) &
F127 AEL*CCZ 2215(3/01) & F127 AEL(9/99) & A13 EXC(1/95) & F455 WFX(3/92)

K6   J.V. PICKFORD.t/a FARESAVER,FOSSEWAY & NEXTBUS

Depots:Camerton Inn,MEADGATE,Somerset &
*   10 Vincients Road,Bumpers Enterprise Centre,CHIPPENHAM,Wiltshire.*

PSV 444	Mercedes-Benz 811D	Whittaker B31F	Arriva Shires 2061 00
TIL 2741	Mercedes-Benz 609D	RB B20F	Arriva Scotland W. 323 00
TIL 2742	Mercedes-Benz 609D	RB B20F	Arriva Scotland W. 346 01
TIL 2744	Mercedes-Benz 709D	RB B25F	Arriva Shires 2043 00
TIL 2745	Mercedes-Benz 609D	RB B24F	Gascoine,Sandford 54 96
TIL 2746	Mercedes-Benz 609D	RB B20F	Evans,Prenton 96
TIL 2747	Mercedes-Benz 609D	RB C16F	Sarang,Leicester 96
D413 TFT	Mercedes-Benz 709D	RB B20F	Munden,Bristol 00
E880 DRA	Mercedes-Benz 811D	Optare B33F	Horrocks,Brockton 01
E 45 UKL	Mercedes-Benz 609D	RB B20F	Arriva Cymru MMM645 01
F328 FCY	Mercedes-Benz 814D	Robin Hood B31F	First Cymru 328 99
F378 UCP	Mercedes-Benz 609D	RB B20F	Whitehead,Hoddlesdon 00
G434 ETW	Ford Transit	Dormobile B16F	Hillman,Tredegar 95
G 75 ONN	Mercedes-Benz 609D	North West C24F	Downton,Dorchester 02
G411 PGG	Mercedes-Benz 811D	RB B33F	Cedar,Bedford 02
G 71 PKR	Mercedes-Benz 609D	RB DP21F	Arriva Kent YFB71 01
G842 UDV	Mercedes-Benz 811D	Carlyle DP29F	Thames Transit 366 02
G844 UDV	Mercedes-Benz 811D	Carlyle DP29F	Davies,Bettws Gwerfil G 01
H185 CNS	Mercedes-Benz 609D	MM B26F	Arriva Scotland W. 308 01
H204 EKO	Mercedes-Benz 709D	Carlyle B25F	Arriva Kent 1204 02
H985 FTT	Mercedes-Benz 811D	Carlyle DP29F	Bluebird Buses 251 01
H103 HDV	Mercedes-Benz 811D	Carlyle B29F	Woods,Wigston 01
H882 LOX	Mercedes-Benz 811D	Carlyle B31F	Dolan,Barrhead 00
H523 SWE	Mercedes-Benz 709D	Whittaker B29F	Arriva Shires 2056 00
J408 PRW	Mercedes-Benz 811D	Wright B33F	Midland Red South 408 02
K865 ODY	Mercedes-Benz 709D	ARB B25F	Stagecoach South 865 02
K542 OGA	Mercedes-Benz 811D	Dormobile B33F	Arriva Cymru MMM842 01
L318 AUT	Mercedes-Benz 709D	ARB B25F	Arriva Fox County 1318 02
L422 CPB	Mercedes-Benz 709D	Dormobile B25F	Arriva Fox County 01
L423 CPB	Mercedes-Benz 709D	Dormobile B25F	Arriva Fox County 01
L428 CPC	Mercedes-Benz 709D	Dormobile B27F	Arriva Cymru MMM728 01
L228 HRF	Mercedes-Benz 709D	Dormobile B27F	Arriva Fox County 1330 02
L229 HRF	Mercedes-Benz 709D	Dormobile B29F	Arriva Midlands Nth 229 02
L231 HRF	Mercedes-Benz 709D	Dormobile B29F	Arriva Fox County 1331 02
M236 KNR	Mercedes-Benz 709D	Alexander B29F	Arriva Fox County 1366 02
M122 YCM	Mercedes-Benz 709D	Alexander B27F	Arriva Cymru MMM730 01

PSV 444*H641 UWE(?/01), TIL 2741*D441 RKE(8/00),
TIL 2742*E50 UKL(8/00), TIL 2744*F128 TRU(8/00),
TIL 2745*F132 KAO(8/00), TIL 2746*F133 KAO(8/00),
TIL 2747*F407 MTY(8/00) & G58 RGG*G673 NUA(5/94)

K7   PLAINGLOBE LTD

Depot:c/o Jewsons,Tyning Road,BATHAMPTON,Somerset.

ERV 249D	Leyland PDR1/1	MCW O43/33F	Bournemouth(Vintage) 01
ERV 251D	Leyland PDR1/1	MCW O43/33F	Bournemouth(Vintage) 02
OJD 405R	Leyland FE30ALR	PR O44/22D	Kinch,Barrow-on-Soar 94
OJD 469R	Leyland FE30ALR	PR O44/24D	London Buses DMS2469 93
HWG 208W	Bristol VRT/SL3/6LXB	ECW H43/31F	Hoar & Savage,Tilsworth 02

K8   POINTMOST LTD.t/a GIRLINGS OF PLYMOUTH

Depot:4 Clock Tower Business Centre,Central Ave.,Lee Mill,IVYBRIDGE,Devon.

FDZ 3014	Volvo B10M-61	Van Hool C53F	Weaver,Newbury 01
KSU 460	Volvo B10M-60	Van Hool C53F	Wallace Arnold 02
LBZ 7534	Volkswagen LT55	Optare C21F	Chester,Plymouth 98
NIL 6486	Volvo B58-56	Plaxton C53F	Travel Final,Blaengarw 01
PJI 8364	Leyland TRCL10/3ARZM	Duple C59F	Filer,Stanton Wick 02
SJI 5617	Volvo B58-61	Plaxton C57F	Solent,Wootton 01
TIL 2177	Volvo B10M-61	Van Hool C57F	Foster,Glastonbury 02
TIL 7904	Volvo B10M-60	Van Hool C48FT	Kings Ferry,Gillingham 00
TIL 7906	Volvo B10M-61	Plaxton C53F	Dawlish Coaches 00
TIL 7907	Volvo B10M-60	Caetano C53F	Dawlish Coaches 00
TIL 7908	DAF MB230LB615	Caetano C49FT	Heaton,Mayford 01
TIL 7909	Volvo B10M-60	Jonckheere C51FT	Berrys,Taunton 01
TIL 9074	Volvo B10M-46	Plaxton C38FT	Rignall,Kingskerswell 02
647 PYC	Volvo B58-56	Plaxton C53F	Cowdrey,Gosport 01
701 UDE	Volvo B58-61	Plaxton C51F	Cowdrey,Gosport 01
ORS 86R	Leyland PSU4D/4R	Alexander DP45F	Perry,Bromyard 50 96
UCA 508V	Bedford YMT	Unicar C53F	Ball,Plymouth 97
GJR 878W	Ford Transit	Dormobile B16F	Walton,Cardiff 89
SGS 510W	Volvo B58-61	Plaxton C32F	Chalfont,Southall 01
VJT 620X	Ford R1114	Plaxton C53F	Chester,Plymouth 98
CVU 302Y	Ford Transit	Dixon Lomas C12F	Lang,Plymouth 95
E248 EGY	Freight Rover Sherpa	Crystals C16F	Brenton,Plymouth 98
G943 TTA	Mercedes-Benz 408D	DC B15F	Torbay Council 02
L919 NWW	Volvo B10M-60	Van Hool C50F	James,Cenarth 01

OTHER VEHICLE OWNED BY THE COMPANY
* * * * * * *

NGR 117T	Leyland PSU5C/4R	Plaxton C-F	Seatstore

FDZ 3014*A175 MNE(4/89),
KSU 460*J691 LGA(2/95) & LSK 502(11/94) & J462 HDS(2/93),
LBZ 7534*D555 TMR(4/96), NIL 6486*KYC 984V(4/01) & KYC 983V(1/81),
PJI 8364*E449 MMM(8/98), SJI 5617*MGD 942V(8/94), TIL 2177*E473 TYC(3/02),
TIL 7904*K42 SBY(2/01) & B13 APT(10/98) & K292 GDT(4/98),
TIL 7906*E592 UHS(2/01), TIL 7907*G996 OKK(2/01),
TIL 7908*E182 KNH(2/01) & HIL 5682(1/99) & E182 KNH(1/97),
TIL 7909*G846 NYC(2/01),
TIL 9074*E594 UHS(4/02) & WJY 530(7/00) & E594 UHS(3/93),
647 PYC*NTT 575W(3/02),
701 UDE*LUA 244V(2/00) & 991 FOT(2/00) & LUA 244V(11/94),
SGS 510W*TIL 9074(4/02) & SGS 510W(4/01) &
L919 NWW*B20 APT(3/00) & L919 NWW(4/98)

K9   J.P. & D.M. POWELL.t/a POWELLS COACHES

Depot:2 The Barris,LAPFORD,Devon.

JUI 3850	Volvo B10M-60	Plaxton C53F	Cleverly,Cwmbran 99
KIW 3080	Leyland TRCTL11/3R	Plaxton C51FT	Hill,Hersham 94
PIJ 4690	Leyland TRCTL11/3R	Plaxton C53F	Ribblesdale,Gt Harwood 90
PIJ 5170	Leyland TRCTL11/3R	Duple C53F	Ribblesdale,Gt Harwood 91

```
RJI 1630  Leyland TRCTL11/3RZ  Plaxton C51F        Holmeswood,Rufford 93
VJI 4012  Mercedes-Benz O303/2  C49FT              Kings Ferry,Gillingham 01
VJI 4014  Leyland TRCTL11/3RZ  Van Hool C53F       Kingdom,Tiverton 97
```
~~~~~~
```
JUI 3850*G117 XRE(2/99), KIW 3080*A381 AKW(12/89),
PIJ 4690*MEO 199Y(8/90), PIJ 5170*B206 AFV(3/91), RJI 1630*B109 NPY(6/93),
VJI 4012*H4 KFC(6/01) &
VJI 4014*YOD 544(5/97) & C219 WPA(5/95) & 2003 RU(8/94) & C228 EME(11/87)
```
~~~~~~

L1   D.W. & J. PRATT.t/a JACKIES COACHES

Depot:The Old Airfield,MORETON VALENCE,Gloucestershire.

```
IUI 7210  Fiat 49-10            RB B25F            Stagecoach Devon 384 98
IUI 7211  Leyland TRCL10/3ARZM  Plaxton C53F       National Holidays 32 01
LBZ 2944  Leyland TRCTL11/3RZ   Plaxton C53F       Gardner,Raynes Park 01
TIL 5930  Mercedes-Benz 811D    Marshall B31F      Arriva Cymru MMM880 02
TIL 5931  Mercedes-Benz 709D    Phoenix B27F       Arriva Cymru MMM229 00
TIL 5932  Mercedes-Benz 709D    Robin Hood DP25F   Arriva Cymru MMM222 00
TIL 5933  Mercedes-Benz 709D    Robin Hood DP25F   Arriva Cymru MMM228 00
TJI 5399  Scania K112CRB        Van Hool C49F      Dodds,Troon 01
B504 MDC  Bedford YMP           Plaxton C35F       Reynolds,Maerdy 99
B 7  OJC  Volvo B10M-61         Plaxton C49F       Harrison,Morecambe 98
B 17 OJC  DAF SB3000DKSB585     Plaxton C49FT      Burton,Haverhill 98
E270 CPU  Ford Transit          Steedrive B2FL     Essex County Council 98
E941 KEU  Fiat 49-10            Robin Hood B21F    Bristol 4941 97
G382 BEV  Ford Transit          Steedrive B2FL     Essex County Council 99
H189 YAL  Ford Transit          LCB B16FL          Nottinghamshire CC 99
```
~~~~~~
OTHER VEHICLE OWNED BY THE COMPANY
* * * * * * *
```
A694 PKE  Ford Transit          Dormobile B12FL    Store
```
~~~~~~
```
IUI 7210*G924 KWF(5/99),
IUI 7211*F717 ENE(12/01) & 552 UTE(2/01) & F717 ENE(2/93),
LBZ 2944*D594 MVR(6/94), TIL 5930*L193 DBC(?/02), TIL 5931*G229 FJC(2/01),
TIL 5932*F222 DCC(12/00), TIL 5933*F428 EJC(12/01),
TJI 5399*E755 TCS(6/95),
B7 OJC*E570 UHS(5/98) & 4360 WF(9/97) & E570 UHS(8/89) &
B17 OJC*D284 XCX(8/98)
```
~~~~~~

L2   PREMIERE COACH TRAVEL LTD

Depot:Milber Trading Estate,Haccombe Path,NEWTON ABBOT,Devon.

```
HIL 8442  Volvo B10M-60         Plaxton C49FT      Renton,Kirknewton 02
IIL 1318  Volvo B10M-61         Plaxton C53F       York Pullman,Elvington 00
KIB 8111  Iveco 391E            Beulas C49FT       Evans,Newton Abbot 01
KIW 8610  Volvo B58-56          Plaxton C53F       Wiseman,Galmpton 00
LIW 4078  Bova FHD12-280        C49FT              Eyres-Scott,Brentwood 99
TIA 6937  Volvo B10M-53         PN CH54/13CT       Bharat,Southall 01
TJI 5843  Mercedes-Benz 0303    Jonckheere C49FT   Bowers,Chapel-en-Frith 00
UCY  629  Auwaerter N122/3      CH57/20CT          Coach Hire,Henfield 99
UDO  475  Volvo B58-61          Duple C57F         Garrett,Newton Abbot 00
UJI 5789  Volvo B10M-61         Van Hool C46FT     Dodds,Ayr 02
WYD 397M  Volvo B58-56          Plaxton C51F       Williams,Camborne 99
PUN 197S  Bedford YMT           Duple C53F         Hookways,Meeth 01
YYL 781T  Bedford YMT           Duple C53F         Treneary,Paignton 00
BVY 164V  DAF MB200DKTL600      Plaxton C56F       Wilkins,Paignton 01
LFH 900V  DAF MB200DKTL600      Plaxton C50FT      Wilkins,Paignton 01
HBH 412Y  Bedford YNT           Duple C53F         Hookways,Meeth 01
A 27 TNK  Bova EL26/581         C49FT              Treneary,Paignton 00
B991 UPS  Volvo B10M-61         Plaxton C53FT      Senior,Witney 01
E134 KRP  LAG Panoramic         C49FT              Shreeve,Lowestoft 00
E674 NNV  LAG Panoramic         C49FT              Shreeve,Lowestoft 00
H 2  LWJ  LAG E180Z             C53FT              Williamson,Catcliffe 00
H329 POG  Scania K113TRB        VH CH53/14CT       Courtney,Bracknell 01
```

```
L332 BFX  MAN 16.290            Berkhof C49F    Ashall,Clayton 99
P 9 YET   Iveco 391E            Beulas C49FT    Yorkshire,Boroughbridge 02
```

```
HIL 8442*K14 FTG(2/99) & K286 XOG(1/93), IIL 1318*C117 DWR(6/92),
KIW 8610*29 DRH(6/93) & OMA 896V(5/88), LIW 4078*B763 JGM(3/91),
TIA 6937*C740 GOP(10/91),
TJI 5843*A17 ETS(10/95) & 3653 RE(4/94) & 203 YKX(5/92) & A126 SNH(3/88),
UCY 629*OES 629Y(3/87) & 9492 SC(10/85) & NES 482Y(7/84),
UDO 475*YPX 112V(1/86), UJI 5789*E318 OPR(5/96),
PUN 197S*MIL 4680(1/02) & PUN 197S(5/96),
A27 TNK*697 BYU(12/97) & A27 TNK(5/96) & 2917 MK(1/89),
B991 UPS*YSU 989(6/94) & B619 AMD(9/90),
E134 KRP*LIL 9454(5/99) & E134 KRP(1/96),
E674 NNV*TIL 9162(1/02) & E674 NNV(3/01) & LIL 9455(1/00) &
        E674 NNV(1/96), H2 LWJ*H747 BCU(3/93) &
H329 POG*H10 WLE(5/98) & H682 FCU(12/96) & KSU 463(10/93) &
        H133 ACU(4/92)
```
~~~~~~

L3   PULHAM & SONS (COACHES) LTD

Depot:Station Road Garage,BOURTON-ON-THE-WATER,Gloucestershire.

```
FDF  965  Volvo B10M-60          Plaxton C55F    New 91
HDF  661  Volvo B10M-60          Plaxton C53F    Bonas,Coventry 93
LDD  488  Volvo B10M-61          Plaxton C53F    New 88
NDD  672  Volvo B10M-56          Plaxton C53F    Marchant,Cheltenham 97
ODF  561  Leyland TRCL10/3ARZA   Plaxton C53F    Metropolitan Police 97
PDF  567  Volvo B10M-60          Plaxton C53F    Bonas,Coventry 93
TJI 8780  Leyland TRCTL11/2R     Plaxton C51F    Southern Vectis 310 97
UDF  936  Volvo B10M-61          Plaxton C53F    New 89
VAD  141  Volvo B10M-56          Plaxton C53F    Smith,Tring 95
VDF  365  Leyland TR2R           Plaxton C53F    Metropolitan Police 97
WDD  194  Volvo B10M-62          Van Hool C49FT  New 96
WDF  946  Leyland TRCTL11/2R     Plaxton C53F    Pilcher,Strood 86
XDG  614  Volvo B10M-62          Plaxton C53F    Trueman,Fleet 01
C193 CYO  Volvo B10M-46          Plaxton C37F    Tellings-GM,Byfleet 89
C 71 XDG  Leyland TRCTL11/3R     Plaxton C53F    New 86
G680 YLP  Ford Transit           Dormobile B16F  LB Harrow 96
J914 MDG  Volvo B10M-60          Plaxton C57F    New 91
L202 MHL  DAF 400                ACL C16F        Mayne,Buckie 98
P618 FTV  Volvo B10M-62          Plaxton C53F    Southern Vectis 905 00
P361 UFH  Toyota HZB50R          Caetano C21F    New 96
P 9  WAC  Volvo B10M-48          Van Hool C38F   Cheyne,Daviot 99
R748 SDF  Volvo B10M-62          Plaxton C53F    New 98
Y852 SDD  Mercedes-Benz O814D    Plaxton C33F    New 01
VU51 FGN  Volvo B10M-62          Plaxton C57F    New 01
```

~~~~~~
```
FDF 965*H345 KDF(4/98), HDF 661*H155 HAC(3/94), LDD 488*F150 RFH(1/93),
NDD 672*A233 MDD(5/97) & A4 DOF(4/94) & A899 YOV(2/93) & 6349 D(2/93) &
        A733 JAY(4/87), ODF 561*J935 CYK(4/98), PDF 567*H156 HAC(4/94),
TJI 8780*WDL 142(10/95) & WDL 310Y(7/92), UDF 936*F401 UAD(1/93),
VAD 141*A22 NRO(11/95), VDF 365*J933 CYK(4/98), WDD 194*N680 RDD(3/01),
WDF 946*A748 JAY(4/95), XDG 614*L671 OHL(1/02),
C193 CYO*ODF 561(4/98) & C193 CYO(1/93),
C71 XDG*XDG 614(1/02) & C71 XDG(1/93) &
P618 FTV*473 CDL(6/99) & P618 FTV(2/99)
```
~~~~~~

L4   R & R COACHES LTD.t/a BEELINE

Depot:Bishopstrow Road,WARMINSTER,Wiltshire.

```
ANZ 3607  Volvo B10M-61          Plaxton C53F    Cropley,Fosdyke 02
BNZ 4922  Volvo B10M-61          Plaxton C49FT   Burton,Haverhill 01
IIL 1353  Bedford YNT            Plaxton C53F    East Surrey,S. Godstone 96
NIL 1387  Bedford YNT            Plaxton C53F    Cooper,Maiden Bradley 98
NIL 9886  Volvo B10M-61          Plaxton C53F    Eastbourne 3 97
RIL 1203  Volvo B10M             Plaxton C53F    ? 01
```

```
RJI 8602   Volvo B10M-61         Plaxton C53F     Goodwin,Witheridge 97
TJI 6312   Volvo B10M-61         Plaxton C53F     Wickson,Clayhanger 02
WJI 2839   Bedford YNT           Plaxton C53F     Cooper,Maiden Bradley 98
XIB 1907   Volvo B10M-56         Plaxton C57F     Smith,Tring 98
YAZ 8922   Volvo B10M-61         Plaxton C50FT    Stagecoach South 8618 99
6220  WY   Volvo B10M-60         Plaxton C53F     Essex Buses 1133 00
832  JYA   Volvo B10M            Plaxton C53F     ? 02
L694 JEC   Mercedes-Benz 609D    Concept C24F     Peruzza,Kendal 98
N604 ADC   Mercedes-Benz 814D    ACL C33F         Costelloe,Dundee 97
N123 DNV   Mercedes-Benz 711D    Plaxton C25F     Country Lion,Northamptn 98
N270 KAM   Mercedes-Benz 811D    Plaxton B33F     New 95
N271 KAM   Mercedes-Benz 811D    Plaxton B33F     New 95
N272 KAM   Mercedes-Benz 811D    Plaxton B33F     New 95
N273 KAM   Mercedes-Benz 811D    Plaxton B33F     New 95
N274 KAM   Mercedes-Benz 811D    Plaxton B33F     New 95
N275 KAM   Mercedes-Benz 814D    Plaxton C33F     New 95
N276 KAM   Mercedes-Benz 814D    Plaxton C33F     New 95
N460 KMW   Mercedes-Benz 814D    ACL C33F         Mayne,Buckie 98
P691 LKL   LDV Convoy            Jaycas C16F      Jaycrest,Sittingbourne 01
P689 VHU   LDV Convoy            LDV B16F         New 97
R767 OHY   LDV Convoy            LDV B16F         New 97
V116 GWP   Mercedes-Benz O814D   Onyx C24F        New 00
```

```
ANZ 3607*B505 CGP(?/01) & EAZ 4709(12/99) & B505 CGP(3/95),
BNZ 4922*D328 UTU(?/02) & VLT 149(11/95) & VLT 229(4/94) &
        D287 UDM(11/87), IIL 1353*D380 BNR(10/97),
NIL 1387*D913 JHW(3/98) & HWV 904(12/97), NIL 9886*C580 KNO(12/97),
RIL 1203*   ? (6/01), RJI 8602*E828 EUT(4/99), TJI 6312*D575 MVR(3/95),
WJI 2839*C288 NFV(2/98) & XMR 558(1/98) & C288 NFV(3/93),
XIB 1907*C24 KBH(8/95),
YAZ 8922*D326 GCD(4/99) & WVT 618(1/99) & D202 LWX(12/90),
6220 WY*F947 WFA(11/95) & 1879 RU(3/95) & F486 LHO(4/92),
832 JYA*   ? (?/02) & N123 DNV*L10 NKK(3/98) & A19 CLN(7/96)
```

L5   M. RAWLINGS.t/a JOHN MARTIN COACHES

Depot:c/o St John Ambulance,Radstock Road,MIDSOMER NORTON,Somerset.

```
TIL 6721   Volvo B10M-61         Plaxton C53F     Burdett,Mosborough 01
TIL 6722   Volvo B10M-61         Berkhof C49FT    Savage,Walderslade 00
VIB 7660   Bova EL26/581         C53F             Phillips,Barking 99
AAL 587A   Leyland TRCTL11/3R    Plaxton C57F     Brown,Motcombe 02
```

```
TIL 6721*F532 GET(?/01) & BAZ 2563(5/01) & F532 GET(10/93),
TIL 6722*780 VHW(11/00) & A573 RVW(1/87),
VIB 7660*APT 416B(4/96) & PMS 1M(10/94) & PMS 371(?/91) &
        LIB 4333(10/89) & OOU 854Y(7/88) & AAL 587A*SDW 920Y(9/85)
```

L6   B.J. & P.J. REDWOOD.t/a REDWOODS TRAVEL

Depot:Unit 3,Industrial Park,Station Road,HEMYOCK,Devon.

```
EOI 4363   Volvo B58-61          Plaxton C53F     Carr,Pluckley 00
USV  330   DAF MB230LB615        Caetano C49FT    Boorman,Henlow 01
USV  331   DAF MB200DKFL600      Plaxton C53F     Filer,Ilfracombe 02
USV  462   Volvo B10M-60         Duple C53FT      Skill,Nottingham 56 01
USV  474   Iveco 59-12           G & M C16F       Wighton,Kingsbury Epis. 01
USV  511   Scania K113TRB        Irizar C51FT     Tarhum,Nailsea 02
USV  556   Volvo B10M-61         Plaxton C53F     J & B,Horsforth 02
USV  562   Mercedes-Benz 408D    Crystals C15F    Dealtop,Clyst St Mary 01
USV  577   Bova EL26/581         C53F             Ladbrook &,Long Sutton 98
USV  605   Volvo B10M-60         Plaxton C53F     Harrison,Morecambe 00
USV  620   Bova FHD12-280        C53F             Baker,Duloe 01
USV  625   Bova EL26/581         C53F             New 85
USV  628   Volvo B10M-61         Van Hool C55F    Nash,South Mimms 97
USV  630   DAF SB2300DHTD585     Plaxton C53F     Matthews,Goytre 99
USV  676   DAF MB230LB615        Plaxton C53F     Cropper,Kirkstall 00
```

```
USV  859   Scania K113CRB      Plaxton C49FT    Leons,Stafford 73 01
T 2  RED   Scania K124IB       Irizar C49FT     New 99
T 3  RED   Volvo B10M-62       Plaxton C49FT    Wallace Arnold 01
W 2  RED   Bova FHD12-370      C49FT            New 00
```
~~~~~~
```
EOI 4363*NFS 373T(4/86) & 12 DLY(4/86) & HGA 830T(5/85),
USV 330*J299 KFP(8/01),
USV 331*C314 LTT(5/02) & MIL 9751(3/02) & C307 VMX(12/01) &
         TJL 800(12/98) & C770 MVH(11/96), USV 462*G56 RTO(4/01),
USV 474*L826 VLP(6/01), USV 511*M34 LHP(3/02),
USV 556*A517 NCL(6/02) & A11 WEH(3/97) & A517 NCL(11/92),
USV 562*F484 MTA(2/02),
USV 577*GVV 461X(9/98) & 224 ASV(8/96) & FBD 958X(10/89),
USV 605*G760 RRN(3/00) & 7622 UK(9/99) & G852 MFV(9/91),
USV 620*C33 VJF(9/01), USV 625*TOI 6513(11/95) & B901 YYC(11/92),
USV 628*ABZ 4842(10/98) & OPC 122W(11/94) & 712 NIP(11/94) &
         OPC 122W(9/84), USV 630*PIL 6501(10/99) & A546 RVH(9/98),
USV 676*HIL 7670(3/01) & F639 OHD(5/92),
USV 859*LOI 9772(4/01) & K680 BRE(1/97) & T3 RED*T531 EUB(9/01)
```
~~~~~~

L7   REXQUOTE LTD.t/a QUANTOCK MOTOR SERVICES

*Depots:Station Works,Station Road,BISHOPS LYDEARD, LANGLEY GREEN &
          Unit 82c,Taunton Trading Estate,NORTON FITZWARREN,Somerset.*

```
IIW  783   AEC Reliance        Willowbrook C51F  Lewis,Greenwich 01
MPK 693P   AEC Reliance        Plaxton C53F      Isaac,Gunn 01
VMJ 967S   AEC Reliance        Plaxton C53F      Hircock,Upwell 19 01
BUR 438T   AEC Reliance        Plaxton C42FT     Gray,Higher Ince 01
EBM 448T   AEC Reliance        Plaxton C57F      Hircock &,Upwell 21 01
JTL 150T   Bristol LHS6L       Plaxton DP33F     Grayscroft,Mablethorpe 01
WDK 562T   AEC Reliance        Plaxton C53F      Smith,West Bromwich 01
FDC 417V   Leyland PSU3E/4R    Plaxton DP53F     Gunn,South Petherton 02
NUB  93V   AEC Reliance        Plaxton C53F      Rawlings,Midsomer Nortn 01
ODV 404W   AEC Reliance        Duple DP53F       Non-PSV 01
A462 ODY   Bedford YNT         Plaxton C53F      Annetts &,Innersdown 02
G 56 TGW   Dennis Dart         Carlyle B28F      Perry,Bromyard 163 02
H539 XGK   Dennis Dart         Plaxton B35F      Go Ahead London DR39 02
N748 OYR   Dennis Dart         East Lancs DP31F  Metropolitan Police 02
```
~~~~~~

OTHER VEHICLE OWNED BY THE COMPANY
                    * * * * * * *
```
GSU  678   Leyland PD2/40      RV                Towing Vehicle
```
~~~~~~
N.B.:- This company also operates a large number of preserved/semi-
           preserved vehicles,which are listed in the preserved section.
~~~~~~
```
GSU 678*ORV 991(1/88),
IIW 783*YYY 563M(3/97) & IIW 670(12/94) & UMT 903M(4/90reb),
BUR 438T*YMJ 554S(9/78),
JTL 150T*NBZ 1671(9/00) & ATH 108T(9/96) & 10 OOX(1/94) &
          FTW 133T(10/90), ODV 404W*MIL 1854(12/97) & ODV 404W(6/96),
A462 ODY*ODY 395(2/97) & A627 YWF(7/93) &
G56 TGW*SIL 1583(1/02) & G56 TGW(12/99)
```
~~~~~~

L8   C.J.,P.A.,B. & B. RICHARDSON.t/a CLH LUXURY TRAVEL

Depot:Torre Station Yard,TORQUAY,Devon.

```
R639 VYB   Bova FHD12-340      C49FT            Moseley(Demonstrator) 98
T765 JYB   Bova FHD12-340      C49FT            New 99
T517 PYD   Bova FHD12-340      C49FT            New 99
W153 RYD   Bova FHD12-370      C49FT            New 00
```
~~~~~~
~~~~~~

L9   G. RIDLER

Depot:Jury Road Garage,DULVERTON,Somerset.

VJI 7010	Toyota HB31R	Caetano C21F	Collins,Windsor 94
VYD 890	Ford R1114	Plaxton C53F	Seaview,Parkstone 91
WFD 46	Leyland TRCL10/3ARZM	Plaxton C53F	Ambassador Travel 97
YYD 154	Ford R1115	Plaxton C35F	Coachmaster,Coulsdon 89
YYD 687	Duple 425	C51FT	Swanbrook,Cheltenham 93
255 CYA	Leyland TRCL10/3ARZM	Plaxton C49FT	Carnell,Sutton Bridge 02
260 FPJ	Leyland TRCL10/3ARZM	Plaxton C53F	National Holidays 31 01
AAA 900V	Ford R1114	Plaxton C53F	Thomas,Upton 99
J725 KBC	Dennis Javelin	Duple C55F	Evans,Tregaron 96
L269 LCW	DAF SB3000WS601	Caetano C49FT	M Jackson,Blackpool 98
M342 JJR	Scania K113CRB	Van Hool C49FT	Coopers,Annitsford 02
P960 PYA	Dennis Javelin	Plaxton C51FT	Chambers,Moneymore(NI) 00

~~~~~~
VJI 7010*G260 XFP(3/00), VYD 890*VWE 138Y(12/91), WFD 46*H379 TNG(2/02),
YYD 154*A754 JAY(6/95), YYD 687*E127 LAD(8/98),
255 CYA*G406 XMK(2/01) & JIL 3964(5/94) & G406 XMK(2/01) & G608 XMD(4/90),
260 FPJ*F716 ENE(6/01) & 491 JVX(2/01) & F716 ENE(2/93),
L269 LCW*L2 JPJ(2/98), M342 JJR*JVN 423(1/00) & M342 JJR(11/97) &
P960 PYA*VJI 7010(3/00)
~~~~~~

M1   R.J. RISK.t/a TARGET TRAVEL

Depot:17 Walkham Business Park,Burrington Way,PLYMOUTH,Devon.

NIL 6560	Mercedes-Benz 709D	G & M C24FL	Gullen,Quintrell Downs 98
PJI 3354	Volvo B10M-60	Plaxton C49FT	Bournemouth 336 00
RIB 4323	DAF SB2305DHTD585	Plaxton C57F	Shaw-Hadwin,Carnforth 98
WCR 819	Volvo B10M-60	Plaxton C49F	Bournemouth 337 00
4011 LJ	Volvo B12T	Jonckheere C46FT	Chester,Plymouth 99
B674 CBD	Fiat 60-10	Caetano C18F	Phillips &,Totnes 98
D542 GFH	DAF SB2300DHS585	Plaxton C53F	Chester,Plymouth 99
D434 OWO	DAF MB200DKFL600	Plaxton C49FT	Chester,Plymouth 99
D353 RCY	DAF SB2300DHTD585	Plaxton C53F	Chester,Plymouth 99
E922 SNY	DAF MB230DKFL615	Plaxton C51FT	Chester,Plymouth 99
F951 HTT	Mercedes-Benz 609D	DC C23F	Dealtop,Exeter 99
F689 OFJ	Mercedes-Benz 609D	RB C23F	Non-PSV(Plymouth) 02
G534 LWU	Volvo B10M-60	Plaxton C48FT	Cheltenham & Glou. 534 98
G546 LWU	Volvo B10M-60	Plaxton C49FT	Cheltenham & Glou. 546 98
G547 LWU	Volvo B10M-60	Plaxton C49FT	Cheltenham & Glou. 547 98
J 86 LLA	Mercedes-Benz 410D	DC C15F	Dealtop,Exeter 02
K374 LWS	DAF 400	G & M C16F	Bournemouth 374 00
K179 SLY	Mercedes-Benz 410D	? C16F	MCH,Uxbridge 98
M359 LFX	Scania K113CRB	Van Hool C49FT	Bournemouth 359 02
M360 LFX	Scania K113CRB	Van Hool C49FT	Bournemouth 360 02
M 12 YCL	Scania K113CRB	Van Hool C49FT	Bournemouth 342 01
S 3 HJC	MAN 18.350	Auwaerter C49FT	Home James,Totton 02

~~~~~~
NIL 6560*F861 ATH(8/97), PJI 3354*H815 AHS(11/92),
RIB 4323*E651 EEO(3/92),
WCR 819*H371 VCG(4/02) & PJI 3354(11/92) & H818 AHS(10/92),
4011 LJ*L702 SUA(4/00) & 4 WA(11/96) & L965 NWW(9/95),
D542 GFH*PSV 111(8/94) & D287 XCX(8/89),
D434 OWO*RJI 1977(12/94) & D954 LTX(11/93),
D353 RCY*PJI 3547(3/95) & D882 BDF(9/92) &
K179 SLY*MCH 85(3/98) & K149 SDF(2/97)
~~~~~~

M2   **D.S. & K.W.M. ROBERTS.t/a BRUCE & ROBERTS**

Depot:The Chalet,LEWDOWN,Devon.

CDV 162T	Bedford VAS5	Plaxton C29F	Perry,Bromyard 111 99
D144 NON	Freight Rover Sherpa	Carlyle B20F	Hookways,Meeth 00
E934 RWR	Freight Rover Sherpa	Carlyle B18F	Hookways,Meeth 01
F329 FDT	MCW Metrorider MF154	DP31F	Perry,Bromyard 149 01

OTHER VEHICLE OWNED BY THE COMPANY
* * * * * * *

GNF 691Y	MAN MT8.136	RB C28F	Storeshed

GNF 691Y*221 WPH(5/89)

M3   **A. ROBISON.t/a BLUELINE COACHES OF DEVON**

Depot:Pine Lodge,NORTH TAWTON,Devon.

DYT 182	DAF MB200DKTL600	Plaxton C51F	Phare,Monkokehampton 00
BDV 671Y	Fiat 60-10	Caetano C18F	New 82
A651 CMY	Bova EL26/581	C49FT	Frost,St Austell 97
C685 HDM	Fiat 315	Robin Hood C28F	Robin Hood(Demonstr.) 87
F222 RJX	DAF SB2305DHTD585	Plaxton C53F	Barnes,Aldbourne 00

DYT 182*WNR 117X(12/86) & F222 RJX*MIL 6084(10/00) & F222 RJX(1/97)

M4   **D.E. ROTHWELL.t/a BURNHAM PARK COACHES & TOWER CABS**

Depot:138 North Road West,PLYMOUTH,Devon.

G303 EOK	DAF 400	Jubilee C16F	Non-PSV(Van) 93
K361 LWS	DAF 400	G & M C16F	Non-PSV(Van) 92
L919 OGW	DAF 400	G & M C16F	Non-PSV(Van) 98
R985 FOT	Renault Master	Onyx C16F	Non-PSV 00
S623 VOM	Renault Master	Jubilee C15F	Jones,Bromsgrove 01

M5   **J.W. RUNNALLS.t/a HAYLE TRAVEL & PRIMROSE COACHES**

Depot:Godolphin Moor,TOWNSHEND,Cornwall.

PJI 6077	Auwaerter N216H	C49FT	Dereham Coaches 92
RIB 6197	Kassbohrer S210HI	C28FT	Jones,Newton Aycliffe 00
HCV 140N	Bedford YRT	Plaxton C53F	Hookways,Meeth 99
YAL 690Y	Bedford YNT	Plaxton C53F	Willis,Bodmin 99
A271 RBK	Mercedes-Benz L608D	Robin Hood B ?FL	Barfoot,West End 98
C761 GOJ	Mercedes-Benz L307D	Taurus B2FL	WMSNT,Birmingham 97
G878 AGL	Van Hool T815H	C49FT	New 89
S649 RCV	Toyota BB50R	Caetano C21F	New 98

PJI 6077*B682 DVL(12/92), RIB 6197*F81 GGC(10/92) &
A271 RBK*987 FOU(5/98) & A271 RBK(5/96)

M6   **M.J. & C. RYAN.t/a CITYTOUR**

Depot:Locksbrook Road,BATH,Somerset.

HIL 3451	Leyland TRCTL11/3RZ	Plaxton C53F	Shearings 595 92
NXI 608	Leyland TRCTL11/2R	Plaxton C53F	Jorvik,Market Weighton 92
RIL 2103	DAF MB230LB615	Plaxton C51FT	Metroline(Brents) 97
WJI 3726	Mercedes-Benz 814D	RB C33F	Hayball,Warminster 99
NUD 106L	Bristol VRT/SL6G	ECW O41/27F	South Midland 905 89
TNJ 995S	Bristol VRT/SL3/6LXB	ECW CO43/27D	Stephenson,Rochford 94

```
TNJ 996S   Bristol VRT/SL3/6LXB   ECW CO43/27D    Brighton & Hove 596 90
TNJ 998S   Bristol VRT/SL3/6LXB   ECW CO43/27D    Stephenson,Rochford 94
UWV 619S   Bristol VRT/SL3/6LXB   ECW CO43/31F    Brighton & Hove 619 99
AHW 199V   Bristol VRT/SL3/6LXB   ECW H43/27D     Brewers 943 94
ANA 565Y   Leyland AN68D/1R       NC O43/32F      GM Buses 8565 91
H380 XHG   Mercedes-Benz 814D     RB C33F         Whitehead,Hoddlesden 97
J243 MFP   Dennis Javelin         Plaxton C53F    Smith,Liss 98
R275 LDE   Dennis Javelin         Plaxton C57F    Davies,Pencader 275 99
Y446 AUY   Mercedes-Benz O814D    Onyx C24F       New 01
Y138 RDG   Mercedes-Benz O814D    Onyx C24F       New 01
Y139 RDG   Mercedes-Benz O814D    Onyx C24F       New 01
```

HIL 3451*D595 MVR(8/94), NXI 608*NDW 145X(10/92), RIL 2103*E64 SJS(4/99) &
WJI 3726*G70 GHG(1/99)

M7   M.G. SADLER.t/a BEAUMONT TRAVEL

Depots:Esso Yard,Meadow Dock,Hempsted &
*   27 Beaumont Road,Longlevens,GLOUCESTER,Gloucestershire.*

```
E300 BWL   Mercedes-Benz 709D     RB DP25F           Thomas,Cheltenham 01
E303 BWL   Mercedes-Benz 709D     RB DP25F           Thomas,Cheltenham 01
G100 KUB   Mercedes-Benz 811D     Optare DP33F       Bentley,Birmingham 00
G920 WGS   Mercedes-Benz 709D     RB B23F            Yorkshire Coastliner 00
G921 WGS   Mercedes-Benz 709D     RB B23F            Yorkshire Coastliner 00
J348 GKH   Dennis Dart            Plaxton B40F       Tayside 32 01
M 12 FUG   Mercedes-Benz 711D     WS DP25F           Bibby,Ingleton 01
P525 UDG   Ford Transit           MinO C14F          New 96
R612 FBX   Renault Master         Cymric C12F        New 97
R 54 OCK   Dennis Dart SLF        East Lancs B35F    Smith,Prenton 01
V181 FVU   Mercedes-Benz O814D    Onyx C24F          New 99
VX51 RDO   Dennis Dart SLF        Alexander B33F     loan from Mistral
```

M8   SEAGERS COACHES LTD

Depot:c/o Webb,Bumpers Way,Bumpers Farm IE,CHIPPENHAM,Wiltshire.

```
G536 YFW   Ford Transit           Bedwas B16FL    Chase,Chasetown 02
J125 OBU   Mercedes-Benz 609D     MM C24F         New 91
L524 BDH   Iveco 49-10            Mellor B16FL    Hillier,Foxham 02
N303 CKP   Iveco 49-10            ? B ?F          Non-PSV 01
N242 WDO   Mercedes-Benz 711D     ACL C24F        Telsons,Whitechapel 02
P899 PWW   DAF DE33WSSB3000       Ikarus C53F     New 96
S637 AHU   LDV Convoy             LDV B16F        New 99
```

M9   F.M. SEARLE.t/a AXE VALLEY MINI TRAVEL

Depot:26 Harbour Road,SEATON,Devon.

```
GBU  8V    MCW Metrobus DR101     H43/30F             Arriva Shires 5358 00
GYE 557W   MCW Metrobus DR101     H43/28D             Arriva Surrey M557 01
KEP 829X   LN NL116AL11/1R        B44F                Eastern Counties 629 99
KYV 685X   MCW Metrobus DR101     H43/28D             Billingshurst Coaches 02
B 87 WUV   Leyland TNLXB/2RR      Leyland H44/26D     Go Ahead London T1087 01
D144 LTA   Dodge S56              RB B23F             Plymouth 44 91
E358 KPO   Fiat 49-10             Robin Hood B25F     Halford,Bridport 00
K331 RCN   Iveco 59-12            Dormobile B27F      Halford,Bridport 01
K332 RCN   Iveco 59-12            Dormobile B29F      Anslow,Pontypool 99
```

N1   I.A. & R.M. SEWARD

Depot:Glendale,DALWOOD,Devon.

GIL 3129	Bedford YMP	Plaxton C35F	Chivers,Radstock 99
SVJ 777S	Bedford YLQ	Plaxton C45F	Denslow,Chard 98
D759 UTA	Leyland TRCTL11/3RZ	Plaxton B54F	MOD 96
D 86 VDV	Leyland TRCTL11/3RZ	Plaxton B54F	MOD 99
E325 CTT	Dennis Javelin	Plaxton DP72F	New 88
G 92 RGG	Volvo B10M-60	Plaxton C53F	Edwards,Whitland 99
J127 DGC	Mercedes-Benz 609D	PMT C25F	Crystal Palace FC 97
K744 RBX	Renault Master	Cymric C16F	New 92
K562 YFJ	Dennis Javelin	WS DP44FA	MOD 02
K458 YPK	Dennis Javelin	Plaxton C53F	LB Lewisham 0998 00
L486 HKN	Bova FHD12-340	C55F	Kings Ferry,Gillingham 99
N335 SDV	Bova FLD12-270	C57F	New 95
N770 VTT	Dennis Javelin	Berkhof C53F	New 96
N771 VTT	Dennis Javelin	Berkhof C41F	New 96
P719 EOD	Toyota HZB50R	Caetano C21F	New 97
R608 OTA	Dennis Javelin	Caetano C57F	New 98
R609 OTA	MAN 11.220	Berkhof C35F	New 98
T953 RTA	MAN 11.220	Caetano C35F	New 99
W346 VOD	Mercedes-Benz O404	Hispano C53F	New 00
W347 VOD	MAN 13.220	Berkhof C41F	New 00
X149 BTA	Iveco 49-10	G & M C16F	New 01
Y906 GFJ	Mercedes-Benz O815D	Sitcar C27F	New 01
Y166 GTT	Dennis R	Plaxton C53F	New 01

GIL 3129*A93 GLD(3/90) & L486 HKN*L8 KFC(11/99)

N2   M.C. & L.C. SIMMONS.t/a WESTWARD TRAVEL

Depot:Cromhall Quarry,CROMHALL,Gloucestershire.

DPV 881	21	Bova EL26/581	C53F	Baird,Prestwood 90
312 XYB	19	DAF SB2300DHS585	Plaxton C55F	Hand,Horsley 89
LHT 730P	38	BL VRT/SL3/6LXB	ECW H43/33F	Ball,Bristol 02
OHR 190R	23	Leyland FE30AGR	ECW H43/31F	Stubbington,Benfleet 93
URB 161S	26	BL VRT/SL3/6LXB	ECW H43/31F	Bugler,Bristol 94
VPF 287S	27	BL VRT/SL3/6LXB	ECW H43/31F	Holliday,Clyst Honitn 95
EAP 989V	28	BL VRT/SL3/6LXB	ECW H43/31F	City of Oxford 446 96
KRU 844W	34	BL VRT/SL3/6LXB	ECW H43/31F	L Munden,Bristol 98
VWX 350X	18	Bova EL26/581	C51F	Wallace Arnold 87
HBH 416Y	20	Leyland TRCTL11/3R	Plaxton C53F	Stevens,Bristol 91
A930 JOD	22	Leyland TRCTL11/3R	Plaxton C57F	Snell,Newton Abbot 92
A661 UHY	30	Bova FLD12-250	C53F	Clayton,Leicester 95
A611 XKU	35	Leyland TRCTL11/3R	Plaxton C57F	Bristol 8211 98
C828 EHU	36	LD TRCTL11/3LZ	WS DP68FA	MOD 99
E650 KCX	33	DAF SB2305DHTD585	Plaxton C57F	Burton,Haverhill 98
F281 ENV	31	LD TRCTL11/3ARZ	Plaxton C53F	Wainfleet,Nuneaton 97

DPV 881*URW 702X(3/84), 312 XYB*A21 KDF(4/86) &
F281 ENV*MIW 5788(4/97) & F203 HSO(3/92)

N3   D.W. & R. SKELTON

Depot:Langland House,90 Broadway,CHILTON POLDEN,Somerset.

FXI 2268	MAN SR280	C53F	Barry,Weymouth 93
RJI 7973	Kassbohrer S215HD	C49FT	Beeston,Hadleigh 02
VJI 8200	MAN SR280	C48FT	Wilts & Dorset 6041 97
E641 LNV	LAG Panoramic	C49FT	Procter,Bedale 99

FXI 2268*NEG 980W(4/91) & 847 XKJ(9/88) & RGB 3W(11/87),
RJI 7973*LSU 256(4/95) & D599 BPA(4/90),
VJI 8200*XLJ 84X(9/97) & HSV 342(5/96) & KMR 3X(6/86) &
E641 LNV*MSU 462(4/98) & E641 LNV(3/96)

N4　　　　　　R.J. SLEEMAN.t/a KERNOW TRAVEL

Depot:Kestle Quarry,SLADESBRIDGE,Cornwall.

PIW 4616	DAF MB200DKL600	Plaxton C51F	Bendry,Ilford 01
RJI 3803	Bova FHD12-280	C49FT	Frimley,Aldershot 01
SIW 2763	DAF MB200DKFL600	Caetano C50FT	Johnson,Newingreen 99
TVD 861R	Bedford YLQ	Duple C45F	Roberts,Lewdown 92
PKD 416S	Volvo B58-61	Plaxton C53F	Truscott,Roche 96
URL 946S	Bedford YMT	Duple C53F	Moore,St Keverne 1 94
XGL 51T	Bedford YMT	Plaxton C53F	Fry,Tintagel 99
FAF 44V	Volvo B58-56	Duple C53F	Webber,Bodmin 01
JAH 769V	Fiat 55-10	Harwin C23F	Gill,Wadebridge 98
JWV 250W	Bristol VRT/SL3/6LXB	ECW H43/31F	Preserved 00
TND 132X	Volvo B58-61	Duple C53F	Gill,Wadebridge 98
FEW 225Y	DAF MB200DKFL600	Plaxton C53F	Whippet,Fenstanton 01
FEW 226Y	DAF MB200DKFL600	Plaxton C53F	Whippet,Fenstanton 01
A254 LLL	Scania K112CRS	Jonckheere C49FT	Castle,Clanfield 01
E139 ATV	Renault S56	RB B25F	Nottingham 139 99
E 67 SUH	Volkswagen LT55	Optare B25F	Forrester,Tighnabruaich 00
E182 UEJ	Volvo B10M-61	Ikarus C53FT	Warren,Neath 00

```
PIW 4616*DFD 953B(5/95) & YEB 103T(1/85),
RJI 3803*C418 FAH(4/01) & NIL 7250(12/99) & C418 FAH(12/98) &
        WOA 521(11/98) & C700 NHJ(1/97) & 2942 FH(11/95) &
        C90 LVX(11/90), SIW 2763*9309 ML(3/96),
TVD 861R*RJI 3803(4/01) & TVD 861R(2/94),
PKD 416S*WXO 37(6/87) & UJP 92S(1/84),
URL 946S*705 AOW(4/92) & TGL 626S(6/89), A254 LLL*6461 ZX(4/88) &
E182 UEJ*9 GUV(1/00) & E182 UEJ(10/94)
```

N5　　　　　　G.A. & R.G. SLEEP.t/a H. & A. SLEEP

Depot:The Garage,Station Hill,BERE ALSTON,Devon.

WNL 110A	Volvo B58-61	Duple C53F	Turner,Bristol 93
WNL 382A	Volvo B58-56	Caetano C53F	DAC,St Anns Chapel 02
UHB 277S	Bedford YMT	Plaxton C53F	Thomas,Barry 82
YRW 777S	Bedford YLQ	Plaxton C45F	Gordon,Rotherham 83
XCG 13V	Bedford YMT	Duple C53F	New 79
TCV 253Y	Volvo B10M-61	Plaxton C53F	Friend,Harrowbarrow 02

```
WNL 110A*SDR 445T(10/84) & WNL 382A*AWB 319T(4/86)
```

N6　　　P.A. SLUGGETT.t/a BASSETT & SLUGGETT COACHES

Depot:Richmar,Trewyn Road,HOLSWORTHY,Devon.

FIL 8471	DAF MB200DKFL600	Plaxton C49FT	Courtney,Binfield 93
JDB 940V	Ford R1114	Plaxton C53F	Turner &,Chulmleigh 96
CMJ 536X	Ford R1014	Plaxton C35F	Gatwick Parking,Horley 94
B440 WUL	Ford R1115	WS DP33F	Hutchings,Kilmington 98
B189 YTC	Volvo B10M-61	Duple C51F	Phillips,Crediton 99
C137 GHS	Dennis Lancet	Van Hool C35F	Meredith,Wrexham 01
D286 RKW	Mercedes-Benz 609D	RB C19F	Thomas,Hayle 91
F201 XBV	Freight Rover Sherpa	Carlyle B20F	Tilley,Wainhouse Corner 97

```
FIL 8471*ANA 462Y(8/93) & B189 YTC*6443 MW(1/92)
```

N7   B.E. & G.W. SMITH

Depots:Pilton Garage,PILTON & Garage House,PYLLE,Somerset.

RIB 3195	Bedford YNT	Plaxton C53F	New 83	
RIB 8740	Bedford YMP	Plaxton C30F	Armchair,Brentford 93	
843 AYA	Leyland TRCL10/3ARZM	Plaxton C53F	New 89	
505 AYB	Volvo B10M-46	Plaxton C43F	Docherty,Auchterarder 01	
916 DYA	Leyland TRCTL11/3RZ	Plaxton C57F	New 87	
217 NYA	Volvo B10M-60	Plaxton C57F	New 91	
OYA 519V	Bedford YMT	Plaxton C53F	New 80	
TKV 15W	Bedford YNT	Plaxton C53F	Phillips,Ruskington 98	
LAE 470X	Leyland PSU5D/5R	WS B60F	MOD 98	
JYC 226Y	Ford R1114	Duple C53F	Bailey,Biddisham 97	
OWO 235Y	Leyland PSU3G/2R	Duple DP53F	Edwards,Tiers Cross 98	
J931 CYK	Leyland TRCL10/3ARZA	Plaxton C53F	Gordon,Rotherham 01	
M750 VYB	Volvo B10M-62	Plaxton C53F	New 95	
N310 DYC	Volvo B10M-62	Plaxton C53F	New 96	
R445 FWT	Volvo B10M-62	Plaxton C53F	Wallace Arnold 02	
R726 TYC	Volvo B10M-62	Plaxton C53F	New 98	
W501 SYB	Volvo B10M-62	Plaxton C53F	New 00	

RIB 3195*LYA 717Y(6/01), RIB 8740*D640 ALR(5/92), 843 AYA*F851 GYB(1/98),
505 AYB*H716 FLD(4/01) & 7119 WD(11/00) & H716 FLD(2/00),
916 DYA*D196 OYD(?/98) & 217 NYA*H197 WYA(3/00)

N8   B.J. SMITH.t/a CREMYLL COACHES

Depot:5 West End,Terrace,MILLBROOK,Cornwall.

D724 JUB	Freight Rover Sherpa	Carlyle B16F	Smith,Liskeard 97
E898 ASU	Ford Transit	Steedrive B16F	Barry,Liskeard 01
E213 BDV	Ford Transit	Mellor B16F	Stagecoach Devon 222 97
K805 AJW	Mercedes-Benz 410D	G & M C16F	Benning,Griffithstown 99
M407 MPD	Mercedes-Benz 410D	Olympus C12F	Houghton,Ealing 01

N9   G.P. SMITH.t/a GRAHAMS OF BRISTOL

Depot:Unit D,Hallen Industrial Estate,Severn Road,Hallen,BRISTOL.

IIW 828	Bova FHD12-290	C57F	Cowdrey,Gosport 97
RJI 5703	Leyland TNLXB/2RR	PR H44/24D	Bennett,Chieveley 98
REU 311S	Bristol VRT/SL3/6LXB	ECW H43/28F	Cheltenham & Glou. 213 01
WKO 128S	Bristol VRT/SL3/6LXB	ECW H43/31F	Maidstone & Dist. 5127 97
ULS 658T	Bristol FE30AGR	ECW H43/32F	Lloyd,Bagillt 97
WTU 495W	Bristol VRT/SL3/501	ECW H43/31F	Baker,Weston-S-Mare 64 98
K758 KRB	DAF SB3000KS601	Caetano C51FT	Reliant,Ibstock 01
Q160 HCP	Ford R1114	Duple C53F	Streets,Chivenor 00

IIW 828*G96 VFP(8/01), RJI 5703*CUL 113V(8/95) & K758 KRB*REL 520(?/01)

R1   SMITHS COACHES (LISKEARD) LTD

Depot:Unit 11,Treburgie Water,DOBWALLS,Cornwall.

DJI 1333	Leyland PSU3E/4R	Plaxton C53F	Tellings-GM,Nuneaton 93
IIL 4153	Bova EL28/581	Duple C49FT	Kinsman,Bodmin 98
WDZ 8521	Bova FHD12-280	C53F	McVay,Edinburgh 99
RKY 878R	Leyland PSU3E/4R	Plaxton C53F	Robinson,High Wycombe 00
C660 JAT	Leyland TRCTL11/3RZ	Duple C49FT	Hayball,Warminster 97
D163 LTA	Dodge S56	RB B27F	Marks,Plymouth 95
E129 KYW	MCW Metrorider MF150	B25F	Walsh,Middleton 00
H187 CNS	Mercedes-Benz 814D	Dormobile C33F	Day,Lake 01
J908 ODH	LDV 400	Crystals C16F	Ryder,West Bromwich 97

```
W 39 EOX   Renault Master        ? C16F          Simpson,Harrow 01
~~~~~~~~~~~~~~~~~~~~~~~~~~~~~~~~~~~~~~~~~~~~~~~~~~~~~~~~~~~~~~~~~~~~~~~~~~~
DJI 1333*BVP 779V(10/91), IIL 4153*B953 ARL(4/93),
WDZ 8521*A912 YOX(4/97) & 124 JPO(3/97) & A22 LKV(12/95),
RKY 878R*NIB 8927(8/94) & SDD 148R(5/90) &
C660 JAT*926 BWV(2/97) & C119 GKH(9/94)
~~~~~~~~~~~~~~~~~~~~~~~~~~~~~~~~~~~~~~~~~~~~~~~~~~~~~~~~~~~~~~~~~~~~~~~~~~~
```

R2   T.J. SNELL.t/a SNELLS COACHES

Depot:Plot 10,West Lynx Industrial Estate,YEOVIL,Somerset.

```
HEO  495   DAF MB200DKTL600       Caetano C53F      Gill,Cheltenham 95
NXI  784   DAF MB200DKFL600       Plaxton C51F      Bendle,Middlestown 00
PIL 7242   DAF MB200DKFL600       Plaxton C53F      Isle of Purbeck,Wareham 98
TIB 9158   Bova EL26/581          C53F              Robinson,Stewkley 97
HPR 686V   Bedford YMT            Plaxton C53F      Seaview,Parkstone 90
PWU 366W   Bedford YMQ            Plaxton C45F      Seward,Dalwood 87
WCA 941W   Leyland PSU5C/4R       Plaxton C57F      Cheney,Banbury 00
JCJ 700X   Bedford YNT            Duple C53F        Wheelband,Weymouth 97
~~~~~~~~~~~~~~~~~~~~~~~~~~~~~~~~~~~~~~~~~~~~~~~~~~~~~~~~~~~~~~~~~~~~~~~~~~~
HEO 495*EDX 805Y(3/93) & 2086 PP(8/85),
NXI 784*FSU 357(2/00) & NIW 6858(2/96) & A540 CSE(4/93),
PIL 7242*MMW 371(11/98) & PAE 553Y(8/86) & TIB 9158*WUT 101X(12/93)
~~~~~~~~~~~~~~~~~~~~~~~~~~~~~~~~~~~~~~~~~~~~~~~~~~~~~~~~~~~~~~~~~~~~~~~~~~~
```

R3   SOMERBUS LTD

Depot:The Old Colliery,Wick Lane,STANTON WICK,Somerset.

```
NHG  541   Mercedes-Benz 208CDI   Mellor B11F       New 02
704  BYL   Optare Solo M850       B30F              New 01
816  SHW   Mercedes-Benz O814D    Plaxton B28F      Tillingbourne,Cranleigh 01
620  UKM   Mercedes-Benz O814D    Onyx C21F         New 99
J 80 BUS   Iveco 480-10-21        AR H52/31F        Dunstan,Middleton 77 02
~~~~~~~~~~~~~~~~~~~~~~~~~~~~~~~~~~~~~~~~~~~~~~~~~~~~~~~~~~~~~~~~~~~~~~~~~~~
816 SHW*V450 FOT(2/02), 620 UKM*S532 GHT(5/99) & J80 BUS*J227 OKX(6/02)
~~~~~~~~~~~~~~~~~~~~~~~~~~~~~~~~~~~~~~~~~~~~~~~~~~~~~~~~~~~~~~~~~~~~~~~~~~~
```

R4   SOUTH WEST COACHES LTD.t/a WAKES

Depots:Southgate Road,WINCANTON & 45 Victoria Road,YEOVIL,Somerset.

```
ANZ 4372   006  DAF SB3000DKV601  Van Hool C49FT    Aztecbird,Guiseley 00
ANZ 4373   007  Volvo B10M-62     Plaxton C53F      Excelsior,Bournemouth 96
ANZ 4374   008  Dennis Javelin    Plaxton C35F      New 89
GLZ 7465   013  Volvo B10M-61     Plaxton C53F      New 89
JIL 8319   017  LD TRCTL11/2R     Plaxton C57F      Torr,Gedling 95
LAZ 5826   040  Volvo B10M-60     Plaxton C49FT     Wellington,Kingsbrdge 02
LIL 2167   019  LD TRCTL11/2R     Plaxton C53F      Torr,Gedling 95
LUI 2527   004  LD TRCTL11/3R     Plaxton C57F      Armchair,Brentford 86
LUI 2528   014  LD TRCTL11/2R     Plaxton C53F      Lodge,High Easter 89
LUI 2529   041  MB 709D           LHE B29F          Arriva Midlands N 166 01
MAZ 6792   045  Volvo B10M-60     Plaxton C51FT     Wellington,Kingsbrdge 02
RAZ 8598   047  Volvo B10M-60     Plaxton C49FT     Wellington,Kingsbrdge 02
RIL 1475   025  LD TRCTL11/2RH    Plaxton C49F      Edwards,Tiers Cross 99
SAZ 2511   046  Volvo B10M-60     Plaxton C51FT     Wellington,Kingsbrdge 02
TIL 9685   015  Volvo B10M-60     Plaxton C53F      New 90
UIL 1335   016  Volvo B10M-60     Plaxton C57F      Excelsior,Bournemouth 92
WSV  323   027  Leyland PSU5C/4R  Plaxton C57F      Ebdon,Sidcup 83
WSV  868   028  LD TRCTL11/3R     East Lancs B59F   Northern,Anston 1355 94
XBJ  860   031  Bedford YMQ       Plaxton C35F      Armchair,Brentford 87
ETL 545T   012  Bedford YLQ       Plaxton C45F      Booth,Hyde 87
LYA 315V   020  Bedford YMT       Duple DP57F       New 79
UYD 950W   026  Bedford YMT       Duple B55F        Osmond,Curry Rivel 88
WYD 103W   029  Leyland PSU3F/5R  Duple DP57F       New 81
WYD 104W   030  Leyland PSU3F/5R  Duple DP57F       New 81
XYC 248W   032  Bedford YMT       Duple C53F        New 80
BYD 795X   010  Leyland PSU3F/5R  Duple C53F        New 82
```

```
PWJ 497X   023  Bedford YNT          Duple B55F        Cowdrey,Gosport 88
EGV 695Y   011  LD TRCTL11/2R        Plaxton C53F      Leiston Motors 96
KYA 284Y   018  LD TRCTL11/3R        Plaxton C57F      New 83
A109 EPA   001  LD TRCTL11/2RH       Plaxton C53F      Q Drive 726 96
A130 EPA   002  LD TRCTL11/2RH       Plaxton C53F      Venner,Minehead 95
A799 REO   003  LD TRCTL11/3R        Marshall B52F     Holmeswood,Rufford 94
A256 VYC   005  LD TRCTL11/3RH       WS B59F           USAF(Lakenheath) 95
B155 AYD   009  LD TRCTL11/3RZ       Plaxton C57F      New 85
F997 KCU   051  MB 609D              DC DP23F          New 88
F734 USF   052  MB 609D              Alexander DP24F   Murray,Glenrothes 89
H484 BND   055  Ford Transit         MM C16F           New 90
L210 OYC   053  MB 410D              Deansgate C16F    New 94
L211 OYC   054  MB 410D              Deansgate C16F    New 94
L716 WCC   042  MB 709D              Marshall B29F     Arriva Cymru MMM716 01
P550 JEG   043  Marshall Minibus     B29F              North Star,Huyton 02
P690 NAV   044  Marshall Minibus     B29F              North Star,Huyton 02
P643 TMV   039  Kassbohrer S250      C49FT             Clarke,Lower Sydenham 02
R652 TYA   057  MB 412D              G & M C16F        New 97
V852 DYB   056  MB O814D             Onyx C24F         New 99
```
~~~~~~

OTHER VEHICLE OWNED BY THE COMPANY
* * * * * * *

```
NYC 824L        Bedford YRT      Willowbrook B-F   Storeshed
```
~~~~~~

N.B.:- Company formed when the Wakes business was acquired by and then
merged with that of Male & Graham 1/00.Dates acquired prior to this
are either for Wakes(001-33) or Male & Graham(051-7).

~~~~~~
```
ANZ 4372*J823 KHD(12/00), ANZ 4373*M375 MRU(1/01) & A17 EXC(11/95),
ANZ 4374*F990 FYB(1/01), GLZ 7465*F555 FYD(3/01), JIL 8319*GNW 121Y(6/95),
LAZ 5826*G329 PEW(1/98), LIL 2167*GNW 122Y(6/95), LUI 2527*A831 PPP(5/01),
LUI 2528*FNM 862Y(5/01), LUI 2529*G166 YRE(5/01), MAZ 6792*G342 FFX(1/98),
RAZ 8598*G343 FFX(12/97), RIL 1475*WJB 490(3/99) & B268 KPF(9/97),
SAZ 2511*G328 PEW(12/97), TIL 9685*G183 OYC(3/01),
UIL 1335*G518 EFX(3/01) & G520 EFX(12/91), WSV 323*LVS 421V(6/92reb),
WSV 868*BDF 205Y(2/95reb), XBJ 860*UUR 341W(2/85), XYC 248W*SYD 1W(12/99),
EGV 695Y*448 HWT(11/96) & EVH 240Y(12/93), P643 TMV*P100 TCC(5/98) &
R652 TYA*P184 LYB(6/97)
```
~~~~~~

R5   STAR-LINE BAND SERVICES LTD

Depot:Unit 3,Tweed Road,CLEVEDON,Somerset.

```
IIL 4317   Auwaerter N116         C8FT           Allen &,Burntwood 01
LIL 7920   Auwaerter N122/3       CH10/6CT       ILG,Ratby 91
LUI 6246   LAG Panoramic          C10FT          Johnson,Henley-in-Arden 94
LUI 6247   Auwaerter N122/3       CH10/6CT       Shaw Hadwin,Carnforth 96
LUI 6248   Volvo B10M-61          VH CH10/6FT    Skylark,Woodfalls 01
PIL 3108   DAF SBR3000DKZ570      VH CH10/6CT    Aztecbird,Guiseley 01
RIL 9458   DAF SBR2300DHS570      VH CH10/6CT    Collis,Bristol 97
RIL 9459   Van Hool TD824         CH10/8CT       Selwyn,Runcorn 99
RIW 1907   Van Hool T818          CH14/-DT       Trathens,Plymouth 00
SJI 8286   Volvo B10M-61          JE CH10/6DT    Skylark,Woodfalls 01
2191  RO   Volvo B10M-61          VH CH10/6DT    Top Brass,Dunstable 98
331  BCH   Van Hool TD824         CH6/7FT        DSB,Lambeth 02
842  DYG   Van Hool TD824         CH10/6CT       Bromwich,Southam 00
A 8  TRA   Volvo B10M-53          PN CH10/6DT    Movers,Harrogate 96
F535 EWJ   Mercedes-Benz 609D     Whittaker C20F Wadman,Throwleigh 92
G544 JOG   Bova FHD12-290         C10FT          Allen &,Burntwood 01
H981 GDV   Auwaerter N122/3       CH10/6CT       Trathens,Plymouth 98
L 3  LWB   Volvo B12R             Plaxton C15FT  Wright,Watford 01
N315 BYA   Volvo B12T             VH CH10/6CT    Trathens,Plymouth 02
N318 BYA   Volvo B12T             VH CH57/14CT   Trathens,Plymouth 02
R909 DOU   Mercedes-Benz 310D     Star-Line B5F  Non-PSV(Van) 01
S138 TYC   Mercedes-Benz 312D     Star-Line B5F  Non-PSV(Van) 01
T172 BWR   Mercedes-Benz 310D     Star-Line B8F  Non-PSV(Van) 01
```
~~~~~~

```
IIL 4317*MEU 603Y(11/92), LIL 7920*E474 YWJ(4/96),
```

```
LUI 6246*G382 JBD(10/01),
LUI 6247*F664 DRN(10/01) & 4150 RU(9/95) & F619 CWJ(1/93),
LUI 6248*A554 YGF(10/01) & LSU 783(5/01) & A547 XUH(3/89),
PIL 3108*F216 RJX(6/98),
RIL 9458*G265 EHD(11/01) & ROI 8358(9/97) & G265 EHD(6/92),
RIL 9459*SEL 702(12/99) & E510 CHS(6/96) & LSK 611(11/95) &
          E407 FSH(5/92) & D579 SUS(8/87), RIW 1907*D860 VHH(4/95),
SJI 8286*4442 MT(1/95) & A384 UNH(1/88),
2191 RO*A871 FSF(10/88) & A817 FSF(10/88) & MSP 333(10/85) &
          A156 XFS(3/85), 842 DYG*D867 FSX(7/90), A8 TRA*F700 COA(4/95),
G544 JOG*LUI 6245(5/02) & G544 JOG(10/01) & 5010 CD(10/98) &
          G544 JOG(7/92) & H981 GDV*LSK 481(12/98) & H981 GDV(11/96)
```

R6   R.O. STENNING

Depot:Merriottsford Garage,MERRIOTT,Somerset.

G373 UVR	Ford Transit	MM C16F	New 90
H381 CDV	Ford Transit	G & M B16F	Holliss,Halwell 97
H914 GNC	Ford Transit	MM C16F	New 91
J342 TFA	Ford Transit	Dormobile B15F	Non-PSV(Abergavenny) 97

R7   D.M. & J.A. STEVENS

Depot:152a Soundwell Road,Soundwell,BRISTOL.

RIB 5084	Volvo B10M-60	Plaxton C53F	MTL London VP334 97
F923 PEU	Volvo B10M-61	Plaxton C57F	New 88
R777 DEN	LDV Convoy	LDV B16F	New 98
R888 DEN	Dennis Javelin	Plaxton C57F	New 98
V777 DEN	Dennis Javelin	Berkhof C57F	New 99

```
RIB 5084*G74 RGG(10/94), R777 DEN*S966 ATC(4/01) & R888 DEN*R683 DWS(1/00)
```

R8   J. STEVENS

Depot:Trevacroft,Alexander Road,ST IVES,Cornwall.

A535 VAF	Mercedes-Benz L608D	DC C18F	Non-PSV(Exeter) 89
C680 KFM	Mercedes-Benz L608D	PMT C25F	Hill,Congleton 92
E251 PRL	Mercedes-Benz 609D	RB C25F	Thomas,Hayle 01
F193 UGL	Mercedes-Benz 609D	G & M C24F	Thomas,Hayle 96

R9   E. STIRK.t/a GOLD STAR COACHES

Depot:Torre Station Yard,TORQUAY,Devon.

G443 WLL	Fiat 49-10	Carlyle DP21F	British Airways BU6043 96
H662 DKO	Ford Transit	G & M B16F	Devon County Council 00
L836 XGV	DAF 400	G & M C16F	Non-PSV 97
S649 ETT	LDV Convoy	G & M C16F	New 98

T1   D.G.,R.M.,C.G. & S.M. STONE

Depot:Lower Bristol Road,BATH,Somerset.

KIB 260	Scania K113TRB	Irizar C49FT	New 95
KIB 734	Scania K113TRB	Irizar C51FT	New 98
TSV 787	DAF SBR3000DKZ570	Van Hool C46FT	New 90
TSV 788	DAF SB3000DKV601	Van Hool C55F	New 89

```
458   VHT   DAF SB2305DHS585      Van Hool C55F      New 88
J467  NJU   Toyota HDB30R         Caetano C19F       New 92
J468  NJU   Toyota HDB30R         Caetano C19F       New 92
L 18  RMS   DAF SB3000WS601       Van Hool C43FT     New 94
R 7   JMJ   Auwaerter N116/3      C49FT              Jones,Burley Gate 01
WA51  JYK   Bova FHD10-340        C ?F               New 02
```

KIB 260*N690 AHL(2/00), KIB 734*R456 YDT(2/00), TSV 787*G952 KJX(4/95),
TSV 788*F244 RJX(3/00) & 458 VHT*E322 EVH(7/95)

T2   T.J.,J.T. & K.J. STONEMAN.t/a CURRIAN TOURS

Depot:Currian Road Garage,NANPEAN,Cornwall.

```
KSU  454    Volvo B10M-60         Plaxton C48FT      National Holidays 76 02
NIW 8794    Volvo B10M-61         Plaxton C53F       Kingdoms,Tiverton 99
YUU  556    Volvo B10M-60         Plaxton C49FT      National Holidays 77 02
513  SRL    Bova FHD12-290        C51FT              Bailey,Biddisham 02
SNJ 590R    Bristol VRT/SL3/6LXB  ECW H43/31F        Reading 562 95
SNJ 593R    Bristol VRT/SL3/6LXB  ECW H43/31F        Reading 563 95
AAP 648T    Bristol VRT/SL3/6LXB  ECW H43/31F        Stephenson,Rochford 98
DDL 677V    Bedford YMT           Duple C53F         Webber,St Austell 01
A600 XGL    Bedford YNT           Plaxton C53F       Gill,Wadebridge 97
P137 XFW    Kassbohrer S250       C48FT              Clarke,Lower Sydenham 01
R455 YDT    Scania K113TRB        Irizar C51FT       WPS,Stafford 00
WK02 UHR    Bova FHD12-340        C49FT              New 02
```

KSU 454*G526 LWU(1/99), NIW 8794*A656 UGD(4/93), YUU 556*G527 LWU(?/01),
513 SRL*G114 VDV(?/02) & 28 XYB(12/01) & G114 VDV(8/95) &
DDL 677V*BAZ 6532(11/01) & DDL 677V(4/94)

T3   STREETS COACHWAYS LTD

Depot:The Old Aerodrome,CHIVENOR,Devon.

```
AHZ 8280    DAF SB2305DHS450      Van Hool C38FT     Stone,Bath 00
PJI 8994    LAG Panoramic         C53F               Bailey,Biddisham 97
WJI 3813    DAF SB2005DHU605      Plaxton C57F       Treneary,Paignton 00
WJI 3814    Bova EL26/581         C53F               Terraneau,South Molton 94
359  DBK    LAG Panoramic         C49FT              Perry,Aldershot 02
D986 DPG    Leyland TRCTL11/3R    Duple C57F         MC Travel,Melksham 00
D404 ERE    Freight Rover Sherpa  PMT B20F           Hearn,Stibb Cross 98
D764 JUB    Freight Rover Sherpa  Dormobile B20F     Allison & Lamb,Rhyl 95
D 66 NOF    Freight Rover Sherpa  Carlyle B20F       Colwill,Penclawdd 00
E723 HBF    Freight Rover Sherpa  PMT B20F           Hearn,Stibb Cross 00
J646 ANW    Leyland ST2R          RB C37F            Hazell,Northlew 01
K541 RJX    DAF SB3000DKVF601     Van Hool C49FT     Hoare,Weymouth 00
K278 VTT    Freight Rover Sherpa  Dormobile C20F     Hazell,Northlew 99
M587 BFL    Mercedes-Benz 709D    Marshall B23F      Richmond,Barley 00
```

AHZ 8280*E600 LVH(9/00) & TSV 788(3/00) & E600 LVH(1/94),
PJI 8994*B732 TEL(5/93),
WJI 3813*OAX 305X(12/00) & GIL 2636(5/98) & OAX 305X(8/90),
WJI 3814*YFJ 639X(11/00) & BOV 415(3/94) & VDV 893X(9/86),
359 DBK*E138 KRP(4/99) & 6501 AD(3/99) & 2052 NF(6/95) & E138 KRP(1/88) &
D986 DPG*538 FCG(2/93) & D145 HML(2/89)

T4   SUMMERCOURT TRAVEL LTD

Depot:Harris Garage,St Austell Street,NEWQUAY,Cornwall.

```
RIL 4396    Mercedes-Benz 709D    Alexander B25F     Blazefield Lancashire 02
RIL 4529    Mercedes-Benz 811D    Mellor DP33F       Petes,West Bromwich 00
RIL 4572    Renault S56           Alexander B24F     Ryder,West Bromwich 01
RIL 4586    Ford Transit          Mellor B16F        Petes,West Bromwich 01
RIL 4599    Renault S56           Alexander B25FL    Ryder,West Bromwich 01
```

```
K130 STY   Ford Transit        Careline B14FL   Non-PSV 98
L305 AUT   Mercedes-Benz 709D  Alexander B25F   Arriva Fox County 1305 02
X584 EJE   LDV Convoy          ? C16F           Non-PSV 02
```

RIL 4396*N459 VOD(?/02), RIL 4529*N628 BWG(9/00), RIL 4572*E452 EAP(8/00),
RIL 4586*E209 BDV(1/01) & RIL 4599*891 EHA(2/00) & E464 CWV(8/98)

T5   T W COACHES LTD

Depot:Hacche Lane,SOUTH MOLTON,Devon.

```
BOV  415   MB O303RHD          C49FT            Deeble,Darley Ford 94
KIB 8964   Leyland TRCTL11/3R  Duple C55F       Tearall,West Buckland 99
MXI 2742   MAN SR280           C46FT            Harris,Harmondsworth 88
PJI 6071   DAF MB200DKTL600    Duple C49FT      Archer,Taunton 00
SOI 1552   MAN SR280           C46FT            Western National 2238 89
YIB 3701   TAZ D3200           C53F             Chalfont,Southall 95
YIB 3702   Volvo B58-61        Duple C57F       Cropley,Fosdike 96
6499  MZ   MB O303/15R         C49FT            New 85
251  AET   LAG Panoramic       C49FT            Thorogood,Barking 01
DAK 216V   Leyland PSU5C/4R    Duple C51F       Russell,Sutton Coldfld 98
KBH 843V   Leyland PSU3E/4R    Plaxton C53F     Steel,Addingham 43 90
KTA 980V   Volvo B58-56        Plaxton C53F     Palmer,Blackwater 98
PWK   3W   Leyland PSU3F/5R    Plaxton C53F     Hearn,Stibb Cross 01
C988 MWJ   Auwaerter N722/3    PN CH53/18DT     Dent &,North Kelsey 01
E 53 GHO   Mercedes-Benz 609D  RB C24F          Seaview,Parkstone 97
F544 HTA   Mercedes-Benz 407D  DC C15F          New 88
V  1 TWC   Mercedes-Benz O814D Mellor C33F      New 99
X 10 TWC   Mercedes-Benz O814D ACL C31F         New 00
```

BOV 415*F66 WCV(3/94), KIB 8964*KGS 484Y(6/88),
MXI 2742*PPD 648W(10/88) & 7107 PH(10/86) & KPC 410W(9/80),
PJI 6071*ACX 781Y(3/93),
SOI 1552*SOI 171(4/85) & HMS 1V(3/85), YIB 3701*F869 ONR(8/96),
YIB 3702*UHJ 648V(8/96) & 7947 RU(11/89) & UHJ 496V(7/89) &
         BWC 800(7/88) & MNK 780V(7/86), 6499 MZ*B295 YOD(2/88),
251 AET*D24 XPF(11/94),
KTA 980V*YMU 134(12/98) & LBU 670V(8/94) & KIW 3675(3/94) &
         LUA 254V(3/93) & C988 MWJ*HE 5362(12/95) & C92 KET(11/89)

T6   TARHUM LTD.t/a BLUE IRIS COACHES

Depots:25 Clevedon Road,NAILSEA & 51 Claverham Road,YATTON,Somerset.

```
D 53 TLV   Freight Rover Sherpa Carlyle B20F    Jones,Yatton 97
E521 TOV   Fiat 49-10          Carlyle B25F     Dowling,Bristol 02
F680 AFY   Mercedes-Benz 408D  North West C15F  Clapton Coaches 92
F617 PWS   Fiat 49-10          Dormobile B20F   Dowling,Bristol 02
K 18 LUE   Volvo B10M-60       Jonckheere C49FT Park,Hamilton 94
L142 JVR   Talbot Pullman      B18F             Hillier,Foxham 00
L 18 LUE   Toyota HZB50R       Caetano C21F     Haldane,Glasgow 01
M 18 LUE   Scania K113TRB      Irizar C51FT     Capital,West Drayton 99
N 18 LUE   Toyota HZB50R       Caetano C18F     New 95
N 88 LUE   Volvo B10M-62       Plaxton C53F     Tillingbourne,Cranleigh 01
P 88 LUE   Scania K124IB       Irizar C49FT     Elizabethan,Walsall 99
R 18 LUE   Toyota BB50R        Caetano C18F     New 97
R872 SDT   Scania L94IB        Irizar C53F      Bus Eireann SI3 01
S344 SET   Scania L94IB        Irizar C53F      Bus Eireann 02
T 18 LUE   Toyota BB50R        Caetano C24F     New 99
T568 SUF   Toyota BB50R        Caetano C22F     Toyota(Demonstrator) 01
V301 EAK   Scania K124IB       Irizar C53F      New 00
V 28 LUE   Scania L94IB        Van Hool C49FT   Chambers,Moneymore(NI) 02
V888 LUE   Scania L94IB        Van Hool C49FT   Chambers,Moneymore(NI) 02
```

K18 LUE*K921 RGE(3/94), L18 LUE*M898 CNS(7/01),
M18 LUE*M304 VET(5/02) & 88 CWR(7/98) & M304 VET(4/98),
N88 LUE*MIL 8584(2/02) & N984 THO(1/00) & A6 XEL(10/99),

P88 LUE*R460 YDT(4/00), R872 SDT*98D 10285(8/01), S344 SET*98D ? (3/02),
V28 LUE*V5 CCH(3/02) & V888 LUE*V4 CCH(3/02)
~~~~~~

T7   TAW & TORRIDGE COACHES LTD

Depots:Merton Garage & Grange Lane Depot,MERTON,Devon.

NDO 856	Volvo B10M-60	Plaxton C46FT	Western National 9817 99
PJI 4713	Bristol LHS6L	Plaxton C33F	British Airways CC304 96
TIW 7681	Bedford YMQ	Plaxton C35F	Perry,Bromyard 128 99
6986 RU	Van Hool T815	C49FT	Chalk,Coombe Bissett 89
7646 RU	Scania K112CRB	Jonckheere C51FT	Dreamline,Blackburn 91
895 FXA	Bova FHD12-280	C49FT	Robinson,Stewkley 97
676 GDV	Volvo B10M-61	Jonckheere C51FT	Wood,Oldbury 02
775 HOD	Van Hool T815	C49FT	Pettigrew,Kirkoswald 93
509 HUO	Volvo B58-61	Van Hool C49DT	Lowland Scottish 631 93
407 JWO	Scania K112CRB	Jonckheere C49FT	Hayward,Horndean 98
ODV 283P	Volvo B58-61	Duple C57F	Newquay Motors 86
JCW 517S	Volvo B58-56	Plaxton C53F	Abbott,Blackpool 01
YTT 178S	Bedford YMT	Plaxton C42FT	Gouldbourn,Royton 88
AFJ 740T	Bristol LH6L	Plaxton C43F	Bruce-Robertson,Exeter 92
AFJ 742T	Bristol LH6L	Plaxton C43F	King,Bordon 92
JMJ 134V	Ford R1114	Duple C53F	Tarka Travel,Bideford 89
RLN 230W	Bristol LHS6L	Plaxton C31F	British Airways CC303 96
C546 BHY	Ford Transit	Dormobile B16F	Badgerline 4546 94
C550 BHY	Ford Transit	Dormobile B16F	Badgerline 4550 94
D100 XRY	MAN MT8.136	GCS C28F	Crudge,Honiton 01
J130 LVM	DAF 400	Deansgate C16F	Wellington,Kingsbridge 01
N855 XMO	Dennis Javelin	Berkhof C53F	Jones,Pontypridd 99
N869 XMO	Dennis Javelin	Berkhof C53F	Monetgrange,Nottingham 99
N870 XMO	Dennis Javelin	Berkhof C49FT	Monetgrange,Nottingham 99
N873 XMO	Dennis Javelin	Berkhof C53F	Monetgrange,Nottingham 99
R 10 TAW	Dennis Javelin	Auwaerter C49FT	New 98
Y 25 TAW	Bova FHD12-370	C49FT	New 01

~~~~~~
A.G. HUNT.t/a AMG COACHES(Associated Company)

NOK 43	Volvo B58-61	Plaxton C57F	Taw & Torridge,Merton 89
ODV 287P	Volvo B58-56	Duple C53F	Taw & Torridge,Merton 89
DMJ 374T	Bedford YMT	Duple C53F	Tanner &,Sibford Gower 83

~~~~~~
NDO 856*L257 UCV(7/00), NOK 43*NGB 5P(5/90), PJI 4713*RLN 231W(10/99),
TIW 7681*81CW 271(5/99) & TIW 7681(12/98) & NPC 387W(5/97),
6986 RU*NOX 740X(7/85), 7646 RU*E699 NNH(3/93),
895 FXA*C104 TFP(12/97) & 4542 VU(7/97) & C104 TFP(5/93),
676 GDV*ONV 652Y(2/02) & TIL 8148(1/02) & ONV 652Y(3/01) & 349 LVO(2/01) &
        ONV 652Y(6/87), 775 HOD*G254 VML(10/95), 509 HUO*RHS 2W(8/94),
407 JWO*E518 KNV(8/98), ODV 283P*509 HUO(8/94) & KDR 487P(7/90),
ODV 287P*676 GDV(2/95) & KTT 316P(2/89) &
YTT 178S*407 JWO(8/98) & XLJ 426S(2/88) & 11 AFC(3/84)
~~~~~~

T8   TAYLORS COACH TRAVEL LTD

Depot:Townsend Garage,TINTINHULL,Somerset.

RIL 1057	Volvo B10M-61	Van Hool C53F	Southern National 7002 00
RJX 318	Bova FHD12-340	C53F	Kings Ferry,Gillingham 01
WJI 1414	DAF SB3000DKV601	Van Hool C57F	James,Cenarth 00
752 FUV	Toyota HB31R	Caetano C20F	Cowdrey,Gosport 00
JHA 216L	Leyland PSU3B/2R	Marshall DP49F	Non-PSV(Dublin) 00
EGD 201T	Ford R1114	Plaxton C53F	Redwood,Hemyock 02
KCH 753V	Volvo B58-61	Plaxton C53F	Cooper,Woolston 02
KHL 460W	Volvo B58-56	Plaxton C53F	Jones,Llanidloes 02
MAX 261X	Leyland TRCTL11/3R	Plaxton C57F	Procter,Bedale 01
D659 WEY	Bedford YNT	Plaxton C53F	Southern National 9045 02
E755 HJF	Dennis Javelin	Duple C57F	Powell,Ledbury 01
F791 GNA	Leyland TRCL10/3ARZ	Duple C53F	Powell,Ledbury 01

```
F729 JWD   Leyland LBM6T/2RS    WS DP33F        Rignall,Kingkerswell 00
F869 YWX   Leyland LBM6T/2RS    RB C37F         Smith,Darenth 01
G275 BEL   Toyota HB31R         Caetano C18F    Forward,Tiverton 00
P224 KTP   Iveco CC95           Indcar C35F     Botley,Bishops Waltham 01
YN51 WGW   Dennis R             Plaxton C53F    New 01
```
~~~~~~
```
RIL 1057*8 TEN(2/99) & E313 OPR(10/93),
RJX 318*L485 HKN(11/01) & L7 KFC(11/99), WJI 1414*G965 KJX(11/99),
752 FUV*E240 NFA(4/96), JHA 216L*73KE 18(12/00) & JHA 216L(10/90),
EGD 201T*USV 800(?/02) & EGD 201T(9/93),
KCH 753V*380 BUO(1/02) & KCH 753V(4/97) & PSV 110(5/95) & WGA 492V(?/89) &
           877 COT(3/88) & VBG 739V(3/85) &
D659 WEY*610 LYB(3/94) & D933 XWP(4/93)
```
~~~~~~

T9   THAMESDOWN DIAL-a-RIDE COMMUNITY TRANSPORT

Depot:Shaftesbury Centre,Percy Street,SWINDON,Wiltshire.

```
E122 CAM   Mercedes-Benz 307D    DC B10FL           New 88
H536 YHT   Talbot Freeway        B16FL              New 91
J221 OTM   Iveco 40-12           DC B12FL           New 92
K246 MMR   Mercedes-Benz 308D    DC B10FL           New 93
N884 NHR   Mercedes-Benz 412D    DC B ?FL           New 96
P897 GOG   Mercedes-Benz 412D    DC B ?FL           Birmingham City Council 01
R760 BVV   Mercedes-Benz 410D    PG B16FL           New 98
R714 FOJ   Mercedes-Benz 410D    ? B8FL             New 97
S859 PHR   Mercedes-Benz 410D    ? B ?FL            New 98
V903 DMR   Mercedes-Benz 410D    ? B ?FL            New 00
Y754 UMR   Mercedes-Benz 411CDI  ? B ?FL            New 01
WX51 EPP   Mercedes-Benz 411CDI  Courtside B ?FL    New 01
```
~~~~~~
~~~~~~

U1   D.J.,K.J. & J.A. THOMAS.t/a SWANBROOK

Depot:Pheasant Lane,GOLDEN VALLEY,Gloucestershire.

```
UJI 1761   Volvo B10M-60         Plaxton C51F    City of Oxford 161 00
UJI 1762   Volvo B10M-60         Plaxton C51F    City of Oxford 162 00
UJI 1763   Volvo B10M-60         Plaxton C53F    City of Oxford 163 00
BYX 186V   MCW Metrobus DR101     H43/28D        London United M186 98
KJW 301W   MCW Metrobus DR102     H43/30F        Arriva Midlands N. 2052 99
KJW 320W   MCW Metrobus DR102     H43/30F        Arriva Midlands N. 2071 00
A900 SUL   MCW Metrobus DR101     H43/28F        Go Ahead London M900 00
A926 SUL   MCW Metrobus DR101     H43/28F        Go Ahead London M926 00
A958 SYF   MCW Metrobus DR101     H43/28D        London United M958 98
A703 THV   MCW Metrobus DR101     H43/28D        London United M1003 98
B120 UUD   Leyland TRCTL11/3RH    Plaxton C51F   City of Oxford 120 96
B149 WUL   MCW Metrobus DR101     H43/32F        Metroline M1149 01
B221 WUL   MCW Metrobus DR101     H43/32F        Arriva London M1221 01
C142 SPB   Leyland TRCTL11/3RH    Berkhof C53F   Coombs,Weston-S-Mare 99
F 71 LAL   Mercedes-Benz 811D     Alexander C33F Tidbury,St Helens 00
G103 TND   Mercedes-Benz 811D     Carlyle B31F   Arriva North West 73 98
H423 GPM   Mercedes-Benz 709D     Phoenix B27F   Ash,Wooburn Moor 01
H683 NEF   Iveco 49-10            Dormobile B25F Non-PSV(Dinorwic) 00
L194 OVO   Mercedes-Benz 811D     Plaxton B33F   Nottingham 194 01
L195 OVO   Mercedes-Benz 811D     Plaxton B33F   Nottingham 195 01
N202 LCK   Optare Excel L1070     B36F           Blackpool 202 00
N205 LCK   Optare Excel L1070     B36F           Blackpool 205 00
R100 PAR   Optare Excel L1150     B40F           New 97
R200 PAR   Optare Excel L1150     B40F           New 97
R300 PAR   Optare Excel L1150     B40F           New 97
R 12 SBK   Dennis Dart SLF        UVG B40F       New 97
T 12 SBK   Dennis Dart SLF        Marshall B37F  New 99
X 96 AHU   Renault Master         Rohill B16F    Op for Gloucestershire CC
Y892 HAE   Renault Master         Rohill B16F    Op for Gloucestershire CC
Y893 HAE   Renault Master         Rohill B16F    Op for Gloucestershire CC
SK51 SBK   Dennis Dart SLF        Marshall B40F  New 01
```

UJI 1761*H957 DRJ(11/95), UJI 1762*H960 DRJ(11/95),
UJI 1763*H958 DRJ(11/95), F71 LAL*WNF 26(9/00) & F71 LAL(2/99) &
R12 SBK*R162 KFH(5/99)

U2   T. THOMAS.t/a FIRST & LAST COACH HIRE

Depot:The Sail Loft,SENNEN COVE,Cornwall.

XIB 4608	DAF MB200DKFL600	Plaxton C57F	Carlton,Carlton-1-Moor. 99
MMK 907W	Volvo B58-56	Plaxton C53F	Thomas,Hayle 99
A388 XMC	Volvo B10M-61	Plaxton C53F	Mundell,Tarbert 00
D954 NOJ	Freight Rover Sherpa	Carlyle DP18F	Thomas,Relubbus 98
D208 VVV	Fiat 79-14	Caetano C19F	Hosking,Ludgvan 99
L710 LFO	Toyota HZB50R	Caetano C21F	Blake,East Anstey 02

OTHER VEHICLE OWNED BY THE COMPANY
* * * * * * *

D512 CLN	Dodge G10	WS B-F	Storeshed

XIB 4608*A659 XWE(9/96) & MMK 907W*90 NOR(12/89) & NPV 444W(1/86)

U3   T.F. THOMAS.t/a BROOKSIDE TRAVEL

Depot:Brookside Garage,RELUBBUS,Cornwall.

OJI 8324	Ford R1014	Plaxton C35F	Moffat &,Gauldry 00
TIW 1743	Bedford YMP	Plaxton C35F	Morley,Maylandsea 01
DJH 475V	DAF SB2005DHU605	Plaxton C55F	Sale Moor,Stretford 96
A 56 NPP	Mercedes-Benz L608D	RB C19F	Harley,Marlborough 97
C593 JAF	Freight Rover Sherpa	Imperial C16F	Best,Penzance 96
G393 EFS	Mercedes-Benz 507D	Alexander B16F	Grenfell,Motherwell 99
G166 HWO	Optare MR01	B31F	Cardiff 166 01
L492 NDT	Iveco 49-10	Mellor DP20FL	Non-PSV(Catford) 01

OJI 8324*NMC 66X(6/92), TIW 1743*D764 TDV(9/96) &
C593 JAF*883 VCV(3/94) & C371 PHF(1/94)

U4   P.A. & L.A. TILLEY

Depot:The Coach Station,WAINHOUSE CORNER,Cornwall.

TIL 1253	Mercedes-Benz 811D	Robin Hood C29F	R & I,Park Royal 085 95
TIL 1254	Mercedes-Benz 811D	Robin Hood C29F	R & I,Park Royal 089 95
TIL 1255	Leyland ST2R	RB C37F	Turbostyle,Crawley 01
TIL 1256	MAN 13.220	Marcopolo C37F	New 01
TIL 1257	Dennis Javelin	Marcopolo C50FT	Chalfont,Southall 01
TIL 1258	Dennis Javelin	Auwaerter C53F	Londoners,Nunhead 02
TIL 1259	Dennis Javelin	Duple C53F	Vince,Burghclere 99
TIL 1260	Dennis Javelin	Caetano C53F	Metroline(Brents) 01
TIL 1261	Optare Solo M850	B30F	New 00
TIL 1262	Mercedes-Benz 709D	Mellor DP27F	New 95
TIL 1263	Mercedes-Benz O817L	SCC C31F	Friedel,Enfield 00
TIL 5081	Mercedes-Benz O814D	ACL C29F	Kingsbury,K. Episcopi 02

TIL 1253*F85 GGC(9/00), TIL 1254*F89 GGC(9/00), TIL 1255*G483 JOP(4/02),
TIL 1257*P559 BAY(11/01), TIL 1258*R7 LON(2/02), TIL 1259*F869 TLJ(9/00),
TIL 1260*P771 BJF(8/01), TIL 1261*W676 DDN(9/00), TIL 1262*M729 UWJ(9/00),
TIL 1263*R997 RHL(6/01) & TIL 5081*W232 KDO(4/02)

U5   I. TOPPING.t/a SUNSET COACHES

Depot:Peace & Quiet,Chapel Euny,BRANE,Cornwall.

DAZ 5055	Fiat 35-8	Elme C16F	Topping,Wavertree 87
D 44 OYA	Fiat 35-8	G & M C14F	Non-PSV(Mousehole) 00
E658 VHF	Fiat 40-8	Wright B18FL	Liverpool City Council 97
H765 GTJ	Fiat 40-8	Mellor B16FL	Liverpool City Council 97
H 16 SUN	Mercedes-Benz 811D	? C24F	Non-PSV(Van) 97
J613 NLH	Mercedes-Benz 609D	Mellor B15FL	City of Westminster 99

DAZ 5055*D893 THF(6/96) & H16 SUN*H967 NTX(9/97)

U6   TRATHENS TRAVEL SERVICES LTD

Depot:Walkham Park Industrial Estate,Burrington Way,PLYMOUTH,Devon.

KSK 984	Volvo B12T	JE CH57/14CT	Park,Hamilton 02
KSK 985	Volvo B12T	JE CH57/14CT	Park,Hamilton 02
LSK 473	Volvo B12T	VH CH57/14CT	New 98
LSK 481	Volvo B12T	VH CH57/14CT	New 98
LSK 498	Volvo B12T	VH CH57/14CT	New 98
LSK 499	Volvo B12T	VH CH57/14CT	New 98
LSK 500	Volvo B10M-62	Jonckheere C49FT	Park,Hamilton 01
LSK 501	Volvo B10M-62	Jonckheere C49FT	Park,Hamilton 01
LSK 502	Volvo B10M-62	Jonckheere C49FT	Park,Hamilton 01
LSK 503	Volvo B10M-62	Jonckheere C49FT	Park,Hamilton 01
LSK 504	Volvo B10M-62	Jonckheere C49FT	Park,Hamilton 02
LSK 505	Volvo B10M-62	Jonckheere C49FT	Park,Hamilton 02
LSK 506	Volvo B10M-62	Jonckheere C49FT	Park,Hamilton 02
LSK 507	Volvo B10M-62	Jonckheere C49FT	Park,Hamilton 02
LSK 508	Volvo B10M-62	Jonckheere C49FT	Park,Hamilton 02
LSK 611	Volvo B12T	VH CH10/6CT	Park,Hamilton 96
LSK 612	Volvo B12T	VH CH10/6CT	Park,Hamilton 96
LSK 613	Volvo B12T	VH CH10/6CT	New 93
LSK 614	Volvo B12T	JE CH10/6CT	Park,Hamilton 96
LSK 615	Volvo B12T	JE CH10/6CT	Park,Hamilton 96
LSK 812	Volvo B12T	VH CH10/6CT	Park,Hamilton 96
LSK 814	Volvo B12T	VH CH10/6CT	Park,Hamilton 96
TSU 603	Van Hool TD824	CH14/8CT	Deeble,Darley Ford 95
290 WE	Volvo B10M-53	VH CH10/6FT	Express Travel,Perth 93
P926 KYC	Volvo B12T	VH CH57/14CT	New 97
P927 KYC	Volvo B12T	VH CH57/14CT	New 97
YN51 XMH	Auwaerter N122/3	CH57/18CT	New 01
YN51 XMJ	Auwaerter N122/3	CH57/18CT	New 01
YN51 XMK	Auwaerter N122/3	CH57/18CT	New 01
YN51 XML	Auwaerter N122/3	CH57/18CT	New 01
YN51 XMU	Auwaerter N122/3	CH57/18CT	New 01
YN51 XMV	Auwaerter N122/3	CH57/18CT	New 01
YN51 XMW	Auwaerter N122/3	CH57/18CT	New 01
YN51 XMX	Auwaerter N122/3	CH57/18CT	New 01
YN51 XMZ	Auwaerter N122/3	CH57/18CT	New 01
YN51 XNC	Auwaerter N122/3	CH57/18CT	New 01
YN51 XND	Auwaerter N122/3	CH57/18CT	New 01
YN51 XNE	Auwaerter N122/3	CH57/18CT	New 01

OTHER VEHICLE OWNED BY THE COMPANY
* * * * * * *

GPT 224S	Volvo B58-61	Plaxton C24F	Trainer

N.B.:- Company owned by Park,Hamilton & YN51 XMH etc carry fleet numbers
521/2/15/6/1-4/7-20 respectively.

LSK 473*R262 OFJ(5/02), LSK 481*R263 OFJ(5/02), LSK 498*R261 OFJ(5/02),
LSK 499*R264 OFJ(5/02), LSK 611*LSK 831(3/96), LSK 612*LSK 832(3/96),
LSK 613*L977 KDT(10/97), TSU 603*E406 FSH(2/90) & D578 SUS(8/87),
290 WE*B418 CGG(3/88) & GPT 224S*891 HUM(5/95) & OJY 577S(1/87)

110

U7   **I. TROTTER.t/a BRUE TRAVEL**

Depot:Styles Farm,The Marsh,HENSTRIDGE,Somerset.

VAZ 9488	Ford Transit	Dormobile C16F	Jacobs,Horton Heath 99
B570 YOD	Mercedes-Benz L307D	RB B8F	CSGB,South Newton 99
G731 PGA	Ford Transit	Dormobile B16F	Staines,Brentwood 97
H874 ABU	Renault Master	Premier B15F	Jenkins,Cinderford 99

VAZ 9488*E205 OEL(9/98)

U8   **TRURONIAN LTD**

Depots:Flambards Theme Park,HELSTON &
Whetter Building,Litherage Hill,Newnham Ind. Est.,TRURO,Cornwall.

XBF 976	Leyland TRCTL11/2R	Plaxton C53F	Powell,Wickersley 6 97
260 ERY	Volvo B10M-62	Caetano C49FT	New 94
NNK 809P	Bedford YRT	Duple B63F	Ede & Paramor,Par 94
AAP 668T	Bristol VRT/SL3/6LXB	ECW H43/28F	Stagecoach South 768 97
AFJ 753T	Bristol VRT/SL3/6LXB	ECW H43/31F	Ryan,Langridge 96
AFJ 771T	Bristol VRT/SL3/6LXB	ECW H43/31F	Wellington,Kingsbridge 96
BKE 851T	Bristol VRT/SL3/6LXB	ECW H43/31F	Wellington,Kingsbridge 96
BKE 857T	Bristol VRT/SL3/6LXB	ECW H43/31F	Tims Travel,Sheerness 98
EAP 985V	Bristol VRT/SL3/6LXB	ECW H43/31F	Stagecoach South 685 98
FKM 876V	Bristol VRT/SL3/6LXB	ECW H43/31F	Maidstone & Dist. 5876 97
SGR 790V	Bristol VRT/SL3/6LXB	ECW H42/31F	Hopley,Mount Hawke 00
PAF 189X	Leyland TRCTL11/3R	Duple C53F	Powell,Wickersley 97
PRC 849X	Bristol VRT/SL3/6LXB	ECW H43/31F	Trent 849 91
PRC 856X	Bristol VRT/SL3/6LXB	ECW H43/31F	Trent 856 91
TPL 762X	Leyland TRBL11/2R	Plaxton C53F	Vale,Cheetham 97
C812 BYY	Leyland ONLXB/1RH	ECW H42/30F	Stagecoach London L12 01
C819 BYY	Leyland ONLXB/1RH	ECW H42/30F	Stagecoach London L19 01
C 23 CHM	Leyland ONLXB/1RH	ECW H42/30F	Stagecoach London L23 01
C 74 CHM	Leyland ONLXB/1RH	ECW H42/30F	Stagecoach London L74 01
C 83 CHM	Leyland ONLXB/1RH	ECW H42/30F	Stagecoach London L83 01
C 87 CHM	Leyland ONLXB/1RH	ECW H42/30F	Stagecoach London L87 01
E872 PGL	Mercedes-Benz 609D	RB C19F	New 87
F314 VCV	Mercedes-Benz 609D	RB C19F	New 88
F315 VCV	Mercedes-Benz 609D	RB C25F	New 88
H920 XYN	Renault G10	WS B28FL	Springham,Dartford 96
H932 XYN	Renault G10	WS B32FL	LB Hackney 422 98
L725 WCV	Mercedes-Benz 811D	Plaxton B31F	New 94
L726 WCV	Mercedes-Benz 811D	Plaxton B31F	New 94
M372 CRL	Volvo B10M-62	Plaxton C49FT	New 95
M373 CRL	Volvo B10M-62	Plaxton C49FT	New 95
N166 KAF	Dennis Dart	Plaxton B37F	New 96
N167 KAF	Dennis Dart	Plaxton B37F	New 96
N168 KAF	Dennis Dart	Plaxton B37F	New 96
N169 KAF	Dennis Dart	Plaxton B37F	New 96
N170 KAF	Mercedes-Benz 711D	Plaxton C25F	New 96
N212 KBJ	Mercedes-Benz 711D	ACL C24F	Galloway,Mendlesham 00
N498 PYS	Volvo B10M-62	Van Hool C49FT	loan from Dawsons
N514 PYS	Volvo B10M-62	Van Hool C49FT	loan from Dawsons
P452 SCV	Dennis Dart SLF	Plaxton B34F	New 97
P453 SCV	Dennis Dart SLF	Plaxton B34F	New 97
P454 SCV	Dennis Dart SLF	Plaxton B34F	New 97
P455 SCV	Dennis Dart SLF	Plaxton B34F	New 97
R 1 TRU	Volvo B10M-62	Van Hool C49FT	New 98
R527 YRP	Dennis Dart SLF	Wright B38F	loan from Dawsons
R530 YRP	Dennis Dart SLF	Wright B41F	loan from Dawsons
S549 SCV	Dennis Dart SLF	Plaxton B29F	New 98
S405 TMB	Dennis Dart SLF	Plaxton B41F	loan from Dawsons
T442 EBD	Dennis Dart SLF	Wright B39F	loan from Dawsons
T 32 JCV	Dennis Dart SLF	Plaxton B35F	New 99
T 34 JCV	Dennis Dart SLF	Plaxton B34F	New 99
T 35 JCV	Dennis Dart SLF	Plaxton B34F	New 99
T 2 TRU	Volvo B10M-62	Plaxton C49FT	New 99

```
T 12 TRU  Dennis Dart SLF      Plaxton B29F      New 99
W  3 TRU  Volvo B10M-62        Plaxton C49FT     New 00
W  4 TRU  Mercedes-Benz O814D  Plaxton C25F      New 00
Y  1 EDN  Dennis Dart SLF      Plaxton B37F      New 01
Y  2 EDN  Dennis Dart SLF      Plaxton B37F      New 01
Y  5 TRU  Volvo B10M-62        Plaxton C49FT     New 01
```
~~~~~~
```
XBF 976*LES 991X(10/96) & WSV 490(5/88) & XAY 875X(1/87) &
       3810 VT(11/86) & GCA 123X(3/85), 260 ERY*L339 WAF(10/01),
PAF 189X*260 ERY(2/99) & 8921 WF(8/88) & NTG 18X(10/85),
N498 PYS*LSK 824(12/98), N514 PYS*LSK 845(12/98) &
S405 TMB*98D 70810(10/01) & S405 TMB(12/99)
```
~~~~~~

U9 A.R. & M.E. TURNER & S.L. & P.C. GILSON.t/a TURNERS TOURS

Depot:Back Lane Industrial Estate,CHULMLEIGH,Devon.

```
GIL 5107  Volvo B10M-56   Plaxton C53F      New 83
GIL 5109  Volvo B10M-60   Plaxton C53F      Dawlish Coaches 01
GIL 5711  Volvo B10M-61   Plaxton C53F      Horseshoe,Kempston 91
LBZ 2939  Volvo B10M-61   Plaxton C49FT     Ralph,Langley 96
LIL 7043  MAN 16.290      Jonckheere C49FT  Coliseum,West End 96
LIW 3460  Volvo B10M-61   Plaxton C49FT     Moon,Warnham 94
PIL 6577  Volvo B10M-61   Caetano C49FT     Chiltern Queen,Woodcote 01
VAZ 2531  MAN 16.290      Jonckheere C49FT  Buddens,Romsey 97
VAZ 2533  Volvo B10M-60   Jonckheere C49FT  Q Drive,Battersea 98
VAZ 2534  Volvo B10M-60   Jonckheere C49FT  Q Drive,Battersea 98
WJI 7955  Ford R1115      Plaxton C35F      Turner,Chesham 99
458  FTA  Volvo B10M-61   Plaxton C49F      Taylor,Rottingdean 89
NMJ 283V  Volvo B58-56    Plaxton C53F      Horseshoe,Kempston 91
HAX 331W  Ford R1114      Plaxton C53F      Bennett &,Gloucester 97
YUY  94W  Ford R1114      Plaxton C53F      Clements,Nailsea 33 01
AEF 260Y  Ford R1015      Plaxton C35F      Walton,Stockton 85
A987 POD  Bedford YNT     Plaxton C53F      New 84
D851 UTA  Dodge G13       WS DP38F          MOD 96
D928 UTA  Dodge G13       WS DP38F          MOD 97
F515 SCW  Mercedes-Benz 407D  RB C15F       Mellor,Harrow 00
J398 GKH  Dennis Dart     Plaxton DP30F     Metroline DR98 01
K892 CSX  Dennis Dart     Alexander B40F    Richmond,Epsom 01
K437 OKH  Dennis Dart     Plaxton B34F      Metroline DRL37 02
L535 YCC  Volvo B10M-60   Jonckheere C49FT  Vale Llangollen,Cefn M. 02
L537 YCC  Volvo B10M-60   Jonckheere C49FT  Vale Llangollen,Cefn M. 02
M629 KVU  Volvo B10M-62   Jonckheere C46FT  Shearings 629 99
M619 ORJ  Volvo B10M-62   Jonckheere C53F   Shearings 619 99
R190 SUT  Volvo B10M-62   Jonckheere C49FT  Mayne,Buckie 01
```
~~~~~~
```
GIL 5107*EFJ 573Y(7/90),
GIL 5109*F788 MAA(2/01) & XEL 6S(12/93) & F453 WFX(9/91),
GIL 5711*B27 BMC(4/92), LBZ 2939*D251 HFX(5/95),
LIL 7043*F202 UOR(2/96) & MIB 651(11/94), LIW 3460*D221 LWY(11/99),
PIL 6577*C114 PUJ(9/98) & SEL 7X(4/93) & C690 KDS(6/90),
VAZ 2531*K228 WNH(8/98), VAZ 2533*H61 XBD(8/98), VAZ 2534*H62 XBD(8/98),
WJI 7955*A383 OFR(12/99) & 84KK 171(12/99) & A383 OFR(1/89),
458 FTA*A943 VMH(10/86), HAX 331W*HAX 335W(6/91),
L535 YCC*VLT 22(10/01) & L5 VLT(3/97),
L537 YCC*VLT 55(11/01) & L6 VLT(3/97) &
R190 SUT*R555 GSM(2/01) & R190 SUT(4/99)
```
~~~~~~

V1   R.S. & R.L. TURNER.t/a BEACON GARAGE

Depot:Beacon Garage,DOLTON,Devon.

```
C740 FBU  Freight Rover Sherpa  MM C16F     Bennett,Warrington 90
E140 WTA  Freight Rover Sherpa  Leith C16F  New 87
F893 CAT  Freight Rover Sherpa  ? C16F      East Yorkshire 293 91
G 72 APO  Mercedes-Benz 709D    Alexander DP25F  McColl,Gartocharn 01
G969 BLE  DAF 400               G & M C16F  Levick,Torrington 97
```

```
G  64 PTT   DAF 400           G & M   C16F       New 89
J608  OOD   DAF 400           DC      C16F       New 92
K176  XOD   DAF 400           Concept C16F       New 93
M497  TVH   DAF 400           Concept C16FL      New 95
P707  YTT   LDV 400           Concept C16FL      New 96
R 39  BYG   LDV Convoy        Concept C16F       New 98
V487  RDN   LDV Convoy        Concept C16F       New 99
```
~~~~~~
~~~~~~

V2   TURNERS COACHWAYS (BRISTOL) LTD

Depot:59 Days Road,St Philips,BRISTOL.

```
MIL 8583  Toyota HZB50R          Caetano C21F       Business,Banwell 00
OYY    3  Volvo B10M-60          Van Hool C57F      North Mymms,Potters Bar 93
BFX 570T  Bristol VRT/SL3/6LXB   ECW H43/31F        Stagecoach Cambus 706 97
D 78 JHY  Leyland TRCTL11/3LZ    Plaxton DP70FA     MOD 98
D202 JHY  Leyland TRCTL11/3LZ    Plaxton DP70FA     MOD 99
E691 NOU  Leyland TRCTL11/3LZ    Plaxton DP56FA     MOD 99
E787 NOU  Leyland TRCTL11/3LZ    Plaxton DP70FA     MOD 99
G826 XWS  Leyland TRCTL11/3LZM   Plaxton DP56FA     MOD 98
G829 XWS  Leyland TRCTL11/3LZM   Plaxton DP56FA     MOD 98
K  5 CJT  Toyota HDB30R          Caetano C21F       New 92
K  6 CJT  Volvo B10M-60          Van Hool C57F      New 93
K  7 CJT  Volvo B10M-60          Van Hool C57F      New 93
L  8 CJT  Volvo B10M-60          Van Hool C49FT     New 94
L  9 CJT  Volvo B10M-60          Van Hool C49FT     New 94
M 10 CJT  Volvo B10M-62          Jonckheere C53F    Park,Hamilton 96
M 11 CJT  Volvo B10M-62          Jonckheere C49FT   Park,Hamilton 96
M 12 CJT  Volvo B10M-62          Jonckheere C53F    Park,Hamilton 96
M 13 CJT  Volvo B10M-62          Jonckheere C49FT   Park,Hamilton 96
M 20 CJT  Volvo B12R             JE CH57/15CT       Excelsior,Bournemouth 98
M 40 CJT  Volvo B12R             JE CH57/15CT       Excelsior,Bournemouth 98
M165 XHW  Dennis Javelin         UVG C ?F           MOD 02
N 14 CJT  Volvo B10M-62          Plaxton C49FT      Tillingbourne,Cranleigh 01
N895 VEG  Mercedes-Benz 811D     Marshall B33F      Richmond,Barley 00
P 15 CJT  Volvo B10M-62          Plaxton C57F       New 97
P 16 CJT  Volvo B10M-62          Plaxton C57F       New 97
R  2 CJT  Volvo B10M-62          Jonckheere C49FT   New 97
R  3 CJT  Volvo B10M-62          Jonckheere C49FT   New 97
R 18 CJT  Volvo B10M-62          Plaxton C57F       New 98
R 19 CJT  Volvo B10M-62          Plaxton C57F       New 98
R 30 CJT  Mercedes-Benz O1120L   Ferqui C35F        New 98
R 90 CJT  Scania K113TRB         Irizar C49FT       Appleby(Halcyon) 01
S 50 CJT  Volvo B10M-62          Berkhof C49FT      New 98
S 60 CJT  Volvo B10M-62          Berkhof C49FT      New 98
S853 PKH  Mercedes-Benz O814D    Plaxton B31F       Plaxton(Demonstrator) 00
W 17 CJT  Volvo B7R-63           Plaxton C53F       Plaxton(Demonstrator) 02
X 70 CJT  Volvo B10M-62          Jonckheere C49FT   New 00
X 80 CJT  Volvo B10M-62          Jonckheere C49FT   New 00
AT02 CJT  Volvo B7R-63           Jonckheere C57F    New 02
BT02 CJT  Volvo B7R-63           Jonckheere C57F    New 02
```
~~~~~~
```
MIL 8583*N14 CJT(11/01), OYY 3*G879 ARO(4/94),
M10 CJT*M983 HHS(3/96) & LSK 825(11/95),
M11 CJT*M984 HHS(3/96) & LSK 821(11/95),
M12 CJT*M985 HHS(3/96) & KSK 977(11/95),
M13 CJT*M987 HHS(3/96) & KSK 985(11/95), M20 CJT*XEL 4(1/98),
M40 CJT*M459 MRU(5/98) & XEL 14(3/98),
N14 CJT*MIL 8583(10/01) & N997 THO(1/00) & A5 XEL(10/99),
R90 CJT*R278 RRH(10/01) & W17 CJT*W38 DOE(4/02)
```
~~~~~~

V3   UNITED BRISTOL HEALTHCARE TRUST

Depot:Bristol General Hospital,Guinea Street,Redcliffe,BRISTOL.

H429 CHW	Ford Transit	DC B16F	New 91
L518 XFB	Iveco 49-10	DC B14F	New 94
M631 BEU	Iveco 49-10	DC B14F	New 94
M479 BTC	Mercedes-Benz 609D	Frank Guy B23F	New 94
N556 KWS	Mercedes-Benz 609D	Frank Guy B23F	New 96
W461 PHW	Mercedes-Benz O814D	Plaxton B31F	New 00

~~~~~~
~~~~~~

V4   I. WATSON.t/a A1 TRAVEL

Depot:31 Oxford Road,Pen Mill Trading Estate,YEOVIL,Somerset.

KIW 3076	Ford R1014	Plaxton C35F	Powell,Thornford 99
PSU 699	Kassbohrer S210HD	C35FT	Kings Ferry,Gillingham 02
XFE 499	Mercedes-Benz L608D	Robin Hood C21F	Rigby,Lathom 95
A847 YJH	Mercedes-Benz L307D	DC C12F	Lever,East Knoyle 96
E816 VSU	MCW Metrorider MF150	C25F	Goodman,Werrington 98
J584 NBX	Renault Master	Cymric C16F	John,Clydach 96
P488 EOX	LDV 400	Jubilee C16F	Tomlin,Worton 97

~~~~~~
KIW 3076*KPP 617V(12/89) & XFE 499*LOW 46Y(2/94)
~~~~~~

V5   D.A. & D.J. WEBBER & E. GARDNER.t/a WEBBERBUS

Depots:Old Storage Depot,Brue Avenue,BRIDGWATER,
        34a Brunel Road,MINEHEAD & The Garage,WHEDDON CROSS,Somerset.

RBZ 4294	Freight Rover Sherpa	Carlyle B20F	Stevens,Withycombe 98
RBZ 4295	Freight Rover Sherpa	Optare C16F	Stevens,Withycombe 98
RIB 6849	Leyland TRCTL11/3R	Plaxton C53F	Filer,Ilfracombe 01
511 SKM	Leyland TRCTL11/3RZ	Duple C50FT	Baker,Yeovil 01
MYD 217V	DAF MB200DKL550	Plaxton C53F	Morley,Minehead 99
SND 281X	Leyland PSU5D/4R	Duple C50F	Hookways,Meeth 01
SND 282X	Leyland PSU5D/4R	Duple C50F	Hookways,Meeth 01
B 73 FGT	Leyland TRCTL11/3R	Duple C48FT	Randolph,Wincanton 00
B247 KUX	DAF MB200DKFL600	Caetano C53F	M Line,Byfleet 00
C906 GYD	Ford Transit	Robin Hood B16F	Southern National 344 98
C908 GYD	Ford Transit	Robin Hood B16F	Southern National 346 98
D127 ACX	DAF MB230DKFL615	Plaxton C53F	Morley,Minehead 99
D630 YCX	DAF MB230DKFL615	Plaxton C53F	Whitehead,Bournemouth 99
E604 CDS	Volvo B10M-61	Plaxton C53F	Repton,New Haw 00
F404 DUG	Volvo B10M-60	Plaxton C53F	Richmond,Barley 99
K218 CBD	MAN 16.290	Jonckheere C51FT	Talbot &,Portsmouth 01
M 41 KAX	Volvo B10M-62	Plaxton C51FT	Lawrence,St Anns Chapel 01
P943 YSB	Mercedes-Benz 814D	Mellor C33F	Lawrence,St Anns Chapel 00
T979 OGA	Mercedes-Benz O814D	Mellor C33F	Lawrence,St Anns Chapel 02

~~~~~~
RBZ 4294*F422 BOP(8/97), RBZ 4295*D704 HUA(9/97), RIB 6849*A282 PDV(4/92),
511 SKM*D135 HML(2/97), SND 281X*RJI 5701(5/01) & SND 281X(9/96),
SND 282X*RJI 5702(4/01) & SND 282X(9/96),
B73 FGT*TJL 800(11/96) & B138 ACK(11/94),
B247 KUX*413 MAB(2/97) & MJI 5013(4/95) & B668 GBD(?/91),
E604 CDS*123 TRL(10/93) & E773 MMH(11/92) &
F404 DUG*892 LTV(8/98) & F404 DUG(8/92)
~~~~~~

V6   R.K. WEBBER.t/a GROUP TRAVEL

Depot:Dunmere Road Garage,Dunmere Road,BODMIN,Cornwall.

LIL 9397	Volvo B10M-61	Caetano C49FT	Webber,Blisland 02
PXI 1421	Volvo B10M-61	Jonckheere C53F	Colton,Dousland 00
THU 514	Volvo B10M-61	Van Hool C53F	National Holidays 69 02
8212 RU	Volvo B10M-61	Jonckheere C49FT	Webber,Blisland 02
WJS 843X	Volvo B58-56	Plaxton C53F	Webber,Blisland 02
D895 VAO	Mercedes-Benz 609D	RB B20F	Gardiner,Spennymoor 97
E714 LYU	Mercedes-Benz 811D	Optare B31F	Bluebird Buses 294 98
F716 FDV	Mercedes-Benz 709D	RB DP25F	Stagecoach Devon 404 99
F730 FDV	Mercedes-Benz 709D	RB DP25F	Stagecoach Devon 414 99
F738 FDV	Mercedes-Benz 709D	RB DP25F	Stagecoach Devon 421 99
F407 KOD	Mercedes-Benz 709D	RB DP25F	Stagecoach Devon 438 99
F616 XMS	Mercedes-Benz 811D	Alexander B31F	Stagecoach Devon 594 98
F641 XMS	Mercedes-Benz 811D	Alexander B31F	Stagecoach Devon 595 98
G387 FSF	Mercedes-Benz 811D	PMT C33F	Bolton School,Bolton 97
H898 LOX	Mercedes-Benz 811D	Carlyle B31F	Hornsby,Ashby B23 98
N629 BWG	Mercedes-Benz 811D	Mellor B31F	Holt,Thornton-le-Dale 02

~~~~~~
LIL 9397*B776 SFA(5/96) & LJI 8160(2/93) & B664 SHE(11/89) & 18 XWC(3/87),
PXI 1421*D614 UGD(3/01), THU 514*D614 MVR(5/95) &
8212 RU*9485 RH(11/91) & MRP 845Y(7/89)
~~~~~~

S.J. & D.E. WELLINGTON & L. HORSWILL.t/a TALLY HO COACHES

Depots:Kingsley Close,East Way,Lee Mill Industrial Estate,IVYBRIDGE &
Station Yard Industrial Estate & Union Road,KINGSBRIDGE,Devon.

AIW 257	DAF MB200DKL600	Plaxton C53F	Nuttall,Modbury 99
ALZ 3248	Renault S56	RB B25F	Mainline 212 97
DCZ 2307	Volvo B58-61	Plaxton C57F	Endicott,Totnes 99
GKZ 3108	Dennis Javelin	Berkhof C53F	Prairie,Hounslow 01
GKZ 3109	Dennis Javelin	Berkhof C53F	Prairie,Hounslow 01
HIB 5017	Leyland PSU5C/4R	Duple C57F	Hearn,Stibb Cross 00
HIL 2897	DAF SB2300DHTD585	Plaxton C53F	Nuttall,Modbury 99
HIL 4966	Mercedes-Benz 609D	Whittaker C23F	Nuttall,Modbury 99
JCZ 3604	Mercedes-Benz 709D	Alexander DP25F	Ribble 568 01
KIW 6512	Ford R1114	Plaxton C53F	Chalkwell,Sittingbourne 96
SIL 4465	Dennis Javelin	Berkhof C53FT	North Western 840 00
VIB 5239	Ford R1114	Plaxton C53F	Chalkwell,Sittingbourne 96
WDR 598	Volvo B58-56	Unicar C55F	Brennan,Bradford 84
YSU 923	Ford R1115	Plaxton C53F	Harrington,Coventry 96
312 KTT	Ford R1115	Plaxton C53F	Harrington,Coventry 96
KJD 410P	Bristol LH6L	ECW B43F	London Buses BL10 86
KJD 413P	Bristol LH6L	ECW B43F	London Transport BL13 82
KJD 414P	Bristol LH6L	ECW B43F	London Buses BL14 86
KJD 419P	Bristol LH6L	ECW B39F	London Buses BL19 92
KJD 420P	Bristol LH6L	ECW B43F	London Transport BL20 82
KJD 422P	Bristol LH6L	ECW B43F	London Buses BL22 86
KJD 431P	Bristol LH6L	ECW B39F	Sidhu &,Bicester 95
OJD 45R	Bristol LH6L	ECW B41F	Tyne & Wear,Gateshead 90
OJD 51R	Bristol LH6L	ECW B43F	London Transport BL51 82
OJD 54R	Bristol LH6L	ECW B43F	Brown,Motcombe 99
OJD 56R	Bristol LH6L	ECW B43F	Tyne & Wear,Gateshead 90
OJD 58R	Bristol LH6L	ECW B45F	London Transport BL58 82
OJD 59R	Bristol LH6L	ECW B41F	London Transport BL59 82
OJD 77R	Bristol LH6L	ECW B43F	London Transport BL77 82
OJD 83R	Bristol LH6L	ECW B41F	Ash,High Wycombe 94
OJD 84R	Bristol LH6L	ECW B43F	Brown,Motcombe 00
RAW 19R	Bedford YMT	Duple C53F	Willis,Bodmin 99
AJD 19T	Bedford YMT	Plaxton C53F	Nuttall,Modbury 99
HFX 411V	Ford R1114	Plaxton C53F	Cole,Winford 98
KPP 619V	Ford R1014	Duple C35F	Hearn,Stibb Cross 00
JCV 433W	Bedford YMT	Plaxton C53F	Nuttall,Modbury 99
PJT 524W	Ford R1114	Plaxton C53F	Powell,Lapford 96
CNH 176X	Leyland PSU3F/4R	ECW C53F	Timeline 22 95

```
CNH 177X   Leyland PSU3F/4R     ECW C49F           Timeline 23 95
RAW 777X   Ford R1114           Plaxton C53F       Pearce,Yatton 96
VMX 234X   Leyland TRCTL11/3RH  Plaxton C51F       Draper,Sidcup 02
TTY 696Y   Ford R1114           Duple C53F         Hearn,Stibb Cross 01
A561 OTA   Dodge S46            Dormobile B20F     Kemp,Kingsbridge 90
B630 DDW   Bedford YNT          Plaxton C53F       Jones,Oakley 00
D184 LTA   Dodge S56            RB B23F            Western National 7006 95
E 39 SBO   Dennis Javelin       Duple C53F         Bebb,Llantwit Fardre 89
E 40 SBO   Dennis Javelin       Duple C53F         Bebb,Llantwit Fardre 89
E210 XWG   Renault S56          RB B25F            Harratt,Kingsteignton 98
G105 DPB   Renault S56          NC B25F            Metrobus,Orpington 55 98
M583 WLV   Dennis Dart          Marshall B40F      Halton 71 01
M584 WLV   Dennis Dart          Marshall B40F      Halton 72 01
M495 XWF   Scania K113CRB       Irizar C49FT       Tarhum,Nailsea 02
N919 DWJ   Scania K113CRB       Irizar C49FT       Buddens,Romsey 02
N 94 PDV   Mercedes-Benz 711D   G & M B22FL        New 95
P423 JDT   Dennis Javelin       Plaxton C49FT      Memories,Stansted 02
```
~~~~~~
```
AIW 257*MIA 626(1/87) & XVW 453S(5/86), ALZ 3248*E212 XWG(9/97),
DCZ 2307*CNA 827T(1/00),
GKZ 3108*J96 UBL(10/01) & 315 ASV(2/01) & J96 UBL(6/98),
GKZ 3109*J97 UBL(10/01) & 848 KMX(2/01) & J97 UBL(6/98),
HIB 5017*DAK 222V(8/95), HIL 2897*A351 RUA(6/99),
HIL 4966*E201 WMB(12/01), JCZ 3604*G568 PRM(6/01),
KIW 6512*SMB 264V(9/91), SIL 4465*K792 YFV(2/00) & K200 SLT(5/97),
VIB 5239*PNW 315W(9/94), WDR 598*ACP 54V(5/84),
YSU 923*HBZ 4299(1/97) & BLJ 717Y(6/94),
312 KTT*HBZ 2459(12/96) & TUK 665Y(6/94),
VMX 234X*TIL 9836(5/02) & ORN 341X(2/01) &
M495 XWF*M18 LUE(4/02) & M495 XWF(2/00)
```
~~~~~~

V8   WESTERN GREYHOUND LTD

Depot:Western Greyhound Garage,St Austell Street,SUMMERCOURT,Cornwall.

```
DSU 107   907   Volvo B10M-60     Van Hool C49FT    Shearings 232 99
TFO 319   919   Volvo B10M-60     Van Hool C53F     Worthing Coaches 02
ULL 933   933   Volvo B10M-60     Van Hool C49FT    Shearings 234 99
UWR 498   498   MB 811D           RB B33F           Arriva Shires 2055 00
WSV 537   937   Volvo B10M-61     Van Hool C50FT    Mitchell,Birmingham 02
XOD 665   665   Volvo B58-56      Plaxton C53F      Plymouth 353 01
674 SHY   674   Volvo B58-56      Plaxton C53F      Plymouth 354 01
RDF 500R   50   Leyland PSU3C/4R  Plaxton C53F      Tippett,St Columb 99
VOD 596S    1   BL VRT/SL3/6LXB   ECW H43/31F       Cheltenham & G. 218 00
EDT 918V    8   BL VRT/SL3/501    ECW H43/31F       Bugler,Bristol 01
LUA 282V   82   Leyland PSU5D/4R  Plaxton C53F      Gill,Wadebridge 98
JWV 259W    2   BL VRT/SL3/6LXB   ECW H43/31F       Brighton & Hove 259 00
TAH 276W    6   BL VRT/SL3/6LXB   ECW H43/31F       Eastern Counties 276 01
VVV 959W    9   BL VRT/SL3/6LXB   ECW H43/31F       Brighton & Hove 279 00
A110 FDL   10   LD ONLXB/1R       ECW CH41/23F      Arriva Shires 5384 02
E301 BWL  301   MB 709D           RB DP25F          Hazell,Northlew 99
R668 DNS  568   MB 614D           Adamson C24F      Reay,Fletchertown 99
R809 HWS  509   MB O814D          Plaxton DP33F     James,Tetbury 01
R810 HWS  510   MB O814D          Plaxton DP33F     James,Tetbury 01
S 30 ARJ  530   MB O814D          Plaxton DP33F     James,Tetbury 01
S 34 BMR  534   MB O814D          Plaxton DP33F     James,Tetbury 01
S501 SRL  501   MB O814D          Plaxton DP27F     New 99
S502 SRL  502   MB O814D          Plaxton DP27F     New 99
S503 SRL  503   MB O814D          Plaxton DP27F     New 99
V 40 WGL  540   MB O814D          Plaxton B31F      Gregg,Boston 02
WK51 AVP  551   MB O814D          Plaxton DP33F     New 01
WK51 HNF  552   MB O814D          Plaxton DP29F     New 02
```
~~~~~~
```
DSU 107*J232 NNC(7/99), TFO 319*L656 ADS(3/02) & HSK 646(11/94),
ULL 933*J234 NNC(6/99), UWR 498*G896 TGG(9/00),
WSV 537*LIW 3459(3/02) & C28 VJF(6/92),
XOD 665*DSR 476V(8/01) & VSR 591(9/97) & DSR 476V(5/84),
674 SHY*DSR 478V(8/01) & PSR 781(9/97) & DSR 478V(5/85),
```

```
RDF 500R*674 SHY(8/01) & RDF 500R(10/92),
A110 FDL*WDL 748(4/91) & A701 DDL(10/87) & V40 WGL*V991 DNB(4/02)
```

V9   C.D. WHITE.t/a CHISLETTS

Depot:Beckery Road,GLASTONBURY,Somerset.

```
TJI 4682  Bedford YNV          Jonckheere C53F  Elliott,Charlton Mackr. 01
D503 FAE  Mercedes-Benz L608D  Dormobile B20F   Bristol(Durbin) 96
F624 FNA  Renault Master       MM C15F          Chislett,Glastonbury 91
G716 XPO  Renault S56          WS DP24F         AWE,Aldermaston 01
G717 XPO  Renault S56          WS DP24F         AWE,Aldermaston 01
```

```
TJI 4682*B465 YUR(5/95)
```

W1   M.R. WILKINSON.t/a HERITAGE TRAVEL

Depot:Valley Road,CINDERFORD,Gloucestershire.

```
RJI 6238  Scania BR116         Jonckheere C48FT Howe,Waddington 95
D298 EKS  DAF SB2305DHS585     Jonckheere C51FT Auty & Maynard,Rushden 00
D352 TEV  Dodge S46            Dormobile B16FL  Basildon District Coun. 93
K348 LGK  Renault Master       O & H B14F       Mole,Kidderminster 00
```

```
RJI 6238*JFL 720Y(4/94) & 972 SYD(12/89) & CEG 60Y(5/88) &
D298 EKS*HIL 4056(5/99) & D96 BNV(12/95)
```

W2   F.R. WILLETTS & CO (YORKLEY) LTD.t/a GEOFF WILLETTS

Depot:Dean Rise,PILLOWELL,Gloucestershire.

```
2464  FH  LN 11351/1R          East Lancs B52F  East Yorkshire 151 94
890  CVJ  Kassbohrer S250      C53F             Brelaton,Hounslow 98
G290 XFH  Leyland TRCL10/3RZA  Plaxton C57F     New 89
H937 DRJ  Volvo B10M-60        Plaxton C53F     Shearings 937 95
X904 ADF  Mercedes-Benz O814D  Plaxton C33F     New 00
```

```
2464 FH*GCY 748N(11/94reb) & 890 CVJ*N200 TCC(6/98)
```

W3   F.T. WILLIAMS.t/a WILLIAMS TRAVEL

Depot:Dolcoath Industrial Park,Dolcoath Road,CAMBORNE,Cornwall.

```
MJI 6251  Scania K112TR        PN CH55/20CT     Head,Lutton 01
PJI 5014  Volvo B10M-61        Van Hool C50FT   Eastville,Bristol 99
RIL 3706  Volvo B10M-60        Jonckheere C51FT Knowles,Paignton 00
XSU  910  Volvo B10M-61        Jonckheere C49FT Viscount,Burnley 10 99
9996  WX  Volvo B10M-61        Van Hool C50FT   Meeds,Tavistock 93
511  HCV  Volvo B10M-61        Plaxton C53F     St Buryan Garage 94
739  JUA  Volvo B58-61         Jonckheere C49FT Safford,Little Gransden 89
SVL 175W  Bristol VRT/SL3/6LXB ECW H43/31F      Eurotaxis,Harry Stoke 97
XPG 295Y  DAF MB200DKTL600     Plaxton C57F     Garrett,Newton Abbot 92
B710 EOF  Volvo B10M-53        JE CH54/13DT     Shaw Hadwin,Carnforth 01
B269 TLJ  Mercedes-Benz L608D  RB C19F          Cheney,Banbury 94
C105 AFX  Volvo B10M-61        Plaxton C53F     Safeguard,Guildford 97
E920 EAY  Volvo B10M-61        Plaxton C53F     Stevens,Colchester 97
G823 MNH  DAF 400              Dormobile B8FL   Bedfordshire CC 98
H165 DJU  Volvo B10M-60        Duple C53FT      Jennings,Bude 98
H794 FAF  Dennis Javelin       WS DP48FL        Non-PSV(Truro) 99
J953 SBU  Dennis Dart          NC DP31D         Dearsley,Barking 97
P347 FOL  Iveco 49-10          Mellor B19F      Petes,West Bromwich 01
P133 KOJ  LDV Convoy           LDV B16F         Non-PSV(BCR) 01
R764 VNT  LDV Convoy           LDV B16F         Non-PSV(Kenning) 01
```

MJI 6251*C351 DWR(7/90), PJI 5014*D616 MVR(1/93),
RIL 3706*RIL 3707(8/99) & G141 MNH(6/99), XSU 910*E507 KNV(4/91),
9996 WX*TCV 137Y(3/86), 511 HCV*C483 HAK(3/90), 739 JUA*XNV 149W(5/87) &
B710 EOF*LSU 939(11/00) & B710 EOF(6/99)

~~~~~~

W4   K.J. WILLS.t/a MID DEVON COACHES

Depot:Midco,Station Road,BOW,Devon.

IIL 4417	Quest VM	Plaxton C53F	Phillips,Hereford 01
LIL 4348	Leyland TRCTL11/3R	Plaxton C55F	Newton,Guildford 02
LIL 9174	Bova FLD12-250	C53F	Chivers,Midsomer Norton 01
MIL 5577	Leyland TRCTL11/3R	Plaxton C49FT	Leyland(Demonstrator) 86
MIL 5578	Leyland TRCTL11/2R	Plaxton C53F	New 83
MIL 5579	Bedford YNT	Plaxton C53F	Wainfleet,Nuneaton 86
MIL 5991	Ford R1114	Duple C53F	Bryant &,Williton 96
MIL 5992	Ford R1114	Plaxton C49F	Bryant &,Williton 96
MIL 6682	Ford R1115	Plaxton C53F	Andrews,Marshfield 98
MIL 6685	Ford R1114	Plaxton C53F	Walker,Riseley 97
NSU 205	Scania K112CRS	Jonckheere C49FT	Harris,Wombwell 99
OIW 1319	Volvo B10M-60	Plaxton C49FT	Wallace Arnold 02
TIL 2812	Leyland TRCTL11/3R	Plaxton C57F	Newton,Guildford 02
TSU 649	Scania K112CRS	Jonckheere C53FT	Flintham,Metheringham 99
WJI 6886	Ford R1114	Plaxton C53F	Davies,Slough 98
WJI 6887	Bedford YRT	Plaxton C53F	Bryant &,Williton 96
WJI 6888	Ford R1114	Plaxton C53F	Warren,Neath 98
WSV 530	Bova FHD12-280	C53F	Hearn,Stibb Cross 00
LHW 504P	Bedford YMT	Plaxton C53F	Willis,Bodmin 99
WAW 354Y	Ford R1114	Plaxton C53F	Pratt,Moreton Valence 02
B100 YUC	Toyota BB30R	Caetano C19F	Druett,Princetown 94
D289 OAK	Freight Rover Sherpa	Whittaker C16F	Duchy Travel,Torquay 98
D366 SFC	Toyota BB30R	Caetano C19F	Pearce,Berinsfield 93
E667 MWP	Scania K112CRB	Plaxton C49FT	Blake,East Anstey 02
G167 XJF	Toyota HB31R	Caetano C18F	Day,North Common 00
K926 TTA	Toyota HDB30R	Caetano C21F	Seward,Dalwood 00

~~~~~~

IIL 4417*A818 LEL(3/93), LIL 4348*A150 RMJ(8/95),
LIL 9174*C160 XRT(3/96) & 2086 PP(10/95) & C126 AHP(10/88),
MIL 5577*A198 RUR(9/96), MIL 5578*FTA 850Y(9/96), MIL 5579*YUT 637Y(8/96),
MIL 5991*HYC 642Y(7/96), MIL 5992*VJT 623X(7/96), MIL 6682*EFK 148Y(4/98),
MIL 6685*JJW 251W(6/97), NSU 205*A57 JLW(5/99), OIW 1319*F35 HGG(9/93),
TIL 2812*A242 SCW(10/00) & BIB 3994(3/00) & A281 GEC(5/86),
TSU 649*C412 LRP(3/90), WJI 6886*PEW 623X(9/98),
WJI 6887*MIL 6684(8/00) & XYD 559N(7/96), WJI 6888*LUA 266V(11/98),
WSV 530*A660 EMY(8/92), WAW 354Y*TIL 5933(12/01) & WAW 354Y(1/01),
E667 MWP*24 PAE(1/93) & E584 OEF(?/92) &
G167 XJF*253 DAF(11/00) & G167 XJF(2/00)

~~~~~~

W5   K.K. WITTE.t/a CALNE TRAVEL

Depot:Unit 5,Penn Hill Farm Trading Estate,CALNE,Wiltshire.

AHZ 1253	Scania K112CRB	Van Hool C49FT	Lodge,High Easter 00
DKZ 9972	Toyota HB31R	Caetano C18F	Silverline,Torquay 01
EEU 359	Leyland TRCTL11/3R	Plaxton C57F	Miles,Stratton St Marg. 01
IUI 7971	DAF MB200DKFL600	Duple C55F	Bristol 8201 98
JIL 2950	Scania K113TRB	PN CH51/16CT	Pygall,Easington Coll. 01
KUI 8145	Scania K112CRB	Van Hool C49FT	Lodge,High Easter 00
NIW 3927	Scania K112CRS	Plaxton C55F	Ridgeon,Stanford-1-Hope 97
PIL 3524	Leyland RT	Plaxton C47FT	L Munden,Bristol 98
PIW 4725	Bova EL26/581	C53F	Lambkin,Queenborough 96
RJI 2721	Bova EL28/581	Duple C53F	Bristol 8206 98
TJI 6311	Volvo B10M-61	Plaxton C53F	Expertpoint,Stratford 02
D907 HOU	Fiat 49-10	Robin Hood B19F	Bristol 4907 96
H210 TCP	DAF SB2305DHTD585	Duple C57F	Perrett,Shipton Oliffe 00

~~~~~~

AHZ 1253*E442 JAR(7/01) & 160 EBK(9/99) & E663 YDT(7/96),

```
DKZ 9972*G152 XJF(?/01), EEU 359*A862 WTX(1/89),
IUI 7971*A455 JJF(4/98) & WYY 752(3/98) & A455 JJF(9/96),
JIL 2950*G30 HKY(3/94),
KUI 8145*E443 JAR(5/01) & 436 UVT(9/99) & 46 AEW(12/98) & E665 YDT(4/95),
NIW 3927*D170 VVO(10/93), PIL 3524*A329 XHE(8/98),
PIW 4725*EPP 818Y(4/95), RJI 2721*B799 MAY(7/93) &
TJI 6311*D594 COS(3/95) & 306 JBP(6/93) & D298 FVT(2/92) & WHA 325(7/91) &
        D876 EEH(1/90)
```

W6   WOOD BROTHERS TRAVEL LTD

Depot:Harewood Garage,Bossell Road,BUCKFASTLEIGH,Devon.

Reg	Chassis	Body	Operator
MIL 9764	Mercedes-Benz 811D	Robin Hood C29F	Woods,Wigston 97
WIA 69	Leyland TRCTL11/3RZ	Plaxton C50F	Morley,Minehead 95
505 ETT	Volvo B10M-61	Van Hool C57F	Mayne,Buckie 95
GPD 310N	Bristol LHS6L	ECW B35F	London Country BN42 83
LTA 731P	Leyland PSU3C/4R	Plaxton C49F	Millmans,Newton Abbot 97
RRL 375S	Leyland PSU3C/4R	Plaxton C53F	Western National 2452 92
AFJ 721T	Bristol LH6L	Plaxton C41F	Truronian,Truro 97
AFJ 724T	Bristol LH6L	Plaxton C41F	Gascoine,Crediton 55 97
FDV 827V	Leyland PSU3E/4R	Willowbrook C49F	Plymouth 356 91
LBH 460Y	Leyland TRCTL11/3R	Plaxton C53F	Western Greyh.,Newquay 02
UOB 894Y	Leyland TRCTL11/2R	Plaxton C53F	Crudge,Honiton 01
D 95 CFA	Ford Transit	Dormobile B16F	Ball,Plymouth 00
E979 WDS	Mercedes-Benz 609D	North West DP24F	Andrews,Trudoxhill 93
F183 RNH	Mercedes-Benz 407D	RB C15F	Sinnott,Leigh 96
F337 SMD	Mercedes-Benz 609D	RB C19F	New 89
G637 UHU	Mercedes-Benz 609D	MM C24F	Anton Travel,Lea 94
N996 AEF	Mercedes-Benz 711D	ACL C25F	Williams,Dutton 97

```
MIL 9764*6962 WF(6/97) & F350 JVS(3/94),
WIA 69*A696 DCN(9/00) & GSU 348(3/90) & A32 FVN(12/87),
505 ETT*E878 FRS(4/95) & YSU 990(2/95) & E616 CDS(7/94) & LSK 876(11/93) &
        E646 UNE(4/92),
LBH 460Y*TFO 319(4/02) & JIL 5289(4/98) & LBH 460Y(6/94) &
        1056 AR(10/93) & THL 291Y(7/89) &
UOB 894Y*USV 474(9/98) & UOB 894Y(11/97) & MJI 2370(10/97) &
        WBF 718X(12/89)
```

W7   ROYAL MAIL POSTBUSES

*Depots:The Platt,WADEBRIDGE,Cornwall, Church Street,HONITON,Devon &
                   Grove Trading Estate,DORCHESTER,Dorset.*

Reg	Fleet No	Chassis	Body	New	Route
P206 ETA	6750005	LDV Convoy	DAF B10F	New 97	Dorchester-Bridport
S604 VJW	8750011	LDV Pilot	DAF B9F	New 98	Honiton-Luppitt
S605 VJW	8750012	LDV Pilot	DAF B9F	New 98	Wadebridge-Penrose

OB   OTHER VEHICLES IN BRISTOL

Reg	Chassis	Body	Operator
MIL 9301	Leyland RT	Leyland C53F	Liddell,Brislington
SIB 9017	Bova EL26/581	C49FT	Haines,Whitehall
B913 AJX	Mercedes-Benz L307D	Devcoplan B12F	Walker,Lawrence Hill
D156 UGB	Volvo B10M-61	Plaxton C53F	Britton,Hartcliffe
E222 ANA	Ford Transit	Mellor C16F	King,Brislington
E929 HPJ	Renault Master	DC B8FL	Pearson,Bedminster
E198 LRV	Mercedes-Benz 811D	Robin Hood C33F	Liddell,Brislington
F596 OHT	Fiat 49-10	Dormobile B26F	S Munden,St Philips
G267 RKJ	Renault Master	Crystals C15F	S Munden,St Philips
H508 AEU	Ford Transit	DC B4FL	Pearson,Bedminster
J 43 BTV	Ford Transit	Mellor B12FL	Pearson,Bedminster
L513 BDH	Iveco 49-10	Mellor B16FL	S Munden,St Philips
M 93 BOU	Toyota HZB50R	Caetano C21F	Britton,Hartcliffe
M122 SKY	Toyota HZB50R	Caetano C21F	King,Brislington

```
N333 EST   Dennis Javelin         Auwaerter C50FT       Acorn,Horfield
P557 BAY   Dennis Javelin         Marcopolo C53F        Haines,Whitehall
R742 EGS   LDV Convoy             LDV B13FL             Singh &,St Philips
R661 YAV   LDV Convoy             LDV B16F              Haines,Whitehall
S342 FAE   Mercedes-Benz 412D     Onyx C16F             Britton,Hartcliffe
T436 FOW   LDV Convoy             LDV B16F              Brown,Knowle
V884 EBX   Renault Master         Cymric C16F           Singh &,St Philips
W  9 CCH   LDV Convoy             ? C16F                Holloway,Coombe Dingle
W839 PWS   LDV Convoy             LDV B16F              Sterry,Stockwood
X991 BNH   Cannon Hi-Line         LCB C33F              Singh &,St Philips
X671 JND   Mercedes-Benz 313CDI   Concept C16F          Fitzpatrick,Hengrove
AT02 BOT   Bova FHD12-370         C53F                  Broadoak,St Philips
```

MIL 9301*C817 FMC(12/96), SIB 9017*A565 TYD(8/93),
CHT 566V*TVV 213(5/90) & EYH 806V(12/89),
D156 UGB*OSK 788(4/97) & D762 COS(11/93) & LSK 483(10/93) &
     D576 MVR(2/93), N3 BOT*N796 ORY(2/99) & N333 EST*N585 AWJ(5/96)

OC   OTHER VEHICLES IN CORNWALL

```
BAZ 6532   Volvo B10M-61          Duple C49FT           Webber,St Austell
FIL 6783   Mercedes-Benz 609D     North West C24F       Friend,Harrowbarrow
FIL 9220   DAF MB200DKFL600        Jonckheere C53F       Frost,St Austell
NIL 2101   Toyota HB31R           Caetano C21F          Lianswood,St Austell
NIL 7056   DAF MB200DKTL600       LAG C53F              Hosking,Ludgvan
RIL 7155   Mercedes-Benz 811D     Phoenix C29F          Bawden,Truro
TIL 1185   Volvo B10M-55          Plaxton B55F          St Buryan Garage
WXF  906   Bedford YNT            Plaxton C53F          Webber,St Austell
6426  DU   Volvo B10M-61          Van Hool C48FT        Friend,Harrowbarrow
FTV  11L   Volvo B58-56           Duple C51F            Clayton,Mabe
YRC 125M   Bristol VRT/SL6G       ECW H43/34F           Johns & Berryman,Flushing
ARL 958T   Volvo B58-61           Duple C57F            Lethbridge,Trewidland
XCC 769V   Volvo B58-56           Plaxton C53F          Hosking,Ludgvan
GPX 557X   Mercedes-Benz L508DG   Robin Hood C18F       Clayton,Mabe
CVU 777Y   Ford A0609             Moseley C25F          Clayton,Mabe
A851 TDS   Volvo B10M-61          VH CH49/6FT           Davies,Par
B438 WTC   Ford Transit           Dormobile B16F        Zambuni,Chapmanswell
C914 BTS   Fiat 79-14             Caetano C22F          Courtis,Breage
C141 KGJ   Bedford YNV            Duple C57F            Webber,St Austell
C507 TJF   Ford Transit           Alexander B16F        Zambuni,Chapmanswell
F167 DET   MCW Metrorider MF154   DP29F                 Hosking,Ludgvan
F  37 PKV  Mercedes-Benz 811D     RB C25F               Bawden,Truro
F866 TNH   Toyota HB31R           Caetano C18F          Courtis,Breage
F405 WAF   Mercedes-Benz L307D    DC C15F               Powell,Redruth
G327 PAV   DAF 400                G & M C16F            Heckbert,Bude
G156 UYK   Toyota HB31R           Caetano C16F          Heckbert,Bude
J727 KBC   Toyota HDB30R          Caetano C18F          Lianswood,St Austell
J367 TOC   Mercedes-Benz 410D     DC B12FL              George,St Just
K  96 OGA  Toyota HDB30R          Caetano C21F          Friend,Harrowbarrow
K757 PUT   Toyota HDB30R          Caetano C21F          Gay,St Agnes
L166 AKN   Ford Transit           Dormobile B16F        Carne,Heamoor
L  91 GAX  Volvo B10M-62          Jonckheere C51FT      Merrell,Newquay
L  93 GAX  Volvo B10M-62          Jonckheere C51FT      Merrell,Newquay
L525 UCV   Iveco 49-10            Mellor B16F           Tavistock Community Tpt
M238 AAF   Mercedes-Benz 308D     G & M C12FL           West Penwith CB
M835 BRL   Mercedes-Benz 407D     ? B17F                Lerryn Area Minibus
M848 LTX   Toyota HZB50R          Caetano C21F          Lianswood,St Austell
N670 BNV   Mercedes-Benz 609D     DC C15FL              St Teath Community Bus
R  6 LEY   Mercedes-Benz 410D     G & M C16F            St Buryan Garage
S  49 BAF  Mercedes-Benz 410D     G & M C16F            Bawden,Truro
T560 CDM   Mercedes-Benz 614D     Olympus C19F          Isles of Scilly,St Just
W493 HOB   Mercedes-Benz 410D     Olympus C16F          St Buryan Garage
W675 PAF   Mercedes-Benz 411CDI   Courtside C15F        Gorran & District CB
X753 URL   Mercedes-Benz 411CDI   Courtside C14FL       Lanteglos Community Bus
Y194 BAF   Mercedes-Benz 411CDI   G & M B15F            Downderry & District CB
WA51 RPZ   Mercedes-Benz 614D     G & M B20F            Charman,Polruan-by-Fowey
WA51 XVX   Mercedes-Benz 413CDI   G & M C15F            Tamar Valley CT
```

```
BAZ 6532*513 SRL(11/01) & C770 SGU(5/01), FIL 6783*E104 WFY(5/89),
FIL 9220*A378 UNH(4/90), NIL 2101*F210 PNR(9/97),
NIL 7056*JYA 298Y(6/97) & 40 FER(11/96) & JYA 298Y(10/93),
RIL 7155*RCJ 830H(8/99) & G360 XRV(8/94), TIL 1185*K102 XPA(9/00),
WXF 906*D840 KSE(5/01) & GIL 5109(2/01) & D840 KSE(11/99),
6426 DU*A330 PFJ(5/95), ARL 958T*5448 CD(8/94) & UTP 771T(9/90),
XCC 769V*OJC 496(2/99) & LUS 909V(2/96),
A851 TDS*3287 EL(6/01) & A851 TDS(4/88) &
C914 BTS*8733 CD(5/89) & C648 KDS(6/88)
```

OD — OTHER VEHICLES IN DEVON

Reg	Chassis	Body	Operator
ALZ 1360	Fiat 315	Lorraine C31F	Hyde,South Molton
BNZ 2799	Mercedes-Benz 609D	? DP24F	Parnell,Axminster
DXI 74	Duple 425	C50FT	Helmore,Paignton
HIL 7620	Scania K112CRB	Van Hool C49FT	Blake,East Anstey
KUI 3720	Leyland LBM6T/2RS	RB C37F	Williams,Plympton
NIW 6506	DAF MB200DKFL600	Caetano C53F	Helmore,Paignton
RIW 2650	Mercedes-Benz 508D	? B12FL	Waite,Newton Abbot
TSV 617	Leyland TRCTL11/3R	Plaxton C53F	Hellaby,Paignton
WJY 530	Volvo B10M-60	Jonckheere C53F	Shutts,Torquay
YTT 1	Mercedes-Benz 412D	G & M B16FL	Thompson,Plymouth
314 ASV	Scania K113CRB	Van Hool C53F	Colton,Dousland
DET 720D	Bedford VAM14	Farrar O18/16RO	Farrar,Ivybridge
DFD 704D	Bedford VAM5	Farrar O18/16RO	Merrivale,Torquay
JTD 395P	Daimler CRL6	NC O49/29F	Merrivale,Torquay
JTH 756P	LN 11351/1R	B52F	Grenville College,Bideford
FYD 120T	Bedford YMT	Duple C53F	Hewitt,Paignton
FLJ 745V	Ford R1114	Plaxton C53F	Easterbrook,Crediton
KRO 644V	Ford Transit	Dormobile B16F	Monnington,Paignton
GTX 758W	Bristol LHS6L	ECW DP29F	Woodrow,Plymouth
CFF 404Y	Bedford YNT	Duple C53F	Hewitt,Paignton
CPD 214Y	Bedford YNV	Plaxton C53F	Woolacott &,Dolton
A 16 CTL	DAF 400	Crystals C16F	Thomas,Plymouth
A428 DWP	DAF MB200DKFL600	Caetano C53F	Helmore,Paignton
A422 LDV	Mercedes-Benz L307D	DC B12F	Gramercy Hall,Churston
C123 DYD	Fiat 35-8	G & M C14F	Stevens,Exeter
C361 HGF	Volvo B10M-46	Plaxton C36F	Clifford,Newton Abbot
C 85 NNV	Fiat 79-14	Caetano C22F	Goodwin,Witheridge
C968 PFS	Freight Rover Sherpa	DL C16FL	Johns,Plympton
C657 XLK	Ford Transit	Robin Hood C16F	Hyde,South Molton
D915 HOU	Fiat 49-10	Robin Hood B19F	Hewitt,Paignton
D 74 KRL	Ford Transit	Dormobile B16F	Carpenter,Uplowman
D815 KWT	Freight Rover Sherpa	Dormobile B16F	Brown,Newton Abbot
D504 NDA	Freight Rover Sherpa	Carlyle B19F	Gutteridge,Kings Nympton
D778 NDV	Ford Transit	Mellor B16F	Parnell,Axminster
D254 OOJ	Freight Rover Sherpa	Carlyle B18F	Woodrow,Plymouth
D 26 PVS	Freight Rover Sherpa	Dormobile B16F	Bibb,Tiverton
E167 GFA	Mercedes-Benz 609D	North West C19F	Goodwin,Witheridge
E213 MFX	Toyota HB31R	Caetano C19F	West,Torquay
E805 YRM	Ford Transit	Mellor C16F	Williams,Plympton
E287 YWA	Ford Transit	Coachcraft C16F	Timms,Plymouth
F595 SHW	Freight Rover Sherpa	Crystals C16F	Blake,East Anstey
G731 KPW	DAF 400	Pearl C16F	Payne,Torquay
G972 KWJ	Mercedes-Benz 811D	Whittaker C23F	Hyslop,Kingkerswell
G974 LWY	Mercedes-Benz 308D	DC B12F	Wills,Kingsbridge
G118 SNV	Toyota HB31R	Caetano C18F	Johns,Plympton
G776 UYV	Fiat 49-10	Robin Hood DP20F	Wilks,Teignmouth
H302 AHU	DAF 400	G & M C16F	Holman,Mary Tavy
H548 EVM	Freight Rover Sherpa	MM C16F	Riches,Plympton
H990 GKN	Ford Transit	G & M B16F	Exe Valley Market CB
J 45 HAM	DAF 400	POW B16F	Johns,Plympton
J404 KBV	DAF 400	Cunliffe B10FL	Thomas,Plymouth
J161 KKE	Ford Transit	G & M B16F	Parnell,Axminster
J189 KLW	Iveco 49-10	Dormobile DP25F	Williams,Plympton
K410 DHH	Mercedes-Benz 410D	G & M C16F	Druett,Princetown
K131 DTW	Mercedes-Benz 410D	G & M C16F	Fall,Paignton
K831 FEE	Mercedes-Benz 410D	ACL C16F	Bennett,Newton Abbot

```
K138 LHT  DAF 400               G & M C16F    Barnes,Bere Alston
L837 YCU  Iveco 49-10           G & M C16F    Holman,Mary Tavy
M553 BRL  Mercedes-Benz 410D    G & M B15F    Johns,Plympton
M361 EHU  Renault Master        ? C16F        Hyslop,Kingkerswell
M644 HFJ  LDV 400               G & M C16F    Rockett,Newton Abbot
M463 KFJ  LDV 400               G & M C16F    LAL Language,Paignton
M150 OKK  LDV 400               Crystals C16F Blake,East Anstey
M616 RCP  DAF DE33WSSB3000      Van Hool C51FT Chadcourt,Torquay
N581 XNT  Iveco ?               G & M C16F    Lock,Dartmouth
P849 ADO  Mercedes-Benz 412D    ACL C16F      Bennett,Newton Abbot
P  9 CAE  Volvo B10M-46         Van Hool C32FT Rignall,Kingskerswell
P308 CFJ  LDV Convoy            G & M C16F    LAL Language,Paignton
P516 CTV  Mercedes-Benz 611D    G & M C16F    Holman,Mary Tavy
R230 DKO  LDV Convoy            G & M C16F    Rockett,Newton Abbot
R371 VOK  Iveco 49-10           Jubilee C19F  Grimwood,Ilfracombe
R636 YAV  LDV Convoy            LDV B16F      Gramercy Hall,Churston
S138 EAF  Mercedes-Benz 412D    DC B15FL      Hyslop,Kingkerswell
S 14 RUT  Bova FHD12-340        C49FT         Marks,Torquay
T562 SBX  Renault Master        Cymric C16F   Ludgate,Brayford
V208 EAL  Iveco 59-12           Mellor C25F   Goodwin,Witheridge
W853 WDV  Ford Transit          G & M C16F    Harbourne Community Tpt
W857 WOD  Renault Master        G & M C14F    LAL Language,Paignton
X868 AEU  Renault Master        ? C16F        Grenville College,Bideford
X613 HFB  Renault Master        ? C16F        Grenville College,Bideford
Y833 DAA  Mercedes-Benz 413CDI  G & M C16FL   Lucky Sun,Torquay
Y362 HBX  Renault Master        Cymric C16F   Country Cousins,Ilfracombe
```

N.B.: DET 720D & DFD 704D have replica London General "B" class body.

```
ALZ 1360*RJI 5724(4/97) & H527 HPM(11/93), BNZ 2799*   ?  (?/??),
DXI 74*E572 BGA(5/92), HIL 7620*E58 VHL(5/92), KUI 3720*F820 TMD(7/00),
NIW 6506*A48 BWJ(7/93), RIW 2650*   ?  (?/??), TSV 617*A529 LPP(12/93),
WJY 530*K915 RGE(7/00) & 93KY 2166(4/00) & K915 RGE(4/94),
YTT 1*N848 KCV(1/98),
314 ASV*YTT 1(1/98) & G269 RHG(9/97) & 90D 8272(5/97),
GTX 758W*19660(10/95) & GTX 758W(12/87),
CPD 214Y*SJI 1960(2/02) & CPD 214Y(5/94) & TIB 4686(3/94) &
        CPD 214Y(3/94) & 3900 PH(12/93) & VGM 245Y(11/89),
A16 CTL*H778 CKO(12/97),
A428 DWP*YCT 502(4/97) & A654 XWN(2/97) & 278 TNY(9/89) & A644 WCY(3/88),
C361 HGF*TXI 6710(9/99) & C361 HGF(10/91),
C657 XLK*WET 590(3/89) & C333 YRU(10/87) & P9 CAE*P465 JWB(11/99)
```

OE   OTHER VEHICLES IN DORSET

```
MIB  612  DAF MB200DKFL600       Van Hool C49F  Powell,Thornford
 21  DGX  Volvo B58-56           Plaxton C53F   Powell,Thornford
BYC 835B  Bedford YLQ            Duple C45F     Davies &,West Bay
CUV 253C  AEC Routemaster        PR CO36/27RD   Letts,Gillingham
NMY 662E  AEC Routemaster        PR H32/24F     Letts,Gillingham
NMY 665E  AEC Routemaster        PR H32/24F     Letts,Gillingham
TFP  25R  Ford R1014             Plaxton C45F   Powell,Thornford
E663 YTT  Freight Rover Sherpa   DC B14F        Hession,Bothenhampton
G276 BEL  Toyota HB31R           Caetano C18F   Johnson,Winfrith
G515 VYE  Dennis Dart            Duple DP28F    Weaver,Weymouth
H 11 POW  DAF 400                Jubilee B10FL  Cox,Portland
J 69 FEU  DAF 400                Whittaker B16F Stiles,Sturminster Newton
L866 NHL  DAF 400                G & M C16F     Hill,Sherborne
M227 BBX  Renault Master         Cymric C16F    Smithers,Wyke Regis
M661 GJF  Toyota HZB50R          Caetano C18F   Lever,Motcombe
M 78 VYD  Renault Master         Jubilee C16F   Forsey,Charmouth
P162 CON  Renault Master         Jubilee C15F   Forsey,Charmouth
S386 BBX  Renault Master         Cymric C8F     Smithers,Wyke Regis
T958 GCK  LDV Convoy             LDV B16FL      Turner,Milton Abbas
W221 KDO  Mercedes-Benz 412D     Ferqui C16F    Forsey,Charmouth
```

```
MIB 612*WSC 912Y(5/90) & WFE 36(3/89), 21 DGX*DJB 863V(8/84),
BYC 835B*VNT 36S(12/89) & H11 POW*M578 MOX(11/96)
```

OG   OTHER VEHICLES IN GLOUCESTERSHIRE

Reg	Chassis	Body	Operator
HIL 7749	Bedford YNV	Plaxton C57F	Perrett,Shipton Oliffe
ILZ 1566	LAG Panoramic	C49FT	Hawker,Patchway
IUI 4767	Renault Master	Cymric C15F	Cowie,Quedgley
JIL 5372	Bedford YMP	Plaxton C37F	Thorne,Aylburton
JIL 8390	Renault Master	Premier C15F	Little,Woodchester
LUI 6203	Volvo B10M-61	Plaxton C53F	Denwell,Cheltenham'
NLP 592	AEC Regent III	PR H28/26RO	Brown,Lydney
SXI 8576	Auwaerter N116	C49FT	Hawker,Patchway
TIB 3019	Ford R1015	Plaxton C33F	Hoskins & Davis,Eastington
TIB 8599	Ford Transit	Dormobile B13FL	DMH,Norcote
UAM 2	DAF SB2300DHS585	LAG C53F	Buchanan,North Common
OWJ 637A	Bristol LD6B	ECW O33/27RD	Brown,Lydney
GRF 32T	Bedford YLQ	Plaxton C45F	Bendall,Kilcot
A 2 ATN	Mercedes-Benz 609D	G & M C16F	Norton,Stonehouse
A675 DCN	Leyland TRCTL11/3RZ	Plaxton C50F	Hoskins & Davis,Eastington
A111 EPA	Leyland TRCTL11/2RH	Plaxton C53F	Perrett,Shipton Oliffe
A398 NNK	Bedford YNT	Plaxton C53F	Hall,Gloucester
B 10 DCT	Mercedes-Benz 609D	Premier C24F	Thorne,Aylburton
C402 XFO	Bedford YNV	Plaxton C57F	Perrett,Shipton Oliffe
D 76 KRL	Ford Transit	Dormobile B16F	Mayo,Kings Stanley
E 94 LDG	Mercedes-Benz 609D	RB C25F	Dix,Gloucester
F212 BWF	Renault Master	Coachcraft C16F	Prout,Dymock
F680 KJO	Mercedes-Benz 609D	North West B15FL	Hoskins & Davis,Eastington
G458 MEG	Fiat 49-10	Phoenix DP16FL	Scrivens,Mitcheldean
G228 UUE	Fiat 45-10	G & M B11FL	Bennett,Cam
H739 DKE	Ford Transit	Dormobile B8FL	Bohan,Gloucester
J153 VOJ	DAF 400	Concept B16FL	Champion,Cheltenham
K 4 ESC	Fiat 35-10	? C14F	Sibbick,Lower Slaughter
K 8 ESC	Toyota BB50R	Caetano C16F	Sibbick,Lower Slaughter
K394 PVL	DAF 400	Cunliffe B18F	Scrivens,Mitcheldean
L683 GKE	Ford Transit	SEM B16F	Villager,Upper Oddington
L297 WFH	Renault Master	? B11FL	Cirencester & District VB
M294 BBX	Renault Master	Cymric C15F	Guttridge,Leckhampton
M943 KDF	Renault Master	Atlas B16F	Cirencester & District VB
M797 LJW	Renault Master	Jubilee B7FL	Guttridge,Leckhampton
N375 BOP	LDV Convoy	LDV B16F	A2B,Cheltenham
N498 YNB	LDV 400	Concept C16F	Prout,Dymock
P556 CUJ	LDV 400	? B16F	Gill,Leckhampton
P684 PBP	LDV Convoy	LDV B16F	West,Wotton-under-Edge
P988 SCK	Volkswagen LT35	? B16F	Guttridge,Leckhampton
P576 TDD	Dennis Javelin	UVG DP ?F	Serco,Gloucester
P492 TNP	Ford Transit	UVG B16F	Villager,Upper Oddington
R574 NAD	LDV Convoy	LDV B16F	Connect,Churchdown
R226 TBC	Mercedes-Benz 412D	Jubilee C16FL	Chauffeurhire,Chipping Sod
R812 UOK	LDV Convoy	UVG B16F	Nth Cotswolds CB,Mickleton
S555 MAL	Mercedes-Benz 413CDI	Excel C16F	Witts,Hardwicke
S297 MHN	Iveco 35-10	? C14F	Red Rose,Nympsfield
S338 RHB	LDV Convoy	LDV B16F	DMH,Norcote
T702 RNP	Ford Transit	CD B16F	Villager,Upper Oddington
T283 ROR	Renault Master	Atlas B13FL	Tetbury Volunteer Bureau
V799 SNY	Mercedes-Benz 412D	UVG B16F	Nth Cotswolds CB,Mickleton
W556 EOL	Mercedes-Benz 412D	Jubilee C11FL	Chauffeurhire,Chipping Sod
W777 MAL	Mercedes-Benz 412D	Ferqui C16F	Witts,Hardwicke
W248 RNT	LDV Convoy	LDV B16F	Walmsley,Bourton-on-Water
W646 UUH	LDV Convoy	LDV B16F	Deane,Thornbury
X869 AEU	Renault Master	Advanced B16F	Webb,Hanham
Y727 VRH	LDV Convoy	Excel C16F	Jenkins,Cinderford
CU51 KLA	Renault Master	Cymric C16F	Denwell,Cheltenham

~~~~~~
HIL 7749*D836 DJU(4/92) & FIL 9378(11/91) & D735 XBC(2/90),
ILZ 1566*G381 JBD(10/01), IUI 4767*M152 CBX(9/97),
JIL 5372*315 RTO(3/00) & E36 PWO(9/96), JIL 8390*D399 VVL(3/95),
LUI 6203*C527 DND(10/01),
SXI 8576*PMB 272Y(9/91) & SEL 133(2/91) & MFM 311Y(5/87),
TIB 3019*WEC 556Y(?/02) & OBV 142(8/94) & CRN 588Y(1/92),
TIB 8599*F628 RBP(11/98), OWJ 637A*ACA 217A(6/88) & 928 CFM(10/84),
GRF 32T*9685 VT(9/93) & LDM 537T(2/85),

A2 ATN*4060 D(12/95) & 3153 D(10/94) & G400 NMW(9/92),
A675 DCN*GSU 346(3/90) & A30 FVN(12/87),
A111 EPA*WDD 194(1/01) & A111 EPA(6/97),
A398 NNK*4 DOF(9/98) & A398 NNK(4/91), B10 DCT*   ?   (9/96) &
K8 ESC*P952 DNR(12/01)
~~~~~~

OS   OTHER VEHICLES IN SOMERSET

NIL 5813	Leyland PSU3	Duple C ?F	Evans,Whitchurch
PJI 8325	Leyland TRCTL11/3R	Plaxton C53F	Brent,Bishops Sutton
UJI 4526	MAN SR280	C49F	Freitas,Bridgwater
WIW 8557	Volkswagen LT35	? B8F	Select Travel,Bath
473 FAE	Leyland AN68A/1R	MCW H43/32F	Evans,Whitchurch
GCL 349N	Bristol RELH6L	ECW DP49F	Cuff,Henstridge
DFH 491T	Ford R1114	Duple C53F	Roberton,Creech St Michael
FVM 191V	Bedford CFL	Plaxton C17F	Babb,Blue Anchor 5
FYX 818W	Leyland PSU3E/4R	Duple C49F	Freitas,Bridgwater
HAX 11W	Bedford YMT	Duple C53F	Grimmett,Minehead
D344 FOT	Ford Transit	Steedrive B8FL	Broadway,Bridgwater
D314 MNC	Freight Rover Sherpa	Dixon Lomas B16F	Gregory,Timsbury
D825 PUK	Freight Rover Sherpa	Carlyle B20F	Babb,Blue Anchor
D454 YPN	Dodge S56	Alexander B25F	Young,Haydon
E881 DGS	Ford Transit	CD C16F	Broadway,Bridgwater
E501 KNV	Volvo B10M-61	Jonckheere C51FT	Taunton School
E979 SVU	Freight Rover Sherpa	MM C16F	C Snape,Bath
F703 COA	Volvo B10M-53	PN CH55/12DT	Taunton School
F164 JOD	DAF SB3000DKV601	Caetano C49FT	Archer,Taunton
F898 KHJ	Mercedes-Benz L307D	PG B8F	Young,Haydon
F165 PFB	Freight Rover Sherpa	Steedrive C16F	Turner,Wincanton
F480 PHU	Mercedes-Benz 609D	RB C29F	King,West Huntspill
F178 RWS	Renault Master	? B12F	Sparkes,Bath
G389 HTX	DAF 400	Concept C16F	Venner,Minehead
H896 DFB	DAF 400	? C15F	Rendall,Wincanton
H675 EAY	DAF 400	Dormobile B2FL	Gazey,Clevedon
H283 HLM	Mercedes-Benz 814L	North West C35F	Young,Haydon
H312 WPN	Renault Master	Oatia B12F	Wood,Keyford
H557 XNN	Iveco 49-10	Carlyle B25F	Bryant,Nailsea
J679 TWK	Iveco 49-10	? B16FL	AC Minibuses,Burnham
K704 RNR	Toyota HDB30R	Caetano C16F	Kingfisher,Yeovil
N707 AOJ	LDV Convoy	LDV B16F	Broadway,Bridgwater
N423 FFS	Mercedes-Benz 711D	Onyx C26F	Stanford,Hatch Green
N 65 FWU	EOS E180Z	C49FT	Norman,Keynsham
N642 GLO	LDV 400	? C15F	Wood,Keyford
P688 DAW	LDV Convoy	Jubilee C16F	Gazey,Clevedon
P620 MDT	LDV Convoy	LDV B16F	Freitas,Bridgwater
P 7 SKC	LDV Convoy	? C16F	Branch,East Harptree
R907 FNB	Mercedes-Benz 412D	Concept C16F	Maggs,Paulton
R694 GMW	Volkswagen LT35	Courtside C16F	Jefferies,Radstock
R757 KCU	Mercedes-Benz 412D	G & M C16F	Jefferies,Radstock
R955 TLD	Mercedes-Benz 412D	ACL C16F	Cosh,Peasedown St John
R 29 TLL	Mercedes-Benz O814D	ACL C29F	Clevedon Retirement
R465 UAK	Volkswagen LT35	Advanced B14F	Jefferies,Radstock
R149 VYC	Toyota BB50R	Caetano C21F	Goodman,Culmhead
S429 VYC	LDV Convoy	LDV B16F	Stanford,Hatch Green
W869 BOH	Mercedes-Benz 410D	Jubilee C16F	Hill,Burnham on Sea
W688 JOG	Mercedes-Benz 410D	Excel C16F	McCreight,Whitchurch
W611 KFE	Mercedes-Benz 412D	ACL C16F	Williams & Green,Nailsea
W557 RYA	Iveco 49-10	Coachsmith B16FL	Exmoor Community Bus Assoc
Y479 HWE	Mercedes-Benz 413CDI	Excel C16F	McCreight,Whitchurch
Y649 UCC	Mercedes-Benz 413CDI	Onyx C16F	Williams & Green,Nailsea
WJ02 KDK	Bova FHD12-340	C49FT	Grimmett,Minehead

~~~~~~
NIL 5813*   ?   (?/??), PJI 8325*ETP 61W(6/93), UJI 4526*A850 VMR(2/96),
WIW 8557*V688 KAM(8/01), 473 FAE*PHF 559T(11/96),
F703 COA*449 GTU(10/00) & F703 COA(10/98) &
K704 RNR*USV 474(8/01) & K704 RNR(2/00) &
~~~~~~

OW   OTHER VEHICLES IN WILTSHIRE

```
OIL 4571   DAF SB2300DHS585      Jonckheere C51FT  Cargill,Warminster
RIL 4099   Volvo B10M-60         Plaxton C53F      Smith,Ford
SIL 3069   Volvo B10M-61         Berkhof C49FT     Smith,Ford
TAZ 4993   Leyland TRCTL11/3RH   Plaxton C51FT     Gardner,Colerne
FAO 420V   Bristol VRT/SL3/6LXB  ECW H43/31F       Vines,Goatacre
JRT 155V   Ford R1114            Plaxton C53F      Gardner,Colerne
LUM 979V   Ford R1114            Duple C49F        Blake,Trowbridge
A986 ARD   Mercedes-Benz L310    ? B12F            Druett,Bradenstoke
A999 GNR   Bedford YNT           Plaxton C51F      Petty,Melksham
C777 MVH   DAF MB200DKFL600      Duple C53F        Petty,Melksham
C 27 VJF   Bova FLD12-250        C53F              Vines,Goatacre
D394 SGS   Freight Rover Sherpa  Dormobile B16F    Connor,Calne
E 61 JHY   Renault Master        DC B4FL           Freeway,Devizes
E780 MLB   Fiat 35-8             DC C13F           Vines,Goatacre
E581 SAT   Mercedes-Benz 307D    Coachcraft C12F   Freeway,Devizes
E690 UNE   Leyland TRCTL11/3R    Plaxton C53F      Petty,Melksham
L 9 CCH    Volvo B10M-61         Berkhof C49FT     Smith,Ford
P283 HFY   LDV Convoy            LDV B16F          West,Corsham
P501 HNE   LDV Convoy            Olympus B11FL     Robinson &,Warminster
R132 KAE   LDV Convoy            LDV B16F          Walsh &,Kington St Michael
S862 BHR   Mercedes-Benz 412D    G & M C16F        Seend Community Bus
S792 CHU   LDV Convoy            LDV B16F          Zeals Garage
T 59 RFB   LDV Convoy            LDV B16F          Three Villages,Edington
Y928 GEU   Renault Master        MinO B7FL         Robinson &,Warminster
```
~~~~~~
```
OIL 4571*A229 RNS(12/98), RIL 4099*F31 HGG(4/01), SIL 3069*J300 CCH(4/01),
TAZ 4993*D802 NBO(2/98), C27 VJF*REL 188(4/98) & C27 VJF(2/88),
E780 MLB*43 FJF(12/94) & E778 VGK(2/92) &
E690 UNE*SBZ 8075(6/00) & E690 UNE(2/98)
```
~~~~~~

INDEX OF ABBREVIATIONS USED IN THIS PUBLICATION

```
ACL   Autobus Classique              ME    Mann Egerton
AR    Alexander                      MinO  Minibus Options
ARB   Alexander Belfast              MM    Made 2 Measure
BL    Bristol                        MW    Martin Walter
BM    Burlingham                     NC    Northern Counties
CD    Chassis Developments           O&H   Oughtred & Harrison
CSM   Coachsmith                     OE    Optare
DC    Devon Conversions              PG    Pilcher Greene
DL    Dixon Lomas                    PN    Plaxton
DN    Duple Northern                 POW   Post Office Works
ECW   Eastern Coach Works            PR    Park Royal
EL    East Lancs                     RB    Reeve Burgess
FR    Freight Rover                  RH    Robin Hood
FGY   Frank Guy                      RV    "Recovery Vehicle"
GCS   G.C. Smith                     SCC   SC Coachbuilders(Caetano UK)
H&P   Huntley & Palmers              SE    Steedrive
JE    Jonckheere                     TSM   Tilling Stevens
LCB   Leicester Carriage Builders    VH    Van Hool
LD    Leyland                        VHM   Van Hool McArdle
LG    Longwell Green                 VR    Van Rooijen
LN    Leyland National               WK    Willowbrook
MB    Mercedes-Benz                  WMB   Walsall Motor Bodies
MC    Metro-Cammell                  WS    Wadham Stringer
MCW   Metro-Cammell Weymann
```

THE ISLANDS

Y1   BLUE BIRD TAXIS LTD

Depot:Braye Road Industrial Estate,Vale,GUERNSEY.

49282	Toyota HB31R	Caetano C16F	Ardenvale,Knowle 94
62812	Toyota HDB30R	Caetano C18F	Hertz,Heathrow 98
64918	Mercedes-Benz O814D	Plaxton B31F	loan from Dawsons
67463	Toyota BBR50R	Caetano C27F	New 01

49282*G700 APB(10/94), 62812*K26 VRY(9/98) & 64918*P856 GRC(9/00)

Y2   A.J. CURTIS.t/a RIDUNA BUSES

Depot:3 Les Courtures,ALDERNEY.

AY	91	Bedford SB3	Duple C41F	MacDonald,Alderney 96
AY	593	Leyland CU435	Duple B31F	Bentley,Birmingham 98
AY	1114	Dodge S56	Mellor B20FL	Guernsey Health Board 99
LEU	263P	Bristol VRT/SL3/6LXB	ECW O43/27D	First Bristol 8622 02

AY 91*AY 750(3/95) & J 43805(4/88),
AY 593*HSC 166X(4/98) & CIB 9623(9/96) & HSC 166X(3/96) &
AY 1114*41898(5/99)

Y3   DELTA TAXIS LTD

Depot:Kings Road,St Peter Port,GUERNSEY.

56650	4	Renault Master	Cymric C14F	New 94
56660	2	Renault Master	Cymric C14F	New 97
56690	3	Renault Master	Cymric C14F	New 95
66959	1	Toyota BBR50R	Caetano C27F	New 01

Y4   ISLAND COACHWAYS LTD

Depot:Hougue a la Perre,St Peter Port,GUERNSEY.

1787	51	Toyota HB31R	Caetano C18F	Manning,Challow 95
3989	49	Iveco 95-18F	Camo C42F	New 94
5779	48	Leyland ST2R	Elme C43F	New 90
6768	50	Renault PP180	Camo C43F	New 95
8225	62	Iveco 49-10	Iveco B18F	New 96
8227	56	Leyland LBM6T/2RS	WS C37F	Howarth,Merthyr Tydf. 97
8228	73	Mercedes-Benz 811D	Optare B31F	Lawrenson,Earlstown 95
8230	47	Renault PP180	Camo C43F	New 98
9438	64	Iveco 49-10	Iveco B18F	New 96
9969	57	Renault PP180	LCB B39F	New 99
12723	71	Optare MR03	B26F	Guernseybus 71 00
12727	72	Optare MR03	B26F	Guernseybus 72 00
17314	67	Optare MR03	B31F	Guernseybus 67 00
18047	83	Optare MR13	B31F	New 96
18264	70	Optare MR03	B26F	Guernseybus 70 00
19660	79	Optare MR03	B26F	Guernseybus 79 00
19662	80	Optare MR03	B26F	Guernseybus 80 00
19675	78	Optare MR03	B25F	Guernseybus 78 00
19676	75	Optare MR03	B25F	Guernseybus 75 00
19677	76	Optare MR03	B25F	Guernseybus 76 00
19678	77	Optare MR03	B25F	Guernseybus 77 00
20716	69	Optare MR03	B31F	Guernseybus 69 00
23196	63	Iveco 49-10	Iveco B18F	New 95
24493	81	MCW MF150	B25F	West Midlands 671 98
24539	82	Optare MR13	B31F	New 96

```
24603    88   Optare MR03         B26F            Guernseybus 88 00
24775    90   Optare MR03         B26F            Guernseybus 90 00
29728    74   Optare MR03         B25F            Guernseybus 74 00
31921   171   Bristol LH6L        Plaxton C45F    Guernseybus 171 00
33541    84   Optare MR03         B29F            Guernseybus 84 00
34518    85   Optare MR03         B29F            Guernseybus 85 00
38290    59   Volkswagen LT55     Optare B25F     Derby 79 94
38328    60   Volkswagen LT55     Optare B25F     Memory Lane,Caerleon 95
38406    53   Leyland ST2R        Elme C43F       New 91
39138    53   Leyland ST2R        Elme C35F       New 92
40527    65   Optare MR03         B31F            Guernseybus 65 00
47979    89   Optare MR03         B26F            Guernseybus 89 00
56206    68   Optare MR03         B31F            Guernseybus 68 00
61973    86   Optare MR01         B33F            Guernseybus 86 00
62067    87   Optare MR01         B33F            Guernseybus 87 00
64991    54   Leyland LBM6T/2RA   WS B41F         West Midlands Police 00
66867    43   Leyland CU302       WS B37F         Amies,Shrewsbury 01
66868    44   DAF 9.13R           WS B37F         LB Redbridge 01
```

1787*G154 ELJ(1/95), 8225*39138(8/99),
8227*E961 PME(6/97) & J 45700(9/89) & E961 PME(11/88),
8228*38406(8/99) & F721 TLW(6/95) & RIB 7017(3/95) & F607 SDP(3/93),
12723*H151 UUA(3/98), 12727*H142 UUA(4/98), 17314*J216 BWU(9/98),
18264*H147 UUA(4/98), 19660*H168 WWT(1/98), 19662*H167 WWT(1/98),
19675*J968 JNL(5/97), 19676*J967 JNL(10/96), 19677*J971 JNL(9/96),
19678*J972 JNL(9/96), 20716*J220 BWU(9/98), 24493*F671 YOG(5/98),
24603*H165 WWT(3/00), 24775*H161 WWT(3/00), 29728*J963 JNL(2/97),
31921*AFJ 736T(1/93), 33541*J962 DWX(3/00), 34518*J960 DWX(3/00),
38290*D854 CRY(2/94), 38328*D346 JUM(3/95), 38406*8228(8/99),
39138*8225(8/99), 40527*J210 BWU(9/98), 47979*H163 WWT(3/00),
56206*J218 BWU(9/98), 61973*J326 PPD(3/00), 62067*G972 WPA(3/00),
64991*F56 BJW(9/00), 66867*F396 RHT(6/01) & 66868*H557 JEV(6/01)

Y5   J.M.T. (1987) LTD

Depot:2-4 Caledonia Place,St Helier,JERSEY.

```
J 11467   69   Dennis Dart         Plaxton B40F    New 98
J 13853   11   Dennis Dart         Plaxton B43F    New 97
J 14639   30   Ford R1014          Duple B45F      New 80
J 14644   31   Ford R1014          Duple B45F      New 80
J 14645   32   Ford R1014          Duple B45F      New 80
J 14650   33   Ford R1014          Duple B45F      New 80
J 15374    1   Leyland ST2R        WS B43F         New 91
J 15884   19   Leyland ST2R        WS B43F         New 91
J 15908    5   Leyland ST2R        WS B43F         New 91
J 16043   46   Leyland ST2R        WS B43F         New 91
J 16439   48   Leyland ST2R        WS B43F         New 91
J 16527   57   Ford R1014          Duple B45F      New 81
J 16582   60   Ford R1014          Duple B45F      New 81
J 16598   59   Ford R1014          Duple B45F      New 81
J 16601   58   Ford R1014          Duple B45F      New 81
J 16861   53   Dennis Dart         Plaxton B40F    Isle of Man 77 00
J 29709   34   Ford R1014          Duple B45F      New 82
J 29710   35   Ford R1014          Duple B45F      New 82
J 29713   36   Ford R1014          Duple B45F      New 82
J 29717   37   Ford R1014          Duple B45F      New 82
J 31271   61   Ford R1014          Duple B45F      New 83
J 31281   62   Ford R1014          Duple B45F      New 83
J 31300   63   Ford R1014          Duple B45F      New 83
J 31312   64   Ford R1014          Duple B45F      New 83
J 34191   24   Ford R1015          WS B41F         Wadham Stringer(Demo) 85
J 40820   17   Ford R1015          WS B45F         New 86
J 40853   18   Ford R1015          WS B45F         New 86
J 40865   25   Ford R1015          WS B45F         New 86
J 40899   39   Ford R1015          WS B45F         New 86
J 42252   41   Ford R1015          WS B45F         New 85
J 42259   42   Ford R1015          WS B45F         New 85
```

```
J 42298   43  Ford R1015        WS B45F         New 85
J 42653   21  Ford R1015        WS B45F         New 85
J 43037   20  Ford R1015        WS B45F         New 84
J 43048   29  Ford R1015        WS B45F         New 84
J 43063   23  Ford R1015        WS B45F         New 84
J 43066   26  Ford R1015        WS B45F         New 84
J 46598    4  Dennis Dart       Plaxton B43F    New 94
J 46631    8  Dennis Dart       Plaxton B43F    New 94
J 46744    6  Dennis Dart       Plaxton B43F    New 94
J 46794   10  Dennis Dart       Plaxton B43F    New 94
J 46828   51  Dennis Dart       Plaxton B43F    New 94
J 58127   56  Ford R1014        Duple B45F      New 79
J 58128   54  Ford R1014        Duple B45F      New 79
J 58917    2  Ford R1014        Duple B45F      New 78
J 58923   52  Ford R1014        Duple B45F      New 78
J 58924   15  Ford R1014        Duple B45F      New 78
J 61334   40  Dennis Dart       Plaxton B40F    New 98
J 64744   49  Dennis Dart       Plaxton B40F    New 98
J 64745   67  Dennis Dart       Plaxton B40F    New 98
J 69267   47  Dennis Dart       Plaxton B43F    New 97
J 70700    3  MCW MF158         B33F            New 89
J 70712   45  MCW MF158         B33F            New 89
J 71210   50  MCW MF158         B33F            New 88
J 74393   22  Dennis Dart       Plaxton B43F    New 97
J 75173   12  Dennis Dart       Plaxton B43F    New 95
J 75197   16  Dennis Dart       Plaxton B43F    New 95
J 75241   27  Dennis Dart       Plaxton B43F    New 95
J 75609    7  Dennis Dart       Plaxton B43F    New 95
J 84709   44  Dennis Dart       Plaxton B43F    New 95
J 85325   68  Dennis Dart       Plaxton B40F    New 98
J 86370   65  Dennis Dart       Plaxton B43F    New 97
J 86372   66  Dennis Dart       Plaxton B43F    New 97
J 90172   14  Dennis Dart       Plaxton B40F    Isle of Man 73 00
J 90241   28  Dennis Dart       Plaxton B40F    Isle of Man 74 00
J 90454   55  Dennis Dart       Plaxton B40F    Isle of Man 79 00
J 93319   38  Dennis Dart       Plaxton B40F    Isle of Man 75 00
J 93500    9  Dennis Dart       Plaxton B40F    Isle of Man 72 00
```

~~~~~~

J 16861*CMN 77X(8/00), J 90172*CMN 73X(10/00), J 90241*CMN 74X(8/00),
J 90454*CMN 79X(8/00), J 93319*CMN 75X(8/00) & J 93500*CMN 72X(10/00),

~~~~~~

Y6   TANTIVY BLUE COACH TOURS LTD

Depots:Car Park,Le Mont de Ste Marie,Greve de Lecq,
*   Silver Springs Hotel,La Route des Genets,St Brelade(6),*
*   Georgetown Park Estate,St Clement,*
*   70-72 Colomberie & 10 Parade,St Helier,JERSEY.*

```
J 10376   32  Bedford SB5       Duple C40F      New 86
J 10429   33  Bedford SB5       Duple C40F      New 86
J 10519   34  Bedford SB5       Duple C40F      New 86
J 10569   46  Bedford SB3       Duple C41F      New 82
J 10603   45  Bedford SB3       Duple C41F      New 82
J 12050   60  Cannon Islander   LCB C43F        Pioneer,St Helier 3 00
J 12633  108  Renault Master    WMB B16F        New 96
J 12695   21  Leyland LBM6T/2RS  WS C41F         Gatwick Parkng,Horley 97
J 13779   55  Leyland LBM6T/2RA  WS C43F         Pioneer,St Helier 11 00
J 14609   66  Leyland LBM6T/2RA  WS C42F         Pioneer,St Helier 7 00
J 14610   68  Leyland LBM6T/2RS  WS C39F         Pioneer,St Helier 15 00
J 14612  130  Renault Master    MM C16F         Pioneer,St Helier 22 00
J 14614  132  Renault Master    MM C16F         Pioneer,St Helier 21 00
J 14616   61  Cannon Islander   LCB C43F        Pioneer,St Helier 4 00
J 14638   67  Leyland LBM6T/2RS  RB C37FL        Pioneer,St Helier 18 00
J 14660  131  Renault Master    MM C16F         Pioneer,St Helier 20 00
J 14679   50  Bedford SB5       WS C40F         Pioneer,St Helier 6 00
J 15582   30  Bedford SB5       Duple C40F      New 86
J 17759   29  Bedford SB5       Caetano C40F    Gatwick Pkg,Horley 91
J 20072   58  Bedford SB5       Duple C41F      New 80
```

```
J 24457    15   Leyland ST2R        WS C41F           New 89
J 24489    14   Leyland ST2R        WS C41F           New 89
J 24573    16   Leyland ST2R        WS C41F           New 89
J 24651    41   Bedford SB5         Duple C40F        New 84
J 26626    44   Bedford SB3         Duple C41F        New 84
J 26678    42   Bedford SB3         Duple C41F        New 84
J 26724    43   Bedford SB3         Duple C41F        New 84
J 29206    47   Bedford SB3         Duple C41F        New 81
J 32069    62   Leyland LBM6T/2RA   WS C41F           Cottrell,Mitcheldean 99
J 32575    8    Leyland ST2R        Elme C43F         New 91
J 33181    105  Renault Master      Coachwork B17F    New 88
J 33630    12   Leyland ST2R        Elme C39F         Clarendon,St Helier 92
J 34317    36   Bedford SB5         WS C40F           New 85
J 39815    3    Iveco 95-18F        WS C40F           New 94
J 41130    6    Leyland ST2R        Elme C39F         Collison,Stonehouse 96
J 43881    35   Bedford SB5         WS C40F           New 85
J 44485    31   Bedford SB5         Duple C40F        New 86
J 47452    4    Leyland ST2R        Elme C43F         New 92
J 47453    5    Leyland ST2R        Elme C43F         New 92
J 48300    9    Leyland ST2R        WS C43F           New 91
J 48388    10   Leyland ST2R        WS C43F           New 91
J 49246    107  Renault Master      Deansgate B16F    New 93
J 49250    109  Renault Master      Kimlon B16F       ? 93
J 55378    106  Renault Master      Coachwork B17F    New 86
J 57331    18   Leyland ST2R        WS C41F           New 89
J 57347    19   Leyland ST2R        WS C41F           New 89
J 57357    17   Leyland ST2R        WS C41F           New 89
J 59934    51   Leyland LBM6T/2RS   WS C39F           Pioneer,St Helier 14 00
J 60112    54   Bedford SB3         Duple C41F        New 80
J 60319    26   Leyland LBM6T/2RA   WS C41F           LDT 3085 98
J 61644    28   Bedford SB5         Caetano C40F      Gatwick Pkg,Horley 91
J 61774    7    Leyland ST2R        Elme C43F         New 91
J 66475    40   Bedford SB5         Duple C40F        New 84
J 73973    65   Leyland ST2R        WS C43F           Pioneer,St Helier 12 00
J 75668    20   Leyland LBM6T/2RS   WS C41F           Heron,Crawley 96
J 77033    25   Leyland LBM6T/2RA   WS C41F           LDT 3084 98
J 80977    11   Leyland ST2R        Elme C39F         Educational,Guernsey 96
J 82047    1    Renault PP180       Camo C43F         New 96
J 82049    2    Renault PP180       Camo C43F         New 96
J 84872    59   Cannon Islander     LCB C43F          Pioneer,St Helier 5 00
J 87196    27   Leyland LBM6T/2RA   WS C43F           Collison,Stonehouse 98
J 88633    38   Bedford SB5         Duple C40F        New 84
J 89654    71   Leyland LBM6T/2RA   WS B39F           Pioneer,St Helier 1 00
J 89771    63   Leyland LBM6T/2RA   WS C43F           Collison,Stonehouse 98
J 89914    22   Leyland LBM6T/2RA   WS C41F           Armchair,Brentford 98
J 90393    64   Leyland LBM6T/2RA   WS C43F           Collison,Stonehouse 98
J 90706    39   Bedford SB5         Duple C40F        New 84
J 91155    23   Leyland LBM6T/2RA   WS C41F           LDT 3086 98
J 91574    70   Leyland LBM6T/2RA   WS B41F           Pioneer,St Helier 30 00
J 91728    37   Bedford SB5         Duple C40F        New 84
J 92914    24   Leyland LBM6T/2RA   WS C41F           LDT 3088 98
```

J 12050*J 491(6/00), J 12633*AY 2246(3/96), J 12695*F131 UMD(7/97),
J 13779*J 2438(2/99) & H510 LPE(6/94),
J 14609*F793 RBK(4/97), J 14610*E962 NMK(2/97), J 14612*M34 MXP(1/95),
J 14638*F723 SML(8/95), J 15582*J 44478(3/00),
J 17759*J 6380(5/00) & D832 CNV(5/91), J 24651*J 42607(?/00),
J 32069*F66 SMC(?/99), J 41130*J515 LCW(3/96), J 43881*J 7328(11/96),
J 49250*G433 UTA(5/93), J 59934*E967 NMK(1/94), J 60319*F155 KGS(8/98),
J 61644*J 7997(3/95) & D834 CNV(5/91), J 66475*J 42753(?/00),
J 73973*J 2620(2/99) & J869 PPC(6/94), J 75668*E968 NMK(4/96),
J 77033*F154 KGS(8/98), J 80977*6430(1/96), J 84872*J 491(11/00),
J 87196*F136 UMD(8/98), J 88633*J 40679(?/00), J 89654*G111 VMM(8/98),
J 89771*F138 UMD(8/98), J 89914*E991 NMK(4/98), J 90393*F139 UMD(8/98),
J 90706*J 40658(3/00), J 91155*F300 MNK(6/98), J 91574*F173 SMT(12/99),
J 91728*J40614(5/00) & J 92914*F301 MNK(6/98)

Y7   WAVERLEY COACHES LTD

Depot:20 Gloucester Street,St Helier,JERSEY.

```
J 27404  15  Bedford SB5         Duple C40F    New 86
J 27414  14  Bedford SB5         Duple C40F    New 86
J 37636  11  Bedford SB5         Duple C40F    New 84
J 37684  12  Bedford SB5         Duple C40F    New 84
J 51771   1  Leyland LBM6T/2RS   WS C41F       New 89
J 51772   2  Leyland LBM6T/2RS   WS C41F       New 89
J 51812   4  Leyland LBM6T/2RS   WS C41F       New 89
J 51819   3  Leyland LBM6T/2RS   WS C41F       New 89
J 51937  19  Bedford SB5         Duple C41F    Mascot,St Helier 25 84
J 69526  17  Mercedes-Benz 811D  PMT C33F      Chisholm,Ramsgate 95
J 75736   5  Leyland LBM6T/2RA   WS C43F       Stark,Bridge of Weir 96
J 75874  16  Mercedes-Benz 811D  PMT C33F      Chisholm,Ramsgate 95
J 79519   7  Renault Master      ? B17F        Non-PSV(Cardiff) 95
J 93747  21  Cannon Islander     LCB C43F      New 01
J 93812  20  Cannon Islander     LCB C43F      New 01
```
~~~~~~
```
J 51937*CXF 257G(4/84), J 69526*H541 NSF(5/96), J 75736*F67 FMC(4/96),
J 75874*H899 NFS(11/95) & J 79519*D617 NKO(4/95)
```
~~~~~~

OI   OTHER VEHICLES ON THE ISLANDS

```
   48641  Toyota HZB50R     Caetano C21F     Intransit,St Peter Port(G)
   52408  Iveco 49-10       Iveco B15F       Intransit,St Peter Port(G)
J  18280  BLC               BLC B33          BLC Amphibians(J)
J  42159  BLC               BLC B28          BLC Amphibians(J)
J  45360  BLC               BLC B28          BLC Amphibians(J)
AY  1950  Bedford VAS5      Marshall B30F    Spandler(AY)
PYH 651Y  Leyland CU435     RB DP32F         Lucas,St Marys(SI)
D149 LTA  Dodge S56         RB DP25F         Twynham,Hugh Town(SI)
G420 RYJ  Iveco 49-10       Phoenix B23F     Elms,High Town(SI)
H466 HBA  Iveco 49-10       Phoenix B24F     Lucas,St Marys(SI)
K334 RCN  Iveco 59-12       Dormobile B27F   Woodcock,Carn Thomas(SI)
P 49 OAV  LDV Convoy        LDV B13F         Woodcock,Carn Thomas(SI)
```
~~~~~~
```
48641*M651 FWK(6/01) & AY 1773*6768(4/95) & WUA 655X(8/88)
```
~~~~~~

P   **PRESERVED VEHICLES IN THIS BOOK AREA**

Reg		Make/Type	Body	Year	Owner/Location
	8229	Albion FT39KAN	Reading FB35F	1958	Neek,Thornbury
CD	7104	Vulcan VSD	Replica B18F	1922	Lee,Exmouth
DD	475	Ford TT	Healey B14	1922	Watts,Lydney
DS	9751	Thornycroft J2	Replica Ch30	1919	Lee,Exmouth
DX	8871	Ransomes D	B31D	1930	Science Mus,Wroughton
FV	5737	Leyland TS7	Duple C31F	1936	Hoare,WETC
GW	713	Gilford 1680T	Weymann C30D	1931	Science Mus,Wroughton
JG	9938	Leyland TS8	Park Royal C32R	1937	Rexquote,Bishops Lyd.
JY	124	TSM B39A7	Beadle B-R	1932	Shears,WETC
OD	5868	Leyland LT5	Weymann B31F	1933	Shears,WETC
OD	7497	AEC Regent I	Short O31/24R	1934	Greet,Broadhempston
OD	7500	AEC Regent I	Brush H30/26R	1934	Shorland,WETC
RL	2727	Thorneycroft A1	Mumford Ch20	1926	Warner,Tewkesbury
RV	6367	Leyland TD4	EEC O26/24R	1935	Harvey,Yeovil
UF	8837	Leyland TS4	RV	1932	Hoare,WETC
UO	2331	Austin SPL	Tiverton B13F	1927	Shears,Bideford
VO	6806	AEC Regal I	Cravens B32F	1931	Science Mus,Wroughton
VW	203	Leyland PLSC3	Mumford B-R	1927	Shears & Tucker,WETC
YC	37	Graham	Fay B15F	1927	Ferguson,Avening
ABH	358	Leyland KP3	Duple C20F	1933	Warner,Tewkesbury
ADR	813	Leyland TD5C	Leyland L27/26R	1938	Tucker,Liskeard
AHU	803	Bristol JO5G	Bristol B35R	1934	Bristol Vintage BG
AJA	132	Bristol L5G	Burlingham B35R	1938	Rexquote,Bishops Lyd.
ASV	900	Dennis Lancet III	Reading C33F	1949	Gunn,South Petherton
ATT	922	Bristol JJW6A	Beadle B35R	1935	Cook,WETC
BAS	563	Bristol LD6G	ECW O33/27R	1956	Rexquote,Bishops Lyd.
BAS	564	Bristol LD6G	ECW O33/27R	1956	Rexquote,Bishops Lyd.
BOW	169	Bristol L5G	RV	1938	Hoare,WETC
BWG	528	Leyland PS1	Alexander C35F	1949	Rexquote,Bishops Lyd.
CFN	121	Dennis Lancet III	Park Royal B35R	1949	Rexquote,Bishops Lyd.
CHG	545	Leyland PS2/14	East Lancs B39F	1954	Rexquote,Bishops Lyd.
CHL	772	Daimler CVD6SD	Willowbrook B35F	1950	Rexquote,Bishops Lyd.
CJY	299	Leyland PD1	Roe L27/28R	1946	Plymouth
CMG	30	Bedford WLB	Duple C20R	1935	Taylor,Tintinhull
CNH	699	Bristol KSW6B	ECW L27/28R	1952	Staniforth,Kemble
CPM	61	AEC 661T	Weymann H28/26R	1939	Science Mus,Wroughton
DCK	219	Leyland PD2/3	EL FCL27/22RD	1951	Rexquote,Bishops Lyd.
DDR	414	Leyland PD1A	Weymann L27/26R	1947	Tucker,Liskeard
DFP	496	Albion PH115	Reading B32F	1939	Bowring,Lydney
DHR	192	Guy Arab II	Weymann H30/26R	1943	Science Mus,Wroughton
DJY	945	Leyland PD2/1	Leyland L27/26R	1948	Tucker,Liskeard
DJY	965	Crossley DD42/5	Crossley L27/26R	1948	Tucker,WETC
DOD	474	AEC Regal I	Weymann B35F	1940	Shorland,WETC
DOD	518	Bristol L5G	Beadle B36R	1940	333 Bus Gp,Cheltenham
DSV	715	Morris PV	Reading C13F	1949	Wye,Warminster
EFJ	241	Leyland TD5	Leyland O30/26R	1938	Shears,WETC
EFJ	666	Leyland TS8	Cravens B32R	1938	Shears,WETC
EMW	284	Bristol L6B	Beadle C32R	1949	Tancock,Temple Cloud
EMW	893	Daimler CVD6SD	Park Royal B35C	1947	Rexquote,Bishops Lyd.
ETT	956	Bristol LL5G	ECW B39R	1938	Cotswold PSVG,Stroud
ETT	995	AEC Regent	Saro H30/26R	1938	WETC
EUF	182	Leyland TD5	RV	1938	Burton,Probus
EUF	204	Leyland TD5	PR H28/26R	1938	BBPG,WETC
FCD	506	Leyland TD5	EL H28/26R	1939	BBPG,WETC
FFS	871	Bedford OB	Burlingham FC-F	1948	O'Callaghan,Bath
FMO	949	Bristol LL6B	ECW B39F	1951	Rexquote,Bishops Lyd.
FTA	634	Bristol K5G	ECW L30/26R	1941	Cook,WETC
FTT	704	Bristol K6A	ECW L27/28R	1945	Bristol Vintage BG
GDL	667	Bedford OB	Duple C29F	1950	Alexcars,Cirencester
GHT	127	Bristol K5G	ECW O33/26R	1941	First Bristol 8583
GHT	154	Bristol K5G	Bristol H30/26R	1940	Bristol Vintage BG
GLJ	957	Leyland PD1A	ECW L27/26R	1948	Leatherdale,WETC
GTA	395	Bristol LL5G	Bristol B39R	1942	Cook,WETC
GWN	432	Dennis Lancet III	Thurgood FC37F	1950	Rexquote,Bishops Lyd.
GWV	101	Bedford OB	Duple C29F	1951	Cooper,Maiden Bradley
HET	513	Crossley DD42/8	Crossley H30/26R	1953	Science Mus,Wroughton
HFJ	142	Leyland PD2/1	Leyland H30/26R	1948	Gobbin,St Austell

HIL	7081	Bedford CFL	Plaxton C15F	1979	Jones,Yatton
HJY	296	Leyland PD2/12	Leyland H30/26R	1953	Burch,WETC
HKL	819	AEC Regal I	Beadle OB35F	1946	Rexquote,Bishops Lyd.
HLX	403	AEC Regent III	PR H30/26R	1948	Tyburn,Bristol
HOD	66	Beadle/Bedford	Beadle B35R	1949	Willis,Bodmin
HTT	487	AEC Regal I	Weymann B35F	1946	Greet,Broadhempston
HUO	510	AEC Regal I	Weymann B35F	1948	Rexquote,Bishops Lyd.
HWO	323	Leyland PS1/1	Lydney C33F	1950	Bowring,Lydney
JDV	754	Bedford OB	Duple C29F	1947	Babb,Blue Anchor
JFJ	875	Daimler CVD6SD	Weymann B35F	1950	Hazell,Northlew
JFM	575	AEC Regal III	Strachan B35R	1948	Rexquote,Bishops Lyd.
JHT	802	Bristol K6A	ECW H31/28R	1946	Green,Charfield
JHT	827	Bristol L5G	Bristol B35R	1946	Burt,Shaftesbury
JLJ	402	Leyland PS2/3	BM FDP35F	1949	Rexquote,Bishops Lyd.
JTA	314	Guy Arab II	Roe H31/25RD	1943	DG314 PG,WETC
JTE	546	AEC Regent III	PR H33/26R	1948	Rexquote,Bishops Lyd.
JUO	943	Bristol L6B	ECW FB39F	1948	Abbey Hill SRC,Yeovil
JUO	992	Leyland PD1A	ECW L27/26R	1947	Rexquote,Bishops Lyd.
JVH	378	AEC Regent III	EL H33/28R	1955	Rexquote,Bishops Lyd.
JXC	323	Leyland PS1	ME B30F	1949	Adams,Kemble
KAN	505	Bedford SBG	Yeates C41F	1956	Binning,Gloucester
KDD	38	AEC Regal III	Harrington FC33F	1950	Helliker,Stroud
KFM	767	Bristol L5G	ECW B35R	1950	Rexquote,Bishops Lyd.
KFM	893	Bristol L5G	ECW B35R	1950	Rexquote,Bishops Lyd.
KGK	529	Leyland 6RT	Leyland H30/26R	1949	Adams,Bristol
KHW	630	Leyland PD1	ECW H30/26R	1948	Staniforth,Kemble
KJH	731	Bedford OB	Duple C29F	1949	Read,Ivybridge
KLB	721	AEC Regent III	PR H30/26R	1950	Adams,Bristol
KOD	585	AEC Regent III	Weymann H30/26R	1949	Greet,Broadhempston
KOD	965	Bedford OB	Duple C27F	1949	Jenkins,Wells
KPT	909	Leyland PD2/1	Leyland L27/26R	1950	Science Mus,Wroughton
KTF	594	AEC Regent III	PR O33/26R	1949	Rexquote,Bishops Lyd.
KXW	478	AEC Regent III	Weymann H30/26R	1950	Cooper,Newquay
LAE	13	Leyland PD1A	ECW H30/26R	1948	Bristol Vintage BG
LBP	500	Bedford OB	Duple C29F	1949	Risk,Plymouth
LDB	796	Leyland PSUC1/1	WK DP43F	1960	Rexquote,Bishops Lyd.
LDV	483	Bedford OB	Duple C29F	1950	Higgs,Cheltenham
LFM	302	Leyland PS1/1	Weymann B35F	1950	Rexquote,Bishops Lyd.
LFM	717	Bristol L5G	ECW B35R	1950	Rexquote,Bishops Lyd.
LFM	734	Bristol LL5G	ECW B39R	1950	Rexquote,Bishops Lyd.
LFM	753	Bristol L6B	ECW DP31R	1950	Staniforth,Kemble
LHT	911	Bristol L5G	Bristol B35R	1948	Amos,Nailsea
LHY	976	Bristol L5G	ECW B33D	1949	Somerbus,Paulton
LJH	665	Dennis Lancet III	Duple C35F	1949	Rexquote,Bishops Lyd.
LKN	550	Bedford OB	Mulliner B28F	1949	Staniforth,Kemble
LOD	495	Albion FT39N	Duple C31F	1950	Hazell,Northlew
LOD	974	Sentinel STC4	Sentinel B40F	1950	Group,Chudleigh
LRR	655	Bedford OB	Duple C24F	1950	Greet,Broadhempston
LRV	992	Leyland PD2/12	MC O33/26R	1956	Stagecoach Devon
LTA	755	Bedford OB	Duple C29F	1950	Greenleas Coll.,Bow
LTA	772	Bristol LWL5G	ECW B39R	1951	Dorset TC,Wroughton
LTA	895	Bristol LL6B	Duple C37F	1951	Hawke,Newquay
LTA	906	Bedford OB	Duple C29F	1949	Greet,Broadhempston
LTA	995	Bristol KSW6B	ECW L27/28R	1953	Haynes,Sparkford
LTV	702	AEC Regal III	East Lancs B35R	1951	Blood,WETC
LUC	187	AEC Regent III	PR H30/26R	1951	Copas,Redruth
LUO	595	AEC Regal III	Weymann B35F	1950	Soanes,WETC
LYF	104	Leyland 7RT	PR H30/26R	1951	Cousens &,Torquay
MAF	544	Austin CXB	ME FC31C	1949	Derrick,WETC
MCO	658	Leyland PD2/12	MC O30/26R	1956	Plymouth
MFM	39	Bedford OB	Duple C29F	1951	Jones,Yatton
MHU	52	Bedford OB	Duple B30F	1950	Greet,Broadhempston
MHU	193	Bedford OB	Mulliner B31F	1949	Greet,Broadhempston
MLL	528	AEC Regal IV	MC B39F	1952	Monk,Lostwithiel
MLL	570	AEC Regal IV	MC B37F	1952	Brown,Shaftesbury
MLL	769	AEC Regal IV	MC B37F	1952	Sharland,Exeter
MLL	935	AEC Regal IV	MC B41F	1952	Dale,Sherborne
MLL	963	AEC Regal IV	MC B39F	1952	Henley,Swindon
MMB	861	Foden PVFE6	Metalcraft FC37F	1951	Foden Coach PG,Stroud

MRL	765	Austin K8VC	Tiverton C12F	1950	Davey, East Huntspill
MTT	640	Leyland PD2/1	Leyland L27/26R	1951	Hazell, Northlew
MVS	972	Leyland PD3/4	MC H39/31F	1961	Chatterton, Foxham
MXX	8	AEC Regal IV	MC B41F	1952	Andress, Chippenham
MXX	319	Guy Special	ECW B26F	1953	Hudgell, Tiverton
MXX	345	Guy Special	ECW B26F	1953	Smith, Melksham
NBB	171	Bedford OB	Duple C29F	1949	Staniforth, Kemble
NBH	746	Bedford OB	Duple C29F	1950	X Country, Castle Eatn
NDB	356	Leyland PSUC1/1	Crossley B44F	1958	Rexquote, Bishops Lyd.
NHU	2	Bristol LSX5G	ECW B44F	1951	Walker, Bath
NLJ	268	Leyland PSU1/13	Burlingham B-F	1953	Hallett, Trowbridge
NLJ	271	Leyland PSU1/13	Burlingham B42F	1954	Rexquote, Bishops Lyd.
NLP	645	AEC Regal IV	PR RDP37C	1953	Science Mus, Wroughton
NTT	661	AEC Regent III	Weymann H30/26R	1952	Platt, Crediton
NTT	679	AEC Regent III	Weymann H30/26R	1953	Greet, Broadhempston
OCO	502	Leyland PD2/40	MC H30/26R	1958	Shears, WETC
OHY	938	Bristol KSW6B	ECW L27/24RD	1952	Green, Kemble
OLG	855	Foden PVRF6	Plaxton C41C	1951	Helliker, Stroud
OLJ	291	Bedford CAV	Bedford B12	1954	Science Mus, Wroughton
OMB	161	Daimler CVD6DD	NC H36/28R	1952	Chatterton, Foxham
OTT	55	Bristol LS5G	ECW B41F	1954	Science Mus, Wroughton
OTT	98	Bristol LS6G	ECW C39F	1953	Dorset TC, Weymouth
RDB	846	AEC Reliance	Alexander DP41F	1961	Rexquote, Bishops Lyd.
RDB	872	Dennis Loline III	AR H39/32F	1961	Preston, Bath
RFO	361	AEC Regent V	PR H41/32F	1962	Jacobs, Saltash 9
RFO	375	Albion FT39N	Heaver B8F	1950	Hart, Bodmin
RTT	996	Bristol LD6B	ECW H33/25RD	1954	Green, Kemble
SHO	800	AEC Reliance	Duple C43F	1958	Hallett, Trowbridge
SWO	986	Bristol MW6G	ECW C39F	1958	Annetts, Parkend
UFJ	293	Guy Arab IV	Massey H-R	1957	Greet, Broadhempston
UFJ	296	Guy Arab IV	PR H31/26R	1957	Greet, Broadhempston
UHY	359	Bristol KSW6G	ECW H32/28R	1955	Staniforth, Kemble
UHY	360	Bristol KSW6G	ECW H32/28R	1955	Rexquote, Bishops Lyd.
UHY	384	Bristol KSW6G	ECW H32/28RD	1955	Walker &, Wookey
UMR	112	Daimler CVG6DD	Weymann H36/28R	1960	Swindon Vintage OS
USK	947	Bedford BYC	H & P B8	1935	Izart, Kingswood
UUO	198	Bedford SBG	Duple C41F	1956	Jacobs, WETC
VCD	984	Bedford C4Z2	Duple C29F	1958	Rundell, Falmouth
VDV	752	Bristol LDL6G	ECW O37/33RD	1957	Rexquote, Bishops Lyd.
VDV	753	Bristol LDL6G	ECW O37/33RD	1957	Rexquote, Bishops Lyd.
VDV	798	AEC Reliance	Weymann B41F	1957	798 Group, Crediton
VDV	817	AEC Regent V	MC H33/26R	1957	Platt, WETC
VDV	818	AEC Regent V	MC O33/26R	1957	Platt, Crediton
VLT	140	AEC Routemaster	PR H36/28R	1960	Gale, Wroughton
WKG	287	AEC Reliance	Willowbrook B41F	1961	Rexquote, Bishops Lyd.
WLW	994	Bedford CA	Kenex B12	1959	Wonnacott, Exeter
WRL	16	Rowe Hillmaster	Reading B42F	1956	Glover, WETC
WSL	115	Bedford OB	Duple C29F	1950	Trigg, Bourton-Water
XDV	851	AEC Reliance	Willowbrook C41F	1958	Hookins, Bampton
XTB	91	Bedford SBG	Duple C41F	1955	Down, Mary Tavy
YHT	929	Bristol LD6B	ECW H33/25R	1957	Burt, Shaftesbury
YHT	958	Bristol LD6B	ECW O-RD	1958	Staniforth, Kemble
YHY	78	Bristol LS5G	ECW DP41F	1957	2920 Bus Group, Stroud
YHY	80	Bristol LS6G	ECW B43F	1957	Neale, Bristol
7682	LJ	Bristol FL6G	ECW H37/33RD	1962	Green, Kemble
3655	NE	Leyland PSUC1/12	Park Royal DP38D	1962	Rexquote, Bishops Lyd.
4092	WJ	Karrier BF3023	Plaxton C14F	1959	Ryland, Gloucester
137	ACY	Bristol MW6G	ECW B45F	1961	Lines, Bristol
890	ADV	AEC Reliance	Willowbrook C41F	1959	Rexquote, Bishops Lyd.
974	AFJ	Guy Arab IV	Massey H31/26R	1960	Blood, WETC
838	AFM	Bristol LD6G	ECW H33/27RD	1957	Rexquote, Bishops Lyd.
972	ANK	Bedford SBG	Duple C41F	1957	Jacobs, Saltash 1
747	ATA	Bedford CAV	? B ?	1958	Trowsdale, Exmouth
872	ATA	Leyland PDR1/1	MC H44/32F	1959	Hulme, Bristol
501	BTA	Bristol LD6G	ECW H33/27RD	1959	Rexquote, Bishops Lyd.
503	BTA	Bristol LD6G	ECW H33/27RD	1959	Rexquote, Bishops Lyd.
878	CDH	Bedford SB3	Duple C41F	1958	Jenkins, Wells
479	CFJ	Leyland PD2A/30	Massey H-R	1961	Ribbs & Lynne, WETC
363	CLT	AEC Routemaster	PR H36/28R	1962	Knight, Hawkesbury U.

497	CLT	AEC Routemaster	PR H32/25RD	1962	Gale,Avonwick
572	CNW	Daimler CVG6LX-30DD	Roe H-F	1962	Rexquote,Bishops Lyd.
445	CTT	Bedford SB3	Duple C41F	1959	Hearn,Stibb Cross
466	DHN	Guy Arab IV	Roe H33/28R	1957	Rexquote,Bishops Lyd.
913	DTT	Leyland PDR1/1	Roe H44/31F	1960	Jacobs,Saltash
509	DVT	Bedford SB3	Duple C41F	1958	Jacobs,Saltash
532	DWW	Bedford SB5	Plaxton C41F	1963	Jacobs,WETC
999	EAE	Leyland PSUC1/2	Burlingham C41F	1959	L Munden,Bristol
504	EBL	Bedford VAL14	Duple C52F	1963	Science Mus,Wroughton
181	ECV	Bedford SB1	Duple C41F	1959	Greet,Broadhempston
338	EDV	Bristol SUL4A	ECW B36F	1960	Cainey,Thornbury 18
484	EFJ	Leyland PD2A/30	Massey H31/26R	1962	Shorland,WETC
569	EFJ	AEC Reliance	Harrington C40F	1962	Rexquote,Bishops Lyd.
969	EHW	Bristol LD6G	ECW H33/25RD	1959	Walker &,Kemble
972	EHW	Bristol LD6B	ECW H33/25R	1959	Peters,Brislington
805	EVT	AEC Reliance	Weymann B41F	1960	Rexquote,Bishops Lyd.
898	FUF	Albion FT39AN	Reading B36F	1954	Greet,Broadhempston
86	GFJ	Leyland PD2A/30	Massey H31/26R	1963	Exeter City Council
931	GTA	Leyland PDR1/1	MC O44/31F	1961	Hulme,Bristol
63	GUO	Bristol MW6G	ECW DP41F	1961	Bissett,Westbury
606	HTC	Bedford SB3	Plaxton C35F	1959	Jacobs,Saltash
536	JHU	Bristol MW5G	ECW B45F	1961	Rexquote,Bishops Lyd.
120	JRB	Daimler D650HS	Burlingham C37F	1959	Rexquote,Bishops Lyd.
815	KDV	Bristol FLF6B	ECW H38/30F	1963	Hoare,WETC
824	KDV	Bristol FLF6G	ECW H38/30F	1963	Stevens,Plymouth
270	KTA	Bristol SUL4A	ECW B37F	1962	Western National 1420
407	LHT	Bristol MW6G	RV	1961	Bissett,Westbury
991	MDV	AEC Reliance	Marshall B41F	1963	991 Group,WETC
904	OFM	Bristol SC4LK	ECW C33F	1960	Taylor,Kemble
862	RAE	Bristol SUS4A	ECW B30F	1962	Staniforth,Kemble
1	RDV	AEC Reliance	Harrington C41F	1964	Allmey,WETC
7	RDV	AEC Reliance	Harrington C41F	1964	Warren,Martock
9	RDV	AEC Reliance	Marshall B49F	1964	Cope,WETC
503	RUO	AEC Regent V	WK H39/30F	1964	Greet,Broadhempston
870	VAR	Bedford SB3	Plaxton C41F	1964	Jacobs,Saltash
891	VFM	Bristol FSF6G	ECW O34/26F	1962	Rexquote,Bishops Lyd.
100	VRL	AEC Reliance	Harrington C43F	1964	Thomas,St Austell
ABD	812A	Maudslay ML3BC	Thurgood C35F	1931	Baldwin,Ilminster
ADM	419A	Bristol LD6G	ECW H33/27RD	1957	Rexquote,Bishops Lyd.
ADV	854A	Leyland PD2/12	Leyland H30/26R	1953	Rexquote,Bishops Lyd.
AFE	719A	AEC Reliance	Weymann OB40F	1962	Rexquote,Bishops Lyd.
AJH	163A	AEC Reliance	Plaxton C51F	1963	Jacobs,Saltash 10
AOR	631A	Bristol LHS6L	Duple C35F	1975	Preston,Bath
AEL	2B	Bristol MW6G	ECW C39F	1964	Mills,Netheravon
AFJ	77B	AEC Reliance	Harrington C41F	1964	Rundell,Falmouth
AHN	455B	Daimler CCG5DD	Roe H33/28R	1964	Rexquote,Bishops Lyd.
AYA	448B	Bedford CA	? B ?	1964	Yeo,Chippenham
BHU	92C	Bristol MW6G	ECW C39F	1965	Walker,Wookey
CTT	513C	AEC Regent V	PR H40/29F	1965	Shears,WETC
CWN	629C	Bristol MW6G	ECW B45F	1965	Neale,Kemble
CYD	724C	AEC Reliance	Harrington C41F	1965	Rexquote,Bishops Lyd.
DAX	610C	Bristol MW6G	ECW B45F	1965	Woodcock,Weymouth
DBC	190C	AEC Renown	EL H44/31F	1965	190 Group,Gloucester
DDR	201C	Leyland PDR1/1	MC H43/34F	1965	Ruby,Plymouth
EDD	685C	Bedford SB13	Duple C41F	1965	Willetts,Pillowell
DFE	963D	Bristol FS5G	ECW H33/27RD	1966	Preston,Bath
DPV	65D	AEC Regent V	Neepsend H37/28R	1966	Rexquote,Bishops Lyd.
EDV	505D	Bristol MW6G	ECW C39F	1966	Johnson,Stroud
FHT	15D	Bristol FLF6G	ECW H-F	1966	Staniforth,Kemble
FHW	158D	Bristol FLF6B	ECW H38/32F	1966	Bristol Ind. Museum
HAD	915D	Bedford VAM5	Plaxton C45F	1966	Sabin,Nailsea
HHW	452D	Bristol MW5G	ECW B45F	1966	Furness,Bristol
MRO	146D	Bedford VAS2	Plaxton C-F	1966	Matthews,Plympton
OJH	306D	Bedford VAS1	Plaxton C29F	1966	Leighfield,Grittenham
HDV	626E	Bristol RELL6G	ECW B53F	1967	Hembry,Hazelbury Bryn
HJA	965E	Leyland PD2/40	Neepsend H36/28R	1967	Rexquote,Bishops Lyd.
JAM	145E	Daimler CVG6-30DD	NC H40/30F	1967	Thamesdown 145
JHW	68E	Bristol FLF6B	ECW H38/32F	1967	Hewgill,Cashes Green
KHW	309E	Bristol RELL6L	ECW B44D	1967	Jennings,Paulton

MRC 565E	Leyland PSU4/3R	Plaxton C20FL	1967	Hayward,Fishponds
BKX 94F	Bedford J2SZ10	Plaxton C20F	1968	Ryland,Gloucester
JCP 60F	Leyland PLSC1	Leyland B31F	1928	Science Mus,Wroughton
KED 546F	Leyland Panther Cub	East Lancs B41D	1967	Amos,Nailsea
LUO 47F	AEC Reliance	WK DP47F	1968	? ,Truro
MAA 260F	Bedford VAL70	Plaxton C52F	1968	Greet,Broadhempston
NRL 101F	Bedford VAS5	Duple C29F	1968	Thomas,Roche
OHU 208F	Bedford CALV	MW B11	1968	M Lucas,Warminster
OHU 770F	Bristol RELL6L	ECW B53F	1968	J Smith,Bristol
PHT 227F	BMC 550FG	LG B22F	1968	UBHT,Bristol
KJH 230G	AEC Reliance	Plaxton C53F	1969	Jacobs,Saltash 7
OTA 290G	Bristol VRT/SL6G	ECW H39/31F	1969	Western National 1056
OUH 177G	Leyland PSU3A/4R	Plaxton C49F	1969	Parsons,Westbury
PHA 505G	BMMO S22	DP45F	1968	Rowley,Yelverton
TYC 250G	AEC Reliance	Willowbrook B45F	1968	Hayward,Fishponds
FVW 705H	Ford R226	Plaxton C49F	1969	Jacobs,Saltash 2
POD 829H	Bristol RELL6G	ECW B53F	1969	Cudlipp,Henstridge
RDV 423H	Bristol RELH6G	ECW C45F	1970	Williams,Cromhall
RLJ 793H	Bristol LH6L	ECW B39D	1970	Mills &,Netheravon
SNT 925H	Bedford VAL70	Plaxton C53F	1970	James,Tetbury
UHU 221H	Bristol RELL6L	ECW B44D	1969	C1119 PG,Gloucester
WHW 374H	Bristol RELH6L	ECW DP49F	1970	Stroud RE Group
AHT 206J	Bristol RELL6L	ECW B50F	1971	Tarling,Westerleigh
CYA 181J	AEC Reliance	Plaxton B47F	1970	Rexquote,Bishops Lyd.
LRN 60J	Bristol VRLLH6L	ECW CH42/18CT	1971	Preston,Kemble
TDK 686J	AEC Reliance	Plaxton C48F	1971	Rexquote,Bishops Lyd.
TDV 217J	Leyland PSUR1B/1R	Marshall B-D	1970	West Country HOTT
UMR 953J	Bedford YRQ	Plaxton C45F	1971	Carrie-C.,Warminster
WHL 666J	Bedford J2SZ10	Plaxton C20F	1971	Leighfield,Grittenham
WJH 129J	Bedford VAL70	DN C-F	1971	Greet,Broadhempston
YHT 802J	Bristol RESL6L	ECW B43F	1970	Stanton,Gloucester
CDD 235K	Bedford VAL70	Plaxton C53F	1972	Grindle,Drybrook
DAE 511K	Bristol RELL6L	ECW B50F	1972	Stroud RE Group
EHU 373K	Bristol RELL6L	ECW B53F	1972	Williams,Bristol
GYC 160K	Bristol LH6L	ECW B-F	1972	Hitchens,Kemble
MJP 59K	AEC Reliance	Plaxton C51F	1972	Tomlinson,Tewkesbury
NWW 163K	Bristol LH6L	Plaxton C45F	1972	Hobbs,Liskeard
VOD 88K	Bristol LHS6L	Marshall B25F	1972	Staddon,Exeter
VOD 124K	Bristol LHS6L	Marshall B33F	1972	Derrick,Plymstock
VOD 125K	Bristol LHS6L	Marshall B33F	1972	Western National 1255
AUP 651L	Bedford VAS5	Plaxton C29F	1973	Babb,Blue Anchor
BCD 820L	LN 1151/1R	B49F	1973	Science Mus,Wroughton
BDV 318L	Bristol LH6L	Marshall C39F	1973	Cocks,Carnmenellis
FDG 468L	AEC Reliance	Plaxton C45F	1973	Rexquote,Bishops Lyd.
GDF 650L	AEC Reliance	Plaxton C53F	1973	Berry & Berry,Bristol
HHW 920L	Bristol RELL6L	ECW B44D	1973	Peters,Bristol
LHT 171L	Bristol RELL6L	ECW B50F	1973	Stanley,Bristol
MJH 280L	Seddon Pennine 4	Plaxton C44F	1973	Greenleas Coll.,Bow
MMH 128L	AEC Reliance	Plaxton C45C	1973	Cainey,Stroud
MRO 200L	Bedford VAL70	Plaxton C53F	1973	Smith,Pylle
MUR 218L	AEC Reliance	Plaxton C51F	1973	Cainey,Stroud
VJT 307L	Bedford SB5	Plaxton C41F	1973	K Lucas,Warminster
NAF 443M	Bedford YRQ	Duple C45F	1973	Tomlinson,Gunnislake
NEL 845M	Bristol LH6L	ECW B43F	1973	Mills &,Netheravon
NFJ 592M	Bristol LH6L	ECW B43F	1973	Delbridge,Buckfastlgh
NTT 135M	Bedford YRQ	Plaxton C45F	1973	Jacobs,Saltash
OAE 954M	Bristol RELL6L	ECW B50F	1973	Peters,Bristol
OAE 957M	Bristol RELL6L	ECW B-F	1973	Hoare,WETC
OCT 990M	Bedford YRQ	Duple C45F	1974	Tomlinson,Gunnislake
OHU 38M	Bristol RELL6L	ECW B44D	1973	Hewlett,Bristol
OWC 719M	Bristol RELL6L	ECW B53F	1973	? ,Gloucestershire
PUO 331M	Bristol LH6L	Plaxton C39F	1974	Staniforth,Kemble
GNM 235N	Bristol LHL6L	Plaxton C51F	1975	Shears & Rowley,WETC
GPD 318N	Bristol LHS6L	ECW B35F	1975	Russell &,Truro
GYB 727N	Bedford YRQ	Plaxton C45F	1974	Smith,Pylle
HTA 844N	LN 11351/1R	B49F	1975	Gilmore &,Plymouth
JBN 947N	LN 11351/1R	B52F	1975	Williams,Bristol
JEU 509N	Bristol RELH6L	Plaxton C49F	1975	Bissett,Westbury
JFJ 498N	Bristol LH6L	Plaxton C45F	1975	Fricker &,Exeter

```
JFJ 502N  Bristol LH6L        Plaxton C45F    1975  Cainey,Stroud
JFJ 507N  Bristol LH6L        Plaxton C45F    1975  Pratt,Buckfastleigh
JFJ 508N  Bristol LH6L        Plaxton C45F    1975  Grey & Allen,Devon
KGR 491N  Bristol LHS6L       Duple C35F      1975  Hembry,Hazelbury Bryn
KHT 122P  LN 11351/1R         B52F            1976  Stanton,Gloucester
KHU 323P  Bristol LH6L        RV              1976  Stroud RE Group
KHU 326P  Bristol LH6L        ECW B43F        1976  Staniforth,Kemble
KOU 791P  BL VRT/SL3/6LXB     ECW H39/31F     1976  Williams,Bristol
KTT  43P  Bristol LH6L        ECW B43F        1975  Greet,Broadhempston
MPX 945R  Ford Transit        Robin Hood C-F  1977  Shears,WETC
MUN 942R  AEC Reliance        Plaxton C57F    1976  Berry & Platt,Bristol
OTG  44R  AEC Reliance        Duple C41F      1976  Greenleas Coll.,Bow
PNU 388R  Bristol LHS6L       ECW B35F        1976  Hayward,Fishponds
PPH 471R  Bristol VRT/SL3/501 ECW H43/31F     1977  M Smith,Bristol
RCV 296R  AEC Reliance        Plaxton C57F    1976  Platt,Crediton
ADD 341S  AEC Reliance        Duple C53F      1977  Platt,WETC
UPB 308S  LN 10351A/1R        B41F            1977  Potten,WETC
UPB 309S  LN 10351A/1R        B41F            1977  Potten,WETC
AFJ 692T  Bristol LH6L        Plaxton C41F    1978  Derrick,Plymstock
AFJ 727T  Bristol LH6L        Plaxton C41F    1979  West Country HOTT
AFJ 739T  Bristol LH6L        Plaxton C43F    1979  Grey & Pratt,Devon
CRM 927T  Leyland-DAB         AB-D            1979  Chambers,Exeter
JAB   5T  Volvo B58-56        Plaxton C53F    1979  Lear,Bratton Clovelly
TWS 910T  BL VRT/SL3/6LXB     ECW H43/27D     1979  Bristol Aero,Kemble
VAE 499T  LN 10351B/1R        B44F            1979  Staniforth,Kemble
AHW 200V  BL VRT/SL3/6LXB     ECW H43/27D     1980  Williams,Kemble
ECV 212V  Leyland PSU3E/4R    Duple C53F      1980  Grey,Exmouth
EHE 526V  Bedford CF          Plaxton C17F    1980  Jones,Yatton
HFG 923V  LN NL116L11/1R      B52F            1980  Vine,Yeovil
LSU 381V  Leyland AN68A/1R    AR H45/33F      1979  Hoare,WETC
DHW 351W  Bristol VRT/SL3/680 ECW H43/31F     1981  Stanley &,Bristol
HUD 496W  BL VRT/SL3/6LXB     ECW H43/27D     1980  Hewlett,Bristol
A686 KDV  Leyland ONLXB/1R    ECW H45/32F     1983  West Country HOTT
A927 MDV  Ford Transit        Carlyle B16F    1983  West Country HOTT
C416 AHT  Ford Transit        Carlyle B16F    1986  Williams,Bristol
C862 DYD  Ford Transit        Robin Hood B16F 1985  West Country HOTT
C519 FFJ  Ford Transit        Carlyle B16F    1986  Fricker,Crediton
C671 FFJ  Ford Transit        Carlyle B16F    1986  Fricker,Crediton
C719 FFJ  Ford Transit        Robin Hood B16F 1986  Platt,WETC
C748 FFJ  Ford Transit        Carlyle B16F    1986  Shears,WETC
C801 FRL  Mercedes-Benz L608D RB B20F         1986  West Country HOTT
D583 EWS  FR Sherpa           Dormobile B16F  1986  Fear,Farmborough
E489 MEL  MCW MF150           B23F            1987  Wilding,Shaftesbury
Q995 CPE  AEC Regent III      Park Royal O-R  1953  Cowdery,Newton Abbot
Q507 VHR  Bristol MW6G        RV              1961  Staniforth,Kemble
```

~~~~~~
```
ASV 900*ETP 184(5/86), BAS 563*MDL 952(1/02), BAS 564*MDL 955(1/02),
CMG 30*JTA 608(5/67) & CMG 30(?/43), DFP 496*653(8/83),
DSV 715*43 EBK(5/85) & ERV 34(?/83),
EMW 284*YSV 610(7/91) & EMW 284(5/86), HIL 7081*DJF 631T(3/02),
MCO 658*ADV 935A(4/92) & MCO 658(6/88),
MLL 528*UVS 678(3/00) & XKE 164A(3/93) & MLL 589(11/89),
MVS 972*PRN 911(2/93), RFO 361*241 AJB(9/96),
RFO 375*Q402 JDV(10/97) & 6436(7/85), WSL 115*KEL 95(1/01),
898 FUF*1787(5/98) & 898 FUF(4/86) & 1787(7/83),
931 GTA*NAT 747A(11/91) & 931 GTA(5/89), ABD 812A*NV 30(6/90),
ADM 419A*ACA 194A(1/89) & 848 AFM(8/84), ADV 854A*HJY 297(2/88),
AFE 719A*325 NKT(2/89), AJH 163A*XBW 242(6/85), AOR 631A*HAX 399N(3/93),
AFJ 77B*8229(4/99) & J 16554(1/81) & AFJ 77B(2/76), JCP 60F*J 4601(7/68),
LRN 60J*ARU 199A(5/95) & ARU 500A(9/90) & IJI 5367(1/90) & LRN 60J(4/88),
VOD 88K*12728(11/98) & VOD 88K(1/85),
VJT 307L*VHR 828(1/98) & VJT 307L(1/91), JBN 947N*MAN 15D(10/94),
JEU 509N*CSV 524(9/87) & GJD 194N(3/85),
JFJ 498N*31909(?/01) & JFJ 498N(5/92),
JFJ 502N*31907(?/01) & 31907(?/90) & JFJ 502N(6/85),
JFJ 507N*31914(?/01) & 12723(?/90) & JFJ 507N(12/84),
JFJ 508N*31915(?/01) & 12727(?/90) & JFJ 508N(2/85),
MPX 945R*6768(8/88) & MPX 945R(4/84),
RCV 296R*244 AJB(2/00) & MUN 942R(5/89),
```

ADD 341S*1223 PL(8/90) & FCG 309S(5/90),
A686 KDV*MAN 57N(8/01) & A686 KDV(3/96), Q995 CPE*NLP 581(5/86) &
Q507 VHR*404 LHT(1/98)

~~~~~~

PI   PRESERVED VEHICLES ON THE ISLANDS

J	7247	Bedford OB	Duple C29F	1950	Tantivy Motors(J)
J	7682	Seddon Pennine 4	Pennine B32F	1968	Bell,St Helier(J)
AY	81	Albion FT39AN	Heaver B35F	1957	Curtis(AY)
VVS	913	Austin CXB	Barnard B33F	1948	Twynham,Hugh Town(SI)

~~~~~~

J 7247*JAB 661(5/97), AY 81*YFF 660(1/96) & 3338(9/94) &
VVS 913*4510(4/93) & 2725(6/84) & 4510(?/80)

~~~~~~

X   OTHER NON-PSV VEHICLES IN THIS BOOK AREA

CSH 739	Volvo B58-61	Plaxton C53F	DTS,Wellington
JIL 7169	Ford R1114	Plaxton C53F	? ,Keynsham
OIW 1303	Bova EL26/581	C ?F	WDTS,Weston-super-Mare
OIW 3286	Bedford YMT	Plaxton C49F	WDTS,Weston-super-Mare
WOI 730	Mercedes-Benz L508D	Deansgate C21F	Broomwood Sea Angling Club
XDG 779	Ford R1114	Duple C35F	Spartans RFC,Gloucester
387 FJF	Bedford SB5	Duple C41F	Deighton Bros,Barnstaple
LDS 162A	AEC Routemaster	Park Royal H-R	Science Museum,Wroughton
CCV 166C	Bedford SB5	Duple C41F	Chris Bonnington,Bude
ETO 463C	Leyland PDR1/2	MC H-D	London Bus Export,Lydney
FPT 581C	AEC Routemaster	Park Royal H-F	Bertie Bus,Tewkesbury
GBU 143D	Leyland PDR1/1	Roe H-F	Protex,Bodmin
KGJ 622D	AEC Routemaster	Park Royal H-F	Bell,Coleford
FJY 914E	Leyland PDR1/1	MC H-F	RNAS Culdrose Gliding Club
GRS 114E	Leyland PDR1/1	AR O43/34F	Golden Coast,Woolacombe
JAM 144E	Daimler CVG6-30	NC H40/30F	Swindon Octobus Project
NNY 761E	AEC Regent V	MC H-F	Bateman,Wolvershill
MWV 150G	Daimler CRG6LX	NC H43/29F	Notaro,North Petherton
OCR 161G	Leyland PDR1/1	EL H45/31F	Cheltenham Fun Bus
OTA 287G	Bristol VRT/SL6G	ECW H-F	Greet,Broadhempsted
VML 4G	Leyland PDR2/1	Park Royal H-F	Longleat House
DDD 756H	Daimler CRG6LX	Park Royal H-C	Night Life,Weymouth
STO 538H	Leyland PDR1A/1	NC H47/30D	Pearce Seeds,Bradford Ab.
ARE 170J	Bedford SB5	Duple C41F	Chris Bonnington,Bude
EGP 36J	Daimler CRG6LXB	Park Royal H-C	Film Wheels,Aylesbeare
FEH 172J	AEC Reliance	Alexander C-F	Bannerdown GC,Hullavington
NDR 509J	Leyland PDR2/1	Park Royal H-F	Real Outreach,Lydney
URO 859J	Bedford YRQ	Duple C45F	Malford Tug of War Team
WOW 535J	Leyland PDR1A/1	East Lancs H-F	Truro Youth Bus
WOW 549J	Leyland PDR1A/1	East Lancs H-F	Bristol Playbus
EOW 404L	Leyland AN68/1R	East Lancs H-F	Taunton Playgroup Assoc.
JHA 238L	Leyland PSU3B/2R	Marshall DP49F	Great Dorset Steam Fair
JHU 848L	LN 1151/2R	B-D	BTCV,Looe
MLH 374L	Daimler CRL6	MCW H-C	Film Wheels,Aylesbeare
NLG 104L	Ford R226	Duple C16F	New Life,Minehead
OCH 271L	Daimler CRG6LXB	Roe H-F	St Austell Speedway
PGP 202L	Bedford VAS5	Plaxton C25F	Street Town FC
PYJ 445L	Daimler CRG6LXB	Alexander H-D	James,St Day
EFH 222M	Bedford YRQ	Plaxton C22F	3 Counties,Gloucester
NAT 349M	Leyland AN68/1R	Roe H43/29F	Fun Bus,Barnstaple
RTA 637M	Bedford YRT	Duple C53F	Plymouth Ambassadors Band
SPT 174M	Bedford YRQ	Plaxton C41F	Chris Bonnington,Bude
WRR 365M	Bedford YRT	Duple C53F	Majorettes,Wiltshire
XRR 131M	Bristol VRT/SL2/6LX	ECW H-F	Bath Community Bus
YNA 277M	Daimler CRG6LXB	NC H-F	Bannerdown GC,Hullavington
GOG 598N	Daimler CRG6	MCW H-F	Triple M Fashions,Redruth
JAT 882N	Bedford YRT	Plaxton C53F	Moonlighting,Symonds Yat
JDV 179N	Bedford YRQ	Duple C-F	St Just Rugby Club
JRW 732N	Ford R1014	Plaxton C45F	Gloucester Spartans
SMU 726N	Daimler CRL6	MCW H-F	Newells Travels,Falmouth
TYG 374N	Bedford VAS5	Duple C29F	Charity Bus,Churchdown

JJG 6P	Leyland AN68/1R	ECW H-F	Bristol Playbus
JOV 718P	Bristol VRT/SL2/6LX	MCW O-F	Showground,Shepton Mallet
KFB 811P	Leyland PSU3C/4R	Plaxton C53F	Creedy,Bridgwater
KUC 907P	Daimler CRL6	MCW H-DL	Kingswood Bus Project
KUC 988P	Leyland FE30ALR	MCW H-F	Soundwell College
LHT 727P	Bristol VRT/SL3/501	ECW H11/16D	Bath Chronicle
LWG 275P	Bedford YRQ	Duple C45F	WDTS,Weston-super-Mare
MVO 790P	Bedford VAS5	Plaxton C ?F	? ,Warminster
MWP 492P	Bedford YRT	Duple C-F	Portbury,Exeter
MYK 38P	Ford R1114	Duple B-T	Hunter Flying Club,Exeter
TBW 450P	Bristol VRT/SL3/6LX	ECW H-F	Bristol Churches Youth Bus
LTK 100R	Leyland AN68A/1R	Roe H-F	Plymouth Playbus
OAM 333R	Bedford YMT	Plaxton C53F	North Petherton RFC
OTC 605R	Bristol LH6L	ECW B43F	Newfoundland Scout,Bristol
OVV 58R	Ford R1014	Duple B43F	Home Office,Moreton-Marsh
OYJ 66R	Leyland AN68A/1R	East Lancs H-F	Bath Playbus
PJA 956R	Ford R1114	Duple C53F	Palm Court Hotel,Falmouth
PNU 389R	Bristol LHS6L	ECW B-F	Godfrey,St Ives
PPE 660R	Bedford YMT	VHM C53F	Majorwrecks,Devizes
RBO 671R	Bedford YLQ	Plaxton C45F	Robinswood Ch,Gloucester
RDC 108R	Bristol VRT/SL3/6LXB	NC H-F	Johnson & Martin,Minehead
REL 402R	Leyland PSU3E/4R	Plaxton B55F	Weston-s-Mare Sea Cadets
UHG 722R	LN 11351A/1R	B-F	Teen CHallenge,Barnstaple
WYA 290R	Bedford SB	Marshall B35F	1446 Squadron ATC,Sidmouth
XMS 152R	Ford R1114	Duple C53F	Robinswood Ch,Gloucester
OCO 115S	Leyland AN68A/1R	Roe H-D	Eggbuckland Bus Project
SVJ 300S	Bedford YMT	Duple C-F	? ,Lydney
TPE 164S	LN 11351A/1R	B-F	Avon Youth Association
TPJ 59S	Bristol LHS6L	ECW B35F	? ,Lee Mill
UPB 303S	LN 10351A/1R	B-F	Avon Youth Association
USO 173S	Ford R1114	Alexander B-F	TC Snacks,Hartcliffe
VRP 527S	LN 11351A/1R	B49F	Broadwey,West Bay
WGY 593S	LN 11351A/3R	B33T	British Aerospace,Filton
WUM 101S	Leyland FE30AGR	Roe H-F	Bristol TV & Film Services
XFP 983S	Bedford YLQ	Caetano C45F	Home Office,Moreton-Marsh
CWU 140T	Leyland FE30AGR	Roe H-F	Bristol TV & Film Services
EGT 452T	LN 11351A/3R	B33T	British Aerospace,Filton
GDF 516T	Bedford YMT	Duple C53F	Gloster Gladiator Band
TFN 987T	Bristol VRT/SL3/6LXB	Willowbrook H-F	Bristol TV & Film Services
TFN 989T	Bristol VRT/SL3/6LXB	Willowbrook H-F	Bristol TV & Film Services
UMR 195T	Leyland FE30AGR	ECW H-F	Thamesdown Youth Christ
BJG 672V	Bristol VRT/SL3/6LXB	ECW H43/31F	Golden Coast,Woolacombe
CJH 167V	MCW Metrobus DR102	H-D	Weymouth College
FDV 828V	Leyland PSU3E/4R	Willowbrook C49F	Avon Youth Association
GPL 522V	Volvo B58-61	Plaxton C51F	? Rugby Club
JDG 111V	Bedford YMT	Plaxton C51F	Young Gloucestershire
LNV 65V	Ford R1114	Duple C-F	Figaro Furniture,Chippenhm
NWX 823V	Bedford SB5	Marshall B37F	VTT,Edington
RYC 69V	Bedford SB5	Marshall B37FA	Friendbury Driver Training
KLJ 667W	Bedford YRQ	Plaxton C45F	Dorset Police
NPV 442W	Bedford YLQ	Duple C-F	BJs Munch Bar
ORY 708W	Bedford YMT	Duple C53F	Spartans RFC,Gloucester
PNB 801W	Ford R1114	Plaxton C53F	Pool School,Camborne
VCA 453W	Bristol VRT/SL3/6LXB	ECW H-F	Bristol TV & Film Services
WYT 133W	Leyland CU335	WS B ?FL	Quantock Produce,Bathealtn
LCV 989X	Bedford SB	Strachan B36F	Doublebois Commercials
LUL 511X	Leyland CU335	WS B-F	St Lukes School,Swindon
NOC 382X	Ford R1114	Caetano C49F	Simpson Plant,St Merryn
SND 83X	Leyland PSU3B/4R	Duple C51F	Penwith College
TAD 991X	Bedford VAS5	WS B ?FL	Cotswold Rambler
TND 107X	Ford R1114	Duple C ?F	Central Riding Sch,Hutton
XHK 224X	Bristol VRT/SL3/6LXB	ECW H-F	Bristol TV & Film Services
SDW 237Y	Dennis Lancet	WS DP35F	Kennet District Council
A632 BCN	MCW Metrobus DR102	H-F	Bristol TV & Film Services
A 2 CNU	CVE Omni	B-F	Unwin,Lufton
A 18 PCT	Van Hool T818	CH-D	Elliott McDougall,Tormantn
A669 XGG	Leyland RT	Roe C-F	Bristol TV & Film Services
B873 UST	Leyland TRCTL11/3RH	Duple C-F	Bristol TV & Film Services
C552 BHY	Ford Transit	Dormobile B-F	Grinter,Yeovil

C130 CAT	Dennis DDA1006	East Lancs H-F	Bristol TV & Film Services
C657 FFJ	Ford Transit	Carlyle B16F	Torquay Fund Raiser
C658 FFJ	Ford Transit	Carlyle B16F	Exeter Community Health
C660 FFJ	Ford Transit	Carlyle B16F	Wheelgate School,Crantock
C735 FFJ	Ford Transit	Carlyle B-F	Davys Snacks,Trevarrian
C755 FFJ	Ford Transit	Carlyle B16F	Embassy Tavern,Paignton
C143 FYC	Dodge S56	RB B10FL	Somerset County Council
C144 FYC	Dodge S56	RB B10FL	Somerset County Council
C219 MDS	Auwaerter N122/3	CH-CT	Colin White,Glastonbury
C515 TJF	Ford Transit	Rootes B16F	? Darts Team,Bodmin
D522 FAE	Mercedes-Benz L608D	Dormobile B20F	Hengrove Athletic Club
D900 GEU	Fiat 49-10	Robin Hood B19F	Johns Garage,Weston-s-Mare
D 86 JHY	Dodge G10	WS B ?F	1st Backwell Scouts
D455 KYB	Fiat 49-10	? B25FL	Somerset County Council
D456 KYB	Fiat 49-10	? B25FL	Somerset County Council
D180 LTA	Dodge S56	RB B23F	T & GWU South West
D806 MNY	Dodge S56	East Lancs DP24F	Warminster Scouts
D144 NDT	Mercedes-Benz L608D	Whittaker C25F	TA Centre,Bridgwater
D 22 PVS	Freight Rover Sherpa	Dormobile B16F	Foxes Hotel,Minehead
D696 RKE	Dodge S46	Dormobile B16FL	2nd Stratton Scout Group
E374 KHT	Mercedes-Benz 609D	WS B9FL	North Somerset Council
E377 KHT	Mercedes-Benz 609D	WS B15FL	Bath & NE Somerset Council
E379 KHT	Mercedes-Benz 609D	WS B15FL	Bath & NE Somerset Council
E407 KHY	Renault S46	WS B20FL	Somerset County Council
E 50 KWS	Mercedes-Benz 609D	Robin Hood B15FL	South Gloucestershire Coun
E 52 KWS	Mercedes-Benz 609D	Robin Hood B11FL	North Somerset Council
E756 MJT	Mercedes-Benz 507D	? B14F	Sherborne Disabled
E110 NWP	Dodge G13	WS B16F	Cheltenham Driver Training
E116 NWP	Dodge G13	WS B39FA	Cotswold Training
E348 SYD	Mercedes-Benz 609D	? B12FL	Barngoose Garage,Redruth
E659 VHF	Fiat 40-8	Wright B18FL	? ,Gloucester
E667 VHF	Fiat 40-8	Wright B12FL	Oak Tree Lodge,Clevedon
E822 WDV	Ford Transit	Mellor B-F	Makeover Bus,Bristol
E676 WFJ	Mercedes-Benz 310	DC B17F	St Aubyns School,Tiverton
E 93 WWD	Dodge G13	WS B39FA	Cotswold Training
E663 XND	Mercedes-Benz 507D	Cunliffe B15FL	Earlfield Lodge,Weston-s-M
F468 EOD	Mercedes-Benz 507D	G & M B11FL	Lelant Home,Plymouth
F457 ETA	Mercedes-Benz 609D	G & M B4FL	Plymouth & Dist. Disabled
F281 FFJ	Fiat 49-10	DC B11FL	Puffins Play School,Exeter
F739 FJO	Mercedes-Benz 609D	? B14F	West Coast,Newquay
F 67 FMW	Talbot Freeway	B6FL	Burton Hill House School
F566 FYA	Mercedes-Benz 407D	DC B16F	Yeovil & District CVS
F394 GTA	Mercedes-Benz 307D	DC B17F	St Johns School,Sidbury
F913 OHW	Leyland RR8-13R	WS B18F	North Somerset Council
F114 SWS	Mercedes-Benz 609D	DC B-FL	Avon Ambulance Service
F115 SWS	Mercedes-Benz 609D	DC B-FL	Avon Ambulance Service
F612 TGL	Renault S46	Dormobile B18FL	Cornwall County Council
F613 TGL	Renault S46	Dormobile B18FL	Cornwall County Council
F 29 TMP	Leyland LBM6T/1RS	RB B24FL	Bath & NE Somerset Council
F975 WEF	CVE Omni	B20D	Calvert Trust,Exmoor
F414 YAJ	CVE Omni	B16F	Churchtown Farm,Lanlivery
G640 CGL	Renault S46	Dormobile B18FL	Cornwall County Council
G641 CGL	Renault S46	Dormobile B18FL	Cornwall County Council
G657 EVN	CVE Omni	DP9F	MSS,Barnstaple
G347 GAJ	CVE Omni	B8F	Churchtown Farm,Lanlivery
G131 GEY	Mercedes-Benz 609D	DC B18FL	St Loyes College,Exeter
G863 LYC	Fiat 49-10	Dormobile B14FL	Somerset County Council
G461 NMW	Mercedes-Benz 308D	DC B10F	Wiltshire Fire Brigade
G465 ODT	Leyland LBM6T/1RS	RB B28FL	North Somerset Council
G468 ODT	Leyland LBM6T/1RS	RB B28FL	Bath & NE Somerset Council
G929 SHR	Mercedes-Benz 508D	G & M B15FL	PHAB,Devizes
G 33 VHT	Mercedes-Benz 609D	Robin Hood B15FL	South Gloucestershire Coun
G731 WOD	Mercedes-Benz 408D	G & M B7FL	Roborough Nursing Home
G253 XDV	Mercedes-Benz 508D	G & M B4FL	Plymouth & Dist. Disabled
G351 XHY	Mercedes-Benz 609D	Steedrive B15FL	Maytrees Home,Bristol
H891 AAE	Mercedes-Benz 609D	Steedrive B15FL	Bath & NE Somerset Council
H529 BOD	Mercedes-Benz 508D	G & M B17FL	Torbay Council
H370 EFK	Iveco 49-10	Mellor B9FL	Bristol Dial-A-Ride
H718 FWD	Talbot Freeway	B ?F	Calne Community Tpt

H597 GDV	Mercedes-Benz 609D	G & M B16FL	Devon County Council
H 51 GLP	Mercedes-Benz 308D	PG B6FL	Bethesda Church,Weston-s-M
H446 SYB	Mercedes-Benz 408D	DC B11FL	Yeovil & District CVS
H428 UYB	Renault S66	WS B8FL	Somerset County Council
J582 FFB	Mercedes-Benz 609D	Steedrive B15FL	Bath & NE Somerset Council
J690 FWS	Mercedes-Benz 410D	DC B12FL	Chippenham & Dist Disabled
J735 KTT	Mercedes-Benz 410D	G & M B10FL	Mount Gould Hospital
J570 LDF	Mercedes-Benz 609D	DC B2FL	Chamwell School,Gloucester
J305 OTT	Mercedes-Benz 508D	DC B9FL	Gloucester Dial-A-Ride
K938 AEP	Mercedes-Benz 408D	PVB B10FL	Yeovil & District CVS
K443 GYD	Mercedes-Benz 410D	Frank Guy B14FL	Yeovil & District CVS
K445 GYD	Mercedes-Benz 508D	Frank Guy B14FL	Mendip CVS
K446 GYD	Mercedes-Benz 410D	? B11FL	Yeovil & District CVS
K245 MMR	Mercedes-Benz 609D	G & M B16FL	PHAB,Devizes
K 46 NEU	Mercedes-Benz 410D	DC B15F	Warmley Tower School
K483 OAF	Mercedes-Benz 609D	DC DP13FL	Cornwall Disabled Assoc.
K966 OEU	Mercedes-Benz 609D	Frank Guy B15FL	Bath & NE Somerset Council
K967 OEU	Mercedes-Benz 609D	Frank Guy B14FL	Bath & NE Somerset Council
K968 OEU	Mercedes-Benz 609D	Frank Guy B14FL	North Somerset Council
L 21 THU	Mercedes-Benz 814D	Mellor B24FL	South Gloucestershire Coun
L 89 TOU	Mercedes-Benz 814D	Mellor B32FL	South Gloucestershire Coun
L 93 TOU	Mercedes-Benz 814D	Mellor B32FL	South Gloucestershire Coun
L943 UEU	Mercedes-Benz 609D	Frank Guy B15FL	Bath & NE Somerset Council
L703 VHY	Mercedes-Benz 814D	Mellor B32FL	South Gloucestershire Coun
L705 VHY	Mercedes-Benz 711D	Mellor B24FL	North Somerset Council
L706 VHY	Mercedes-Benz 711D	Mellor B24FL	North Somerset Council
L707 VHY	Mercedes-Benz 711D	Mellor B24FL	North Somerset Council
L709 VHY	Mercedes-Benz 711D	Mellor B24FL	North Somerset Council
L710 VHY	Mercedes-Benz 711D	Mellor B24FL	South Gloucestershire Coun
L711 VHY	Mercedes-Benz 711D	Mellor B24FL	Bath & NE Somerset Council
L153 XDD	Iveco 49-10	Dormobile B16FL	Cheltenham Lions Club
M405 BNJ	Mercedes-Benz 410D	Bacon B5FL	Leonard Cheshire,Timsbury
M977 CCV	Iveco 49-10	DC B12FL	Cornwall County Council
M549 DAF	Iveco 40-10	DC B12FL	Cornwall County Council
M550 DAF	Iveco 40-10	DC B12FL	Cornwall County Council
M552 DAF	Iveco 40-10	DC B12FL	Cornwall County Council
M988 GDF	Mercedes-Benz 308D	DC B ?FL	Gloucester Chinese Women
M221 GTT	Mercedes-Benz 410D	? B ?FL	Torr Home Blind,Plymouth
M597 JDV	Mercedes-Benz 410D	G & M B12FL	Dame Hannah Rogers School
M917 OCV	Iveco 49-10	? B ?F	Duchy,Stoke Climsland
M 56 PCY	Mercedes-Benz 711D	? B29F	Somerset County Council
M582 SSX	Iveco 59-12	Keillor B13FL	Somerset County Council
M371 VYB	Mercedes-Benz 410D	Deansgate B12FL	Yeovil & District CVS
M626 XCM	Iveco 49-10	? B ?FL	Star Centre,Ullenwood
N779 CKB	Iveco 40-10	Whittaker B ?FL	Star Centre,Ullenwood
N586 DYD	Iveco 49-10	G & M B6FL	Penrose School,Bridgwater
N323 FEH	Mercedes-Benz 410D	Whittaker B5FL	Disabled Group,Patchway
N395 JWS	Mercedes-Benz 609D	TBP B15FL	North Somerset Council
N396 JWS	Mercedes-Benz 609D	TBP B15FL	Bath & NE Somerset Council
N812 KHW	Mercedes-Benz 611D	TBP B12FL	Bath & NE Somerset Council
N813 KHW	Mercedes-Benz 814D	Mellor B24FL	South Gloucestershire Coun
N531 KWS	Mercedes-Benz 609D	TBP B ?FL	North Somerset Council
N926 LEU	Mercedes-Benz 609D	Crystals C24F	Our Lady of Lourdes School
N919 PHB	Iveco 59-12	Bedwas DP24FL	Municipal Hire,Shirehamptn
N654 TTA	Iveco 49-10	Pentagon B ?FL	Somerset County Council
N655 TTA	Iveco 49-10	Pentagon B ?FL	Somerset County Council
N648 UOE	Talbot Freeway	B ?F	Calne Community Tpt
N650 UOE	Peugeot Boxer(3)	TBP B15FL	Sherborne Disabled
P719 COD	Mercedes-Benz 412D	G & M B16FL	Devon County Council
P984 EOD	Iveco 40-10	? B14FL	Somerset County Council
P798 JYD	Mercedes-Benz 412D	? B15F	British Red Cross,Yeovil
P806 JYD	Mercedes-Benz 412D	Frank Guy B16FL	Blagdon Valley Minibus
P677 OCV	Iveco 35-10	DC B12FL	Redruth Senior Citizens
P736 PAF	Iveco 40-10	Mellor B16FL	Cornwall County Council
P533 RAF	Iveco 49-10	Mellor B ?FL	Cornwall County Council
P575 RUL	Volkswagen LT35	DC B12FL	Bath Community Transport
P827 SAF	Iveco 59-12	Mellor B25F	Duchy,Stoke Climsland
P501 SCV	Iveco 35-10	Mellor B12FL	Cornwall County Council
P913 SUM	Optare Excel L1070	B34F	British Telecom,Goonhilly

```
P914 SUM  Optare Excel L1150   B48F                 British Telecom,Goonhilly
P915 SUM  Optare Excel L1150   B48F                 British Telecom,Goonhilly
P288 SUV  Volkswagen LT35      ? B ?FL              Newent Dial-a-Ride
P276 THW  Iveco 40-10          Euromotive B16F      Colstons Collegiate School
P 43 VDF  Mercedes-Benz 412D   ? B6FL               Spa-Trek,Cheltenham
P556 WWS  Iveco ?              UVG B ?FL            Stow Disabled Association
Q130 REU  Bedford SB5          Marshall B18F        Six Pilgrims,Weston-s-Mare
R558 ACV  Iveco 40-10          G & M B14F           Wedmore Community Tpt
R 61 FAE  Mercedes-Benz 310D   Mellor B12F          Avon Autistic Foundation
R624 HKX  Mercedes-Benz 410D   Whitacre B12FL       Mendip Community Tpt
R865 KGU  Volkswagen LT35      ? B ?F               Thornbury & District CB
R915 KGU  Volkswagen LT35      ? B ?FL              Bath Community Transport
R110 NMR  Mercedes-Benz 410D   Frank Guy B16F       Yeo Valley Lions,Clevedon
R101 PBW  Volkswagen LT35      Whitacre B11FL       Orchard Homes,Henbury
R918 SDF  Mercedes-Benz 410D   Whitacre B ?FL       Gloucester Dial-a-Ride
R488 UYA  Volkswagen LT35      Kirkham B13FL        Yeovil & District CVS
R109 UYC  Iveco 35-12          Courtside B16F       Somerset Rural Youth
R110 UYC  Iveco 35-12          Courtside B16F       Somerset Rural Youth
R112 UYC  Iveco 35-12          Courtside B11F       Somerset Rural Youth
R129 WYD  Iveco 49-10          G & M B8FL           Somerset County Council
R130 WYD  Iveco 49-10          G & M B8FL           Somerset County Council
R131 WYD  Iveco 49-10          G & M B8FL           Somerset County Council
S687 KHY  Mercedes-Benz O814D  ? DP12FL             Bath & NE Somerset Council
S688 KHY  Mercedes-Benz O814D  ? DP12FL             Bath & NE Somerset Council
S842 SNM  Mercedes-Benz 410D   Euromotive B ?FL     Clevedon Community Tpt
S696 WYC  Iveco 49-10          G & M B12FL          Somerset County Council
S697 WYC  Iveco 49-10          G & M B5FL           Somerset County Council
T762 AFJ  Mercedes-Benz 814D   G & M B ?FL          Vranch House School,Exeter
T163 CGX  Volkswagen LT35      Courtside B11FL      Bath Community Transport
T561 CGX  Volkswagen LT35      ? B ?FL              Newent Dial-a-Ride
T158 JCV  Dennis Javelin       SCC C48DL            Cornwall Disabled,Truro
T440 JLD  Iveco 40-10          Courtside B11FL      Age Concern,Barnstaple
T483 JYC  Iveco 45-10          G & M B14FL          Penrose School,Bridgwater
T806 JYD  Mercedes-Benz 412D   Frank Guy DP15FL     Blagdon Valley Bus
T999 OSM  Mercedes-Benz 410D   ? B15FL              Ottery District Hospital
T191 RFB  Iveco 49-10          Frank Guy B11FL      Bristol Dial-a-Ride
T192 RFB  Iveco 49-10          Frank Guy B11FL      Bristol Dial-a-Ride
V250 GGS  Mercedes-Benz 411CDI ? B ?FL             Gloucester Dial-a-Ride
V870 HKV  Mercedes-Benz 410D   Mellor B14FL         Weston-s-Mare Dial-a-Ride
V739 KGU  Volkswagen LT46      Courtside B16FL      Bristol Community Tpt
V348 UUD  Volkswagen LT46      Courtside B16FL      Bristol Community Tpt
W178 BVP  Mercedes-Benz O814D  Mellor B16FL         Mendip District Council
W201 RWS  Iveco 59-12          Frank Guy B8FL       South Gloucestershire Coun
W202 RWS  Iveco 59-12          Frank Guy B8FL       South Gloucestershire Coun
W549 RYA  Iveco 49-10          G & M B6FL           Baysfield Children,Yeovil
W563 RYA  Iveco 49-10          ? B16FL              Sherborne Disabled
W277 SYA  Volkswagen LT46      Courtside B12FL      Yeovil & District CVS
W551 UFH  Volkswagen LT46      Advanced B14FL       Tewkesbury Association
W495 UGY  Volkswagen LT46      ? B16FL              Taunton East Action
W514 VGU  Volkswagen LT35      Courtside B16FL      Bristol Community Tpt
W679 VGW  Volkswagen LT35      ? B ?FL              Bath Community Transport
W736 XGS  Mercedes-Benz 412D   Courtside B ?FL      Gloucester Dial-a-Ride
X771 ADG  Dennis Dart SLF      East Lancs B-F       Gloucester Fire Brigade
X751 AHT  Iveco 59-12          Frank Guy B10FL      South Gloucestershire Coun
X529 BYD  Volkswagen LT ?      G & M B10FL          Somerset County Council
X689 BYD  Iveco 35S11          G & M B13FL          Somerset County Council
X437 CDW  Mercedes-Benz 411CDI UVG B15FL            Yate,Sodbury & District CT
X594 CWN  Mercedes-Benz 614D   Cymric B15FL         South Gloucestershire Coun
X595 CWN  Mercedes-Benz 614D   Cymric B9FL          South Gloucestershire Coun
X596 CWN  Mercedes-Benz 614D   Cymric B11FL         South Gloucestershire Coun
X597 CWN  Mercedes-Benz 614D   Cymric B11FL         South Gloucestershire Coun
X827 EBY  Mercedes-Benz 311CDI ? B16F               Royal High School,Bath
X233 HEU  Mercedes-Benz O814D  Frank Guy B10FL      South Gloucestershire Coun
X235 HEU  Mercedes-Benz O814D  Frank Guy B10FL      South Gloucestershire Coun
X237 HEU  Mercedes-Benz O814D  Frank Guy B10FL      South Gloucestershire Coun
X447 YWV  Volkswagen LT35      ? B ?F               Thomas Hardye,Dorchester
Y814 DRB  Mercedes-Benz 411CDI Frank Guy B16FL      RAFA Home,Weston-s-Mare
Y146 HAE  Iveco 40C11          Euromotive B16FL     Bath & NE Somerset Council
Y148 HAE  Iveco 40C11          Euromotive B16FL     Bath & NE Somerset Council
```

```
Y187 HAE  Volkswagen LT46        ? B16FL           Harry Foundation, ?
Y209 HAE  Volkswagen LT35        ? B16F            Ashton Park School
Y 61 HBT  Optare Solo M850       B26F              Exeter Airport 1
Y 62 HBT  Optare Excel L1150     B29D              Exeter Airport 2
Y 63 HBT  Optare Excel L1150     B29D              Exeter Airport 3
Y 64 HBT  Optare Excel L1150     B29D              Exeter Airport 4
Y297 MBM  Mercedes-Benz 314      ? B3FL            Disabled Hengrove
Y945 NYA  Iveco 45-10            G & M B6FL        Somerset County Council
Y994 NYA  Iveco 49-10            G & M B13FL       Somerset County Council
Y995 NYA  Iveco 49-10            G & M B13FL       Somerset County Council
Y871 PWT  Optare Solo M920       B29F              Bath & NE Somerset Council
Y872 PWT  Optare Solo M920       B29F              Bath & NE Somerset Council
Y873 PWT  Optare Solo M920       B29F              Bath & NE Somerset Council
Y874 PWT  Optare Solo M920       B29F              Bath & NE Somerset Council
Y875 PWT  Optare Solo M920       B29F              Bath & NE Somerset Council
CN51 BUA  Mercedes-Benz 413CDI UVG B ?FL           ? ,Tewkesbury
WA51 HXS  Volkswagen LT46        Courtside B10FL   Apollo Swimming,Yeovil
WA51 HXV  Volkswagen LT46        Courtside B12FL   Arthritis Care,Yeovil
WA51 HXX  Volkswagen LT46        Courtside B13FL   Yeovil & District CVS
WX51 EKM  Iveco ?                Euromotive B14FL  Bath & NE Somerset Council
UK02 EMT  Dennis R               Plaxton C-F       European Mobile Training
UR02 EMT  Dennis R               Plaxton C-F       European Mobile Training
```
```
CSH 739*PKH 601M(5/85),
JIL 7169*AVT 69S(8/95) & 5317 EH(10/92) & WVM 551S(?/87),
OIW 1303*    ? (?/??), OIW 3286*    ? (?/??),
WOI 730*982 RUO(3/94) & NNE 59W(3/92),
XDG 779*UJW 822Y(5/94) & OHA 106(2/94) & CVH 732Y(9/92),
LDS 162A*WLT 794(11/89), DDD 756H*PLA 9(2/89) & SOE 899H(3/86),
EFH 222M*YCT 502(?/86) & NCJ 400M(5/84),
RTA 637M*8405 CD(7/87) & YJH 709M(8/79),
REL 402R*CSU 244(4/00) & REL 402R(8/87reb),
GDF 516T*5469 AD(4/93) & HGG 998T(5/88),
GPL 522V*XLH 570(4/96) & GPL 522V(4/84), SND 83X*HNE 644N(12/81reb),
A2 CNU*G653 EVN(7/92), A18 PCT*D267 GBP(8/98),
A669 XGG*MSU 464(5/91) & A164 TGE(4/89),
C130 CAT*CMN 53T(2/00) & C130 CAT(9/93) &
C219 MDS*YSV 570(5/96) & C564 NCA(12/91) & SEL 853(11/91) & C721 JTL(6/90)
```

XI   OTHER NON-PSV VEHICLES ON THE ISLANDS

```
  5597  Bristol LHS6L        Marshall B28F   Aurigny Airlines A1(J)
 31738  Dodge S56            Rootes B22FL    Morley Youth Hostel(G)
J  3159 Bedford SB3          Duple C41F      De La Salle College(J)
J 28091 Mercedes-Benz 407D   ? B19F          ITC Schools,St Brelade(J)
J 33643 Bedford SB3          Strachan C41F   Apart Hotels,Grouville(J)
J 35352 Bedford SB5          Duple C41F      Powell Driving School(J)
J 55137 Bedford VAS5         Duple C27F      De La Salle College(J)
J 79630 Mercedes-Benz 609D   RB B24F         De La Salle College(J)
PSC 310G Leyland PDR1A/1     Alexander H-D   British Show Jumping(G)
GHV 502N Bristol LHS6L       ECW B26F        St Marys Airport(S)
OJD 905R LN 10351A/2R        B21DL           Aurigny Airlines(J)
THX 121S LN 10351A/2R        B21DL           Jersey Airport(J)
AYR 308T LN 10351A/2R        B21DL           Jersey Airport(J)
BYW 403V LN 10351A/2R        B21DL           Jersey Airport(J)
```
```
5597*VOD 90K(1/85), J 35352*VOD 774K(6/78), J 55137*KGG 718N(8/91) &
J 79630*J 14675(12/97)
```

OPERATOR LOCATION INDEX

BRISTOL

BRISTOL   1(x4), 2,25,44,49,57,68,90,A1,E3,K2(x2),K3,N9,R7,V2,
                        V3

CORNWALL

BLACKWATER	K5	PADSTOW	3
BODMIN	3,V6	PAR	A3
BOSCOPPA	74	PELYNT	D7
BRANE	U5	PENRYN	J8
BUDE	C9,E9	PENZANCE	3,K1
CALLINGTON	3	RELUBBUS	U3
CAMBORNE	3,W3	ST AUSTELL	3,12,74
CARBIS BAY	A2	ST IVES	R8
CROWLAS	K4	ST JUST	3
DELABOLE	3	ST KEVERNE	J7
DOBWALLS	R1	SALTASH	70,F5
DULOE	22	SENNEN COVE	U2
FALMOUTH	3	SLADESBRIDGE	N4
GUNNISLAKE	79	SUMMERCOURT	V8
HELSTON	3,U8	TORPOINT	3
ILLOGAN HIGHWAY	51	TOWNSHEND	M5
LAUNCESTON	3	TREWOON	65
LISKEARD	3,88,H2	TRURO	3,U8
MILLBROOK	C8,N8	UPTON CROSS	87,88,J5
MOUNT HAWKE	F1	WADEBRIDGE	W7
NANPEAN	T2	WAINHOUSE CORNER	U4
NEWQUAY	3,T4		

DEVON

BARNSTAPLE	3	LEWDOWN	M2
BERE ALSTON	N5	LYNTON	H5
BIDEFORD	E5	MARY TAVY	95
BOW	W4	MEETH	E9
BRIXHAM	D9	MERTON	T7(x2)
BUCKFASTLEIGH	W6	MONKTON	G6
BUCKLAND BREWER	E7	MORETONHAMPSTEAD	E2
CHIVENOR	T3	NEWTON ABBOT	9,98,C5,L2
CHULMLEIGH	U9	NORTH TAWTON	M3
CLYST ST MARY	86	NORTHLEW	E4
COMBE MARTIN	H4	OKEHAMPTON	6
CULLOMPTON	6	OTTERY ST MARY	6,96
DALWOOD	N1	PAIGNTON	C1
DARTMOUTH	3	PAYHEMBURY	76
DAWLISH	84	PLYMOUTH	3, 4,48,50,72,C6,
DOLTON	V1		F8,M1,M4,U6,
EXETER	6,E9,J3	ROUSDON	G1
EXMOUTH	6	SAMPFORD PEVERELL	C2
GUNN	F3	SEATON	M9
HALWILL	D5	SHUTE	41
HARTLAND	E5	SIDMOUTH	6
HEATHFIELD	10,J2	SOUTH MOLTON	T5
HEMYOCK	L6	STIBB CROSS	E6
HOLSWORTHY	N6	TAVISTOCK	3
HONITON	2,G6,W7	TEDBURN ST MARY	H3
ILFRACOMBE	3,A9	TIVERTON	6,G3
IVYBRIDGE	26,K8,V7	TORQUAY	6,43,85,D9,L8,R9
KINGKERSWELL	G5	TOTNES	3, 8,81,A5
KINGSBRIDGE	3,V7	WILLAND	2,F4(x2)
LAPFORD	K9		

DORSET

BRIDPORT	2,D6	HAZELBURY BRYAN	J9
CHICKERELL	38	SHAFTESBURY	46(x2)
DORCHESTER	2,63(x2),92,97, W7	STURMINSTER NEWTON WEYMOUTH	2,J9 2,27,94
EAST CHALDON	93		

GLOUCESTERSHIRE

ANDOVERSFORD	20	MILKWALL	19
BERRY HILL	99	MINCHINHAMPTON	82
BOURTON-ON-WATER	L3	MITCHELDEAN	71,83
BUSSAGE	30	MORETON VALENCE	L1
CHELTENHAM	5,H8	NAILSWORTH	D8
CINDERFORD	29,31,78,D3,W1	NEWPORT	16
CIRENCESTER	5,11	NORTON	89
CLAYPITS	42	OLDBURY ON SEVERN	52
COALWAY	67	PATCHWAY	A1
CROMHALL	N2	PILLOWELL	W2
EBLEY	F7,G8	STROUD	5
GLOUCESTER	5,32,56,M7(x2)	TETBURY	F6
GOLDEN VALLEY	U1	TEWKESBURY	40,89
HARTPURY	E1	TOCKINGTON	69
HORSLEY	D8	WESTERLEIGH	A6
KILCOT	A7	WINCHCOMBE	55
LYDNEY	36	WOTTON-UNDER-EDGE	1
MARSHFIELD	14	YATE	1

SOMERSET

BATH	1,18,J4,M6,T1	MINEHEAD	2,V5
BATHAMPTON	K7	NAILSEA	62,T6
BIDDISHAM	21	NORTON FITZWARREN	73,L7
BISHOPS LYDEARD	L7	PAULTON	33
BLAGDON	37	PEASEDOWN ST JOHN	17
BRIDGWATER	2,24,V5	PILTON	N7
BRUTON	53	PYLLE	N7
BURNETT	28	RADSTOCK	1,59,60,61
BURNHAM-ON-SEA	2	SOUTH PETHERTON	D4
CHARD	2,G6	STANTON WICK	A8,C7,R3
CHILTON POLDEN	N3	TAUNTON	2,35
CLEVEDON	R5	THORNEY	G4
DULVERTON	L9	TINTINHULL	T8
FARMBOROUGH	J4	TRUDOXHILL	13
FROME	1,C4,F2	WELLINGTON	G6
GLASTONBURY	C3,V9	WELLS	1
HENSTRIDGE	77,91,H1,U7	WELTON	58
HORTON	D2	WESTON-SUPER-MARE	1,24,69,G7
KINGSBURY EPISCOPI	G4	WHEDDON CROSS	V5,
LANGLEY GREEN	L7	WILLITON	47
LULSGATE	45	WINCANTON	2,R4
MARTOCK	2	WINFORD	66
MEADGATE	K6	WIVELISCOMBE	2
MERRIOTT	R6	YATTON	F9,T6
MIDSOMER NORTON	L5	YEOVIL	2,J6,R2,R4,V4

WILTSHIRE

ASHTON KEYNES	A4	MIDDLEHALL	J1
BOX	J1	MINETY	G2
BRINKWORTH	D1	NETTLETON	64
CALNE	W5	SHRIVENHAM	34
CASTLE EATON	75	STRATTON ST MARG.	H9
CHIPPENHAM	5,K6,M8	STRATTON ST MARY	34
CHRISTIAN MALFORD	15	SWINDON	5, 7,80,G9(x2),T9
CORSHAM	15	TROWBRIDGE	1,18
DEVIZES	1	WARMINSTER	L4
FOXHAM	E8	WESTBURY	23
LONGBRIDGE DEVER.	54	WORTON	39
LOWER WANBOROUGH	H7	WROUGHTON	H6

The only depot outside the area of this publication is: ROSS-ON-WYE(5)

OTHER BOOKS FROM THE PUBLISHERS

1:LONDON: 12950+ Vehicles	£14.00
2:SOUTHERN ENGLAND: 8750+ Vehicles	£14.00
3:SOUTH WEST ENGLAND: 7100+ Vehicles	£12.00
4:EAST ANGLIA: 8700+ Vehicles	£14.00
5:WEST MIDLANDS: 8600+ Vehicles	£ *
6:WALES: 5700+ Vehicles	£10.00
7:EAST MIDLANDS: 7750+ Vehicles	£12.00
8:NORTH WEST ENGLAND: 10750+ Vehicles	£14.00
9:NORTH EAST ENGLAND: 9500+ Vehicles	£14.00
10:SCOTLAND: 10300+ Vehicles	£14.00

The above books with prices are available from us,those marked * being sold out.
Please add 80p postage on one volume,two or more post free,orders to:

TAG PUBLICATIONS
36 Poole Road
West Ewell
Surrey
KT19 9SH

POST FREE STANDING ORDERS are also available from us if you wish to receive our titles as soon as we get them back from the printers,we'll send them to you and invoice you for the cost.

REGISTRATION INDEX

KPT	909	P	LRR	655	P	MIL	4680	E9	NIL	5069	J3	OLG	855	P			
KSK	984	U6	LRV	992	P	MIL	5577	W4	NIL	5381	24	OLJ	291	P			
KSK	985	U6	LSK	473	U6	MIL	5578	W4	NIL	5382	24	OMB	161	P			
KSU	454	T2	LSK	481	U6	MIL	5579	W4	NIL	5651	79	OTT	55	P			
KSU	460	K8	LSK	498	U6	MIL	5991	W4	NIL	5652	79	OTT	98	P			
KSU	468	E7	LSK	499	U6	MIL	5992	W4	NIL	5813	OS	OXI	483	K1			
KSU	476	E6	LSK	500	U6	MIL	6682	W4	NIL	6094	8	OXI	499	K1			
KTF	594	P	LSK	501	U6	MIL	6685	W4	NIL	6486	K8	OXI	626	K1			
KUI	3720	OD	LSK	502	U6	MIL	7609	95	NIL	6560	M1	OXI	630	K1			
KUI	8145	W5	LSK	503	U6	MIL	7610	95	NIL	7056	OC	OXI	725	K1			
KUI	8150	A1	LSK	504	U6	MIL	8583	V2	NIL	7228	G6	OXI	726	K1			
KXW	478	P	LSK	505	U6	MIL	9301	OB	NIL	8237	J3	OXI	7058	K1			
KYC	618	G3	LSK	506	U6	MIL	9574	C2	NIL	8254	C7	OXI	8095	K1			
LAE	13	P	LSK	507	U6	MIL	9750	A9	NIL	8255	C7	OYY	3	V2			
LAZ	2370	27	LSK	508	U6	MIL	9751	A9	NIL	8259	C7	PBZ	9154	98			
LAZ	5826	R4	LSK	611	U6	MIL	9764	W6	NIL	9886	L4	PDF	567	L3			
LAZ	5827	E6	LSK	612	U6	MJI	3833	64	NIW	2235	19	PIB	2470	35			
LBP	500	P	LSK	613	U6	MJI	6251	W3	NIW	3927	W5	PIB	3360	35			
LBZ	2571	86	LSK	614	U6	MLL	528	P	NIW	6506	OD	PIB	4019	35			
LBZ	2936	20	LSK	615	U6	MLL	570	P	NIW	8290	E9	PIB	5767	35			
LBZ	2939	U9	LSK	812	U6	MLL	769	P	NIW	8793	76	PIB	8117	D1			
LBZ	2944	L1	LSK	814	U6	MLL	935	P	NIW	8794	T2	PIJ	660	61			
LBZ	7534	K8	LTA	755	P	MLL	963	P	NIW	8795	G3	PIJ	4690	K9			
LDB	796	P	LTA	772	P	MMB	861	P	NJI	3653	59	PIJ	5170	K9			
LDD	488	L3	LTA	895	P	MRL	765	P	NJI	8067	D3	PIL	3108	R5			
LDV	483	P	LTA	906	P	MTT	640	P	NJI	8874	E5	PIL	3215	H7			
LEN	616	27	LTA	995	P	MVS	972	P	NJI	9479	75	PIL	3216	H7			
LFM	302	P	LTV	702	P	MXI	2742	T5	NLJ	268	P	PIL	3453	H7			
LFM	717	P	LUC	187	P	MXX	8	P	NLJ	271	P	PIL	3454	H7			
LFM	734	P	LUI	1519	27	MXX	319	P	NLP	592	OG	PIL	3524	W5			
LFM	753	P	LUI	2527	R4	MXX	345	P	NLP	645	P	PIL	4420	23			
LHT	911	P	LUI	2528	R4	NBB	171	P	NOK	43	T7	PIL	6501	E4			
LHY	976	P	LUI	2529	R4	NBH	746	P	NSU	205	W4	PIL	6577	U9			
LIB	6445	33	LUI	4653	27	NBZ	1286	77	NTT	661	P	PIL	6581	E9			
LIL	2167	R4	LUI	4655	D1	NBZ	1639	8	NTT	679	P	PIL	6831	21			
LIL	3060	E8	LUI	4658	D2	NDB	356	P	NXI	608	M6	PIL	7242	R2			
LIL	3287	22	LUI	5601	11	NDD	672	L3	NXI	784	R2	PIL	9537	G6			
LIL	4348	W4	LUI	5603	79	NDO	856	T7	OCO	502	P	PIW	4616	N4			
LIL	5851	2	LUI	5812	27	NDZ	3134	5	ODF	561	L3	PIW	4725	W5			
LIL	5930	D6	LUI	6203	OG	NDZ	3136	5	ODW	459	11	PIW	5455	A4			
LIL	6536	98	LUI	6246	R5	NDZ	3152	6	ODZ	8911	2	PJI	2803	J2			
LIL	6537	86	LUI	6247	R5	NDZ	3153	6	ODZ	8912	2	PJI	2804	J2			
LIL	6538	86	LUI	6248	R5	NDZ	3162	2	ODZ	8913	2	PJI	2805	J2			
LIL	6637	G7	LUI	9675	18	NDZ	3163	2	ODZ	8914	2	PJI	3354	M1			
LIL	7043	U9	LUI	9676	18	NDZ	3164	2	ODZ	8915	2	PJI	4713	T7			
LIL	7234	8	LUI	9952	88	NDZ	3165	2	ODZ	8916	1	PJI	5013	A1			
LIL	7802	86	LUI	9953	88	NDZ	3166	3	ODZ	8918	1	PJI	5014	W3			
LIL	7920	R5	LUO	595	P	NDZ	3167	3	ODZ	8919	1	PJI	5016	A1			
LIL	8052	86	LXI	4455	E5	NDZ	3168	3	ODZ	8920	1	PJI	5625	20			
LIL	8556	20	LYF	104	P	NDZ	3169	1	ODZ	8921	1	PJI	5861	8			
LIL	8823	86	MAF	544	P	NER	621	3	ODZ	8922	1	PJI	6071	T5			
LIL	8876	86	MAZ	6792	R4	NHG	541	R3	ODZ	8923	1	PJI	6077	M5			
LIL	9017	86	MBZ	7140	2	NHU	2	P	ODZ	8924	1	PJI	6084	59			
LIL	9174	W4	MCO	658	P	NIB	7615	F3	OHY	938	P	PJI	6909	E8			
LIL	9267	40	MFM	39	P	NIB	8459	D4	OIB	3510	64	PJI	8324	21			
LIL	9270	40	MHU	52	P	NIB	8657	J6	OIL	3924	E8	PJI	8325	OS			
LIL	9271	40	MHU	193	P	NIB	8773	J6	OIL	3927	E8	PJI	8360	A8			
LIL	9397	V6	MIB	612	OE	NIL	1095	8	OIL	4571	OW	PJI	8361	A8			
LIL	9843	H8	MIB	9068	K1	NIL	1387	L4	OIL	5267	27	PJI	8362	A8			
LIL	9990	86	MIJ	9795	98	NIL	1787	8	OIL	6847	87	PJI	8364	K8			
LIW	3221	E5	MIL	1031	8	NIL	2101	OC	OIL	6849	87	PJI	8994	T3			
LIW	3460	U9	MIL	1054	J9	NIL	4981	24	OIL	9262	A1	POI	4905	46			
LIW	4078	L2	MIL	2066	J2	NIL	4982	24	OIL	9263	A1	PSU	527	A1			
LJH	665	P	MIL	2088	J2	NIL	4983	24	OIL	9264	A1	PSU	699	V4			
LJI	3799	E8	MIL	2529	G2	NIL	4984	24	OIW	1303	X	PSV	444	K6			
LKN	550	P	MIL	3010	J2	NIL	4985	24	OIW	1319	W4	PXI	1421	V6			
LKW	13	21	MIL	3012	J2	NIL	4986	24	OIW	3286	X	RAZ	3998	31			
LOD	495	P	MIL	3292	98	NIL	4987	95	OJI	8324	U3	RAZ	7203	87			
LOD	974	P	MIL	3727	E9	NIL	4988	95	OJI	8786	2	RAZ	7349	87			

RAZ	8598	R4	RIL	9776	40	SJI	8286	R5	TIW	1743	U3	USK	947	P			
RAZ	8723	87	RIL	9864	29	SOI	1552	T5	TIW	2114	F5	USU	487	13			
RAZ	9649	87	RIL	9865	29	SWO	986	P	TIW	7681	T7	USV	330	L6			
RBZ	2673	K5	RIW	1907	R5	SXI	8576	OG	TJF	757	55	USV	331	L6			
RBZ	2675	22	RIW	2650	OD	TAZ	4992	K2	TJI	3134	2	USV	462	L6			
RBZ	4294	V5	RIW	4963	D5	TAZ	4993	OW	TJI	3135	2	USV	474	L6			
RBZ	4295	V5	RJI	1630	K9	TAZ	6696	D6	TJI	3136	2	USV	511	L6			
RDB	846	P	RJI	1648	59	TAZ	6963	49	TJI	3137	2	USV	556	L6			
RDB	872	P	RJI	2721	W5	TDZ	3265	1	TJI	3138	2	USV	562	L6			
RFO	361	P	RJI	3046	D4	TFO	319	V8	TJI	4680	G3	USV	577	L6			
RFO	375	P	RJI	3047	G3	THU	514	V6	TJI	4681	D5	USV	605	L6			
RFX	23	G7	RJI	3803	N4	TIA	6937	L2	TJI	4682	V9	USV	620	L6			
RHV	462	67	RJI	4563	95	TIB	3019	OG	TJI	4683	2	USV	625	L6			
RIB	3195	N7	RJI	4668	E5	TIB	4947	D1	TJI	4838	3	USV	628	L6			
RIB	4323	M1	RJI	5701	E9	TIB	8564	F4	TJI	5399	L1	USV	630	L6			
RIB	5084	R7	RJI	5702	E9	TIB	8599	OG	TJI	5813	E6	USV	676	L6			
RIB	5086	95	RJI	5703	N9	TIB	9158	R2	TJI	5843	L2	USV	821	2			
RIB	6197	M5	RJI	5716	24	TIL	1185	OC	TJI	6311	W5	USV	823	2			
RIB	6849	V5	RJI	6328	W1	TIL	1253	U4	TJI	6312	L4	USV	859	L6			
RIB	8740	N7	RJI	7973	N3	TIL	1254	U4	TJI	6925	68	UTA	199	E5			
RIB	8809	58	RJI	8581	21	TIL	1255	U4	TJI	8780	L3	UTT	806	K1			
RIB	8816	58	RJI	8602	L4	TIL	1256	U4	TJI	9141	E9	UUO	198	P			
RIB	8817	58	RJI	8606	A9	TIL	1257	U4	TJY	761	3	UWB	183	3			
RIB	8819	58	RJI	8611	E4	TIL	1258	U4	TPR	354	2	UWR	498	V8			
RIJ	579	60	RJI	8615	21	TIL	1259	U4	TRX	615	49	VAD	141	L3			
RIL	1053	2	RJI	8716	E3	TIL	1260	U4	TSU	603	U6	VAN	524	87			
RIL	1056	2	RJI	8725	D5	TIL	1261	U4	TSU	649	W4	VAZ	2531	U9			
RIL	1057	T8	RJX	318	T8	TIL	1262	U4	TSV	302	F1	VAZ	2533	U9			
RIL	1069	2	ROI	1229	68	TIL	1263	U4	TSV	617	OD	VAZ	2534	U9			
RIL	1172	3	ROI	1417	68	TIL	1898	11	TSV	787	T1	VAZ	9488	U7			
RIL	1203	L4	ROI	1913	68	TIL	2177	K8	TSV	788	T1	VCD	984	P			
RIL	1279	8	ROI	2929	68	TIL	2326	G7	TTL	262	58	VCO	772	F9			
RIL	1475	R4	ROI	7435	68	TIL	2506	27	TXI	8761	G6	VCO	802	F9			
RIL	1841	A5	ROI	8235	68	TIL	2741	K6	TXI	9303	22	VDF	365	L3			
RIL	2102	17	ROI	8358	68	TIL	2742	K6	UAM	2	OG	VDJ	660	61			
RIL	2103	M6	RTT	996	P	TIL	2744	K6	UCT	838	38	VDV	752	P			
RIL	2201	G3	RUH	346	3	TIL	2745	K6	UCY	629	L2	VDV	753	P			
RIL	3148	64	SAZ	2511	R4	TIL	2746	K6	UDF	936	L3	VDV	798	P			
RIL	3702	11	SAZ	3952	C7	TIL	2747	K6	UDL	718	E5	VDV	817	P			
RIL	3706	W3	SBZ	8075	27	TIL	2812	W4	UDO	475	L2	VDV	818	P			
RIL	4022	17	SDZ	3017	34	TIL	3383	93	UFH	277	8	VHY	437	62			
RIL	4099	OW	SHO	800	P	TIL	3866	C7	UFJ	293	P	VIB	5239	V7			
RIL	4396	T4	SIB	6741	G7	TIL	4679	C7	UFJ	296	P	VIB	7660	L5			
RIL	4411	D9	SIB	8357	74	TIL	5081	U4	UFX	330	2	VIB	9378	G6			
RIL	4472	8	SIB	8398	35	TIL	5930	L1	UFX	940	2	VIL	1486	96			
RIL	4529	T4	SIB	8941	70	TIL	5931	L1	UHW	661	3	VJI	2997	96			
RIL	4572	T4	SIB	9017	OB	TIL	5932	L1	UHY	359	P	VJI	4012	K9			
RIL	4586	T4	SIB	9309	35	TIL	5933	L1	UHY	360	P	VJI	4014	K9			
RIL	4599	T4	SIB	9313	35	TIL	6721	L5	UHY	384	P	VJI	7010	L9			
RIL	4958	95	SIL	3066	J2	TIL	6722	L5	UIB	3169	96	VJI	8200	N3			
RIL	4960	95	SIL	3069	OW	TIL	6877	F6	UIL	1335	R4	VJI	8683	88			
RIL	4961	D1	SIL	4456	20	TIL	6880	76	UJI	1757	J3	VJI	8684	88			
RIL	5087	42	SIL	4457	20	TIL	7904	K8	UJI	1761	U1	VLT	140	P			
RIL	5090	E7	SIL	4458	20	TIL	7906	K8	UJI	1762	U1	VOO	273	3			
RIL	5288	60	SIL	4460	J2	TIL	7907	K8	UJI	1763	U1	VOT	762	E5			
RIL	6390	46	SIL	4465	V7	TIL	7908	K8	UJI	1765	E4	VPH	900	C2			
RIL	7155	OC	SIL	4466	J2	TIL	7909	K8	UJI	1778	39	VWF	328	25			
RIL	7643	17	SIL	4470	J2	TIL	7910	75	UJI	3791	24	VYD	890	L9			
RIL	7644	17	SIL	5960	64	TIL	7915	75	UJI	3793	47	VYU	454	15			
RIL	8182	E7	SIL	5970	64	TIL	7916	23	UJI	3794	86	WAF	156	D7			
RIL	9343	E7	SIL	6715	24	TIL	8706	G3	UJI	4519	39	WCR	819	M1			
RIL	9429	46	SIL	6716	24	TIL	8707	G3	UJI	4526	OS	WDD	194	L3			
RIL	9458	R5	SIW	2763	N4	TIL	8708	G3	UJI	5789	L2	WDF	946	L3			
RIL	9459	R5	SIW	2778	E8	TIL	8709	G3	ULL	933	V8	WDR	145	49			
RIL	9671	60	SJI	1969	D9	TIL	9066	23	UMR	112	P	WDR	598	V7			
RIL	9772	40	SJI	5617	K8	TIL	9074	K8	UMS	394	76	WDZ	5236	98			
RIL	9773	40	SJI	7467	D2	TIL	9685	R4	UOP	948	73	WDZ	8521	R1			
RIL	9774	40	SJI	8117	E9	TIL	9833	G3	UPP	938	64	WFD	46	L9			
RIL	9775	40				TIL	9834	G3	UPV	487	24	WGR	565	G2			

148

WIA	69	W6	XIB	8385	58	9891	CD	95	843	AYA	N7	895	FXA	T7
WIA	4122	E5	XIB	8387	58	8909	DF	87	505	AYB	N7	964	FXM	75
WIB	2951	39	XJI	5457	24	6426	DU	OC	300	AYG	69	865	GAT	1
WIB	4393	8	XJI	5458	24	6130	EL	25	331	BCH	R5	422	GDV	H1
WIW	8557	OS	XJI	5459	24	2464	FH	W2	471	BET	27	676	GDV	T7
WJI	1414	T8	XJI	6330	24	5970	FH	64	501	BTA	P	86	GFJ	P
WJI	2321	24	XJI	6331	24	7968	FH	64	503	BTA	P	931	GTA	P
WJI	2839	L4	XJI	6332	24	1434	HP	E9	704	BYL	R3	63	GUO	P
WJI	3490	24	XJI	6333	24	2603	HP	E9	878	CDH	P	894	GUO	3
WJI	3491	24	XLF	622	73	3315	HP	E9	479	CFJ	P	511	HCV	W3
WJI	3492	24	XLH	570	24	3427	HP	E9	115	CLT	75	900	HGG	34
WJI	3493	24	XMW	120	7	3785	HP	E9	363	CLT	P	620	HOD	2
WJI	3494	24	XOD	665	V8	4415	HP	E9	497	CLT	P	775	HOD	T7
WJI	3495	24	XSU	746	J8	4691	HP	E9	572	CNW	P	298	HPK	77
WJI	3496	24	XSU	761	22	4846	HP	E9	751	CRT	88	606	HTC	P
WJI	3497	24	XSU	910	W3	5351	HP	E9	761	CRT	88	224	HUM	56
WJI	3726	M6	XTB	91	P	6230	HP	E9	924	CRT	88	509	HUO	T7
WJI	3813	T3	XUD	367	39	6740	HP	E9	445	CTT	P	86	JBF	55
WJI	3814	T3	XYC	561	A8	7105	HP	E9	890	CVJ	W2	533	JBU	F3
WJI	6879	24	XYD	169	G3	7346	HP	E9	255	CYA	·L9	536	JHU	P
WJI	6880	24	YAF	624	H1	7876	HP	E9	137	DAF	85	654	JHU	38
WJI	6886	W4	YAZ	6391	46	9743	HP	E9	578	DAF	85	595	JPU	2
WJI	6887	W4	YAZ	6392	46	9878	HP	E9	927	DAF	85	120	JRB	P
WJI	6888	W4	YAZ	6393	46	9880	HP	E9	359	DBK	T3	748	JTA	E9
WJI	7690	75	YAZ	6394	46	7740	KO	24	21	DGX	OE	739	JUA	W3
WJI	7955	U9	YAZ	8922	L4	2411	KR	25	466	DHN	P	407	JWO	T7
WJI	8913	59	YBZ	9558	17	1560	KX	76	931	DHT	25	832	JYA	L4
WJY	530	OD	YCV	500	D7	4011	LJ	M1	2	DOF	A7	815	KDV	P
WKG	287	P	YDZ	4234	G4	7682	LJ	P	4	DOF	A7	824	KDV	P
WLJ	926	H1	YHA	320	27	8683	LJ	2	29	DRH	D8	362	KHT	77
WLT	713	40	YHT	929	P	6499	MZ	T5	74	DRH	D8	270	KTA	P
WLW	994	P	YHT	958	P	3655	NE	P	904	DRH	D8	312	KTT	V7
WNN	734	3	YHY	78	P	2052	NF	82	913	DTT	P	573	LCV	J8
WOI	730	X	YHY	80	P	2191	RO	R5	509	DVT	P	407	LHT	P
WOI	8022	28	YIA	258	E6	1256	RU	91	532	DWW	P	991	MDV	P
WRL	16	P	YIB	3701	T5	4708	RU	27	672	DYA	11	315	MWL	24
WSL	115	P	YIB	3702	T5	6185	RU	63	916	DYA	N7	340	MYA	24
WSV	323	R4	YJI	8595	38	6986	RU	T7	783	DYE	28	936	NTT	G3
WSV	408	3	YJI	8596	38	7646	RU	T7	842	DYG	R5	217	NYA	N7
WSV	529	79	YOR	456	A3	8212	RU	V6	999	EAE	P	831	OCV	K4
WSV	530	W4	YSU	923	V7	290	WE	U6	504	EBL	P	904	OFM	P
WSV	537	V8	YSU	987	39	4529	WF	40	181	ECV	P	280	OHT	49
WSV	728	76	YSV	645	27	5904	WF	40	338	EDV	P	511	OHU	5
WSV	868	A4	YTT	1	OD	4092	WJ	P	484	EFJ	P	530	OHU	3
WXF	906	OC	YUU	556	T2	9996	WX	W3	569	EFJ	P	797	ONU	E5
WXI	3860	E9	YXI	2730	24	3408	WY	92	969	EHW	P	586	PHU	49
WYY	752	1	YXI	2732	24	6220	WY	L4	972	EHW	P	562	PTU	95
XAD	761	54	YXI	7381	47				206	EJO	60	647	PYC	K8
XBF	976	U8	YXI	9258	D4				152	EKH	17	862	RAE	P
XBJ	860	R4	YYD	154	L9				863	EKX	25	1	RDV	P
XBZ	4253	17	YYD	687	L9	516	ACH	11	841	ERL	J8	7	RDV	P
XBZ	4254	17	YYD	699	A1	137	ACY	P	260	ERY	U8	8	RDV	84
XBZ	4256	17				890	ADV	P	505	ETT	W6	9	RDV	P
XBZ	7729	7				251	AET	T5	805	EVT	P	503	RUO	P
XBZ	7730	7				974	AFJ	P	473	FAE	OS	94	SHU	25
XBZ	7731	7	1092	AD	82	838	AFM	P	789	FAY	E9	816	SHW	R3
XBZ	7732	7	3134	AD	82	508	AHU	F1	728	FDV	A3	674	SHY	V8
XDG	614	L3	3672	AD	82	237	AJB	A3	228	FHT	79	511	SKM	V5
XDG	779	X	5469	AD	82	239	AJB	A3	660	FHU	17	513	SRL	T2
XDV	851	P	6501	AD	82	241	AJB	A3	984	FJB	42	24	THU	25
XFE	499	V4	8727	AD	82	244	AJB	A3	387	FJF	X	804	TYA	G3
XFF	283	3	9210	AD	82	111	ALP	30	156	FMU	K5	640	UAF	F1
XFJ	466	86	4221	BY	67	267	ALP	30	260	FPJ	L9	645	UCV	D7
XIA	857	6	3271	CD	95	684	ALP	30	409	FRH	E9	701	UDE	K8
XIB	1907	L4	3504	CD	95	972	ANK	P	926	FRH	53	385	UFM	E6
XIB	4608	U2	3594	CD	95	705	AOW	J7	458	FTA	U9	620	UKM	R3
XIB	5178	98	5448	CD	95	314	ASV	OD	898	FUF	P	635	UNU	E5
XIB	8380	58	8405	CD	95	747	ATA	P	682	FUV	F3	688	UYB	H1
XIB	8381	58	8515	CD	95	872	ATA	P	752	FUV	T8	682	VAF	K4

870 VAR P	DFE 963D P		OAE 957M P	LHT 730P N2
710 VCV D7	DPV 65D P	AHT 206J P	OCT 990M P	LHW 504P W4
891 VFM P	EDV 505D P	ARE 170J X	OHU 38M P	LTA 731P W6
458 VHT T1	ERV 249D K7	CYA 181J P	OWC 719M P	LWG 275P X
666 VHU 99	ERV 251D K7	EGP 36J X	PUO 331M P	MHS 4P 5
958 VKM 24	FHT 15D P	FEH 172J X	RCV 493M E9	MHS 5P 5
426 VNU 49	FHW 158D P	LRN 60J P	RTA 637M X	MPK 693P L7
100 VRL P	GBU 143D X	NDR 509J X	SPT 174M X	MVO 790P X
873 VRL J8	HAD 915D P	TDK 686J X	WRR 365M X	MWP 492P X
946 WAE A9	HHW 452D P	TDV 217J P	WYD 397M L2	MYK 38P X
539 WCV D7	KGJ 603D 46	UMR 953J X	XRR 131M X	NNK 808P F1
307 WHT 62	KGJ 622D X	URO 859J X	YNA 277M X	NNK 809P U8
613 WHT 25	MRO 146D P	WHL 666J X	YRC 125M OC	ODV 283P T7
791 WHT 24	OJH 306D P	WJH 129J P		ODV 287P T7
800 XPC 68		WOW 535J X		PYA 645P P
990 XYA E9		WOW 549J X		PYA 646P 35
28 XYB 21		YHT 802J P	GCL 349N OS	TBW 450P X
312 XYB N2			GNM 235N P	
	FJY 914E X		GOG 598N X	
	GRS 114E X		GPD 310N W6	
	HDV 626E P		GPD 318N P	LTK 100R X
	HJA 965E P	CDD 235K P	GWF 759N F3	MOU 739R 98
AAL 520A 40	JAM 144E X	DAE 511K P	GYB 727N P	MOU 747R K2
AAL 587A L5	JAM 145E P	EHU 373K P	HCV 140N M5	MPX 945R P
AAX 466A 1	JHW 68E P	GYC 160K P	HGD 899N J7	MUN 942R P
ABD 812A P	KHW 309E P	MJP 59K P	HTA 844N P	NFB 113R K2
ABM 470A A7	MRC 565E P	NWW 163K P	JAT 882N X	NFB 115R 28
ACH 53A 11	NMY 662E OE	VOD 88K P	JBN 947N P	NTC 573R 3
ACH 69A 11	NMY 665E OE	VOD 124K P	JDV 179N X	OAM 333R X
ADM 419A P	NNY 761E X	VOD 125K P	JEU 509N P	OHE 933R 65
ADV 854A P			JFJ 498N P	OHR 183R 7
AFE 719A P			JFJ 502N P	OHR 190R N2
AJH 163A P			JFJ 507N P	OJD 45R V7
AOR 631A P	BKX 94F P	ATA 555L 2	JFJ 508N P	OJD 51R V7
DYA 221A 41	JCP 60F P	ATA 559L 2	JRW 732N X	OJD 54R V7
LDS 162A X	KED 546F P	AUP 651L P	KGR 491N P	OJD 56R V7
OWJ 637A OG	LUO 47F P	BCD 820L P	SMU 726N X	OJD 58R V7
WNL 110A N5	MAA 260F P	BDV 318L P	TYG 374N X	OJD 59R V7
WNL 382A N5	NRL 101F P	EOW 404L X		OJD 77R V7
	OHU 208F P	FDG 468L P		OJD 83R V7
	OHU 770F P	FTV 11L OC		OJD 84R V7
	PHT 227F P	GDF 650L P		OJD 405R K7
AEL 2B P		HHW 920L P	JHW 107P 1	OJD 469R K7
AFJ 77B P		JHA 216L T8	JHW 108P 1	OMR 221R A4
AHN 455B P		JHA 238L X	JHW 109P 1	ORS 86R K8
AYA 448B P	JUR 599G D2	JHU 848L X	JJG 6P X	OTC 605R X
BYC 802B 58	KJH 230G P	KUM 533L 82	JOV 718P X	OTG 44R P
BYC 828B 17	MWV 150G X	LHT 171L P	JTD 395P OD	OVV 58R X
BYC 835B OE	OCR 161G X	MJH 280L X	JTH 756P OD	OYJ 66R X
	OTA 287G X	MLH 374L X	KFB 811P X	PEU 518R 3
	OTA 290G X	MMH 128L P	KHT 122P P	PHN 570R 88
	OUH 177G P	MRO 200L P	KHU 323P P	PJA 956R X
BHU 92C P	PHA 505G P	MUR 218L P	KHU 326P P	PNU 388R P
CCV 166C X	TYC 250G P	NLG 104L X	KJD 410P V7	PNU 389R X
CTT 513C P	VML 4G X	NUD 106L M6	KJD 413P V7	PPE 660R X
CUV 253C OE		NYC 824L R4	KJD 414P V7	PPH 471R P
CWN 629C P		OCH 271L X	KJD 419P V7	RAN 646R 98
CYD 724C P		PGP 202L X	KJD 420P V7	RAW 19R V7
DAX 610C P	DDD 756H X	PYJ 445L X	KJD 422P V7	RBO 671R X
DBC 190C P	FVW 705H P	VJT 307L P	KJD 431P V7	RCV 296R P
DDR 201C P	POD 829H P		KMW 175P 7	RDC 108R X
EDD 685C P	RDV 423H P		KOU 427P 65	RDF 500R V8
ETO 463C X	RLJ 793H P		KOU 791P P	REL 402R X
FBC 1C 8	SNT 925H P	EFH 222M X	KTT 43P P	RKY 878R R1
FPT 581C X	STO 538H X	NAF 443M P	KUC 907P X	SFJ 106R 3
	UHU 221H P	NAT 349M X	KUC 988P X	SNJ 590R T2
	VUB 382H F5	NEL 845M P	LEU 256P 1	SNJ 593R T2
	WHW 374H P	NFJ 592M P	LEU 269P 1	SRY 759R 52
DET 720D OD		NTT 135M P	LHC 427P E5	TFP 25R OE
DFD 704D OD		OAE 954M P	LHT 727P X	

```
TVD 861R  N4      VRP 527S  X       BKE 857T  U8                        HDB 101V  75
TVD 862R  35      WGY 593S  X       BKH 981T  A3      AAA 900V  L9      HFG 923V  P
UHG 722R  X       WKO 128S  N9      BKH 983T  A3      AHU 516V  3       HFX 411V  V7
UYC 860R  35      WPW 202S  25      BTX 182T  D1      AHW 198V  K2      HHU  31V  24
VCG 127R  A4      WUM 101S  X       BUR 438T  L7      AHW 199V  M6      HHU 146V  24
WYA 290R  X       WWY 123S  3       BVR  89T  75      AHW 200V  P       HPL 422V  24
XMS 152R  X       XBU  19S  75      BVR  98T  7       ATH   4V  F2      HPR 686V  R2
                  XDV 601S  3       CDV 162T  M2      AVK 150V  88      JAH 769V  N4
                  XDV 608S  3       CEL 919T  38      BEP 966V  3       JDB 940V  N6
                  XDV 609S  3       CRM 927T  P       BEP 968V  3       JDG 111V  X
ADD 341S  P       XFP 983S  X       CWU 140T  X       BJG 672V  X       JKV 415V  58
AYA 912S  35      YRW 777S  N5      DAD 256T  88      BMR 201V  7       JLS   5V  77
DUP 143S  19      YTT 178S  T7      DFH 491T  OS      BMR 202V  7       JMJ 134V  T7
ESC 847S  98                        DMJ 374T  T7      BMR 203V  7       JRT 155V  OW
FFR 165S  A1                        DNT 717T  77      BMR 204V  7       JRU 373V  J6
GPT 224S  U6                        EBM 448T  L7      BMR 205V  7       JWT 758V  3
JCW 517S  T7      AAF 409T  K4      EFX 336T  E7      BVA 787V  88      KAD 352V  26
OCO 115S  X       AAP 648T  T2      EGD 201T  T8      BVY 164V  L2      KAD 355V  J2
PHY 697S  3       AAP 668T  U8      EGT 452T  X       BYX 186V  U1      KBH 843V  T5
PKD 416S  N4      AFH 186T  F7      ERB 548T  24      CJH 167V  X       KCH 753V  T8
PUN 100S  F5      AFH 390T  A3      ETA 874T  98      CRL 917V  91      KDB 138V  75
PUN 197S  L2      AFJ 692T  P       ETL 545T  R4      CYH 800V  D5      KOO 785V  3
REU 311S  N9      AFJ 697T  3       EUE 338T  21      DAK 216V  T5      KOO 791V  K2
RHT 503S  3       AFJ 698T  3       FYD 120T  OD      DDL 677V  T2      KOO 792V  K2
RRL 375S  W6      AFJ 699T  3       GDF 516T  X       DJB 865V  19      KOO 793V  K2
RTH 929S  3       AFJ 700T  3       GRF  32T  OG      DJH 475V  U3      KPP 619V  V7
RTH 931S  1       AFJ 701T  3       JAB   5T  P       DMS  22V  2       KRO 644V  OD
SCN 276S  88      AFJ 703T  3       JTL 150T  L7      DOF   1V  A7      KTA 980V  T5
STG 345S  E5      AFJ 704T  3       LHG 438T  F5      DYW 167V  98      KTL  25V  H8
SVJ 300S  X       AFJ 705T  3       MBT 676T  65      EAM 418V  53      KTL  26V  H8
SVJ 777S  N1      AFJ 706T  3       MSF 359T  42      EAP 985V  U8      KVF 248V  F1
TNJ 995S  M6      AFJ 712T  E3      NCW 151T  D1      EAP 989V  N2      LDG 700V  19
TNJ 996S  M6      AFJ 721T  W6      NGR 117T  K8      ECV 212V  P       LFH 719V  55
TNJ 998S  M6      AFJ 724T  W6      STK 133T  91      EDT 918V  V8      LFH 720V  55
TPE 164S  X       AFJ 727T  P       TFN 987T  X       EHE 526V  P       LFH 900V  L2
TPJ  59S  X       AFJ 733T  46      TFN 989T  X       EPC 909V  D3      LNV  65V  X
TWN 936S  3       AFJ 739T  P       TWH 698T  7       EPD 530V  41      LSU 381V  P
UFX 857S  28      AFJ 740T  T7      TWH 699T  7       EYP  33V  23      LUA 239V  D5
UFX 860S  1       AFJ 742T  T7      TWS 910T  P       FAF  44V  N4      LUA 240V  E6
UHB 277S  N5      AFJ 744T  3       TWS 914T  79      FAO 420V  OW      LUA 282V  V8
UPB 303S  X       AFJ 745T  3       TWS 915T  3       FDC 417V  L7      LUA 287V  38
UPB 308S  P       AFJ 747T  3       ULS 658T  N9      FDV 779V  2       LUM 979V  OW
UPB 309S  P       AFJ 749T  3       UMR 195T  X       FDV 780V  2       LYA 315V  R4
UPK 138S  69      AFJ 750T  3       UMR 199T  7       FDV 781V  2       MYD 217V  V5
URB 161S  N2      AFJ 751T  3       UMR 200T  7       FDV 787V  J7      NMJ 283V  U9
URL 946S  N4      AFJ 753T  U8      VAE 499T  P       FDV 807V  3       NUB  93V  L7
USO 173S  X       AFJ 760T  3       VEU 231T  29      FDV 808V  3       NWX 823V  X
UWV 604S  81      AFJ 761T  3       VTH 942T  3       FDV 814V  3       NYC 398V  17
UWV 614S  81      AFJ 762T  3       WAM 519T  A4      FDV 815V  3       OYA 519V  N7
UWV 619S  M6      AFJ 764T  2       WDA 979T  F3      FDV 827V  W6      RSG 815V  2
VDV 111S  2       AFJ 766T  2       WDK 562T  L7      FDV 828V  X       RYC  69V  X
VDV 114S  3       AFJ 767T  2       WTG 360T  28      FDV 837V  2       RYD  51V  17
VDV 116S  3       AFJ 768T  2       WTH 943T  3       FKM 876V  U8      SGR 790V  U8
VDV 117S  3       AFJ 770T  2       WTH 946T  3       FLJ 745V  OD      UCA 508V  K8
VDV 118S  3       AFJ 771T  U8      WTH 950T  3       FTO 552V  24      VBG 114V  2
VDV 121S  3       AFJ 773T  2       WTH 961T  3       FTO 555V  G2      VBG 118V  2
VDV 122S  2       AJD  19T  V7      WUH 171T  99      FVM 191V  OS      VBG 120V  2
VDV 134S  2       AJH 854T  A3      XAK 912T  K2      GAF  69V  G6      VBG 127V  2
VDV 137S  1       AJH 855T  3       XAN  48T  A3      GBU   2V  71      VJY 921V  24
VDV 141S  3       AKK 175T  19      XAN 431T  3       GBU   6V  71      VUO 455V  D5
VDV 142S  2       ANA  21T  7       XCT 251T  98      GBU   7V  71      VUO 612V  74
VDV 143S  1       ARL 958T  OC      XGL  51T  N4      GBU   8V  M9      XAA  27V  93
VJT 458S  C2      AUJ 745T  H1      XHT  48T  23      GHE 844V  D3      XCC 769V  OC
VMJ 967S  L7      BAT  54T  67      YAM 897T  23      GPL 522V  X       XCG  13V  N5
VNT  18S  24      BCL 213T  28      YDL 673T  49      GRU 162V  7       XUY 289V  82
VOD 594S  2       BCV  91T  A3      YPL 420T  16      GRU 163V  7       YFB 972V  29
VOD 596S  V8      BFX 569T  G2      YYL 781T  L2      GRU 164V  7
VOD 597S  34      BFX 570T  V2                        GRU 165V  7
VPF 287S  N2      BKE 851T  U8                        GRU 166V  7
```

Code	No.	Val
ATK	153W	A3
ATK	156W	A3
ATK	157W	A3
ATK	160W	4
ATK	161W	4
CAB	2W	A7
DHW	351W	P
EWS	739W	K2
EWS	741W	K2
EWS	747W	3
FYX	818W	OS
GGM	78W	K2
GGM	79W	K2
GJR	878W	K8
GTX	758W	OD
GYE	261W	A1
GYE	277W	16
GYE	557W	M9
HAX	11W	OS
HAX	331W	U9
HUD	495W	A3
HUD	496W	P
HUD	501W	A3
HWG	208W	K7
JCV	433W	V7
JTH	44W	3
JWV	250W	N4
JWV	259W	V8
KCK	202W	G2
KDL	204W	77
KHL	460W	T8
KJW	301W	U1
KJW	320W	U1
KLJ	667W	X
KRU	844W	N2
LAK	304W	98
LFJ	841W	3
LFJ	842W	3
LFJ	843W	3
LFJ	844W	3
LFJ	845W	3
LFJ	846W	3
LFJ	847W	3
LFJ	862W	K2
LFJ	871W	3
LFJ	872W	3
LFJ	873W	3
LNU	578W	24
LNU	579W	24
LNU	582W	24
LSJ	872W	F7
MMK	907W	U2
MPH	5W	J7
NJT	123W	A4
NPA	228W	D4
NPV	442W	X
ODJ	584W	87
ODV	203W	4
ODV	404W	L7
ORY	708W	X
OUF	359W	24
PFH	90W	56
PJT	524W	V7
PNB	801W	X
PRF	361W	C6
PWK	3W	T5
PWU	366W	R2
PWY	38W	3
PWY	40W	G2
RAH	267W	3
RLN	230W	T7
RNE	692W	F9
RTT	693W	D5
RUA	451W	H8
RUA	452W	H8
RUA	457W	H8
RUA	458W	32
RUE	300W	79
RVW	89W	75
SGS	510W	K8
SLH	42W	24
SLH	43W	24
STW	33W	K2
STW	34W	3
SVL	175W	W3
SWW	187W	C6
TAH	276W	V8
TKV	15W	N7
UAR	586W	3
UAR	588W	3
UAR	589W	3
UAR	590W	3
UAR	597W	3
UYD	950W	R4
VCA	453W	X
VCA	463W	25
VVV	959W	V8
VYC	852W	D4
WCA	941W	R2
WRP	225W	E6
WTU	467W	81
WTU	495W	N9
WYD	103W	R4
WYD	104W	R4
WYT	133W	X
XLV	143W	2
XYC	248W	R4
XYC	249W	17
YUY	94W	U9
AMJ	191X	27
BYD	795X	R4
CMJ	536X	N6
CNH	176X	V7
CNH	177X	V7
GPX	557X	OC
GSC	644X	34
HTU	416X	G4
JCJ	700X	R2
JEO	587X	F7
JHU	899X	5
JHU	902X	2
JHU	903X	2
JHU	904X	2
JHU	905X	1
JHU	906X	1
JHU	909X	1
JHU	910X	1
JHU	911X	1
JHU	912X	5
JHU	913X	1
JHU	914X	1
KEP	829X	M9
KMW	361X	C6
KUY	443X	E9
KYV	444X	6
KYV	462X	6
KYV	469X	6
KYV	473X	6
KYV	685X	M9
LAE	470X	N7
LCV	989X	X
LTY	551X	24
LTY	552X	24
LUL	511X	X
MAX	261X	T8
NDW	39X	E6
NHL	305X	C7
NOC	382X	X
NRS	307X	3
NRS	313X	3
OBO	631X	E9
OUH	770X	65
OWO	37X	F7
PAF	189X	U8
PAF	276X	H3
PNT	825X	63
PRC	849X	U8
PRC	856X	U8
PWF	240X	J2
PWJ	497X	R4
RAW	777X	V7
SND	83X	X
SND	281X	V5
SND	282X	V5
SND	489X	C7
SUJ	434X	C8
TAD	991X	X
TAY	888X	24
TND	107X	X
TND	125X	C2
TND	132X	N4
TND	403X	56
TPD	112X	25
TPD	120X	A1
TPD	125X	A1
TPG	313X	J1
TPL	762X	U8
TSO	17X	H8
TSO	31X	H8
TTT	162X	4
TTT	163X	4
TTT	164X	4
TTT	165X	4
TTT	166X	4
TTT	167X	4
TTT	168X	4
TTT	169X	4
TTT	170X	4
TTT	171X	4
UJT	987X	A4
URS	320X	3
URS	327X	3
URS	328X	3
URU	650X	38
UWW	3X	5
UWW	7X	5
UWY	83X	F6
VBC	984X	24
VEX	287X	3
VEX	288X	3
VEX	297X	3
VJT	620X	K8
VMX	234X	V7
VWX	350X	N2
WDD	17X	29
WDF	998X	H8
WDF	999X	H8
WJS	843X	V6
XEL	542X	24
XFJ	843X	E5
XHK	220X	3
XHK	221X	K2
XHK	222X	K2
XHK	223X	3
XHK	224X	X
XHK	225X	3
XHK	228X	3
XHK	230X	3
XRT	685X	19
XWY	475X	49
YNW	33X	E9
YYA	122X	D4
AEF	203Y	H3
AEF	260Y	U9
AFP	440Y	64
ANA	158Y	79
ANA	437Y	F3
ANA	565Y	M6
BDV	671Y	M3
BFR	958Y	16
BMS	511Y	J5
BMS	513Y	J5
BPF	131Y	A1
BRT	787Y	91
BUD	57Y	67
CFF	404Y	OD
CJU	110Y	F3
CPD	214Y	OD
CUB	25Y	1
CUB	31Y	1
CUB	40Y	1
CUB	45Y	1
CVU	302Y	K8
CVU	777Y	OC
DAD	600Y	52
EEH	902Y	32
EGV	695Y	R4
EJV	32Y	5
EJV	34Y	5
ENF	570Y	J1
ENF	571Y	74
ENF	573Y	79
EWY	77Y	1
FEW	225Y	N4
FEW	226Y	N4
FUM	486Y	3
FUM	487Y	3
FUM	491Y	3
FUM	492Y	3
FUM	499Y	3
FYD	523Y	A4
GNF	691Y	M2
GTA	528Y	E5
GTT	417Y	D4
HAV	1Y	D5
HBH	412Y	L2
HBH	416Y	N2
HHJ	372Y	2
HHJ	373Y	3
HHJ	375Y	2
HHJ	376Y	2
HHJ	381Y	2
HHJ	382Y	2
HTT	672Y	D5
JBW	211Y	G2
JEY	124Y	H8
JKL	942Y	J6
JNM	745Y	J9
JYC	226Y	N7
KBM	14Y	A7
KYA	284Y	R4
LBH	460Y	W6
LOU	437Y	E5
LWS	32Y	1
LWS	33Y	5
LWS	34Y	5
LWS	35Y	5
LWS	36Y	5
LWS	37Y	5
LWS	38Y	5
LWS	39Y	5
LWS	40Y	5
LWS	41Y	5
LWS	43Y	2
LWS	44Y	1
LWS	45Y	1
NDE	147Y	71
NTC	129Y	1
NTC	130Y	1
NTC	131Y	1
NTC	132Y	5
NTC	133Y	1
NTC	134Y	1
NTC	135Y	1
NTC	136Y	1
NTC	138Y	1
NTC	139Y	2
NTC	140Y	2
NTC	141Y	2
NTC	142Y	1
NUW	585Y	6
NUW	660Y	6
OFS	668Y	A1
OFS	701Y	32
OFS	702Y	32
OHV	707Y	16
OHV	766Y	A1
OHV	768Y	16
OHV	798Y	A1
OWO	235Y	N7
PHT	114Y	24
PHT	885Y	16
RBO	506Y	K2
RBO	508Y	K2
SDW	237Y	X
SGC	970Y	19
SHR	638Y	H1
SJR	617Y	32
TCV	253Y	N5
TTY	696Y	V7
UOB	366Y	2
UOB	894Y	W6
URL	375Y	A5
WAW	354Y	W4
XFG	25Y	F7
XFG	30Y	F7
XPG	295Y	W3
XSS	333Y	3
XSS	334Y	3

XSS 338Y 3	A398 NNK OG	A661 UHY N2	B514 OEH E8	C942 DHT E9
XSS 340Y 3	A 56 NPP U3	A379 UNH 25	B 7 OJC L1	C911 DVF C1
XSS 341Y 3	A983 NYC D4	A535 VAF R8	B 17 OJC L1	C110 DWR 33
YAL 690Y M5	A462 ODY L7	A750 VAF 3	B111 ORU 91	C112 DWR 33
YPD 119Y 27	A691 OHJ 2	A751 VAF 3	B678 OVU G9	C123 DYD OD
YPD 140Y F6	A694 OHJ 2	A752 VAF 3	B 94 PLU E3	C862 DYD P
YPD 144Y E8	A695 OHJ 2	A753 VAF 3	B436 RJU D8	C681 EHU A1
YRY 1Y 24	A162 OOT E5	A754 VAF 3	B910 SPR 35	C822 EHU A1
	A188 OOT E5	A755 VAF 3	B533 TEO 73	C828 EHU N2
	A561 OTA V7	A756 VAF 1	B269 TLJ W3	C 28 EUH A1
	A104 OUG J2	A757 VAF 1	B184 TRU 93	C 29 EUH A1
A114 ACV D5	A168 PAE 84	A337 VHB 56	B395 UPO 56	C 30 EUH A1
A989 AET H1	A169 PAE 84	A513 VKG A6	B991 UPS L2	C740 FBU V1
A 60 AFS E9	A 18 PCT X	A256 VYC R4	B873 UST X	C708 FDV D5
A690 AHB 2	A694 PKE L1	A 61 WMW 7	B120 UUD U1	C519 FFJ P
A 5 ALP 30	A987 POD U9	A 63 WMW 7	B175 VDV 4	C657 FFJ X
A 10 APL 15	A271 RBK M5	A669 XGG X	B176 VDV 4	C658 FFJ X
A986 ARD OW	A799 REO R4	A423 XGL H3	B164 VHG 18	C660 FFJ X
A 2 ATN OG	A820 RTP 92	A600 XGL T2	B697 WAR J7	C671 FFJ P
A632 BCN X	A673 RWL F2	A611 XKU N2	B438 WTC OC	C694 FFJ 10
A651 CMY M3	A206 SAE 3	A388 XMC U2	B304 WTP 89	C705 FFJ 10
A 2 CNU X	A945 SAE 1	A847 YJH V4	B149 WUL U1	C708 FFJ C1
A 16 CTL OD	A946 SAE 1	A622 YOX 2	B221 WUL U1	C713 FFJ E6
A689 CWP 56	A948 SAE 1	A624 YOX 2	B440 WUL N6	C719 FFJ P
A635 DCN OG	A949 SAE 1	A649 YOX 2	B 87 WUV M9	C724 FFJ 51
A 1 DWO K4	A950 SAE 1	A696 YOX 2	B108 WUV 5	C735 FFJ X
A428 DWP OD	A951 SAE 2	A523 YSD F7	B112 WUV 5	C745 FFJ 10
A 6 ECS F7	A952 SAE 1		B842 WYO G9	C748 FFJ P
A 9 ECS F7	A953 SAE 1		B156 YFJ E5	C752 FFJ 10
A 16 EFA 16	A954 SAE 1		B570 YOD U7	C755 FFJ X
A 18 EFA 16	A298 SPS J6	B 41 AAF 3	B189 YTC N6	C759 FFJ 10
A 19 EFA 16	A838 SUL 5	B 85 ACX J6	B823 YTC K2	C219 FMF 35
A109 EPA R4	A854 SUL 5	B913 AJX OB	B883 YTC A1	C796 FRL 3
A111 EPA OG	A900 SUL U1	B299 AMG 64	B991 YTC 58	C801 FRL P
A130 EPA R4	A926 SUL U1	B 7 AND D8	B100 YUC W4	C344 FTT C8
A158 EPA 69	A931 SUL 28	B 8 AND D8	B895 YYD 2	C143 FYC X
A110 FDL V8	A947 SUL 28	B 9 AND D8		C144 FYC X
A888 FFP 47	A892 SYE A1	B 21 AUS F7		C451 GGT 80
A101 FPL 40	A943 SYE A1	B155 AYD R4		C453 GGT G9
A 7 FRX J3	A976 SYE 6	B194 BAF 3	C 17 ACT 9	C137 GHS N6
A 10 FRX 57	A958 SYF U1	B195 BAF 3	C 18 ACT 9	C308 GOC D5
A 14 FRX 38	A851 TDS OC	B196 BAF 3	C 19 ACT 9	C761 GOJ M5
A 15 FRX 38	A610 THV 16	B197 BAF 3	C105 AFX W3	C894 GYD X
A646 GLD J9	A632 THV 6	B 7 BEN 32	C416 AHT P	C906 GYD V5
A999 GNR OW	A703 THV U1	B919 BGA 27	C875 ARJ C6	C908 GYD V5
A707 GPR 52	A740 THV 28	B655 BYB 47	C631 BEX C1	C913 GYD 2
A 16 GVC C7	A809 THW 1	B674 CBD M1	C 68 BFX 91	C924 GYD 2
A320 HFP H3	A810 THW 1	B112 CCS J1	C473 BHY 1	C927 GYD 2
A735 HFP 14	A811 THW 1	B934 CGL 65	C546 BHY T7	C947 GYD 2
A624 HNF 78	A812 THW 1	B 10 DCT OG	C550 BHY T7	C685 HDM M3
A 20 JAB 36	A813 THW 1	B630 DDW V7	C552 BHY X	C361 HGF OD
A459 JJF H3	A814 THW 1	B710 EOF W3	C522 BNX H3	C593 JAF U3
A930 JOD N2	A955 THW 1	B608 EYB J6	C914 BTS OC	C660 JAT R1
A 9 JVA 59	A956 THW 1	B715 FCF G9	C239 BWS 18	C744 JYA 91
A684 KCP 65	A957 THW 1	B 73 FGT V5	C812 BYY U8	C680 KDS 38
A685 KDV 2	A958 THW 1	B205 FMW A4	C819 BYY U8	C680 KFM R8
A686 KDV P	A959 THW 1	B591 FOG 2	C474 CAP 71	C141 KGJ OC
A665 KUM 3	A961 THW 1	B 6 GBD 99	C130 CAT X	C609 LFT 5
A422 LDV OD	A962 THW 1	B 65 GHR 7	C256 CFG 1	C610 LFT 5
A817 LEL 14	A963 THW 1	B 66 GHR 7	C 23 CHM U8	C624 LFT 5
A254 LLL N4	A964 THW 1	B 67 GHR 7	C 42 CHM 28	C641 LFT 5
A927 MDV P	A965 THW 1	B 68 GHR 7	C 48 CHM 28	C650 LFT 5
A 18 MHD 83	A966 THW 1	B289 KPF 69	C 74 CHM U8	C659 LFT 5
A523 MJK 27	A967 THW 1	B247 KUX V5	C 83 CHM U8	C149 LJR F2
A191 MNE 38	A968 THW 1	B330 LSA 88	C 87 CHM U8	C 78 MAK F4
A 11 MSN 19	A 67 THX 6	B331 LSA J5	C849 CSN 88	C219 MDS X
A342 MWD 64	A 27 TNK L2	B 39 MBY G9	C193 CYO L3	C737 MEJ H9
A126 NAC H3	A693 TPO 38	B504 MDC L1	C195 CYO 93	C547 MNH E9
A 2 NBT 39	A 8 TRA R5	B549 NDG 56	C286 DFJ 9	C777 MVH OW

C988	MWJ	T5	D705	GHY	1	D809	PUK	C6	E756	CCA	D6	E714	LYU	V6
C 85	NNV	OD	D706	GHY	1	D825	PUK	OS	E604	CDS	V5	E489	MEL	P
C 86	NNV	E3	D707	GHY	1	D 22	PVS	X	E589	CFW	59	E213	MFX	OD
C248	OFE	E9	D708	GHY	1	D 26	PVS	OD	E458	CGM	52	E339	MHU	33
C968	PFS	OD	D709	GHY	1	D353	RCY	M1	E461	CGM	28	E756	MJT	X
C194	RVV	F4	D710	GHY	1	D696	RKE	X	E477	CGM	28	E780	MLB	OW
C142	SPB	U1	D711	GHY	1	D286	RKW	N6	E716	CPC	E9	E803	MOU	2
C311	SPL	77	D221	GLJ	F2	D970	RNC	47	E492	CPE	78	E808	MOU	3
C507	TJF	OC	D771	GTC	37	D753	RTT	C2	E270	CPU	L1	E809	MOU	1
C515	TJF	X	D260	HFX	35	D 73	RYA	47	E325	CTT	N1	E812	MOU	3
C158	TLF	1	D128	HML	A9	D308	SDS	69	E506	CTT	J2	E815	MOU	2
C159	TLF	1	D907	HOU	W5	D366	SFC	W4	E678	DCU	28	E817	MOU	1
C432	VGX	24	D910	HOU	10	D394	SGS	OW	E276	DDV	A5	E818	MOU	2
C 27	VJF	OW	D914	HOU	10	D397	SGS	C8	E881	DGS	OS	E823	MOU	1
C345	VNR	67	D915	HOU	OD	D352	TEV	W1	E654	DGW	94	E667	MWP	W4
C 71	XDG	L3	D513	HUB	3	D413	TFT	K6	E223	DMV	50	E 32	NEF	J5
C402	XFO	OG	D514	HUB	3	D 53	TLV	T6	E880	DRA	K6	E674	NNV	L2
C657	XLK	OD	D 78	JHY	V2	D327	TRN	69	E 33	DSS	G7	E691	NOU	V2
			D 86	JHY	X	D160	UGA	71	E920	EAY	W3	E787	NOU	V2
			D202	JHY	V2	D156	UGB	OB	E248	EGY	K8	E110	NWP	X
			D280	JME	93	D759	UTA	N1	E343	EVH	J6	E116	NWP	X
D127	ACX	V5	D724	JUB	N8	D851	UTA	U9	E200	FCF	E5	E 42	ODE	33
D947	ARE	C6	D764	JUB	T3	D928	UTA	U9	E244	FLD	76	E296	OMG	84
D272	BJB	E8	D784	JUB	78	D726	VAM	F6	E382	GAB	F8	E170	OMU	J1
D 95	CFA	W6	D613	KJT	97	D895	VAO	V6	E167	GFA	OD	E872	PGL	U8
D463	CKV	94	D 74	KRL	OD	D 89	VCC	J5	E 53	GHO	T5	E133	PLJ	47
D512	CLN	U2	D 76	KRL	OG	D 42	VDV	J6	E723	HBF	T3	E322	PMD	H8
D 21	CTR	69	D815	KWT	OD	D 86	VDV	N1	E755	HJF	T8	E323	PMD	H8
D 22	CTR	69	D455	KYB	X	D208	VVV	U2	E768	HJF	38	E324	PMD	H8
D 23	CTR	69	D456	KYB	X	D212	VVV	D5	E929	HPJ	OB	E325	PMD	H8
D986	DPG	T3	D501	LNA	2	D659	WEY	T8	E203	HRY	10	E251	PRL	R8
D891	DWP	5	D502	LNA	2	D510	WNV	E9	E963	HTP	10	E515	PWR	51
D298	EKS	W1	D503	LNA	2	D517	WNV	E9	E667	JAD	D1	E 44	RDW	51
D 12	ELL	A4	D101	LTA	C2	D283	XCX	K2	E211	JDD	K2	E680	RGL	J7
D 14	ELL	A4	D102	LTA	C9	D290	XCX	14	E 61	JHY	OW	E934	RWR	M2
D875	ELL	2	D103	LTA	C9	D100	XRY	T7	E400	JNR	K4	E581	SAT	OW
D404	ERE	T3	D114	LTA	C9	D217	YCW	D3	E908	KBF	D6	E 39	SBO	V7
D583	EWS	P	D137	LTA	E9	D630	YCX	V5	E650	KCX	N2	E 40	SBO	V7
D586	EWS	C1	D144	LTA	M9	D454	YPN	OS	E953	KDP	F4	E922	SNY	M1
D503	FAE	V9	D163	LTA	R1	D 75	YRF	C1	E941	KEU	L1	E 67	SUH	N4
D522	FAE	X	D180	LTA	X				E131	KGM	35	E968	SVU	26
D344	FOT	OS	D184	LTA	V7				E371	KHT	44	E979	SVU	OS
D 33	FYH	F7	D817	LWX	13				E372	KHT	44	E348	SYD	X
D982	FYR	G9	D930	LYC	79	E128	AAL	H6	E373	KHT	44	E318	SYG	F6
D900	GEU	X	D509	MJA	C6	E478	AFJ	71	E374	KHT	X	E402	TCV	88
D542	GFH	M1	D314	MNC	OS	E149	AGG	J4	E377	KHT	X	E608	TCV	H3
D801	GHU	58	D572	MNK	C6	E222	ANA	OB	E378	KHT	44	E510	TOV	C8
D100	GHY	1	D806	MNY	X	E461	ANC	D6	E379	KHT	X	E521	TOV	T6
D101	GHY	1	D910	MVU	48	E991	ANC	H6	E407	KHY	X	E200	TUE	D1
D102	GHY	1	D915	MVU	C6	E131	ANU	H6	E995	KJF	52	E343	TYD	50
D103	GHY	1	D803	NBO	71	E898	ASU	N8	E501	KNV	OS	E182	UEJ	N4
D104	GHY	1	D504	NDA	OD	E139	ATV	N4	E358	KPO	M9	E 45	UKL	K6
D105	GHY	1	D144	NDT	X	E202	BDV	1	E134	KRP	L2	E694	UND	1
D106	GHY	1	D778	NDV	OD	E204	BDV	1	E354	KRP	26	E690	UNE	OW
D107	GHY	1	D 66	NOF	T3	E213	BDV	N8	E 50	KWS	X	E323	UUB	36
D108	GHY	1	D954	NOJ	U2	E215	BDV	10	E 51	KWS	44	E331	UYC	47
D109	GHY	1	D144	NON	M2	E941	BHR	A4	E 52	KWS	X	E658	VHF	U5
D111	GHY	1	D 22	NWO	76	E200	BOD	3	E 53	KWS	44	E659	VHF	X
D112	GHY	1	D289	OAK	W4	E201	BOD	3	E 55	KWS	44	E667	VHF	X
D113	GHY	1	D516	ODV	66	E202	BOD	3	E129	KYW	R1	E816	VSU	V4
D215	GHY	A6	D241	OOJ	88	E203	BOD	3	E944	LAE	1	E979	WDS	W6
D500	GHY	1	D254	OOJ	OD	E205	BOD	3	E 94	LDG	OG	E801	WDV	C8
D501	GHY	1	D510	OTA	76	E215	BTA	3	E500	LFL	5	E815	WDV	10
D503	GHY	1	D434	OWO	M1	E216	BTA	3	E501	LFL	5	E822	WDV	X
D700	GHY	1	D 44	OYA	U5	E217	BTA	1	E502	LFL	5	E676	WFJ	X
D701	GHY	1	D309	PEJ	88	E300	BWL	M7	E641	LNV	N3	E753	WKB	93
D702	GHY	1	D915	PGB	48	E301	BWL	V8	E718	LOU	25	E707	WKC	70
D703	GHY	1	D101	PTT	98	E303	BWL	M7	E198	LRV	OB	E145	WKK	39
D704	GHY	1	D779	PTU	10	E122	CAM	T9	E901	LVE	11	E574	WOK	47

E140	WTA	V1	F566	FYA	X	F394	RHT	44	F193	UGL	R8	G641	CGL	X
E 93	WWD	X	F627	GKM	89	F405	RHT	44	F468	UPB	96	G640	CHF	4
E814	XHS	2	F200	GMR	J4	F814	RJF	13	F734	USF	R4	G643	CHF	4
E663	XND	X	F770	GNA	92	F222	RJX	M3	F314	VCV	U8	G247	CLE	32
E478	XTT	72	F791	GNA	T8	F251	RJX	58	F315	VCV	U8	G293	CLE	32
E210	XWG	V7	F101	GRM	3	F252	RJX	58	F405	WAF	OC	G916	CLV	G3
E 58	YAM	42	F394	GTA	X	F309	RMH	71	F975	WEF	X	G301	CPL	97
E731	YBH	G9	F152	GVO	15	F183	RNH	W6	F476	WFX	35	G250	CPS	63
E732	YBH	78	F600	GVO	4	F602	RPG	7	F487	WPR	E4	G833	CVX	10
E954	YGA	A6	F601	GVO	4	F603	RPG	7	F 92	XBV	88	G993	DDF	H8
E204	YGC	F6	F602	GVO	4	F604	RPG	7	F 93	XBV	88	G226	DGM	E5
E752	YGY	1	F603	GVO	4	F605	RPG	7	F 94	XBV	88	G555	DLV	H6
E805	YRM	OD	F604	GVO	4	F606	RPG	7	F 95	XBV	88	G556	DLV	H6
E469	YTA	D6	F605	GVO	4	F608	RPG	7	F201	XBV	N6	G105	DPB	V7
E663	YTT	OE	F606	GVO	4	F600	RTC	1	F968	XEW	G9	G607	EDC	92
E287	YWA	OD	F607	GVO	4	F604	RTC	3	F616	XMS	V6	G609	EDC	92
E565	YYA	D4	F194	HNN	J4	F605	RTC	3	F630	XMS	39	G393	EFS	U3
			F202	HSO	D4	F606	RTC	3	F641	XMS	V6	G519	EFX	C3
			F389	HTA	H5	F607	RTC	3	F643	XMS	3	G216	EOA	C6
			F544	HTA	T5	F608	RTC	3	F657	XMS	3	G217	EOA	C4
			F545	HTA	C5	F609	RTC	1	F666	XMS	3	G229	EOA	1
F 50	ACL	4	F951	HTT	M1	F610	RTC	1	F667	XMS	3	G230	EOA	10
F 51	ACL	4	F542	HYD	C3	F611	RTC	1	F668	XMS	3	G107	EOG	A1
F127	AEL	K5	F425	JFT	A6	F612	RTC	1	F669	XMS	3	G174	EOG	A1
F680	AFY	T6	F336	JMV	F8	F613	RTC	1	F680	XMS	3	G177	EOG	A1
F165	AWO	34	F164	JOD	OS	F614	RTC	1	F682	XMS	3	G296	EOG	A1
F293	AWW	99	F731	JTT	50	F615	RTC	1	F683	XMS	3	G303	EOK	M4
F701	BAT	6	F729	JWD	T8	F616	RTC	1	F684	XMS	3	G434	ETW	K6
F702	BAT	6	F128	KAO	D9	F617	RTC	1	F706	XMS	3	G650	EVN	92
F705	BAT	6	F997	KCU	R4	F618	RTC	1	F898	XOE	A7	G657	EVN	X
F891	BCY	63	F 90	KDS	62	F619	RTC	1	F158	XYG	3	G283	FKD	62
F892	BCY	10	F898	KHJ	OS	F620	RTC	1	F414	YAJ	X	G387	FSF	V6
F218	BHF	62	F680	KJO	OG	F621	RTC	1	F225	YHG	D3	G347	GAJ	X
F946	BMS	3	F407	KOD	V6	F622	RTC	1	F339	YTG	66	G131	GEY	X
F948	BMS	3	F 71	LAL	U1	F623	RTC	1	F361	YTJ	2	G264	GKG	C1
F949	BMS	3	F278	LND	A6	F624	RTC	1	F362	YTJ	2	G265	GKG	98
F952	BMS	3	F319	LOD	43	F625	RTC	1	F363	YTJ	2	G150	GOL	15
F953	BMS	3	F512	LTT	84	F626	RTC	2	F869	YWX	T8	G151	GOL	3
F954	BMS	3	F439	LTU	E7	F627	RTC	2				G152	GOL	3
F212	BWF	OG	F538	LUF	A1	F628	RTC	2				G895	HHB	G6
F706	CAG	6	F544	LUF	A1	F629	RTC	2				G 90	HJC	A6
F893	CAT	V1	F554	MBC	E9	F630	RTC	1	G101	AAD	5	G713	HOP	A2
F195	CEA	F4	F 77	MFJ	X	F631	RTC	1	G102	AAD	5	G717	HOP	A2
F703	COA	OS	F254	MGB	63	F632	RTC	1	G103	AAD	5	G932	HRN	87
F949	CUA	94	F357	MUT	39	F660	RTL	H8	G104	AAD	5	G389	HTX	OS
F680	CYC	E4	F 28	NLE	E5	F301	RUT	81	G105	AAD	5	G166	HWO	U3
F681	CYC	22	F316	NPF	G9	F309	RVT	76	G878	AGL	M5	G544	JOG	R5
F215	DCC	E9	F659	NPF	G6	F178	RWS	OS	G485	ANM	26	G 38	KAK	38
F221	DCC	E9	F432	OBK	49	F515	SCW	U9	G105	APC	E9	G 58	KET	F4
F221	DDY	D6	F689	OFJ	M1	F325	SHU	39	G114	APC	56	G731	KPW	OD
F167	DET	OC	F596	OHT	OB	F595	SHW	OD	G116	APC	75	G 90	KTH	90
F258	DKG	51	F913	OHW	X	F337	SMD	W6	G 72	APO	V1	G100	KUB	M7
F404	DUG	V5	F923	OHW	44	F169	SMT	D6	G275	BEL	T8	G106	KUB	94
F425	DUG	63	F882	OHY	K3	F114	SWS	X	G276	BEL	OE	G222	KWE	10
F281	ENV	N2	F578	OOU	54	F115	SWS	X	G277	BEL	87	G340	KWE	16
F468	EOD	X	F579	OOU	54	F612	TGL	X	G382	BEV	L1	G823	KWF	A1
F457	ETA	X	F 95	OYO	E6	F613	TGL	X	G 82	BHP	55	G827	KWF	A1
F714	EUG	E9	F923	PEU	R7	F765	TLB	14	G969	BLE	V1	G972	KWJ	OD
F318	EWF	32	F165	PFB	OS	F 29	TMP	X	G552	BSJ	48	G220	LGK	39
F535	EWJ	R5	F480	PHU	OS	F 30	TMP	44	G448	CDG	H8	G706	LKW	34
F328	FCY	K6	F 37	PKV	OC	F 31	TMP	44	G559	CEF	92	G847	LNP	6
F329	FDT	M2	F616	PRE	K3	F 32	TMP	44	G560	CEF	92	G261	LUG	3
F716	FDV	V6	F590	PSE	D2	F 34	TMP	44	G746	CEF	92	G534	LWU	M1
F730	FDV	V6	F617	PWS	OD	F 35	TMP	44	G747	CEF	92	G546	LWU	M1
F738	FDV	V6	F715	RDG	29	F866	TNH	OC	G828	CEF	92	G547	LWU	M1
F751	FDV	10	F875	RFP	63	F455	TOY	3	G829	CEF	92	G974	LWY	OD
F281	FFJ	X	F154	RHK	2	F378	UCP	K6	G830	CEF	92	G863	LYC	X
F739	FJO	X	F800	RHK	3	F167	UDG	29	G831	CEF	92	G685	LYG	48
F 67	FMW	X	F802	RHK	3	F183	UFH	71	G640	CGL	X	G458	MEG	OG
F624	FNA	V9												

G823 MNH W3	G906 TWS 1	H889 AAE 44	H 51 GLP X	H914 WYB 2	
G517 MYD 27	G907 TWS 1	H890 AAE 44	H606 GLT A6	H915 WYB 2	
G165 NAG 79	G908 TWS 1	H891 AAE X	H914 GNC R6	H916 WYB 2	
G426 NGE A8	G909 TWS 1	H874 ABU U7	H422 GPM A1	H539 XGK L7	
G434 NGE 22	G910 TWS 1	H508 AEU OB	H423 GPM U1	H639 XGX 40	
G978 NGN G8	G837 UDV 98	H821 AHS H4	H642 GRO 69	H380 XHG M6	
G900 NHG 92	G840 UDV A1	H822 AHS H4	H765 GTJ U5	H969 XHR 7	
G461 NMW X	G842 UDV K6	H287 AHU 76	H177 GTT 4	H970 XHR 7	
G154 NRC 15	G844 UDV K6	H302 AHU OD	H178 GTT 4	H971 XHR 7	
G693 NUB 69	G258 UFB A6	H 15 ALP 30	H 34 HBG A1	H972 XHR 7	
G699 NUB 69	G637 UHU W6	H 19 AND D8	H103 HDV K6	H973 XHR 7	
G 84 NUX 20	G690 UHU 20	H672 ATN 27	H718 HGL 3	H557 XNN OS	
G897 NYC 29	G639 UKL 89	H354 BDV 43	H723 HGL 3	H402 XTU C4	
G412 OAM 54	G410 USE 56	H362 BDV D7	H726 HGL 3	H920 XYN U8	
G413 OAM 54	G228 UUE OG	H731 BHW 25	H283 HLM OS	H932 XYN U8	
G414 OAM 54	G373 UVR R6	H484 BND R4	H324 HVT 3	H189 YAL L1	
G465 ODT X	G176 UWS 92	H491 BND C6	H346 JFX E9	H536 YHT T9	
G466 ODT 44	G156 UYK OC	H529 BOD X	H348 JFX E9	H633 YHT 1	
G467 ODT 44	G776 UYV OD	H920 BPN 84	H 23 JMJ F7	H634 YHT 1	
G468 ODT X	G860 VAY 74	H437 BVU 79	H180 JRE 3	H636 YHT 1	
G469 ODT 44	G861 VAY 27	H132 CDB 10	H481 JRE 3	H637 YHT 1	
G110 OGA 70	G958 VBC 86	H133 CDB 10	H508 KSG 39	H638 YHT 1	
G997 OKK D4	G221 VDX 46	H381 CDV R6	H345 LJN 3	H639 YHT 1	
G 50 ONN H8	G449 VEE 17	H429 CHW V3	H346 LJN 3	H640 YHT 1	
G 51 ONN H8	G 33 VHT X	H347 CKP 63	H962 LOC G3	H641 YHT 1	
G 75 ONN K6	G902 VKJ 63	H185 CNS K6	H882 LOX K6	H642 YHT 1	
G651 ORR 25	G907 VKJ 63	H187 CNS R1	H893 LOX 3	H643 YHT 1	
G612 OTV 4	G100 VMM 40	H759 CTA G6	H894 LOX 3	H644 YHT 1	
G614 OTV 4	G891 VNA 13	H162 DAP C9	H895 LOX 3	H645 YHT 1	
G615 OTV 4	G501 VRV 27	H896 DFB OS	H896 LOX 3	H646 YHT 1	
G621 OTV 4	G992 VWV A1	H165 DJU W3	H898 LOX V6	H647 YHT 1	
G623 OTV 4	G993 VWV A1	H739 DKE OG	H 2 LWJ L2	H648 YHT 1	
G182 PAO C9	G515 VYE OE	H650 DKO H5	H874 MHB D9	H649 YHT 1	
G201 PAO 74	G423 WFP D2	H655 DKO 27	H403 MRW 5	H650 YHT 1	
G327 PAV OC	G920 WGS M7	H662 DKO R9	H683 NEF U1	H651 YHT 1	
G526 PDH C2	G921 WGS M7	H652 DOD 98	H329 POG L2	H652 YHT 1	
G326 PEW 3	G443 WLL R9	H932 DRJ 71	H 11 POW OE	H653 YHT 1	
G731 PGA U7	G992 WLU E9	H937 DRJ W2	H 82 PTG A6	H654 YHT 1	
G732 PGA 48	G731 WOD X	H112 DVM G6	H236 RUX A5	H655 YHT 1	
G411 PGG K6	G249 XDV 70	H177 DVM 98	H 16 SUN U5	H656 YHT 1	
G113 PGT 98	G253 XDV X	H199 DVM 23	H523 SWE K6	H657 YHT 1	
G 71 PKR K6	G290 XFH W2	H429 DVM E6	H446 SYB X	H658 YHT 1	
G399 PRM G8	G351 XHY X	H675 EAY OS	H139 TAB E8	H659 YHT 1	
G577 PRM G8	G167 XJF W4	H 49 ECW 53	H996 TAK 19	H660 YHT 1	
G 64 PTT V1	G803 XLO 2	H370 EFK X	H202 TCP A4	H661 YHT 1	
G803 RDB 97	G804 XLO 2	H204 EKO K6	H210 TCP W5	H662 YHT 1	
G 92 RGG N1	G215 XOD 96	H548 EVM OD	H123 TYD 47	H368 YHY 44	
G906 RHH 60	G165 XOR 27	H794 FAF W3	H124 TYD 47	H610 YTC 1	
G267 RKJ OB	G716 XPO V9	H187 FDV H5	H688 UAK J4	H611 YTC 1	
G793 RNC 58	G717 XPO V9	H251 FDV OV	H141 UUA 39	H612 YTC 1	
G929 SHR X	G337 XRE 3	H338 FLH A6	H613 UWR 3	H613 YTC 1	
G118 SNV OD	G629 XWS A6	H913 FTT 46	H614 UWR 3	H614 YTC 1	
G 41 SSR 39	G783 XWS A6	H985 FTT K6	H615 UWR 3	H615 YTC 1	
G 42 SSR F6	G826 XWS V2	H987 FTT 98	H633 UWR A8	H616 YTC 1	
G218 SWL E4	G828 XWS A6	H989 FTT 98	H644 UWR 37		
G 56 TGW L7	G829 XWS V2	H715 FWD K3	H651 UWR 71		
G900 TJA A1	G732 YAC G1	H718 FWD X	H932 UWX 54		
G103 TND U1	G524 YAE A6	H544 FWM A1	H428 UYB X		J888 ALL 25
G417 TNJ H3	G525 YAE A6	H 4 GBD 99	H155 UYC 72		J646 ANW T3
G115 TNL F7	G782 YAE F6	H 5 GBD 99	H476 VDM A6		J 43 BTV OB
G983 TSE 92	G536 YFW M8	H 6 GBD 99	H 39 VNH 11		J 80 BUS R3
G274 TSL G8	G680 YLP L3	H 7 GBD 99	H312 WPN OS		J302 BVO 99
G940 TTA G6	G936 YRY 2	H 8 GBD 99	H906 WYB 2		J303 BVO 99
G943 TTA K8	G606 YTA 6	H 9 GBD 99	H907 WYB 2		J304 BVO 99
G901 TWS 2	G818 YTA 6	H597 GDV X	H908 WYB 2		J305 BVO 99
G902 TWS 2		H801 GDV 3	H909 WYB 2		J173 BYD 47
G903 TWS 2		H802 GDV 2	H910 WYB 2		J701 CWT 3
G904 TWS 2		H981 GDV R5	H912 WYB 2		J702 CWT 3
G905 TWS 1	H887 AAE 44	H990 GKN OD	H913 WYB 2		J729 CWT H4

J732	CWT	H4	J234	KDL	94	J106	SOE	31	K555	GSM	E4	K338	OAF	3
J763	CWT	J6	J238	KDL	94	J132	SRE	31	K443	GYD	X	K339	OAF	3
J931	CYK	N7	J415	KEC	H6	J133	SRE	31	K445	GYD	X	K340	OAF	3
J934	CYK	55	J813	KHD	29	J253	TDA	A6	K446	GYD	X	K341	OAF	3
J127	DGC	N1	J853	KHD	E8	J261	TDA	83	K650	HNW	42	K342	OAF	3
J211	DYL	58	J161	KKE	OD	J342	TFA	R6	K835	HUM	D4	K343	OAF	3
J 2	EST	E4	J189	KLW	OD	J367	TOC	OC	K840	HUM	J1	K483	OAF	X
J 41	EYB	47	J140	KPX	10	J988	TVU	A1	K721	HYA	69	K859	ODY	99
J819	EYC	35	J141	KPX	10	J679	TWK	OS	K722	HYA	69	K865	ODY	K6
J969	EYD	2	J145	KPX	10	J 93	UBL	63	K758	KRB	N9	K 29	OEU	1
J 69	FEU	OE	J735	KTT	X	J 98	UBL	62	K328	KYC	1	K966	OEU	X
J 71	FEU	44	J570	LDF	X	J 28	UNY	64	K329	KYC	1	K967	OEU	X
J581	FFB	44	J185	LGE	2	J153	VOJ	OG	K330	KYC	1	K968	OEU	X
J582	FFB	X	J112	LKO	94	J 78	VTX	J3	K606	LAE	1	K969	OEU	44
J870	FGX	86	J 86	LLA	M1	J 42	VWO	E9	K607	LAE	1	K 96	OGA	OC
J811	FOU	25	J135	LLK	E9	J601	WHJ	28	K608	LAE	1	K542	OGA	K6
J812	FOU	G3	J329	LLK	2	J606	WHJ	A1	K609	LAE	1	K437	OKH	U9
J850	FTC	1	J517	LRL	E2	J608	WHJ	28	K610	LAE	1	K100	OMP	G7
J851	FTC	1	J511	LRY	93	J375	WWK	3	K611	LAE	1	K101	OMW	7
J852	FTC	1	J518	LRY	32	J212	XKY	20	K612	LAE	1	K102	OMW	7
J853	FTC	1	J130	LVM	T7	J759	YWA	50	K613	LAE	1	K103	OMW	7
J854	FTC	1	J177	MCW	99	J762	YWA	E8	K614	LAE	1	K104	OMW	7
J855	FTC	1	J471	MDB	58	J764	YWA	E2	K615	LAE	1	K105	OMW	7
J857	FTC	1	J914	MDG	L3				K616	LAE	1	K106	OMW	7
J858	FTC	1	J688	MFE	55				K617	LAE	1	K108	OMW	7
J859	FTC	1	J689	MFE	55				K618	LAE	1	K109	OMW	7
J690	FWS	X	J243	MFP	M6	K938	AEP	X	K619	LAE	1	K110	OMW	7
J241	FYA	2	J321	MLF	A6	K776	AFS	2	K620	LAE	1	K344	ORL	3
J580	FYA	2	J597	MNA	31	K805	AJW	N8	K621	LAE	1	K345	ORL	3
J601	FYA	2	J170	MNX	92	K 18	AND	D8	K622	LAE	1	K346	ORL	3
J 21	GCX	32	J824	MOD	86	K321	AUX	29	K623	LAE	1	K347	ORL	3
J 61	GCX	53	J825	MOD	86	K576	AVP	92	K624	LAE	1	K348	ORL	3
J 62	GCX	53	J595	MVU	H6	K578	AVP	92	K625	LAE	1	K349	ORL	3
J409	GFG	J4	J584	NBX	V4	K579	AVP	92	K626	LAE	1	K350	ORL	3
J348	GKH	M7	J 61	NJT	63	K583	AVP	92	K627	LAE	1	K351	ORL	3
J398	GKH	U9	J467	NJU	T1	K586	AVP	92	K628	LAE	1	K352	ORL	3
J693	CTC	25	J468	NJU	T1	K589	AVP	92	K629	LAE	1	K353	ORL	3
J 45	HAM	OD	J470	NJU	60	K 62	BAX	J1	K630	LAE	1	K354	ORL	3
J662	HFW	90	J613	NLH	U5	K 2	BCC	32	K348	LGK	W1	K601	ORL	3
J290	HJX	89	J297	NNB	A1	K 10	BMS	3	K138	LHT	OD	K602	ORL	3
J822	HMC	6	J236	NNC	A1	K271	BRJ	A6	K153	LHT	E2	K603	ORL	3
J823	HMC	6	J237	NNC	A1	K171	CAV	6	K 18	LUE	T6	K604	ORL	3
J824	HMC	6	J263	NNC	G1	K173	CAV	6	K361	LWS	M4	K605	ORL	3
J825	HMC	6	J272	NNC	69	K218	CBD	V5	K370	LWS	48	K606	ORL	3
J826	HMC	6	J275	NNC	69	K 5	CJT	V2	K373	LWS	E2	K607	ORL	3
J827	HMC	6	J278	NNC	69	K 6	CJT	V2	K374	LWS	M1	K608	ORL	3
J828	HMC	6	J125	OBU	M8	K 7	CJT	V2	K771	MAE	C2	K609	ORL	3
J829	HMC	6	J850	OBV	1	K892	CSX	U9	K245	MMR	X	K610	ORL	3
J610	HMF	3	J908	ODH	R1	K901	CVW	3	K246	MMR	T9	K611	ORL	3
J860	HWS	1	J200	OMP	66	K902	CVW	3	K 46	NEU	X	K612	ORL	3
J861	HWS	1	J608	OOD	V1	K905	CVW	3	K 51	NEU	45	K613	ORL	3
J862	HWS	1	J221	OTM	T9	K537	CWN	A9	K867	NEU	1	K614	ORL	3
J863	HWS	1	J305	OTT	X	K539	CWN	A9	K868	NEU	1	K615	ORL	3
J864	HWS	1	J803	PFJ	3	K410	DHH	OD	K869	NEU	1	K616	ORL	3
J865	HWS	1	J430	PPF	A1	K275	DSG	90	K870	NEU	1	K617	ORL	3
J866	HWS	1	J571	PRU	63	K 7	DTS	K5	K871	NEU	1	K618	ORL	3
J229	JJR	F7	J408	PRW	K6	K131	DTW	OD	K872	NEU	1	K619	ORL	3
J230	JJR	F7	J416	PRW	3	K807	EET	E4	K873	NEU	1	K620	ORL	3
J933	JJR	39	J610	PTA	3	K526	EFL	63	K874	NEU	1	K621	ORL	3
J459	JOW	3	J953	SBU	W3	K527	EFL	15	K875	NEU	1	K622	ORL	3
J573	JUY	C6	J140	SJT	3	K339	EJV	A9	K876	NEU	1	K623	ORL	3
J725	KBC	L9	J141	SJT	3	K597	EKU	98	K474	NTP	K2	K624	ORL	3
J727	KBC	OC	J142	SJT	3	K 4	ESC	OG	K331	OAF	3	K625	ORL	3
J732	KBC	2	J143	SJT	3	K 8	ESC	OG	K332	OAF	3	K801	ORL	3
J404	KBV	OD	J144	SJT	3	K239	FAW	A1	K333	OAF	3	K802	ORL	3
J601	KCU	D4	J145	SJT	3	K831	FEE	OD	K334	OAF	3	K803	ORL	3
J624	KCU	28	J146	SJT	3	K712	FNO	94	K335	OAF	3	K804	ORL	3
J632	KCU	28	J148	SJT	3	K338	FYG	G6	K336	OAF	3	K497	OSU	A6
J637	KCU	28	J 46	SNY	64	K721	GBE	G4	K337	OAF	3	K792	OTC	2

K861	PCN	28	K926	VDV	6	L839	CDG	5	L709	FWO	5	L463	RDN	32
K862	PCN	28	K929	VDV	2	L840	CDG	5	L711	FWO	5	L230	RDO	K5
K326	PHT	A1	K751	VFJ	2	L841	CDG	5	L712	FWO	5	L 18	RMS	T1
K327	PHT	A1	K 34	VFV	32	L842	CDG	5	L 91	GAX	OC	L625	RPX	39
K329	PHT	A1	K715	VNH	94	L548	CDV	3	L 93	GAX	OC	L778	RWW	A1
K345	PJR	F6	K278	VTT	T3	L815	CFJ	3	L683	GKE	OG	L779	RWW	A1
K757	PUT	OC	K803	WFJ	F6	L816	CFJ	3	L780	GMJ	39	L801	SAE	1
K393	PVL	90	K806	WFJ	F6	L817	CFJ	3	L945	GNF	J4	L802	SAE	1
K394	PVL	OG	K816	WFJ	6	L330	CHB	5	L959	GOP	80	L803	SAE	1
K744	RBX	N1	K998	WNC	A6	L 8	CJT	V2	L889	GYH	72	L804	SAE	1
K331	RCN	M9	K809	WPF	77	L 9	CJT	V2	L486	HKN	N1	L806	SAE	1
K332	RCN	M9	K301	WTA	4	L649	CJT	3	L494	HRE	1	L807	SAE	1
K505	RJX	E8	K723	WTT	3	L650	CJT	2	L495	HRE	1	L808	SAE	1
K518	RJX	25	K804	WTT	3	L651	CJT	2	L228	HRF	K6	L809	SAE	1
K541	RJX	T3	K805	WTT	3	L652	CJT	2	L229	HRF	K6	L820	SAE	1
K695	RNR	A1	K424	WUT	32	L435	CND	31	L231	HRF	K6	L822	SAE	1
K704	RNR	OS	K974	XND	G6	L858	COD	86	L455	HVT	1	L824	SAE	1
K712	RNR	32	K176	XOD	V1	L422	CPB	K6	L554	HVT	1	L825	SAE	1
K370	RTY	28	K622	XOD	E8	L423	CPB	K6	L556	HVT	1	L826	SAE	1
K371	RTY	A1	K432	XRF	3	L428	CPC	K6	L694	JEC	L4	L289	SEM	94
K356	SCN	39	K433	XRF	3	L929	CTT	6	L543	JFS	G6	L292	SEM	94
K357	SCN	39	K434	XRF	1	L930	CTT	6	L948	JFU	G6	L293	SEM	94
K101	SFJ	4	K435	XRF	3	L931	CTT	6	L967	JFU	G1	L631	SEU	1
K102	SFJ	4	K441	XRF	1	L932	CTT	6	L542	JJV	K5	L632	SEU	1
K103	SFJ	4	K442	XRF	1	L933	CTT	6	L703	JSC	A6	L633	SEU	1
K104	SFJ	4	K443	XRF	3	L934	CTT	6	L714	JUD	6	L634	SEU	1
K105	SFJ	4	K447	XRF	3	L935	CTT	6	L715	JUD	6	L635	SEU	1
K107	SFJ	4	K752	XTA	3	L936	CTT	6	L716	JUD	6	L636	SEU	1
K108	SFJ	4	K753	XTA	3	L937	CTT	6	L717	JUD	6	L637	SEU	1
K109	SFJ	4	K754	XTA	3	L938	CTT	6	L718	JUD	6	L638	SEU	1
K110	SFJ	4	K755	XTA	3	L939	CTT	6	L719	JUD	6	L639	SEU	1
K241	SFJ	4	K332	YDW	A9	L940	CTT	6	L720	JUD	6	L640	SEU	1
K242	SFJ	4	K562	YFJ	N1	L941	CTT	6	L721	JUD	6	L641	SEU	1
K243	SFJ	4	K308	YKG	5	L942	CTT	6	L722	JUD	6	L642	SEU	1
K244	SFJ	4	K311	YKG	5	L943	CTT	6	L142	JVR	T6	L643	SEU	1
K245	SFJ	4	K319	YKG	G8	L189	DDW	A2	L269	LCW	L9	L644	SEU	1
K246	SFJ	4	K458	YPK	N1	L193	DDW	39	L710	LFO	U2	L645	SEU	1
K247	SFJ	4				L194	DDW	39	L 23	LSG	2	L646	SEU	1
K803	SKN	94				L196	DDW	39	L 24	LSG	2	L647	SEU	1
K179	SLY	M1				L471	DOA	E8	L 26	LSG	2	L648	SEU	1
K264	SSD	J9	L223	AAB	1	L466	DOA	92	L 18	LUE	T6	L649	SEU	1
K130	STY	T4	L224	AAB	1	L484	DOA	92	L 3	LWB	R5	L650	SEU	1
K216	SUY	36	L225	AAB	1	L336	DTG	A9	L202	MHL	L3	L651	SEU	1
K237	SUY	36	L226	AAB	1	L796	DTT	84	L882	MWB	69	L652	SEU	1
K104	TCP	E8	L227	AAB	1	L519	EHD	32	L329	MYC	2	L653	SEU	1
K926	TTA	W4	L228	AAB	1	L945	EOD	6	L330	MYC	2	L654	SEU	1
K676	TTT	H5	L229	AAB	1	L947	EOD	6	L492	NDT	U3	L201	SHW	2
K879	UDB	A1	L230	AAB	1	L948	EOD	6	L866	NHL	OE	L202	SHW	2
K882	UDB	99	L322	AAB	1	L949	EOD	6	L340	NMV	A6	L203	SHW	1
K884	UDB	99	L166	AKN	OC	L 67	EPR	2	L 92	NSF	2	L204	SHW	1
K690	UFV	1	L360	ANR	G6	L 68	EPR	2	L916	NWW	23	L205	SHW	1
K691	UFV	1	L345	ATA	86	L 69	EPR	3	L919	NWW	K8	L206	SHW	1
K692	UFV	1	L305	AUT	T4	L193	FDV	6	L920	NWW	35	L207	SHW	1
K693	UFV	1	L318	AUT	K6	L194	FDV	6	L924	NWW	H4	L208	SHW	1
K694	UFV	1	L513	BDH	OB	L195	FDV	6	L945	NWW	19	L209	SHW	1
K922	UFX	84	L524	BDH	M8	L197	FDV	6	L946	NWW	19	L103	SKB	69
K711	UTT	6	L267	BFJ	43	L201	FDV	6	L919	OGW	M4	L104	SKB	69
K714	UTT	E8	L332	BFX	L2	L203	FDV	6	L 32	OKV	G6	L106	SKB	69
K718	UTT	6	L201	BPL	34	L204	FDV	6	L194	OVO	U1	L670	SMC	3
K719	UTT	6	L225	BUT	E4	L208	FDV	6	L195	OVO	U1	L998	TEU	44
K725	UTT	6	L 9	CCH	OW	L209	FDV	6	L210	OYC	R4	L121	TFB	1
K726	UTT	E8	L248	CCK	5	L210	FDV	6	L211	OYC	R4	L122	TFB	1
K727	UTT	15	L685	CDD	6	L211	FDV	6	L238	OYC	35	L123	TFB	1
K730	UTT	15	L691	CDD	6	L212	FDV	6	L182	PMX	84	L124	TFB	1
K732	UTT	E8	L692	CDD	6	L214	FDV	6	L 2	POW	7	L125	TFB	1
K775	UTT	86	L693	CDD	6	L447	FFR	6	L667	PWT	58	L126	TFB	1
K760	UVR	E2	L694	CDD	6	L448	FFR	6	L669	PWT	G3	L127	TFB	1
K596	VBC	H4	L695	CDD	6	L 24	FNC	A6	L800	RAG	76	L128	TFB	1
K922	VDV	1	L696	CDD	6	L139	FOJ	92	L 3	RDC	A6	L129	TFB	1

L130	TFB	1	L881	VHT	1	L830	WHY	1	M850	ATC	1	M418	CCV	3
L132	TFB	1	L883	VHT	1	L819	WMW	70	M851	ATC	1	M419	CCV	3
L133	TFB	1	L884	VHT	1	L778	XCV	88	M852	ATC	1	M420	CCV	3
L134	TFB	1	L885	VHT	1	L779	XCV	88	M853	ATC	1	M421	CCV	3
L135	TFB	1	L886	VHT	1	L153	XDD	X	M854	ATC	1	M422	CCV	3
L136	TFB	1	L887	VHT	1	L803	XDG	5	M855	ATC	1	M423	CCV	3
L877	TFB	1	L889	VHT	1	L804	XDG	5	M856	ATC	1	M424	CCV	3
L973	TFB	44	L890	VHT	1	L805	XDG	5	M857	ATC	1	M425	CCV	3
L978	TFB	44	L891	VHT	1	L806	XDG	5	M858	ATC	1	M426	CCV	3
L988	TFB	44	L892	VHT	1	L518	XFB	V3	M859	ATC	1	M501	CCV	3
L991	TFB	44	L893	VHT	1	L836	XGV	R9	M860	ATC	1	M502	CCV	3
L998	TFB	44	L895	VHT	1	L255	XHR	H9	M861	ATC	1	M503	CCV	3
L 21	THU	X	L896	VHT	1	L530	XUT	A8	M862	ATC	1	M977	CCV	X
L 24	THU	44	L897	VHT	1	L535	YCC	U9	M863	ATC	1	M259	CDE	15
L 89	TOU	X	L898	VHT	1	L537	YCC	U9	M864	ATC	1	M 10	CJT	V2
L 93	TOU	X	L899	VHT	1	L837	YCU	OD	M865	ATC	1	M 11	CJT	V2
L113	TOU	44	L901	VHT	1	L511	YHA	31	M866	ATC	1	M 12	CJT	V2
L838	UCD	40	L902	VHT	1	L112	YOD	4	M867	ATC	1	M 13	CJT	V2
L525	UCV	OC	L903	VHT	1	L113	YOD	4	M868	ATC	1	M 20	CJT	V2
L943	UEU	X	L904	VHT	1	L114	YOD	4	M870	ATC	1	M 40	CJT	V2
L944	UEU	44	L905	VHT	1	L115	YOD	4	M871	ATC	1	M657	COR	E8
L945	UEU	44	L906	VHT	1	L116	YOD	4	M872	ATC	1	M372	CRL	U8
L917	UGA	54	L907	VHT	1	L117	YOD	4	M873	ATC	1	M373	CRL	U8
L102	UHF	69	L908	VHT	1	L118	YOD	4	M874	ATC	1	M765	CWS	2
L108	UHF	C4	L210	VHU	2	L119	YOD	4	M920	ATC	45	M845	CWS	49
L110	UHF	69	L211	VHU	1	L120	YOD	4	M662	BAF	K4	M548	DAF	G3
L390	UHU	1	L212	VHU	1	L121	YOD	4	M227	BBX	OE	M549	DAF	X
L155	UNS	3	L213	VHU	1	L122	YOD	4	M294	BBX	OG	M550	DAF	X
L355	VCV	3	L214	VHU	1	L123	YOD	4	M 45	BEG	1	M552	DAF	X
L356	VCV	3	L215	VHU	1	L124	YOD	4	M 46	BEG	1	M582	DAF	J2
L357	VCV	3	L216	VHU	1	L125	YOD	4	M 48	BEG	1	M413	DEU	2
L358	VCV	3	L217	VHU	1	L126	YOD	4	M631	BEU	V3	M 85	DEW	5
L359	VCV	3	L218	VHU	1	L248	YOD	4	M882	BEU	1	M 86	DEW	5
L360	VCV	3	L219	VHU	1	L249	YOD	4	M587	BFL	T3	M 87	DEW	A1
L401	VCV	3	L220	VHU	1	L250	YOD	4	M112	BMR	7	M301	DGP	6
L402	VCV	3	L221	VHU	1	L251	YOD	4	M113	BMR	7	M302	DGP	6
L403	VCV	3	L223	VHU	1	L252	YOD	4	M114	BMR	7	M303	DGP	6
L404	VCV	3	L224	VHU	1	L253	YOD	4	M115	BMR	7	M304	DGP	6
L405	VCV	3	L225	VHU	1	L254	YOD	4	M116	BMR	7	M305	DGP	6
L406	VCV	3	L503	VHU	1	L255	YOD	4	M117	BMR	7	M306	DGP	6
L628	VCV	3	L504	VHU	1	L256	YOD	4	M118	BMR	7	M307	DGP	6
L629	VCV	3	L505	VHU	1	L257	YOD	4	M119	BMR	7	M308	DGP	6
L630	VCV	3	L506	VHU	1	L258	YOD	4	M711	BMR	7	M309	DGP	6
L631	VCV	3	L507	VHU	1	L259	YOD	4	M405	BNJ	X	M310	DGP	6
L632	VCV	3	L508	VHU	1	L260	YOD	4	M 92	BOU	2	M311	DGP	6
L633	VCV	3	L701	VHY	44	L302	YOD	4	M 93	BOU	OB	M312	DGP	6
L634	VCV	3	L702	VHY	44	L543	YUS	H8	M301	BRL	3	M313	DGP	6
L635	VCV	3	L703	VHY	X				M302	BRL	3	M314	DGP	6
L636	VCV	3	L704	VHY	44				M303	BRL	3	M315	DGP	6
L637	VCV	3	L705	VHY	X				M553	BRL	OD	M316	DGP	6
L638	VCV	3	L706	VHY	X	M238	AAF	OC	M835	BRL	OC	M317	DGP	6
L639	VCV	3	L707	VHY	X	M 14	ABC	2	M479	BTC	V3	M318	DGP	6
L640	VCV	3	L708	VHY	44	M 19	ABC	2	M 5	BUS	12	M319	DGP	6
L641	VCV	3	L709	VHY	X	M 7	ALP	30	M 12	BUS	84	M509	DHU	1
L642	VCV	3	L710	VHY	X	M831	ATC	2	M289	CAM	G6	M510	DHU	1
L643	VCV	3	L711	VHY	X	M832	ATC	2	M105	CCD	6	M511	DHU	1
L644	VCV	3	L712	VHY	44	M833	ATC	1	M106	CCD	6	M512	DHU	1
L645	VCV	3	L139	VRH	6	M834	ATC	1	M108	CCD	6	M513	DHU	1
L646	VCV	3	L140	VRH	6	M835	ATC	1	M407	CCV	3	M514	DHU	1
L647	VCV	3	L141	VRH	6	M836	ATC	1	M408	CCV	3	M515	DHU	1
L648	VCV	3	L611	WCC	A2	M837	ATC	1	M409	CCV	3	M516	DHU	1
L649	VCV	3	L612	WCC	A2	M838	ATC	1	M410	CCV	3	M517	DHU	1
L650	VCV	3	L716	WCC	R4	M843	ATC	1	M411	CCV	3	M518	DHU	1
L651	VCV	3	L725	WCV	U8	M844	ATC	1	M412	CCV	3	M519	DHU	1
L618	VEU	92	L726	WCV	U8	M845	ATC	1	M413	CCV	3	M830	DRL	E2
L966	VGE	G3	L297	WFH	OG	M846	ATC	1	M414	CCV	3	M102	ECV	3
L878	VHT	1	L422	WHR	86	M847	ATC	1	M415	CCV	3	M103	ECV	3
L879	VHT	1	L827	WHY	1	M848	ATC	1	M416	CCV	3	M697	EDD	6
L880	VHT	1	L829	WHY	1	M849	ATC	1	M417	CCV	3			

M698	EDD	6	M629	HDV	6	M359	LFX	M1	M226	UTM	6	M857	XHY	1
M699	EDD	6	M630	HDV	6	M360	LFX	M1	M227	UTM	6	M314	XSX	F8
M701	EDD	6	M636	HDV	6	M797	LJW	OG	M228	UTM	6	M495	XWF	V7
M702	EDD	6	M637	HDV	6	M817	LNC	89	M229	UTM	6	M 12	YCL	M1
M703	EDD	6	M638	HDV	6	M139	LNP	55	M230	UTM	6	M122	YCM	K6
M704	EDD	6	M639	HDV	6	M 39	LOA	63	M231	UTM	6			
M705	EDD	6	M640	HDV	6	M104	LOA	H6	M232	UTM	6			
M386	EDH	70	M641	HDV	6	M105	LOA	H6	M233	UTM	6			
M312	EEA	21	M644	HFJ	OD	M106	LOA	H6	M234	UTM	6	N633	ACF	2
M361	EHU	OD	M822	HNS	A8	M107	LOA	H6	M235	UTM	6	N634	ACF	2
M843	EMW	5	M823	HNS	A9	M108	LOA	H6	M236	UTM	6	N635	ACF	2
M844	EMW	5	M825	HNS	A9	M109	LOA	H6	M237	UTM	6	N636	ACF	2
M845	EMW	5	M829	HNS	98	M153	LPL	39	M238	UTM	6	N637	ACF	2
M137	FAE	1	M 51	HOD	4	M901	LTT	3	M239	UTM	6	N604	ADC	L4
M138	FAE	1	M 52	HOD	4	M902	LTT	3	M240	UTM	6	N990	AEF	A6
M140	FAE	1	M 53	HOD	4	M848	LTX	OC	M241	UTM	6	N996	AEF	W6
M141	FAE	1	M127	HOD	4	M 18	LUE	T6	M242	UTM	6	N313	AMC	5
M142	FAE	1	M128	HOD	4	M725	LYP	33	M243	UTM	6	N317	AMC	5
M292	FAE	3	M129	HOD	4	M407	MPD	N8	M244	UTM	6	N318	AMC	5
M520	FFB	1	M130	HOD	4	M248	NNF	2	M245	UTM	6	N319	AMC	5
M521	FFB	1	M131	HOD	4	M249	NNF	2	M246	UTM	6	N320	AMC	5
M522	FFB	1	M132	HOD	4	M343	NOD	6	M247	UTM	6	N707	AOJ	OS
M523	FFB	1	M261	HOD	4	M917	OCV	X	M248	UTM	6	N 3	ARJ	F6
M524	FFB	1	M262	HOD	4	M150	OKK	OD	M249	UTM	6	N541	BFY	A6
M525	FFB	1	M263	HOD	4	M738	OKK	25	M250	UTM	6	N542	BFY	A6
M526	FFB	1	M264	HOD	4	M646	OOM	A6	M345	UVX	G6	N543	BFY	A6
M527	FFB	1	M265	HOD	4	M781	OOM	92	M134	UWY	H4	N506	BJA	6
M528	FFB	1	M266	HOD	4	M782	OOM	92	M802	UYA	2	N507	BJA	6
M529	FFB	1	M267	HOD	4	M619	ORJ	U9	M803	UYA	2	N508	BJA	6
M530	FFB	1	M268	HOD	4	M 56	PCY	X	M804	UYA	2	N509	BJA	6
M531	FFB	1	M269	HOD	4	M684	PDA	12	M805	UYA	2	N510	BJA	6
M532	FFB	1	M270	HOD	4	M778	PDC	A6	M215	UYD	C3	N511	BJA	6
M533	FFB	1	M271	HOD	4	M220	PMS	2	M278	UYD	2	N512	BJA	6
M534	FFB	1	M272	HOD	4	M 46	POL	A1	M279	UYD	2	N513	BJA	6
M535	FFB	1	M273	HOD	4	M272	POS	C7	M281	UYD	2	N514	BJA	6
M536	FFB	1	M274	HOD	4	M674	RAJ	2	M282	UYD	2	N515	BJA	6
M537	FFB	1	M 43	HSU	23	M675	RAJ	2	M 79	VAK	80	N516	BJA	6
M538	FFB	1	M191	HTT	6	M676	RAJ	3	M561	VUM	H6	N517	BJA	6
M439	FHW	2	M192	HTT	6	M677	RAJ	3	M562	VUM	H6	N518	BJA	6
M440	FHW	2	M193	HTT	6	M678	RAJ	3	M563	VUM	H6	N 11	BLC	37
M 85	FMR	A4	M194	HTT	6	M851	RAW	C4	M631	VUM	H6	N 22	BLU	3
M 41	FTC	2	M255	HVP	G8	M606	RCP	1	M632	VUM	H6	N670	BNV	OC
M764	FTT	3	M345	JBO	6	M608	RCP	F7	M226	VWU	3	N375	BOP	OG
M765	FTT	3	M360	JBO	6	M616	RCP	OD	M246	VWU	3	N629	BWG	V6
M766	FTT	3	M950	JBO	6	M740	RCP	38	M239	VYA	2	N315	BYA	R5
M768	FTT	3	M706	JDG	6	M741	RCP	38	M240	VYA	2	N318	BYA	R5
M769	FTT	3	M707	JDG	6	M775	RCP	25	M241	VYA	2	N319	BYA	3
M809	FTT	3	M597	JDV	X	M809	RCP	32	M242	VYA	2	N320	BYA	35
M 9	FUG	71	M 91	JHB	G6	M413	RND	2	M508	VYA	2	N967	BYC	69
M 12	FUG	M7	M 93	JHB	39	M122	SKY	OB	M509	VYA	2	N970	BYC	69
M988	GDF	X	M342	JJR	L9	M569	SRE	52	M371	VYB	X	N132	BYD	C3
M752	GDV	86	M510	JRY	39	M582	SSX	X	M750	VYB	N7	N462	CBU	20
M661	GJF	OE	M 41	KAX	V5	M345	TDO	79	M 78	VYD	OE	N 14	CJT	V2
M 45	GRY	A6	M943	KDF	OG	M675	TNA	A6	M419	VYD	A1	N779	CKB	X
M 46	GRY	A6	M463	KFJ	OD	M676	TNA	A6	M421	VYD	84	N303	CKP	M8
M 47	GRY	A6	M465	KFJ	72	M 34	TRR	A3	M 85	WBW	5	N182	CMJ	6
M 48	GRY	A6	M236	KNR	K6	M305	TSF	2	M 86	WBW	5	N183	CMJ	6
M590	GRY	38	M158	KOD	86	M497	TVH	V1	M103	WBW	6	N541	CYA	69
M221	GTT	X	M304	KOD	4	M534	TVH	F4	M583	WLV	V7	N757	CYA	C3
M 6	HAT	E8	M305	KOD	4	M201	TYB	35	M584	WLV	V7	N758	CYA	35
M 8	HAT	E8	M325	KRY	A3	M572	TYB	69	M887	WWB	11	N751	DAK	A9
M847	HDF	5	M582	KTG	G6	M573	TYB	69	M626	XCM	X	N614	DKR	G6
M622	HDV	6	M587	KTT	84	M842	TYC	G6	M372	XEX	2	N801	DNE	2
M623	HDV	6	M381	KVR	2	M843	TYC	G6	M373	XEX	2	N802	DNE	6
M624	HDV	6	M382	KVR	2	M861	TYC	A1	M861	XFY	E4	N817	DNE	5
M625	HDV	6	M386	KVR	2	M862	TYC	A1	M549	XHC	11	N818	DNE	5
M626	HDV	6	M392	KVR	2	M792	TYD	G6	M153	XHW	E8	N123	DNV	L4
M627	HDV	6	M393	KVR	2	M968	TYG	G6	M165	XHW	V2	N605	DOR	69
M628	HDV	6	M629	KVU	U9	M968	USC	1	M349	XHY	C4	N911	DWJ	39

N919	DWJ	V7	N878	HWS	1	N212	KBJ	U8	N978	NAP	6	N211	UFX	92
N172	DWX	G6	N879	HWS	1	N392	KHT	44	N979	NAP	6	N212	UFX	92
N599	DWY	6	N880	HWS	2	N471	KHU	2	N980	NAP	6	N648	UOE	X
N199	DYB	35	N881	HWS	2	N472	KHU	2	N981	NAP	6	N650	UOE	X
N201	DYB	84	N882	HWS	2	N473	KHU	2	N982	NAP	6	N167	UTA	E2
N202	DYB	84	N883	HWS	2	N474	KHU	2	N145	NFB	80	N101	UTT	4
N310	DYC	N7	N884	HWS	2	N812	KHW	X	N884	NHR	T9	N102	UTT	4
N586	DYD	X	N885	HWS	2	N813	KHW	X	N319	NHY	2	N103	UTT	4
N383	EAK	G2	N886	HWS	2	N814	KHW	44	N320	NHY	2	N104	UTT	4
N617	ESN	C4	N887	HWS	2	N913	KHW	2	N321	NHY	2	N105	UTT	4
N333	EST	OB	N889	HWS	2	N914	KHW	2	N322	NHY	2	N107	UTT	4
N908	EWD	22	N890	HWS	2	N460	KMW	L4	N789	NYS	20	N108	UTT	4
N 24	EYB	A1	N891	HWS	2	N998	KUS	E4	N 46	OAE	2	N109	UTT	4
N556	EYB	2	N892	HWS	2	N 76	KVS	E4	N205	OAE	E4	N110	UTT	4
N557	EYB	2	N893	HWS	2	N531	KWS	X	N748	OYR	L7	N112	UTT	4
N558	EYB	2	N894	HWS	2	N556	KWS	V3	N958	PCG	92	N307	UTT	4
N559	EYB	2	N895	HWS	2	N821	KWS	2	N959	PCG	92	N197	UUK	92
N561	EYB	2	N896	HWS	2	N822	KWS	2	N 94	PDV	V7	N208	UUK	92
N323	FEH	X	N897	HWS	2	N202	LCK	U1	N275	PDV	4	N895	VEG	V2
N423	FFS	OS	N898	HWS	2	N205	LCK	U1	N276	PDV	4	N751	VNA	J4
N119	FHK	D3	N899	HWS	2	N976	LCL	K4	N277	PDV	4	N456	VOD	G6
N803	FLW	1	N901	HWS	2	N401	LDF	5	N278	PDV	4	N457	VOD	G6
N804	FLW	1	N902	HWS	2	N402	LDF	5	N279	PDV	4	N810	VOD	3
N805	FLW	1	N903	HWS	2	N403	LDF	5	N281	PDV	4	N811	VOD	3
N806	FLW	1	N904	HWS	2	N404	LDF	5	N282	PDV	4	N644	VSS	5
N807	FLW	1	N905	HWS	2	N405	LDF	5	N283	PDV	4	N770	VTT	N1
N808	FLW	1	N906	HWS	2	N406	LDF	5	N284	PDV	4	N771	VTT	N1
N809	FLW	1	N907	HWS	2	N407	LDF	5	N285	PDV	4	N242	WDO	M8
N810	FLW	1	N219	HWX	H4	N408	LDF	5	N286	PDV	4	N232	WFJ	3
N811	FLW	1	N220	HWX	H4	N409	LDF	5	N287	PDV	4	N233	WFJ	3
N428	FOW	3	N226	HWX	H4	N614	LEU	57	N288	PDV	4	N410	WJL	69
N993	FWT	25	N232	HWX	63	N926	LEU	X	N289	PDV	4	N971	WJL	H9
N 28	FWU	1	N121	JHR	7	N930	LEU	44	N919	PHB	X	N 2	WKC	98
N 29	FWU	1	N122	JHR	7	N222	LFR	F6	N498	PYS	U8	N583	WND	2
N 34	FWU	1	N123	JHR	7	N243	LHT	1	N514	PYS	U8	N584	WND	2
N 65	FWU	OS	N124	JHR	7	N244	LHT	1	N527	PYS	33	N585	WND	2
N605	GAH	2	N393	JWS	44	N245	LHT	1	N 4	RDC	11	N586	WND	2
N609	GAH	2	N394	JWS	44	N246	LHT	1	N718	RDD	5	N608	WND	3
N611	GAH	2	N395	JWS	X	N247	LHT	1	N719	RDD	5	N610	WND	3
N613	GAH	2	N396	JWS	X	N248	LHT	1	N720	RDD	5	N612	WND	3
N622	GAH	2	N226	KAE	2	N249	LHT	1	N721	RDD	5	N791	WNE	63
N623	GAH	2	N227	KAE	2	N250	LHT	1	N722	RDD	5	N989	WNE	J4
N188	GFR	6	N228	KAE	1	N549	LHU	1	N723	RDD	5	N501	WOE	92
N189	GFR	6	N229	KAE	1	N550	LHU	1	N724	RDD	5	N502	WOE	92
N190	GFR	6	N230	KAE	1	N551	LHU	1	N725	RDD	5	N503	WOE	92
N642	GLO	OS	N231	KAE	1	N552	LHU	1	N726	RDD	5	N504	WOE	92
N719	GRV	3	N232	KAE	1	N553	LHU	1	N727	RDD	5	N505	WOE	92
N539	HAE	1	N233	KAE	1	N554	LHU	1	N728	RDD	5	N731	XDV	6
N540	HAE	1	N234	KAE	1	N556	LHU	1	N729	RDD	5	N732	XDV	6
N541	HAE	1	N235	KAE	1	N557	LHU	1	N730	RDD	5	N733	XDV	6
N542	HAE	1	N236	KAE	1	N558	LHU	1	N731	RDD	5	N734	XDV	6
N543	HAE	1	N237	KAE	1	N559	LHU	1	N732	RDD	5	N735	XDV	6
N544	HAE	1	N238	KAE	1	N561	LHU	3	N733	RDD	5	N736	XDV	6
N545	HAE	1	N239	KAE	1	N562	LHU	3	N734	RDD	5	N737	XDV	6
N546	HAE	1	N240	KAE	1	N563	LHU	3	N735	RDD	5	N738	XDV	6
N547	HAE	1	N241	KAE	1	N564	LHU	3	N862	RFU	16	N739	XDV	6
N184	HBX	89	N242	KAE	1	N780	LHY	25	N762	SAV	3	N740	XDV	6
N351	HBX	18	N166	KAF	U8	N125	LMW	7	N890	SBB	39	N742	XDV	6
N348	HGK	6	N167	KAF	U8	N126	LMW	7	N335	SDV	N1	N743	XDV	6
N349	HGK	6	N168	KAF	U8	N127	LMW	7	N556	SJF	33	N744	XDV	6
N350	HGK	5	N169	KAF	U8	N128	LMW	7	N622	SOP	92	N855	XMO	T7
N351	HGK	5	N170	KAF	U8	N 18	LUE	T6	N626	SOP	92	N857	XMO	E8
N239	HHT	44	N270	KAM	L4	N 88	LUE	T6	N628	SOP	92	N860	XMO	27
N 8	HMC	A4	N271	KAM	L4	N410	MBW	6	N631	SOP	92	N862	XMO	27
N463	HRN	6	N272	KAM	L4	N411	MBW	6	N 40	TCC	86	N869	XMO	T7
N464	HRN	6	N273	KAM	L4	N435	MGF	39	N653	THO	36	N870	XMO	T7
N875	HWS	1	N274	KAM	L4	N152	MTG	5	N654	TTA	X	N873	XMO	T7
N876	HWS	1	N275	KAM	L4	N153	MTG	5	N655	TTA	X	N581	XNT	OD
N877	HWS	1	N276	KAM	L4	N230	MUS	64	N210	UFX	92	N231	YCT	84

N358	YNB	F8	P 32	EDV	96	P445	KYC	2	P618	PGP	6	P900	TCC	12
N498	YNB	OG	P317	EFL	5	P446	KYC	2	P619	PGP	6	P441	TCV	3
N837	YRC	G6	P318	EFL	5	P447	KYC	2	P636	PGP	6	P442	TCV	3
			P319	EFL	5	P448	KYC	2	P639	PGP	6	P443	TCV	3
			P719	EOD	N1	P926	KYC	U6	P640	PGP	6	P444	TCV	3
			P984	EOD	X	P927	KYC	U6	P534	PLB	E8	P445	TCV	3
P830	ADO	80	P937	EOP	80	P928	KYC	84	P 2	POW	33	P446	TCV	3
P849	ADO	OD	P420	EOX	89	P929	KYC	84	P521	PRL	3	P576	TDD	OG
P613	AJL	H9	P488	EOX	V4	P934	KYC	86	P522	PRL	3	P161	TDW	5
P 50	AND	D8	P206	ETA	W7	P688	LKL	G3	P899	PWW	M8	P187	TGD	3
P 7	ARL	17	P798	FCF	80	P689	LKL	G3	P960	PYA	L9	P189	TGD	3
P321	ARU	E8	P799	FCF	80	P691	LKL	K4	P533	RAF	X	P276	THW	X
P302	AUM	1	P562	FDA	92	P985	LKL	87	P270	RBX	G5	P643	TMV	R4
P303	AUM	1	P563	FDA	92	P 88	LUE	T6	P494	RHU	G6	P492	TNP	OG
P304	AUM	1	P565	FDA	92	P179	LYB	2	P 8	RJH	93	P167	TNY	5
P305	AUM	1	P567	FDA	92	P180	LYB	2	P183	RSC	A6	P171	TNY	5
P557	BAY	OB	P568	FDA	92	P181	LYB	2	P340	RTC	44	P525	UDG	M7
P558	BAY	79	P887	FMO	E5	P182	LYB	2	P341	RTC	44	P655	UFB	1
P 4	BBC	38	P758	FOD	6	P183	LYB	2	P342	RTC	44	P656	UFB	1
P389	BEL	92	P760	FOD	6	P620	MDT	OS	P343	RTC	44	P657	UFB	1
P390	BEL	92	P762	FOD	6	P407	MLA	2	P344	RTC	44	P658	UFB	1
P391	BEL	92	P347	FOL	W3	P408	MLA	3	P345	RTC	44	P659	UFB	1
P392	BEL	92	P110	FRS	6	P409	MLA	3	P346	RTC	44	P660	UFB	1
P393	BEL	92	P618	FTV	L3	P410	MLA	3	P575	RUL	X	P361	UFH	L3
P394	BEL	92	P690	FUJ	12	P411	MLA	3	P212	RWR	A4	P 92	URG	5
P395	BEL	92	P821	FVU	5	P473	MNA	A6	P944	RWS	2	P932	VAE	45
P396	BEL	92	P822	FVU	5	P474	MNA	A6	P945	RWS	2	P 43	VDF	X
P158	BFJ	G6	P823	FVU	5	P107	MOV	89	P946	RWS	2	P159	VHR	7
P234	BFJ	3	P824	FVU	5	P644	MSC	2	P 87	SAF	F1	P160	VHR	7
P845	BJF	12	P825	FVU	5	P563	MSX	6	P827	SAF	X	P161	VHR	7
P 12	BSL	21	P826	FVU	5	P564	MSX	6	P988	SCK	OG	P689	VHU	L4
P701	BTA	6	P827	FVU	5	P690	NAV	R4	P452	SCV	U8	P505	VUS	11
P702	BTA	6	P828	FVU	5	P476	NCR	22	P453	SCV	U8	P506	VUS	11
P703	BTA	6	P104	GHE	57	P696	NDX	G4	P454	SCV	U8	P 73	VWO	39
P704	BTA	6	P115	GHE	45	P232	NKK	G6	P455	SCV	U8	P 74	VWO	E8
P705	BTA	6	P116	GHE	45	P133	NVM	J4	P501	SCV	X	P 76	VWO	15
P706	BTA	6	P816	GMU	6	P970	OAK	21	P 7	SKC	OS	P304	VWR	67
P707	BTA	6	P817	GMU	6	P677	OCV	X	P901	SMR	5	P344	VWR	84
P708	BTA	6	P819	GNC	5	P427	ORL	3	P902	SMR	5	P786	VYS	94
P709	BTA	6	P820	GNC	5	P428	ORL	3	P903	SMR	5	P 9	WAC	L3
P710	BTA	6	P 86	GOF	H6	P429	ORL	3	P904	SMR	5	P298	WFG	E8
P711	BTA	6	P897	GOG	T9	P430	ORL	3	P905	SMR	5	P556	WWS	X
P712	BTA	6	P744	GOH	G3	P431	ORL	3	P906	SMR	5	P137	XFW	T2
P713	BTA	6	P283	HFY	OW	P432	ORL	3	P907	SMR	5	P466	XHW	37
P714	BTA	6	P501	HNE	OW	P433	ORL	3	P908	SMR	5	P687	XLJ	92
P 9	CAE	OD	P306	HWG	G6	P434	ORL	3	P909	SMR	5	P688	XLJ	92
P944	CEG	G6	P423	JDT	V7	P435	ORL	3	P910	SMR	5	P689	XLJ	92
P590	CFH	36	P429	JDT	86	P436	ORL	3	P911	SMR	5	P690	XLJ	92
P308	CFJ	OD	P550	JEG	R4	P437	ORL	3	P912	SMR	5	P691	XLJ	92
P627	CGM	2	P211	JKL	G6	P438	ORL	3	P913	SMR	5	P692	XLJ	92
P628	CGM	2	P470	JWB	96	P439	ORL	3	P914	SMR	5	P693	XLJ	92
P629	CGM	2	P719	JYA	C3	P440	ORL	3	P 3	SMS	31	P801	XTA	6
P630	CGM	2	P725	JYA	24	P251	PAE	1	P151	SMW	7	P802	XTA	6
P631	CGM	2	P726	JYA	24	P252	PAE	1	P152	SMW	7	P803	XTA	6
P 15	CJT	V2	P727	JYA	35	P253	PAE	1	P153	SMW	7	P804	XTA	6
P 16	CJT	V2	P 87	JYC	69	P254	PAE	1	P154	SMW	7	P805	XTA	6
P532	CLJ	47	P 89	JYC	69	P255	PAE	1	P155	SMW	7	P806	XTA	6
P719	COD	X	P798	JYD	X	P256	PAE	1	P156	SMW	7	P913	XUG	K3
P162	CON	OE	P806	JYD	X	P257	PAE	1	P157	SMW	7	P 9	YET	L2
P235	CTA	3	P117	KBL	G6	P258	PAE	1	P158	SMW	7	P536	YEU	49
P236	CTA	3	P915	KKY	D2	P259	PAE	1	P913	SUM	X	P943	YSB	V5
P403	CTA	C3	P133	KOJ	W3	P260	PAE	1	P914	SUM	X	P944	YSB	F4
P308	CTT	4	P785	KRW	83	P261	PAE	1	P915	SUM	X	P964	YTA	96
P516	CTV	OB	P224	KTP	T8	P262	PAE	1	P288	SUV	X	P707	YTT	V1
P556	CUJ	OG	P828	KTP	1	P263	PAE	1	P100	SYD	E4	P826	YUM	1
P688	DAW	OS	P829	KTP	1	P264	PAE	1	P 10	TCC	H8	P827	YUM	1
P141	DDV	G5	P950	KVP	43	P736	PAF	X	P200	TCC	55	P833	YUM	1
P341	DOF	92	P442	KYC	2	P684	PBP	OG	P777	TCC	92	P834	YUM	1
P853	DTT	3	P443	KYC	2	P256	PBX	89				P836	YUM	2

			R451	CCV	3	R307	JAF	3	R107	NTA	6	R764	VNT	W3
			R452	CCV	3	R308	JAF	3	R108	NTA	6	R371	VOK	OD
			R453	CCV	3	R309	JAF	3	R109	NTA	6	R460	VOP	1
Q995	CPE	P	R454	CCV	3	R310	JAF	3	R110	NTA	6	R629	VYB	G3
Q160	HCP	N9	R455	CCV	3	R962	JCU	H6	R112	NTA	6	R632	VYB	24
Q130	REU	X	R456	CCV	3	R963	JCU	H6	R113	NTA	6	R639	VYB	L8
Q507	VHR	P	R457	CCV	3	R550	JDF	5	R114	NTA	6	R149	VYC	OS
			R458	CCV	3	R551	JDF	5	R115	NTA	6	R 35	WDA	A6
			R459	CCV	3	R552	JDF	5	R116	NTA	6	R865	WHY	44
			R460	CCV	3	R553	JDF	5	R 54	OCK	M7	R866	WHY	44
R558	ACV	X	R461	CCV	3	R554	JDF	5	R113	OFJ	4	R867	WHY	44
R222	AJP	K2	R462	CCV	3	R807	JDV	6	R114	OFJ	4	R501	WJF	97
R943	AMB	54	R463	CCV	3	R902	JDV	6	R115	OFJ	4	R502	WJF	J3
R 12	AND	D8	R464	CCV	3	R903	JDV	6	R116	OFJ	4	R526	WYB	C3
R 30	ARJ	F6	R 2	CJT	V2	R904	JDV	6	R117	OFJ	4	R129	WYD	X
R 2	AVC	84	R 3	CJT	V2	R 7	JMJ	T1	R118	OFJ	4	R130	WYD	X
R297	AYB	1	R 18	CJT	V2	R 57	JSG	F6	R119	OFJ	4	R131	WYD	X
R298	AYB	3	R 19	CJT	V2	R132	KAE	OW	R120	OFJ	4	R199	WYD	35
R299	AYB	1	R 30	CJT	V2	R757	KCU	OS	R121	OFJ	4	R202	WYD	35
R355	AYC	C3	R 90	CJT	V2	R606	KDD	5	R122	OFJ	4	R208	WYD	84
R701	BAE	1	R477	CKN	16	R607	KDD	5	R123	OFJ	4	R209	WYD	84
R702	BAE	1	R920	COU	1	R610	KDD	5	R124	OFJ	4	R372	XYD	24
R703	BAE	1	R777	DEN	R7	R615	KDD	6	R125	OFJ	4	R373	XYD	24
R704	BAE	1	R888	DEN	R7	R727	KDD	E1	R126	OFJ	4	R380	XYD	35
R705	BAE	1	R203	DHB	5	R667	KFE	G6	R767	OHY	L4	R636	YAV	OD
R706	BAE	1	R204	DHB	5	R865	KGU	X	R667	OJM	80	R661	YAV	OB
R707	BAE	1	R205	DHB	5	R915	KGU	X	R680	OJM	80	R455	YDT	T2
R708	BAE	1	R206	DHB	5	R275	LDE	M6	R608	OTA	N1	R470	YDT	57
R709	BAE	1	R207	DHB	5	R 6	LEY	OC	R609	OTA	N1	R851	YDV	3
R710	BAE	1	R208	DHB	5	R814	LFV	49	R100	PAR	U1	R527	YRP	U8
R711	BAE	1	R230	DKO	OD	R943	LHT	2	R200	PAR	U1	R530	YRP	U8
R712	BAE	1	R668	DNS	V8	R 18	LUE	T6	R300	PAR	U1	R801	YUD	6
R714	BAE	1	R909	DOU	R5	R479	MCW	6	R101	PBW	X	R803	YUD	6
R715	BAE	1	R101	DTC	44	R480	MCW	6	R 2	POW	33	R804	YUD	6
R716	BAE	1	R102	DTC	44	R481	MCW	6	R 3	POW	33	R805	YUD	6
R717	BAE	1	R305	DUA	J4	R482	MCW	6	R 4	POW	33	R807	YUD	6
R718	BAE	1	R583	DYG	A6	R103	MEH	50	R719	RAD	1	R808	YUD	5
R566	BAF	72	R376	EBX	89	R677	MEW	45	R650	RKX	61	R809	YUD	5
R 9	BBC	38	R 87	EDW	15	R678	MEW	45	R 12	SBK	U1	R810	YUD	5
R751	BDV	6	R742	EGS	OB	R679	MEW	45	R748	SDF	L3	R811	YUD	5
R400	BEN	32	R990	EHU	25	R680	MEW	45	R918	SDF	X	R812	YUD	5
R500	BEN	32	R 61	FAE	X	R778	MFH	24	R851	SDT	11	R823	YUD	6
R600	BEN	32	R612	FBX	M7	R974	MGB	63	R872	SDT	T6	R824	YUD	6
R901	BOU	1	R901	FDV	6	R221	MSA	1	R309	STA	4			
R902	BOU	1	R907	FNB	OS	R222	MSA	1	R170	SUT	36			
R903	BOU	1	R714	FOJ	T9	R574	NAD	OG	R190	SUT	U9			
R904	BOU	1	R985	FOT	M4	R315	NGM	7	R601	SWO	5	S665	AAE	1
R905	BOU	1	R130	FUP	1	R317	NGM	7	R602	SWO	5	S667	AAE	1
R906	BOU	1	R431	FWT	H8	R319	NGM	7	R603	SWO	6	S668	AAE	1
R907	BOU	1	R432	FWT	H8	R661	NHY	1	R 10	TAW	T7	S669	AAE	1
R908	BOU	1	R452	FWT	H8	R662	NHY	1	R226	TBC	OG	S670	AAE	1
R909	BOU	1	R445	FWT	N7	R663	NHY	1	R650	TDV	3	S671	AAE	1
R910	BOU	1	R694	GMW	OS	R664	NHY	1	R852	TFJ	3	S672	AAE	1
R912	BOU	1	R915	GMW	5	R708	NJH	39	R853	TFJ	3	S673	AAE	1
R913	BOU	1	R916	GMW	5	R110	NMR	X	R179	TKU	92	S674	AAE	1
R914	BOU	1	R917	GMW	5	R501	NPR	2	R955	TLD	OS	S675	AAE	1
R915	BOU	1	R918	GMW	5	R502	NPR	2	R 29	TLL	OS	S676	AAE	1
R916	BOU	1	R 91	GWO	H9	R503	NPR	2	R 1	TRU	U8	S677	AAE	1
R917	BOU	1	R164	HHK	X	R504	NPR	2	R652	TYA	R4	S678	AAE	1
R918	BOU	1	R624	HKX	X	R505	NPR	2	R726	TYC	N7	S679	AAE	1
R919	BOU	1	R 95	HUA	H9	R506	NPR	2	R465	UAK	OS	S680	AAE	1
R501	BUA	G6	R807	HWS	F6	R507	NPR	2	R913	ULA	84	S681	AAE	1
R760	BVV	T9	R808	HWS	F6	R508	NPR	2	R920	ULA	84	S682	AAE	1
R 39	BYG	V1	R809	HWS	V8	R101	NTA	6	R812	UOK	OG	S683	AAE	1
R 46	BYG	12	R810	HWS	V8	R102	NTA	6	R488	UYC	X	S684	AAE	1
R447	CCV	3	R813	HWS	2	R103	NTA	6	R109	UYC	X	S685	AAE	1
R448	CCV	3	R814	HWS	2	R104	NTA	6	R110	UYC	X	S686	AAE	1
R449	CCV	3	R304	JAF	3	R105	NTA	6	R112	UYC	X	S687	AAE	1
R450	CCV	3	R305	JAF	3				R627	VNN	58	S688	AAE	1

S689	AAE	1	S871	NOD	3	T560	CDM	OC	T789	RDV	3				V448	DYB	69
S690	AAE	1	S872	NOD	3	T163	CGX	X	T 2	RED	L6				V852	DYB	R4
S691	AAE	1	S100	PAF	D7	T561	CGX	X	T 3	RED	L6				V832	DYD	2
S720	AFB	1	S924	PDD	5	T 24	COF	G1	T726	REU	1				V833	DYD	2
S721	AFB	1	S925	PDD	5	T442	EBD	U8	T727	REU	1				V834	DYD	2
S722	AFB	1	S926	PDD	5	T 91	EFJ	C5	T728	REU	1				V835	DYD	2
S723	AFB	1	S927	PDD	5	T128	EFJ	4	T729	REU	1				V 91	EAK	57
S724	AFB	1	S928	PDD	5	T129	EFJ	4	T730	REU	1				V 92	EAK	G5
S725	AFB	1	S929	PDD	5	T130	EFJ	4	T731	REU	1				V301	EAK	T6
S637	AHU	M8	S930	PDD	5	T131	EFJ	4	T 59	RFB	OW				V208	EAL	OD
S111	AJP	K2	S859	PHR	T9	T132	EFJ	4	T191	RFB	X				V210	EAL	61
S 30	ARJ	V8	S853	PKH	V2	T133	EFJ	4	T192	RFB	X				V187	EAM	7
S 49	BAF	OC	S925	RBE	K3	T134	EFJ	4	T565	RFS	49				V188	EAM	7
S386	BBX	OE	S649	RCV	M5	T135	EFJ	4	T 58	RJL	H9				V189	EAM	7
S857	BDV	G6	S584	RDG	E1	T136	EFJ	4	T163	RMR	7				V190	EAM	7
S862	BHR	OW	S969	RDG	20	T137	EFJ	4	T164	RMR	7				V191	EAM	7
S 11	BLC	37	S 18	RED	E4	T138	EFJ	4	T165	RMR	7				V884	EBX	OB
S 34	BMR	V8	S338	RHB	OG	T139	EFJ	4	T702	RNP	OG				V318	EEU	44
S162	BMR	7	S 14	RUT	OD	T140	EFJ	4	T283	ROR	OG				V319	EEU	44
S181	BMR	7	S806	RWG	1	T 14	ELL	A4	T953	RTA	N1				V 2	EFA	16
S182	BMR	7	S807	RWG	1	T801	FHW	1	T830	RYC	2				V761	EFB	44
S183	BMR	7	S808	RWG	1	T436	FOW	OB	T831	RYC	2				V802	EFB	2
S184	BMR	7	S809	RWG	1	T615	FPY	H6	T 12	SBK	U1				V803	EFB	2
S185	BMR	7	S311	SCV	3	T620	FPY	H6	T562	SBX	OD				V804	EFB	2
S186	BMR	7	S312	SCV	3	T958	GCK	OE	T568	SUF	T6				V805	EFB	2
S995	BTA	G6	S313	SCV	3	T446	HRV	11	T 2	TRU	U8				V806	EFB	2
S792	CHU	OW	S549	SCV	U8	T104	JBC	2	T 12	TRU	U8				V807	EFB	2
S 50	CJT	V2	S344	SET	T6	T105	JBC	2	T404	UCS	6				V808	EFB	2
S 60	CJT	V2	S842	SNM	X	T106	JBC	2	T920	UEU	24				V809	EFB	2
S138	EAF	OD	S314	SRL	3	T 32	JCV	U8	T198	VAE	44				V810	EFB	1
S686	EAF	K4	S315	SRL	3	T 34	JCV	U8	T713	YDV	D6				V155	EFV	72
S649	ETT	R9	S501	SRL	V8	T 35	JCV	U8	T472	YTT	3				V744	EJF	20
S659	ETT	38	S502	SRL	V8	T158	JCV	X	T473	YTT	3				V287	ENT	E1
S671	ETT	86	S503	SRL	V8	T469	JCV	3							V288	ENT	E1
S342	FAE	OB	S405	TMB	U8	T470	JCV	3							V957	EOD	A9
S234	FGD	A6	S138	TYC	R5	T471	JCV	3							V732	FAE	1
S127	FTA	4	S164	UBU	H6	T501	JEL	92							V733	FAE	1
S538	FTA	44	S169	UBU	H6	T722	JHE	G2							V734	FAE	1
S 3	HJC	M1	S171	UBU	H6	T440	JLD	X				V444	AJP	K2	V735	FAE	1
S117	JFJ	6	S326	UEW	74	T536	JND	H6				V600	CBC	63	V736	FAE	1
S118	JFJ	6	S838	VAG	7	T850	JWB	57				V948	DDG	5	V737	FAE	1
S687	KHY	X	S604	VJW	W7	T761	JYB	24				V949	DDG	5	V738	FAE	1
S688	KHY	X	S605	VJW	W7	T762	JYB	24				V950	DDG	5	V215	FEU	45
S311	KNR	E6	S623	VOM	M4	T765	JYB	L8				V951	DDG	5	V216	FEU	45
S923	KOD	86	S429	VYC	OS	T766	JYB	35				V952	DDG	5	V701	FFB	1
S924	KOD	86	S340	WYB	2	T483	JYC	X				V953	DDG	5	V181	FVU	M7
S925	KOD	86	S944	WYB	86	T806	JYD	X				V954	DDG	5	V606	GGB	1
S926	KOD	86	S696	WYC	X	T316	KCV	3				V955	DDG	5	V607	GGB	1
S817	KPR	2	S697	WYC	X	T575	KGB	6				V956	DDG	5	V608	GGB	1
S818	KPR	2	S824	WYD	2	T 46	KYB	C4				V957	DDG	5	V610	GGB	1
S819	KPR	2	S825	WYD	2	T892	LKJ	E8				V958	DDG	5	V250	GGS	X
S820	KPR	2	S748	XYA	J2	T893	LKJ	E8				V959	DDG	5	V116	GWP	L4
S821	KPR	2	S762	XYA	39	T894	LKJ	E8				V960	DDG	5	V956	HEB	H2
S822	KPR	2				T 18	LUE	T6				V777	DEN	R7	V870	HKV	X
S823	KPR	2				T131	MGB	6				V939	DFH	5	V801	KAF	3
S916	KRG	H6				T132	MGB	6				V940	DFH	5	V802	KAF	3
S917	KRG	H6	S762	AFJ	X	T366	NUA	2				V941	DFH	5	V803	KAF	3
S919	KRG	H6	S826	AFX	2	T367	NUA	2				V942	DFH	5	V739	KGU	X
S726	LEF	D6	S827	AFX	2	T368	NUA	2				V943	DFH	5	V 28	LUE	T6
S863	LRU	2	S828	AFX	2	T369	NUA	2				V944	DFH	5	V888	LUE	T6
S864	LRU	2	S829	AFX	2	T370	NUA	2				V945	DFH	5	V801	LWT	25
S555	MAL	OG	S310	AHY	2	T825	OBL	A9				V946	DFH	5	V 54	MOD	79
S297	MHN	OG	T 2	ALJ	64	T979	OGA	V5				V947	DFH	5	V200	OCC	55
S865	NOD	3	T 54	AUA	25	T999	OSM	X				V961	DFH	5	V689	OJW	17
S866	NOD	3	T 59	AUA	32	T419	PDG	32				V962	DFH	5	V487	RDN	V1
S867	NOD	3	T 7	BBC	38	T993	PFH	82				V968	DFX	92	V799	SNY	OG
S868	NOD	3	T 65	BCU	G1	T 4	POW	33				V969	DFX	92	V 1	TWC	T5
S869	NOD	3	T975	BHY	44	T517	PYD	L8				V903	DMR	T9	V348	UUD	X
S870	NOD	3	T172	BWR	R5	T788	RDV	G6				V543	DYA	C3	V 40	WGL	V8

164

V328	XDO	80	W806	PAF	3	W312	SBC	11	X 11	BLC	37	Y921	FDV	G6						
V483	XJV	84	W807	PAF	3	W311	SDV	4	X991	BNH	OB	Y626	FOD	C5						
V980	XUB	1	W808	PAF	3	W312	SDV	4	X149	BTA	N1	Y208	GEU	44						
V 36	YJV	61	W809	PAF	3	W554	SJM	E8	X529	BYD	X	Y209	GEU	44						
			W811	PAF	3	W646	STA	C5	X584	BYD	C3	Y226	GEU	44						
			W812	PAF	3	W277	SYA	X	X689	BYD	X	Y928	GEU	OW						
			W813	PAF	3	W501	SYB	N7	X141	CDV	4	Y334	GFJ	G6						
W592	AAY	31	W814	PAF	3	W631	SYC	C4	X142	CDV	4	Y906	GFJ	N1						
W804	AAY	61	W815	PAF	3	W 3	TRU	U8	X201	CDV	4	Y166	GTT	N1						
W818	AAY	E8	W347	PFB	44	W 4	TRU	U8	X202	CDV	4	Y146	HAE	X						
W 2	BBC	38	W811	PFB	1	W551	UFH	X	X203	CDV	4	Y148	HAE	X						
W869	BOH	OS	W812	PFB	1	W495	UGY	X	X204	CDV	4	Y187	HAE	X						
W178	BVP	X	W813	PFB	1	W646	UUH	OG	X436	CDW	H2	Y209	HAE	X						
W 9	CCH	OB	W814	PFB	1	W501	VDD	5	X437	CDW	X	Y892	HAE	U1						
W201	CDN	25	W815	PFB	1	W504	VDD	5	X143	CFJ	X	Y893	HAE	U1						
W 17	CJT	V2	W816	PFB	1	W508	VDD	5	X424	CFJ	84	Y 4	HAT	E8						
W678	DDN	36	W817	PFB	1	W509	VDD	5	X 70	CJT	V2	Y 36	HBT	1						
W 14	ELL	A4	W818	PFB	1	W805	VDD	5	X 80	CJT	V2	Y 37	HBT	1						
W506	EOL	17	W819	PFB	1	W514	VGU	X	X564	CUY	29	Y 38	HBT	1						
W556	EOL	OG	W821	PFB	1	W679	VGW	X	X594	CWN	X	Y 39	HBT	1						
W 39	EOX	R1	W822	PFB	1	W809	VMA	1	X595	CWN	X	Y 61	HBT	X						
W414	HOB	E8	W823	PFB	1	W346	VOD	N1	X596	CWN	X	Y 62	HBT	X						
W415	HOB	E8	W824	PFB	1	W347	VOD	N1	X597	CWN	X	Y 63	HBT	X						
W416	HOB	E8	W825	PFB	1	W953	WDS	A6	X615	CWN	H6	Y 64	HBT	X						
W493	HOB	OC	W826	PFB	1	W853	WDV	OD	X616	CWN	H6	Y362	HBX	OD						
W921	JNF	H2	W827	PFB	1	W857	WOD	OD	X617	CWN	H6	Y 69	HHE	11						
W922	JNF	H2	W828	PFB	1	W259	WRV	86	X618	CWN	H6	Y621	HHU	69						
W391	JOG	55	W829	PFB	1	W348	XEE	79	X827	EBY	X	Y144	HWE	G5						
W688	JOG	OS	W831	PFB	1	W736	XGS	X	X584	EJE	T4	Y479	HWE	OS						
W221	KDO	OE	W832	PFB	1				X216	EKK	G1	Y201	KNB	99						
W599	KFE	80	W833	PFB	1				X201	HAE	1	Y707	KNC	82						
W611	KFE	OS	W834	PFB	1				X202	HAE	1	Y847	LDP	80						
W401	LDV	44	W702	PHT	1				X203	HAE	1	Y848	LDP	80						
W449	LDV	44	W703	PHT	1	X 83	AAK	32	X233	HEU	X	Y297	MBM	X						
W777	MAL	OG	W704	PHT	1	X377	ADF	E1	X235	HEU	X	Y818	NAY	84						
W801	PAE	1	W705	PHT	1	X502	ADF	5	X237	HEU	X	Y835	NAY	84						
W802	PAE	1	W706	PHT	1	X503	ADF	5	X191	HFB	2	Y218	NYA	68						
W803	PAE	1	W707	PHT	1	X506	ADF	5	X192	HFB	2	Y223	NYA	93						
W804	PAE	1	W708	PHT	1	X507	ADF	5	X193	HFB	2	Y227	NYA	24						
W805	PAE	1	W461	PHW	V3	X511	ADF	5	X194	HFB	2	Y228	NYA	24						
W806	PAE	1	W371	PHY	69	X512	ADF	5	X613	HFB	OD	Y229	NYA	24						
W807	PAE	1	W372	PHY	69	X513	ADF	5	X314	HOU	A6	Y945	NYA	X						
W808	PAE	1	W102	PMS	6	X518	ADF	5	X671	JND	OB	Y994	NYA	X						
W809	PAE	1	W931	PPT	93	X904	ADF	W2	X412	KRD	80	Y995	NYA	X						
W811	PAE	1	W839	PWS	OB	X771	ADG	X	X413	KRD	80	Y313	NYD	4						
W812	PAE	1	W 2	RED	L6	X868	AEU	OD	X474	SCY	3	Y314	NYD	4						
W813	PAE	1	W253	RHT	92	X869	AEU	OG	X475	SCY	3	Y644	NYD	4						
W814	PAE	1	W709	RHT	1	X966	AFH	5	X476	SCY	3	Y645	NYD	4						
W815	PAE	1	W711	RHT	1	X967	AFH	5	X477	SCY	3	Y646	NYD	4						
W816	PAE	1	W712	RHT	1	X968	AFH	5	X478	SCY	3	Y647	NYD	4						
W817	PAE	1	W713	RHT	1	X969	AFH	5	X 10	TWC	T5	Y648	NYD	4						
W818	PAE	1	W714	RHT	1	X971	AFH	5	X753	URL	OC	Y736	OBE	E8						
W819	PAE	1	W715	RHT	1	X972	AFH	5	X447	YWV	X	Y871	PWT	X						
W821	PAE	1	W716	RHT	1	X973	AFH	5				Y872	PWT	X						
W822	PAE	1	W717	RHT	1	X974	AFH	5				Y873	PWT	X						
W823	PAE	1	W248	RNT	OG	X975	AFH	5				Y874	PWT	X						
W824	PAE	1	W107	RTC	33	X976	AFH	5				Y875	PWT	X						
W601	PAF	3	W183	RWP	H9	X977	AFH	5	Y446	AUY	M6	Y138	RDG	M6						
W602	PAF	3	W201	RWS	X	X978	AFH	5	Y194	BAF	OC	Y139	RDG	M6						
W603	PAF	3	W202	RWS	X	X751	AHT	X	Y200	BCC	32	Y434	RDG	20						
W604	PAF	3	W549	RYA	X	X996	AHT	44	Y300	BCC	32	Y852	SDD	L3						
W605	PAF	3	W557	RYA	OS	X997	AHT	44	Y400	BCC	32	Y 25	TAW	T7						
W606	PAF	3	W563	RYA	X	X998	AHT	44	Y 2	BUS	E2	Y 5	TRU	U8						
W607	PAF	3	W153	RYB	L8	X 96	AHU	U1	Y833	DAA	OD	Y649	UCC	OS						
W608	PAF	3	W154	RYB	21	X468	AHY	44	Y922	DCY	F1	Y 38	UEU	45						
W609	PAF	3	W157	RYB	84	X212	AWB	80	Y 14	DLC	86	Y754	UMR	T9						
W675	PAF	OC	W161	RYB	35	X501	BFJ	3	Y814	DRB	X	Y192	VMR	7						
W804	PAF	3	W416	RYC	G6	X502	BFJ	3	Y153	EAY	C7	Y193	VMR	7						
W805	PAF	3	W562	RYC	84	X503	BFJ	3	Y 1	EDN	U8	Y194	VMR	7						
						X504	BFJ	3	Y 2	EDN	U8									

Y195	VMR	7	VU51	GGK	K3	WX51	AJU	2	AT02	CJT	V2	WU02	KVG	1
Y196	VMR	7	VX51	AMB	99	WX51	AJV	2	BT02	CJT	V2	WU02	KVH	1
Y197	VMR	7	VX51	AWO	H8	WX51	AJY	2	BX02	CME	55	WU02	KVJ	1
Y727	VRH	OG	VX51	NXR	5	WX51	AKY	2	DR02	DRH	D8	WU02	KVK	1
Y151	XAE	25	VX51	NXS	5	WX51	EKM	X	FY02	LCT	H9	WU02	KVL	1
Y341	XAG	12	VX51	NXT	5	WX51	EPP	T9	HJ02	HCG	93	WU02	KVM	1
			VX51	RDO	M7	WX51	YGN	25	OO02	ELL	A4	WU02	KVO	1
			WA51	ACO	4	YN51	MFZ	57	UK02	EMT	X	WU02	KVP	1
			WA51	ACU	4	YN51	WGW	T8	UR02	EMT	X	WU02	KVR	1
AV51	AVA	C3	WA51	ACV	4	YN51	WGX	35	VU02	TRV	H2	WU02	KVS	1
BC51	BBC	38	WA51	ACX	4	YN51	WHJ	80	VU02	UVM	55	WU02	KVT	1
BU51	AYE	57	WA51	ACY	4	YN51	WHK	80	WJ02	HYW	3	WU02	KVV	1
CN51	BUA	X	WA51	EOT	44	YN51	XMH	U6	WJ02	KDF	84	WU02	KVW	1
CU51	KLA	OG	WA51	HXS	X	YN51	XMJ	U6	WJ02	KDK	OS	WV02	ANX	58
FJ51	JXX	68	WA51	HXV	X	YN51	XMK	U6	WJ02	KDX	79	WV02	BEY	C4
FX51	AXP	83	WA51	HXX	X	YN51	XML	U6	WJ02	KDZ	86	WV02	EUP	1
HF51	AWA	92	WA51	JYH	20	YN51	XMU	U6	WJ02	KUE	86	WV02	EUR	1
HF51	AWC	92	WA51	JYK	T1	YN51	XMV	U6	WJ02	UVV	57	WV02	EUT	1
HF51	AWG	92	WA51	OSE	6	YN51	XMW	U6	WJ02	VRP	21	WV02	EUU	1
HF51	AWH	92	WA51	OSF	6	YN51	XMX	U6	WK02	TYD	3	WV02	NJK	44
HF51	AWM	92	WA51	RPZ	OC	YN51	XMZ	U6	WK02	TYF	3	WV02	NNA	7
HF51	AWN	92	WA51	XVX	OC	YN51	XNC	U6	WK02	TYH	3	WV02	NNB	7
HF51	AWO	92	WK51	AVP	V8	YN51	XND	U6	WK02	UHR	T2	WV02	NNC	7
HF51	AWS	92	WK51	HNF	V8	YN51	XNE	U6	WK02	YYK	84	WV02	OGG	69
PG51	GAR	C5	WP51	WXY	17				WR02	RVX	33	WV02	OGH	69
SF51	PVY	79	WU51	CZC	C4				WR02	XXO	F6	YG02	DLV	3
SK51	SBK	U1	WU51	OMB	30				WU02	KVE	1	YR02	UMU	32
VU51	FGN	L3	WU51	VAX	44	AT02	BOT	OB	WU02	KVF	1	YR02	UNY	17

ISLANDS REGISTRATION INDEX

1787	Y4	J 10429	Y6	J 35352	XI	J 74393	Y5
3989	Y4	J 10519	Y6	J 37636	Y7	J 75173	Y5
5597	XI	J 10569	Y6	J 37684	Y7	J 75197	Y5
5779	Y4	J 10603	Y6	J 39815	Y6	J 75241	Y5
6768	Y4	J 11467	Y5	J 40820	Y5	J 75609	Y5
8225	Y4	J 12050	Y6	J 40853	Y5	J 75668	Y6
8227	Y4	J 12633	Y6	J 40865	Y5	J 75736	Y7
8228	Y4	J 12695	Y6	J 40899	Y5	J 75874	Y7
8230	Y4	J 13779	Y6	J 41130	Y6	J 77033	Y6
9438	Y4	J 13853	Y5	J 42159	OI	J 79519	Y7
9969	Y4	J 14609	Y6	J 42252	Y5	J 79630	XI
12723	Y4	J 14610	Y6	J 42259	Y5	J 80977	Y6
12727	Y4	J 14612	Y6	J 42298	Y5	J 82047	Y6
17314	Y4	J 14614	Y6	J 42653	Y5	J 82049	Y6
18047	Y4	J 14616	Y6	J 43037	Y5	J 84709	Y5
18264	Y4	J 14638	Y6	J 43048	Y5	J 84872	Y6
19660	Y4	J 14639	Y5	J 43063	Y5	J 85325	Y5
19662	Y4	J 14644	Y5	J 43066	Y5	J 86370	Y5
19675	Y4	J 14645	Y5	J 43881	Y6	J 86372	Y5
19676	Y4	J 14650	Y5	J 44485	Y6	J 87196	Y6
19677	Y4	J 14660	Y6	J 45360	OI	J 88633	Y6
19678	Y4	J 14679	Y6	J 46598	Y5	J 89654	Y6
20716	Y4	J 15374	Y5	J 46631	Y5	J 89771	Y6
23196	Y4	J 15582	Y6	J 46744	Y5	J 89914	Y6
24493	Y4	J 15884	Y5	J 46794	Y5	J 90172	Y5
24539	Y4	J 15908	Y5	J 46828	Y5	J 90241	Y5
24603	Y4	J 16043	Y5	J 47452	Y6	J 90393	Y5
24775	Y4	J 16439	Y5	J 47453	Y6	J 90454	Y5
29728	Y4	J 16527	Y5	J 48300	Y6	J 90706	Y6
31738	XI	J 16582	Y5	J 48388	Y6	J 91155	Y6
31921	Y4	J 16598	Y5	J 49246	Y6	J 91574	Y6
33541	Y4	J 16601	Y5	J 49250	Y6	J 91728	Y6
34518	Y4	J 16861	Y5	J 51771	Y7	J 92914	Y6
38290	Y4	J 17759	Y6	J 51772	Y7	J 93319	Y5
38328	Y4	J 18280	OI	J 51812	Y7	J 93500	Y5
38406	Y4	J 20072	Y6	J 51819	Y7	J 93747	Y7
39138	Y4	J 24457	Y6	J 51937	Y7	J 93812	Y7
40527	Y4	J 24489	Y6	J 55137	XI		
47979	Y4	J 24573	Y6	J 55378	Y6		
48641	OI	J 24651	Y6	J 57331	Y6		
49282	Y1	J 26626	Y6	J 57347	Y6	AY 81	PI
52408	OI	J 26678	Y6	J 57357	Y6	AY 91	Y2
56206	Y4	J 26724	Y6	J 58127	Y5	AY 593	Y2
56650	Y3	J 27404	Y7	J 58128	Y5	AY 1114	Y2
56660	Y3	J 27414	Y7	J 58917	Y5	AY 1950	OI
56690	Y3	J 28091	XI	J 58923	Y5		
61973	Y4	J 29206	Y6	J 58924	Y5		
62067	Y4	J 29709	Y5	J 59934	Y6		
62812	Y1	J 29710	Y5	J 60112	Y6	VVS 913	PI
64918	Y1	J 29713	Y5	J 60319	Y6	PSG 310G	XI
64991	Y4	J 29717	Y5	J 61334	Y5	GHV 502N	XI
66867	Y4	J 31271	Y5	J 61644	Y6	LEU 263P	Y2
66868	Y4	J 31281	Y5	J 61774	Y6	OJD 905R	XI
66959	Y3	J 31300	Y5	J 64744	Y5	THX 121S	XI
67463	Y1	J 31312	Y5	J 64745	Y5	AYR 308T	XI
		J 32069	Y6	J 66475	Y6	BYW 403V	XI
		J 32575	Y6	J 69267	Y5	PYH 651Y	OI
		J 33181	Y6	J 69526	Y7	D149 LTA	OI
J 3159	XI	J 33630	Y6	J 70700	Y5	G420 RYJ	OI
J 7247	PI	J 33643	XI	J 70712	Y5	H466 HBA	OI
J 7682	PI	J 34191	Y5	J 71210	Y5	K334 RCN	OI
J 10376	Y6	J 34317	Y6	J 73973	Y6	P 49 OAV	OI

TRADING NAMES OF INDEPENDENT OPERATORS

A1 TRAVEL	V4	DENE VALLEY COACHES	F3
A-LINE COACHES	C8	DIAL A BUS	43
ABUS	K2	DOWNTON TRAVEL	97
AD-RAINS	D1	EAGLE COACHES	25
ALLENS TRAVEL	12	EAGLE LINE	20
ALPHA COACHES	41	EASTVILLE COACHES LTD	A1*
ALVAJOAN COACHES	J3	EBLEY COACH SERVICES	F7
AMG COACHES	T7*	ECONOMY TRAVEL	58
ANDREWS COACHES	14	EMERALD TRAVEL	E3
ANDYBUS	F6	ESJ MERLIN TOURS	F5
APPLEGATES INTERNATIONAL	16	DAVID FIELD TRAVEL	A7
AVALON COACHES	C3	FARESAVER	K6
AXE VALE COACHES	21	FIELDS OF NEWPORT	A7
AXE VALLEY MINI TRAVEL	M9	FILERS TRAVEL	A9
AYREVILLE COACHES	50	FIRST & LAST COACH HIRE	U2
AZTEC	K3	FORWARD TRAVEL	C2
BAKERS COACHES	J6	FOSSEWAY	K6
BAKERS DOLPHIN	24	G LINE HIRE	H6
BASSETT & SLUGGETT COACHES	N6	GIRLINGS OF PLYMOUTH	K8
BATH MINI TRAVEL	J4	GOLD STAR COACHES	R9
BATH MINIBUSES	J4	GRAHAMS OF BRISTOL	N9
BATH TRAVEL SERVICES	18	GREENSLADES	E9
BEACON GARAGE	V1	GREY CARS	J2
BEAUMONT TRAVEL	M7	GROUP TRAVEL	V6
BEAVIS HOLIDAYS	30	HAMBLYS OF KERNOW	D7
BEELINE	L4	HARVEYS MINI BUS SERVICES	E2
BELFITT MINIBUS HIRE	31	HATTS COACHES	E8
BENNETTS COACHES	32	HATTS EUROPA LTD	E8*
BLUE IRIS COACHES	T6	HAYLE TRAVEL	M5
BLUELINE COACHES OF DEVON	M3	HEARDS COACHES	E5
BMS COACHES	H9	HEMMINGS COACHES	E7
C. BODMAN & SONS	39	HERITAGE TRAVEL	W1
BRC ENTERPRISES LTD	69*	HIGHWAY TRAVEL	91
BROOKSIDE TRAVEL	U3	HILLS SERVICES	E6
BRUCE & ROBERTS	M2	HOOKWAYS JENNINGS	E9
BRUE TRAVEL	U7	A.G. HUNT	T7*
BRYANTS COACHES	47	HUTTON COACH HIRE	G7
BUGLERS	49	JACKIES COACHES	L1
BURNHAM PARK COACHES	M4	JC TOURS	74
C & B	F2	JVA SUNSEEKER TOURS & HOLIDAYS	59
CALNE TRAVEL	W5	KB COACHES	42
CARADON RIVIERA TOURS	88	KERNOW TRAVEL	N4
CARMEL COACHES	E4	KILMINGTON COACHES	G6
PETER CAROL	68	KTM COACHES	22
CB's ILLOGAN COACHES	51	KWT COACHES	19
CHANDLERS COACH TRAVEL	23	LINCO TRAVEL	77
CHISLETTS	V9	LITTLE BLUE BUS	J5
PAUL CHIVERS COACHING	60	LOVERINGS COACHES	H4
CITYTOUR	M6	JOHN MARTIN COACHES	L5
CLASSIC TOURS	G5	MICHAELS TRAVEL	83
CLH LUXURY TRAVEL	L8	MID DEVON COACHES	W4
COACHMANS TRAVELS	34	MIKES TRAVEL	52
COASTLINE COACHES	C9	NEXTBUS	K6
DANNY COCKS COACHES	65	NORTH SOMERSET COACHES	62
COLOMBUS	G9	OATES TRAVEL	K4
COOKS COACHES	G6	OTS MINIBUS & COACH HIRE	J8
COOMBS COACHES	69	OTTER COACHES	96
COTSWOLD EXPERIENCE TOURS	G8	P & CJ TRAVEL	F8
COUNTY LINE	J5	PALM TREE TRAVEL	D9
COURTESY COACHES	78	PARAMOUNT MINI COACHES	72
CREMYLL COACHES	N8	PLYM COACHES	26
CROWN COACHES	K2	POWELLS COACHES	K9
CURRIAN TOURS	T2	PRIMROSE COACHES	M5
DARLEY FORD TRAVEL	87	QUANTOCK MOTOR SERVICES	L7
DARTINGTON & TOTNES OMNIBUS CO	A5	RAYS COACHES	C6
DARTLINE	86	REDWOODS TRAVEL	L6
DAVRON COACHES	54	RIDUNA BUSES	Y2

RIVIERA COACH & MINIBUS HIRE	C1	TOWN & COUNTRY COACHES LTD	98*
ROSELYN COACHES	A3	TURNERS TOURS	U9
ROVER	D8	UNICORN TRAVEL	53
SAFEWAY SERVICES	D4	VISTA COACHWAYS	F9
SHAFTESBURY & DISTRICT	46	WAKES	R4
H. & A. SLEEP	N5	R.C. & N.J. WARNER LTD	40*
SNELLS COACHES	R2	WARNERS BUS & COACH CO	40
SOUTH GLOUCESTERSHIRE BUS &	A1	L. WATTS	63*
SOVEREIGN COACHES	G1	WEBBERBUS	V5
SPEARINGS COACHES	F4	WESSEX BUS	94
STAMPS COACHES	76	WESTERN PRIVATE HIRE	48
SUNSET COACHES	U5	WESTWARD TRAVEL	N2
SWALLOW COACHES	85	WEYMOUTH BUS COMPANY	94
SWANBROOK	U1	WHEAL BRITON COACHES	K5
TALLY HO COACHES	V7	WHEELS CARE	G9
TARGET TRAVEL	M1	GEOFF WILLETTS	W2
TAUNTON COACHES	73	F.T. WILLIAMS TRAVEL	W3
TEDBURN COACHES	H3	WINFORD QUEEN COACHES	66
TIVVY COACHES	G3	Z-CARS OF BRISTOL	57
TJs COACHES	J9	ZOAR COACHES	J7
TOWER CABS	M4		

STOP PRESS